TEXTUAL AND CRITICAL INTERSECTIONS

UNIVERSITY PRESS OF FLORIDA

Florida A&M University, Tallahassee
Florida Atlantic University, Boca Raton
Florida Gulf Coast University, Ft. Myers
Florida International University, Miami
Florida State University, Tallahassee
New College of Florida, Sarasota
University of Central Florida, Orlando
University of Florida, Gainesville
University of North Florida, Jacksonville
University of South Florida, Tampa
University of West Florida, Pensacola

Textual and Critical Intersections

Conversations with Laurence Sterne and Others

Melvyn New

UNIVERSITY PRESS OF FLORIDA

Gainesville · Tallahassee · Tampa · Boca Raton
Pensacola · Orlando · Miami · Jacksonville · Ft. Myers · Sarasota

Copyright 2023 by Melvyn New
All rights reserved
Published in the United States of America.

28 27 26 25 24 23   6 5 4 3 2 1

Library of Congress Cataloging-in-Publication Data
Names: New, Melvyn, author.
Title: Textual and critical intersections : conversations with Laurence
   Sterne and others / Melvyn New.
Description: 1. | Gainesville : University Press of Florida, 2023. |
   Includes bibliographical references and index. | Summary: "In this
   collection of wide-ranging essays representing fifty years of
   scholarship on Laurence Sterne, Melvyn New brings Sterne into
   conversation with other authors from the past three centuries."—
   Provided by publisher.
Identifiers: LCCN 2023010639 (print) | LCCN 2023010640 (ebook) | ISBN
   9780813069838 (hardback) | ISBN 9780813070605 (pdf)
Subjects: LCSH: Sterne, Laurence, 1713–1768—Criticism and interpretation.
   | Authors, English—18th century—Criticism and interpretation. | BISAC:
   LITERARY CRITICISM / European / English, Irish, Scottish, Welsh |
   LITERARY CRITICISM / Modern / 18th Century | LCGFT: Literary criticism.
Classification: LCC PR3716 .N49 2023 (print) | LCC PR3716 (ebook) | DDC
   823/.6—dc23/eng/20230727
LC record available at https://lccn.loc.gov/2023010639
LC ebook record available at https://lccn.loc.gov/2023010640

The University Press of Florida is the scholarly publishing agency for the State University System of Florida, comprising Florida A&M University, Florida Atlantic University, Florida Gulf Coast University, Florida International University, Florida State University, New College of Florida, University of Central Florida, University of Florida, University of North Florida, University of South Florida, and University of West Florida.

University Press of Florida
2046 NE Waldo Road
Suite 2100
Gainesville, FL 32609
http://upress.ufl.edu

Contents

List of Figures vii

List of Abbreviations ix

Introduction 1

STERNE: TEXTUAL CONVERSATIONS

  1. Sterne and the Narrative of Determinateness 15
  2. The Odd Couple: Laurence Sterne and John Norris of Bemerton 33
  3. Laurence Sterne's Sermons and *The Pulpit-Fool* 62
  4. "The Unknown World": The Poem Laurence Sterne Did Not Write 80

DIGRESSIONS IN THE MANNER OF STERNE

  5. Taking Care: A Slightly Levinasian Reading of *Dombey and Son* 101
  6. Johnson, T. S. Eliot, and the City 136

STERNE: CRITICAL CONVERSATIONS

  7. Reading Sterne through Proust and Levinas 165
  8. Sterne and the Modernist Moment 196
  9. Richardson's *Sir Charles Grandison* and Sterne: A Study in Influence 212
  10. Boswell and Sterne in 1768 250
  11. Single and Double: *Memoirs of Martinus Scriblerus* and *Tristram Shandy* 278
  12. "The Life of a Wit is a warfare upon earth": Sterne, Joyce, and Their Portraits of the Artist 314

CODA

"A Genius of That Cast": Celebrating Sterne 347

List of Permissions 367

Index 369

Figures

1. "The Unknown World," from the *Gentleman's Magazine* 81
2. "The Unknown World," from the *Gentleman's Magazine* 82
3. "The Unknown Θ," from *Vallis Eboracensis* 83
4. "The Unknown Θ," from *Vallis Eboracensis* 84
5. *Uncle Toby and the Widow Wadman,* by Charles Robert Leslie 103
6. "Joe B is sly, Sir, devilishly sly," by Phiz (Hablot Browne) 104
7. *Sleeping Adela and Edzio,* by Bruno Schulz 205

Abbreviations

Where possible, citations to Laurence Sterne's works refer to the Florida Edition of the Works of Laurence Sterne. These citations appear in the text, using the abbreviations below:

Letters
The Letters. Part 1, *1739–1764;* Part 2, *1765–1768.* Florida Edition, vols. 7 and 8. Edited by Melvyn New and Peter de Voogd. Gainesville: University Press of Florida, 2009.

MW
Miscellaneous Writings and Sterne's Subscribers: An Identification List. Florida Edition, vol. 9. Edited by Melvyn New and W. B. Gerard. Gainesville: University Press of Florida, 2014.

Sermons
The Sermons of Laurence Sterne. Florida Edition, vol. 4. Edited by Melvyn New. Gainesville: University Press of Florida, 1996.

Sermons, Notes
The Sermons of Laurence Sterne: The Notes. Florida Edition, vol. 5. Edited by Melvyn New. Gainesville: University Press of Florida, 1996.

SJ, BJ
A Sentimental Journey through France and Italy and Continuation of the Bramine's Journal. Florida Edition, vol. 6. Edited by Melvyn New and W. G. Day. Gainesville: University Press of Florida, 2002.

TS
The Life and Opinions of Tristram Shandy, Gentleman. Florida Edition, vols. 1–2. Edited by Melvyn New and Joan New. Gainesville: University Presses of Florida, 1978. References to the text are to the original volume and chapter, in most instances also followed by the page number in the Florida Edition; thus, *TS* 2.2.98 indicates volume 2, chapter 2, page 98 of the Florida Edition.

TS, Notes
The Life and Opinions of Tristram Shandy, Gentleman: The Notes. Florida Edition, vol. 3. Edited by Melvyn New, with Richard A. Davies and W. G. Day. Gainesville: University Presses of Florida, 1984.

Introduction

Against the Word the unstilled world still whirled
About the centre of the silent Word.

T. S. Eliot, *Ash-Wednesday*

Maybe the whole art of writing . . . is the perfection of imprecise forms.

Olga Tokarczuk, *The Books of Jacob*

It was a truth universally acknowledged in the eighteenth century that claims to be publishing at the urging of friends are nonsense. I strongly suspect the same is true in 2022, so that few will believe me when I write that the book in their hands is the result of one friend's persistence. For half a century Richard Brantley and I have participated in one another's careers despite differences that might well have separated us: obvious things like my work with fiction, his with poetry; his interest in Romanticism and, later, American authors like Ralph Waldo Emerson and Emily Dickinson, mine at first in Laurence Sterne and at last, still in Laurence Sterne; or, more biographically, his heritage in the Protestant South, especially Methodism and all those dissenters, mine in Jewish Manhattan, with an especial interest in Catholicism. We arrived in Gainesville within three years of one another (1966 for me, 1969 for him) and have never moved from there.

It is, however, in the formal outputs of our careers that the most interesting differences have occurred. He has had the patience to publish seven monograph studies in the last fifty years, displaying one unifying idea: the chiastic movement from faith in experience (Locke) to the experience of faith (Wesley) as the glue that binds English and American literature from the Romantics to the Moderns. My own limited attention span explains my predilection for notes, essays, and reviews, some two hundred by last count, but only one book-length study, published in 1969 and based on my doctoral dissertation. Since then, I've seen through the press nine volumes of works by Sterne (1978–2013) and four volumes of *Sir Charles Grandison* by Samuel Richardson (2022), two authors who alone may indicate that Roderick Random's bouncing tennis ball is an apt description of my own publishing career. Confirming this restlessness are two other editions, *The Complete Novels and Selected Writings of Amy Levy* (1993); and Mary Astell and John Norris's *Letters concerning the Love of God* (2005). Levy was a late nineteenth-century Anglo-Jewish writer who committed suicide at age twenty-seven; Astell and Norris were, in this exchange of letters, Christian Neoplatonists—about Norris you will learn more in the essays that follow than you have ever wanted to know. Let me also note at this point that I have had more shared publications during my career than most, so that each project has called for me to step outside my own individual interests into that of a joint enterprise. I will here acknowledge the long line of colleagues, most still conversing with me, with whom I shared months—and at times years—of merging our thoughts: Norman Fry, Richard A. Davies, W. G. Day, Robert Bernasconi, Richard A. Cohen, Derek Taylor, Peter de Voogd, W. B. Gerard, Gerard Reedy, Robert G. Walker (numerous times!), Judith Hawley, Mary Newbould, Elizabeth Kraft, and Anthony W. Lee. Of course, all this collaboration began with the first two volumes of the Florida Edition of the Works of Laurence Sterne, the text of *Tristram Shandy,* with Joan New, a sixty-one-year marriage of minds that only ceased with her death in 2020.

To suggest that a scholar who has spent his scholarly career as an editor—a career spanning more than five decades and reflecting an obsession with one author above all others—has a short attention span may sound counterintuitive, so let me explain. Samuel Johnson's "harmless drudge," his self-deprecating definition of a lexicographer, embodies a truth I think I recognize, namely that for him, every word was a new challenge, and what kept his mind active, drudging away, was precisely that novelty. We recall that he too was an editor—and an essayist—and that his longest sustained work, *Rasselas* (1759), is, as Mrs. Shandy says of Walter, "very short." I am not, of course, comparing myself to Johnson in any way but that we both lacked whatever is necessary to write lengthy monographs, fiction or fact, and that writing historical dictionaries and editing texts have something in common in their piecemeal activity: we construct our texts one word, one line, one paragraph at a time. The same applies to annotation;

no unifying idea(s) should interfere with this work of individual problem-solving, where progress is measured by pages finished and pages yet to go, and where each annotation is an "idea" started and ended within the confines of a sentence or paragraph. I do love notes that run on for a page or two, but they are indulgent exceptions to the annotative practice of concise non-digressiveness.

Let us call it digressiveness, then, this restless need to start anew each day, and it might account for the years it took to convince me to gather some of my essays into a second collection, a bookend to a similar collection I put together thirty years ago at the urging of a very optimistic chief editor for the University Press of Florida, titled *Telling New Lies: Seven Essays in Fiction, Past and Present* (1992). Even there, restless impatience was on display: there are several to-be-expected essays on the eighteenth-century novel, but also an essay on George Orwell and anti-Semitism, another on Thomas Pynchon's *V.* (1963), and one essay (the sole previously unpublished piece) on Jonathan Swift's *Tale of a Tub* (1704) and Thomas Mann's *Magic Mountain* (1924)—still, to my biased mind, one of the best essays I ever wrote. Had it appeared in *Swift Studies* it would have been read by Swiftians; as it is, it is not even listed in the MLA International Bibliography: "alas, poor Castorp!" Like Tristram lamenting his "ten cartloads ... of ... volumes still—still unsold" (*TS* 8.6.663), I can offer what is left of my remaindered copies at a sizable discount.

If any unifying thesis emerges in my nonediting career, I would trace its roots to that Swift-Mann essay, along with another essay included in my earlier collection, on Proust and Sterne, previously published in *MLN*.[1] I began to develop at this time a penchant for bringing authors together by sheer contiguity of my own reading—the nighttime habit of engaging, as a novice, with modern fiction, alongside my eighteenth-century scholarship; to read Thomas Mann after a day of reading eighteenth-century sermons is God's gift to a harmless drudge. During the 1980s and 1990s, I also designed a series of courses in modern authors (mostly fiction writers, but dramatists and poets as well), the only connection among them being their last names would have to begin with the same letter. For example, one term's reading was Stendhal, Strindberg, Sholokhov, Silone, Schulz, Saint-Exupéry, Sartre, Svevo, Solzhenitsyn, and Soyinka. I am not sure what the students gained from these courses, but I hope it was a love of good authors, indeed, of some of the best authors in the Western tradition.

If present-day literature teachers do not recognize all these names, it is the problem of our training, one that began when literature departments started doing away with courses grounded in the best that had been thought and written before us. I will return to Matthew Arnold shortly.

My own gain was twofold: first, I was able to listen in on conversations that Bruno Schulz and Italo Svevo were holding with Sterne and develop further the conversation I had heard between Sterne and Proust. I began to develop some generalizations about Sterne's relationship to those writers we usually think of as modernists, and several essays herein are the result: namely, my second attempt at Proust and Sterne, this time putting both in conversation with Emmanuel Levinas, whom I consider the most important French philosopher of the second half of the twentieth century; an essay on Sterne and modernism, which puts him into conversation with Virginia Woolf and Bruno Schulz; and a third essay on Sterne and James Joyce. By way of Shandean digression, there is also an essay on Johnson and another modernist, T. S. Eliot. I also published an essay in the *Shandean,* not reprinted here, on Sterne and two additional modernists—Svevo, who was Joyce's good friend in Trieste, and Viktor Shklovsky, a name familiar to theorists of the novel, although few will know that he also wrote a memoir of his experiences during the Russian Revolution titled *A Sentimental Journey.*[2]

These two somewhat unifying notions of literary genius talking to literary genius, and of Sterne's relationship with modernism, will result in some necessary duplication in the essays that follow, but I felt it important that I present each essay as it was originally conceived and executed rather than attempt to turn my collection of essays into the monograph I have resisted during an entire career. Perhaps, by reading my separate essays in proximity to one another, readers will come to the flattering conclusion that even editor-annotators can at times have unifying thoughts—even a theory or two. However, I still prefer to approach new subjects as independent, freestanding challenges to be analyzed ab ovo when possible, or—since we carry our biases with us—at least with a feint toward starting ab novo.

Unfortunately, neither as an editor nor as a theorist do I have any but the most inadequate ideas of how we can define literary genius or how we can distinguish it from mediocrity. Toward the end of my career, I taught a steady dose of William Shakespeare and Charles Dickens precisely to find out what separates those two transcendent writers from the popular (or "relevant") writers of today edging their way into our curriculums. That difficulty of distinction, I discovered, was partially explained for me in the writings of John Norris of Bemerton (1657–1711), cleric, poet, sermon writer, and Neoplatonic philosopher, and the first to question John Locke's *Essay concerning Human Understanding* (1690). I found in Norris a source for much that I considered most important in Sterne's writings, both his sermons and his fictions, as will become embarrassingly apparent to readers of this volume. In recent years, wherever I happened to begin an essay on Sterne I seemed almost always to have brought Norris into the discussion, and I apologize again for the repetitiveness that results when essays published separately over time are gathered together. Norris—and Anglican theology more generally—became entwined with my reading of Levinas and moved me toward coediting (with two Levinas scholars, Robert Bernasconi and Richard A. Cohen), a collection of essays, *In Proximity: Emmanuel Levinas and the Eighteenth Century,* in which the modern philosopher and eighteenth-century authors are put in conversation with one another; and a second collection, edited with Gerard Reedy, SJ, with a subtitle that defines much of my work editing Sterne's sermons: *Theology and Literature in the Age of Johnson: Resisting Secularism.*[3] In our many discussions about literature and theology, I believe a Jesuit and a Jew arrived by different routes at the most viable meaning of one of the Society's mottoes: *Unus non sufficit orbis* (one world is not enough).

Is it possible that eighteenth-century literature was governed as much by ontology as by epistemology? I have no desire to redo Ian Watt's great *Rise of the Novel* (revisions of which have become a cottage industry for other eighteenth-century scholars),[4] but I will suggest that Norris's ontological separation of a natural world we can and should know from a spiritual world we cannot know (a distinction in many ways echoing Levinas's philosophical, apophatic separation of being from "otherwise than being") governs Enlightenment literature as much, if not more, than does Lockean epistemology. The literature of the eighteenth century from beginning to end can be defined as "resisting secularism." And this, I would argue, is the effort that binds their output to that of the modernists, and, borrowing from Brantley's work, joins the entire literary transatlantic world from John Milton to Emily Dickinson in an awareness that without a means of remystifying the words we write, the literature of genius cannot be dis-

6 · Textual and Critical Intersections

tinguished from all those billions of generated words that are not great literature.

In the eighteenth century the mundane world was more and more converted into a laboratory for the development of truths derived from observation and experience of the natural world (science); at the same time the spiritual world continued to base truths on its received religion. Science has had many successes, but its failure to deal with death's inevitability and the inadequacies of human justice pointed to a lapse that would emerge full blown in the twentieth century, where our increasingly desperate dependence on scientific solutions ended with *final solutions* in Germany and Russia. On the other hand, Christianity (and more generally, religion) has always failed to deal with its most basic contradiction, an unknowable, ineffable God ("I am that I am"), who is nonetheless revealed in His anger, His love, His beard. God is unknown, but here is what He is like and what He wants from us. This making the Word into flesh has been the task of the priests of all religions, all sects. But even good priests, acting within their belief in divinely sanctioned Truth, are bad literature professors, and our greatest concern for our profession should be to demonstrate the important divide between the two.

I have suggested that for several centuries now Western literature has resisted secularism, but I suspect the very essence of all enduring art is that it leaves room for whatever is not being, whatever is not definable or knowable. To read the Book of Job or *Tristram Shandy* and admit that one does not understand their greatness even as one admires them as works of genius is to perform the true function of a professor of literature: a learned confession that this product of the human mind surpasses all efforts to grasp it, quite a different pedagogy from the transfer of knowledge that takes place in other academic disciplines. The works we receive as our canon have been met for generations with the same *learned* unknowingness, an awareness that this work will never fully reveal itself because in its essence it contains the same Mystery locked into a God defined only as "I am that I am." John Keats had his own elegant restatement of the Mystery: Truth is Beauty, and Beauty is Truth. Our knowing stops on the surface of the Grecian urn (and, as teachers, we should master and provide for our students every available fact and speculation about that surface); our unknowingness begins with that mystery, which keeps the poem in our conversation. Our function as teachers of literature, perhaps the last bastion of unknowingness in the university (although I would like to think it resides in astrophysics departments as well), is to explore with our students the value, the beauty, and, above all, the Truth, of what we can never know. Dickens is a genius not because he deplored Britain's industrialization, which was easy enough to see, but because we continue to affirm, with every rereading, what it is that keeps us—and should keep us—in constant conversation with him.

How then can we know what to teach? We can imitate the priests and indoctrinate our students with our own gospels, our own truths, which is what we are more and more tending to do, turning our curriculums into communion and Sunday school classes. In good faith, we want to teach our students as many truths as is possible within a twelve-week semester, but too many instructors today embrace mediocre texts that reveal themselves in full support of what they believe, texts they can trust because of their dominating knowledge of them. This mastery is on display to their students, and if any conversation takes place ("student participation is required in this course"), it is between the knowledge-filled instructor and the soon-to-be-filled student.

The rather common bumper sticker *Question Authority* has always elicited from me a bemused, "Why?" But knowledge-filled instructors will almost always endorse that view, especially when the authority in question is a received cultural canon, works they will be unable to convince their students they fully understand—their authority as a teacher would be questioned, which is not what they meant at all by their bumper wisdom. Dismissing genius and embracing mediocrity because the one is knowable and the other is not, ostracizing those who disagree with our truths and joining in sects with those who agree, dismissing all qualitative distinctions among artists because such discriminations, in our own ethical judgment, are bad for society—all this makes absolute sense if we believe there is no further dimension to our existence, no essence beyond existence, to reawaken a shibboleth from my youth.

But what if we thought of the canon as embodying the Truth that resides in unknowable immateriality, in works read for centuries with intense interest but with no conclusion as to anything but their worthiness to be read? If we should not impose our local truths (Dostoevsky's Grand

8 · Textual and Critical Intersections

Inquisitor comes readily to mind), perhaps we can learn to teach *not know-ingness,* doing so by reexamining the literature that survives precisely, I would argue, because it posits the Truth as its own measurement, even as it refuses to "know" it. The literature of genius, the literature that has survived time and change over many centuries, is the writing that continually probes the Word (Beauty and Truth) *not made flesh,* always acknowledging the never reachable "I am that I am," letting us know that Truth is always just beyond the last sentence, the last verse, the last chord, the last brushstroke. I continue to believe, therefore, that Matthew Arnold's best that has been thought and written should be what guides us in our curriculums, the canon we will never fully understand, neither the mystery of its development, how it includes and excludes, nor the full meaning of its content.

All this is a far cry from my own favorite essay in this collection, "'The Unknown World': The Poem Laurence Sterne Did Not Write," which appeared in the *Huntington Library Quarterly* in 2011. It is the last essay in the first of three divisions, "Sterne: Textual Conversations," which contains essays in which I function primarily as an editor working to find sources and analogues, or, in this last instance, to redefine an author's canon. This essay also, rather accidentally, furthers the argument I have been making, because here I was able to establish with absolute certainty the mundane truth that Sterne was not the author of the poem and that it was probably written in the 1720s, when Sterne was an adolescent. What this has to do with unknowingness might raise an eyebrow, but the title itself, "Unknown World," fits almost too precisely into my argument. Eighteenth-century scholars who treat the literature of the period from their purely secular perspective have read the poem as indicating Sterne's dubious faith: how can a cleric be sincere if he admits he does not know what comes after death? It turns out to be a misattribution, but even if it were Sterne's poem, that would be a magnificently ignorant misreading. The poem was written by a Baptist minister—a cleric without a Shandy bone in his body—shortly before his death in 1728, and sent to another dedicated Christian, Elizabeth Rowe, who commented to a friend after learning of his death that he was gone "to make the important discovery in the invisible world."

Sixty years ago, I was tempted into the study of literature by the Quem quaeritis? trope ("whom are you seeking?"; the origin of liturgical drama and the ensuing mystery plays), the wonderful scholarly introduction of a "fact" into a discipline that seemed to have few of them. I continue after all that time still to believe that facts matter and that the only instructor more culpable than one unwilling to acknowledge the "invisible world" of literary genius is the one who provides fictions in the place of those facts that are already known—or knowable with time and effort. To teach unknowingness is first to be able to separate what can be known from what cannot, and to believe the truths and the Truth inherent in both worlds. I would like to believe that the four essays in my first division were written under the aegis of Quem quaeritis?—a question with an answer.

The second division, "Digressions in the Manner of Sterne," contains essays in which I listen first to a conversation between Levinas and Dickens, and then to one between Johnson and Eliot. It will be observed, however, that a portrait of Sterne's Uncle Toby and the Widow Wadman hangs on the wall in Dombey's dining room, captured by Phiz, Dickens's famous illustrator—and that this portrait plays a role in my reading of *Dombey and Son* (1848). I rarely leave Sterne far behind. And thus he also makes a brief appearance in the second essay, into which I also managed to include Amy Levy's best poem—giving her a moment of conversation with two of the canon's most illustrious lights (and, yes, I do keep in mind that Eliot was too often anti-Semitic), in which, I believe, her poem holds its own. These interlopings should indicate that I am aware that there is always a third party present at these overheard conversations, a listener who, like the scientist in his laboratory, affects the interchange by his presence.

The third division, "Sterne: Critical Conversations," contains six essays in which I listen to conversations between Sterne and others: the Scriblerians, Samuel Richardson and James Boswell (his contemporaries); and the modernists Marcel Proust, Levinas, Woolf, Schulz, and Joyce. The final essay, bringing Sterne and Joyce together, is a revised version of a tribute to Peter de Voogd, acknowledging his long career in both Sterne and Joyce scholarship. If I have succeeded at all in bringing this Anglican cleric and Catholic rebel into proximity with one another, it might help reinforce for others my belief that if we quiet our own voices sufficiently, we just might overhear the literary geniuses of any time and any place talking to one another. The canon we inherit comes to us from those authors, themselves inheritors, who listened to what was given to them, shaped their own words in relation to those who came before, and finally contributed their own version of this world, informed by the unknowable world that will always accompany the known. If Sterne and Joyce cannot teach us how to teach literature as unknowing instructors, I suspect we are unteachable.

Having spent my lifetime in the classroom, I have always thought differently, that we are indeed teachable (although "teachable moment" is a solecism I would hope never to read in a student's essay). Hence, I decided to end this collection with a coda, a talk I gave as a keynote address for Sterne's tercentenary celebration at Royal Holloway, University of London, in 2013. It differs from my scholarly essays in being an unrevised oral presentation, spurred by the organizers' suggestion that the event be a working conference; since the primary work of the participants was teaching, and our workplace the classroom, I directed my remarks to what I think happened to our profession during the past several decades. The address was originally included for publication as the introductory essay to a collection derived from the occasion, edited by Peter de Voogd, Judith Hawley, and me for the University of Delaware Press.[5] The late Don Mell, the outstanding editor of that press, who singlehandedly made it a powerhouse of eighteenth-century studies, was very supportive of the piece, but it was finally deemed too politically sensitive, and we withdrew it from the collection.

Peter de Voogd published the address in the *Shandean* in 2015, a year before the collection appeared. Given their history over the last century, Europeans like Peter may have been more concerned with the interdiction of ideas than were Americans in 2013, although now, just a decade later, we are witnessing the very rapid rise of political figures intent on weaponizing censorship as a strategy for maintaining power. Removing the essay from the tercentenary collection was, sadly enough, a validation of my lamentations about our profession. I shall not repeat its argument in this brief introduction except to say that if my thoughts about our academic enterprise continue to offend some readers today, that offense is not a license for censorship. Surely, if a society should not condone those on the Far Right who are now censoring what they are offended by in schoolbooks, then literature professors—of all academics—cannot allow their sensibilities to turn them into the sort of book burners they purport to despise. We might profitably recall that *A Sentimental Journey* was put on the *Index Librorum Prohibitorum* in 1819; and, since one can find anything on the internet, I will conclude with the poor soul who in 2004 recommended banning *Tristram Shandy,* only to recant a few months later: "Sorry. I take it back about *Tristram Shandy.* On deeper examination, I loved it. Batty and clever as all hell."[6] Perhaps literary genius can best be defined as those authors who continue to respond to "deeper examination."

Notes

1 Melvyn New, "Proust's Influence on Sterne: Remembrance of Things to Come," *MLN* 103, no. 5 (1988): 1031–55.

2 Melvyn New, "Three Sentimental Journeys: Sterne, Shklovsky, Svevo," *Shandean* 11 (1999–2000): 125–34; Viktor Shklovsky, *A Sentimental Journey: Memoirs, 1917–1922,* trans. and intro. Richard Sheldon, intro. Sidney Monas (Funks Grove, IL: Dalkey Archive Press, 2004).

3 Melvyn New, ed., *In Proximity: Emmanuel Levinas and the Eighteenth Century,* with Robert Bernasconi and Richard A. Cohen (Lubbock: Texas Tech University Press, 2001); Melvyn New and Gerard Reedy, SJ, eds., *Theology and Literature in the Age of Johnson: Resisting Secularism* (Newark: University of Delaware Press, 2012).

4 Ian Watt, *The Rise of the Novel: Studies in Defoe, Richardson and Fielding* (London: Chatto and Windus, 1957).

5 Melvyn New, Peter de Voogd, and Judith Hawley, eds., *Sterne, Tristram, Yorick: Tercentenary Essays on Laurence Sterne* (Newark: University of Delaware Press, 2016).

6 Liana, reply to "Banned Book Week," ABCtales.com, November 22, 2004, https://www.abctales.com/forum/tue-2004-09-21-1145/banned-book-week.

Sterne

Textual Conversations

I

Sterne and the Narrative of Determinateness

The reader who demands to know exactly what Sterne really thinks of a thing . . . must be given up for lost.

Friedrich Nietzsche

I will begin with a seemingly noncontroversial observation by a recent critic of *Tristram Shandy,* anonymous simply because it is the sort of comment any one of a hundred might write today: "Sterne's point," he asserts, "is clear enough: life is a confused muddle of intent and accident." It is the sort of generalization many have accepted at least since E. M. Forster in 1927 declared "muddle" to be the God ruling over the work.[1] However, a closer examination of this particular formulation, not a jot different from that of countless others, might suggest an interesting problem. Simply put, if the point of *Tristram Shandy* is *clear,* then the work must be significantly divorced from the life—defined as a "confused muddle of intent and accident"—it portrays. Or, from another perspective, critics who find Sterne's point "clear enough" are themselves divorced from a work they argue is a muddle—and from a life that also does not allow the *clarity* they believe it can have in *Tristram Shandy.* Can one reformulate the observation? Perhaps we might say that "Sterne's point is obscure and muddled; life is a confused muddle and so I, as a reflective reader, become muddled when I try to understand his imitation of that muddle; it is seemingly successful as an imitation, although I cannot be quite clear on that point either." Frankly, I do not foresee this becoming the new mode of critical discourse. In this essay I would like to suggest why not, drawing on what I believe to be Sterne's own encounter with the paradox of the indeterminate text in human hands.

Using *Tristram Shandy* as my model, I specifically want to explore a key means by which its narrative, while pretending to suspend judgment about itself (to remain muddle), simultaneously reminds us of the impossibility of reading without judgment; we are unable to refrain from seeking the definitive statement of what is *clear* about the work. Since the narrative of *Tristram Shandy* is nowadays taken as a prime illustration of disruptive, fragmented, open, disjunctive narrative,[2] it helps us at times to keep our attention not on any particular interpretation, but more broadly on the contrasting "stories" people tell about the work, the narratives they initiate in order to organize or possess or subdue Sterne's mysterious text. In brief, while these modernist readers insist that *Tristram Shandy* is an open narrative, they all impose strategies of closure and *clarity* in their own writing on it.[3]

Sterne had anticipated just such efforts in the characters of Walter and Toby Shandy, both of whom ride very hard the hobby-horse of explication and explanation. What Toby wants to do on the bowling green is to make very *clear* to the observer exactly what happened during the muddle of a real-life battle; what Walter wants to do with his theories, his consultations, his documents, is to find very *clear* solutions to the muddle of a real life. In addition, the text of *Tristram* contains numerous interwoven narrative subtexts that serve as commentaries on the primary narrative— the marriage contract, the Memoire of the Sorbonne doctors, the sermon, Ernulphus's curse, passages from Burton and Rabelais, Montaigne and Chambers's *Cyclopædia,* and on and on.[4] These "narratives" restage the narrative strategies of the reader/critic, since they are almost always reifications, efforts to organize and control the flux of events and attitudes ("the life and opinions") by narrating them into a fixed (that is, a clear and explicable) order and arrangement. What Sterne shows us, I suggest, is that the instinct or desire to order the story is always more powerful than our capacity to rest in muddle, to celebrate disorder without a contrary urge to tidy up the place. Hence, for both character and reader, the interpolated narrative is almost always considered part of the larger narrative, a relevant commentary (limitation) on it, rather than a further dislocation or random interference.

Sterne's technique is tied, I believe, to the classical doctrine associated with the skeptic Sextus Empiricus, concerning the inner suspension of judgment (ἐποχή) about the conformity of appearance to reality, that is, the meanings of narrative representations.[5] Like Hume, Sterne seems to suggest that such suspension, while highly desirable and useful, is not often within the human being's capacity—we cannot refrain from believing in the truth of our own perceptions, our own narratives.[6] As Terence Penelhum comments rather wryly in *God and Skepticism:* "Neither the plain man nor the philosopher can refrain from believing that they are veridical. We cannot make our own assertions *un*dogmatically."[7] *Tristram Shandy* explores the delusions of the undogmatic, indeterminate narrative, even while denying its possibility.

If Sterne embraces many strategies of indeterminacy as part of his general skeptical embrace of the mysteries and riddles of experience,[8] he is equally attracted to—indeed, fascinated by—the narrative instinct, the "art" of storytelling, as an emblem of that divine harmony to which he seems to have remained committed. Our narratives are "truths" in so far as they make life possible for us. The inner compulsion not to contradict these truths, the instinct to narrate our stories to some useful conclusion, would seem inbred in our use of language; we *are* this instinct, since our being is our narrative. But where twentieth-century philosophy strives to keep our eye fixed always on the naivete of assuming such narratives are true (the epistemological issue), Sterne's interest was at least equally focused on the comic and tragic impotence that results from insisting they are not—ultimately, an ontological issue. In particular, Sterne seems intent upon ridiculing those critics and nonbelievers *determined* to practice modes of *indeterminacy* and blind to the paradox of doing so.

Several years ago, in the course of a short essay on the process of annotating *Tristram Shandy*'s bawdy, I asked:

> Is there, then, nothing for the annotator to do with Sterne's game of sexual discovery? Is all such mediation an unwarrantable intrusion between the reader and the text, most especially so when the reader's capacity to "get" the text is the game being played? Sterne confronts the problem in the first volume . . . when he sends madam back to reread a chapter, punishment for having missed a clue concerning intrauterine baptism. Here the author plays his own annotator or mediator, forcing all his readers to "get" a text I am certain all will miss on first reading. Sterne's humor depends on requiring from his readers a knowledge they could not possibly be expected to have.[9]

18 · Textual and Critical Intersections

Jonathan Lamb, a recent exuberant proponent of the indecipherable text of *Tristram Shandy* (as his recent book-length explication makes *absolutely clear*),[10] takes me to task for these comments in this manner: "The annotator [argues New] does his duty by 'forcing all his readers to "get" a text I am certain all will miss on first reading.' . . . The absolute jostling [of] the reader in that sentence seems at odds with the relativising tone [New] adopted elsewhere." It is indeed at odds, since the "jostling" reflects Sterne's humorous "theory" of annotating, the "relativizing" my serious response to its unacceptability. Lamb, however, is in no mood for such subtle distinctions: "I think it is a pity to strip initiatives from readers in this way, especially in view of the great lengths taken by Sterne to extend them," he laments.[11]

I present this exchange between Lamb and my own text not in order to defend the Florida volume of *Notes,* which proved quite useful to him in the course of his study despite his quarrel with its editor, but to argue against his fundamental premise, that Sterne goes to "great lengths" to extend the "initiatives" of the readers. Certainly, that is not true in the present instance: Madam is given absolutely no choice but to read the text in one way—Mrs. Shandy was not a papist, and the documentation for that reasoned conclusion is provided—signed, sealed, and delivered—in French *and* English. Does the reader have a choice? Can it be somehow argued that the text (the Sorbonne's, Sterne's, Madam's) remains undetermined at this point? But the very issue being discussed by the Sorbonne is an emblem of absolute determinacy; not a scintilla of doubt will be able to survive the work of the doctors. Every question, every doubt, every possible avenue of uncertainty, will be put to rest, brought to a satisfying conclusion, canonized into law; doubt will be turned into certainty before it is allowed to leave the womb.

The world that Sterne represents may be a muddle as has been suggested, but it is peopled by multitudes (inside the book *and* holding the book) with brooms and pens, *petites canulles* and swords, diagrams and models and paradigms, all intent on tidying up the place, making it neat and *clear.* There is, in short, no sufficient difference between the learned doctors of the Sorbonne and the learned doctors of today's academy: all work to establish the laws, the principles (the "double principle," in Lamb's case) that will make the muddle of life and its literature *clearer* and hence—no slight benefit—keep the proponents of such principles in positions of authority and acclaim. Sterne celebrates this tendency in Toby and Walter, in the doctors of the Sorbonne, in encyclopedists, in classical and theological scholars, in men like Obadiah Walker[12] and Bishop Warburton.[13] His book celebrates them all, but the appreciation is tempered by his jealous rivalry with their seemingly boundless energies; and by his chastising reminders—satiric and Christian—that human wisdom is a constant dupe to its own aspirations.

The pattern of indeterminacy being put to rest by one means or another is, to my mind, as prevalent in *Tristram Shandy* as the opposing tendency, undeniably present, of shattering certainties into fragments of ambivalence and belief. The modern critical agenda, however, focuses all its interest on the second tendency. There is not a serious work of literature, from Homer to Dante, from Shakespeare to Joyce, that has not been shown to be indeterminate, a uniformity which alone might give wisdom pause, as might the absolute *sameness* with which the prevalence of *difference* is everywhere celebrated. Such paradoxes hover at the edges of Sterne's particular plan to confront us with our inability to remain in "uncertainties, mysteries, doubts, without any irritable reaching after fact and reason."[14] And from the very beginning Sterne offers us a series of documents within *Tristram* that mimic—in their absoluteness and totality, their clarity, their principles of elucidation and discovery—the discourse of criticism that has accompanied Sterne's work from the beginning; the cant of criticism, a wonderful pun, he calls it at one important point.[15]

We are told, by Tristram and others, that this is the most cooperative book ever written, that we are joint sharers in its creation, half and half with its author.[16] But surely in the instance of the Sorbonne doctors, we have no such creative freedom. Even if we refuse to return with Madam to reread the passage, I do not think a similar option is available to deny Tristram's purpose in introducing the Memoire (*TS* 1.20.67–69), namely, to document certainty, not induce uncertainty. Such moves are seen everywhere in *Tristram,* beginning perhaps in chapter 4 of the first volume, where Tristram consults a "memorandum in my father's pocket-book" concerning his whereabouts in the months prior to his son's conception. Then, in chapter 15, we are given, verbatim, the article in the marriage settlement that defines Mrs. Shandy's movements—and the codicil offered by Toby

20 · Textual and Critical Intersections

which slams shut the one slight evasion she might have exercised. Moreover, these documents do work: they confront issues which are undecided, and they decide them. Would we want to enter into a dispute with the Sorbonne doctors concerning the legitimacy of their findings? Are we invited to question the authorship of Walter's memorandum? Are we tempted to challenge the marriage settlement in court? Clearly Sterne is here not sharing his storytelling with the reader, but, quite the contrary, setting out one boundary at which language does serve human purposes—authorization, communication, control.

To be sure, these documents are parodies of the real things—or real documents in parodic situations, as is the case with the major interpolated document in volume 2, the "Abuses of conscience" sermon. For ultimately, Sterne is not putting his faith in human language as the ultimate source of certitude; no one, not Locke in his much misunderstood (among Sterneans) *Essay concerning Human Understanding,* or even Swift, with his maligned academy, believed in such a possibility, the eternal contradiction between "human" and "certitude" being essential to a religious construct all three accepted. But neither does Sterne put his faith in gesture, sentiment, or sympathy, the popular answers of the Shaftesburian "evasion," the fallacies of which the "Abuses" sermon directly addresses.[17]

Nor, finally, does he seem quite at home, this rural Anglican clergyman, in the indeterminate, existential, absurd, phenomenological, solipsistic universe where we nowadays seem to find him. Rather, the documents interpolated everywhere into the world of *Tristram Shandy* seem to me overt examples of one of Sterne's richest observations: the human being produces such texts, in one form or another, *endlessly, necessarily, inevitably.* The copy of *Tristram* we hold in our hands is one such document, Walter Shandy's *Tristrapædia* is another, Slawkenbergius's tome and this brief essay are also examples, and the works of Rabelais and Montaigne and Burton, whose texts reappear in *Tristram* as part of its "documentation," are all restagings of the instinct, the drive to order and comprehend through our language whatever is not yet our language. The urge not merely to begin but to *complete* the narrative of ourselves is evident everywhere in *Tristram Shandy.* That we fail to do so could easily be explained for Sterne within the Christian narrative of sin (human limitation) and death (its consequence). Why we nonetheless continue to *essay* to "tell all" (and it is Montaigne who most clearly literalizes this urge), to make absolutely, positively certain that we have found the fullest measure of explanation and definition, the ever-replenishing cornucopia of endless discourse, that is a question less easily answered and the one I believe particularly fascinated Sterne.[18]

I believe I could make my point with the "Abuses" sermon; or with Ernulphus's curse (a memorial to the urge for closure and the resourcefulness of language); or with "Slawkenbergius's Tale," perhaps Sterne's most extended analysis of the noise and dangers of endless commentary.[19] Indeed, almost all Sterne's interpolated documents respond to what I have defined as a quest for certainty and determinacy (documentation), perhaps because their received form as "supporting evidence" is the outcome of our own need to define, explain, and comprehend. Can we imagine, for example, a discussion of the "Abuses" sermon that suggests it has absolutely nothing to do with *Tristram Shandy?* Could we substitute another sermon in its place (perhaps by Sterne, perhaps by Donne) and argue that it would not matter? Such hypothetical silliness can often serve to test the more serious absurdities of our present critical environment.

I would like to focus attention, however, on two interpolated documents rarely commented on among Sterneans, the first, Rubenius's *De Re Vestiaria Veterum,* which Walter is said to consult for the breeching of Tristram in volume 6; and the second, Spencer's *De Legibus Hebræorum Ritualibus,* which comes into play in chapter 28 of volume 5, after Tristram's accident with the window sash.

Albert Rubens (1614–57) catalogs the clothing of the ancients in a large quarto that wavers between the old style of learning and the new, between the universal citing of past authorities in the hope that truth would emerge from the welter of contrary opinions, and the beginnings of a more scientific orientation that accumulates and catalogs data as the foundation for further generalization. As such, *De Re Vestiaria Veterum, Præcipue de Lato Clavo* (*Of the Clothing of the Ancients, Particularly of the Latus Clavus,* 1665) is typical of late seventeenth-century learning, and Sterne seems brilliantly to have caught its genius in his reduction of Rubenius to lists, the cataloging of knowledge in a manner that suggests above all the growing importance of distinction and difference. For example, Sterne lists eighteen different types of shoe, beginning with

The open shoe.
The close shoe.
The slip shoe.
The wooden shoe. . . .

(*TS* 6.19.531)

This listing, with its vertical presentation—an echo, perhaps, of similar lists in Rabelais—is of especial interest because Walter cannot find in it or in the various other lists of *De Re Vestiaria* the advice concerning breeches that he is looking for. What he does find is a wealth of argumentation, the concentration of energy into a single point on which the learned of the world converge in their determination to settle a point—absolutely, definitively, and with the greatest clarity possible, namely, the identification of the *Latus Clavus:*

> *Rubenius* told him, that the point was still litigating amongst the learned:—That *Egnatius, Sigonius, Bossius Ticinensis, Bayfius, Budæus, Salmasius, Lipsius, Lazius, Isaac Causabon,* and *Joseph Scaliger,* all differed from each other,—and he from them: That some took it to be the button,—some the coat itself,—others only the colour of it. (*TS* 6.19.532)

Walter—and indeed Rubens before him—finds in this collection of data not a point of certainty but simply another list, this time of a community of scholars, a source of comfortable companionship that enables Walter to proceed with his life, whatever obstacles he encounters. Moreover, if the first list suggests to us the elusiveness, indeed impossibility, of the quest for Truth, for "the key," the second list just as certainly and dramatically indicates the refusal of the human mind to surrender to that impossibility.[20] The great satirists of scholastic learning who preceded Sterne—Rabelais and Swift—share with him an ambivalence toward learning that perhaps only the best ironists (and best skeptics) can have.

We must, however, qualify the list of authorities in two ways. In the first place, Sterne informs us that "the great *Bayfius*," listed among the disputants, in reality "honestly said, he knew not what it was,—whether a fibula,—a stud,—a button,—a loop,—a buckle,—or clasps and keepers" (*TS* 6.19.532). In a disputatious world of thesis and antithesis, statement and counterstatement, the admission of "ignorance," of "doubt," gives particular weight to the word "honestly." But Walter's response, typical of the learned world in general, indicates that "doubt" is simply not a satisfactory resting place for the restless mind: "——My father lost the horse, but not the saddle——They are *hooks and eyes,* said my father——and with hooks and eyes he ordered my breeches to be made" (*TS* 6.19.533). The skeptical moment of ἐποχή, the suspension between equally interesting alternatives, is unsustainable because "interest," a word weighted with theological as well as moral meaning in the eighteenth century,[21] denies us the pleasure and satisfaction we might otherwise take in stasis. For Sterne, the idea is embodied most often in the concept of the hobby-horse: to be thrown from one's horse, like Dr. Slop in volume 3 or Walter in this passage, is typical of the Shandy world; to dismount, as Bayfius appears to have done, is a heroic moment rarely encountered—except in the important normative actions of Yorick.

Second, and surely of no small significance to our present discussion, it is to be suspected that Sterne's discussion of clothing is indeed not from Rubens, that his citation is a false one. The Florida annotation (*TS,* Notes 417–22, n. to 529.17ff.) suggests that while the list of authorities might have been gleaned from the first chapter of *De Re Vestiaria,* Sterne's other lists and the language of his discussion follow much more closely Lefèvre de Morsan's *The Manners and Customs of the Romans. Translated from the French* (1740). This is a handbook of Roman costume probably intended for schools; and precisely its commonplace nature suggests that Sterne may have used not it, but a similar "textbook" not yet discovered. In rather stark contrast to the "honesty" celebrated in Bayfius, we have here a seeming instance of basic scholarly dishonesty: deliberate miscitation. Walter's authorization to move forward collapses, the cited author and his text disappear, the determinations and absolutes of the learned prove to be indeterminate after all. Here, perhaps, is the muddle that Forster identified, the loss of "author(ity)" that makes *Tristram Shandy* seem so modern a work. I suggest, however, that the discovery on which this collapse depends is not something Sterne could—or would—count on. Indeed, quite the opposite. The annotator here creates an indeterminacy (two hundred years after the work's appearance) that Sterne made every effort to foreclose in a most time-honored manner—by citing learned authority. It seems important to Sterne's conception of Walter that he participate in the community of scholars represented by Rubenius, that his researches be thorough and his consultations authentic; at the very least, there is nothing in the text that serves as a clue to the imposition of Rubenius on unsuspecting readers.[22] One might argue, of course, that none of Sterne's citations is to be trusted, that the unreliability of Tristram as a narrator is constructed from the materials of false learning, but this is precisely to confuse the ontological question with the epistemological.

Sterne's point depends on the reality of his documentation, the fact that the Sorbonne Memoire, the "Abuses" sermon, Ernulphus's curse, all actually exist; how true they are to the reality they attempt to define is a quite separate matter. But while it serves Sterne's purpose for the reader to recognize, for example, Tristram's attack on plagiary at the opening of volume 5 as a "steal" from Burton,[23] here his purpose seems best served by the sense of closure and determinateness produced in Walter after his consultation with "authority." Or again, where we are not asked to think of Slawkenbergius as anything other than a fabrication, here we are quite directed to the narrator's learning, not his invention, as a source of knowledge. Such distinctions are vital to our reading of Sterne because they indicate a more balanced perspective on, among other things, the documentation that is so inherently a part of the *Shandy* text itself. It is, indeed, no wonder that Tristram and his annotators should so often cross paths, since he, like them, expends much energy in the pursuit of authority, documentation, and closure; unfortunately, in this instance, the annotator may have opened a door (extended an "initiative" in Lamb's terminology) that Sterne had gone to "great lengths" to close.

Unlike the other disasters that befall Walter and Tristram, the falling window sash finds the father quite prepared. He does not write about it, as we might assume—that response is reserved for Tristram, who *"completes"* (my emphasis) the *Tristrapædia* with his own chapter on sash-windows and chamber pots (*TS* 5.26.458–59). Rather, he turns to his library, to some heavy folios, while Mrs. Shandy runs for the "lint and basilicon." What is Walter looking for in these tomes, and specifically in John Spencer's *De Legibus Hebræorum Ritualibus* (*On the Ritual Laws of the Hebrews*), published twenty years after Rubenius on Roman costumes? Not simply consolation or curatives, for he has not proceeded very long before he is deep in controversy, a war of words, the futility and frustration of both history and language.

The parodic use of the documents we noted before is especially apparent here, because of both the subject matter and Yorick's guiding presence. Most important, Yorick knows the text beforehand, and the learning represented by four Greek footnotes is in response to his familiarity with Spencer's learned work. Hence, when Walter is about to let us know just what the theologians have debated, Yorick interrupts: "Theologically? said *Yorick*,—or speaking after the manner of apothecaries?—statesmen?—or washer-women?" (*TS* 5.28.461). The three groups are footnoted, Sterne (Yorick) responding to phrases he found in Spencer, one having to do with disease (anthrax), another with population, a third with cleanliness (*TS,* Notes 374, n. to 461.16–17). Yorick's position is significantly ambivalent, however; he knows the text (as did Sterne, obviously),[24] but he can wish he did not, and when Toby suggests it is all "*Arabick*" to him, Yorick chimes in, "I wish . . . 'twas so, to half the world." At this point, Walter's reading lapses quite into controversy. Having more or less ignored the opportunity to discuss whether the Jews or Egyptians practiced circumcision first (which certainly occupies pages of Spencer and would occupy Bishop Warburton among many others [*TS, Notes* 372–73, n. to 460.9–11]), he finds himself suddenly on the shoals of Ilus's identity and the controvertists' "two and twenty reasons" for his circumcising his entire army—a question which, significantly, immediately involves Toby's "determinate" nature as well: "Not without a court martial?" (*TS* 5.28.462). Perhaps Spencer, perhaps Walter's obvious enjoyment of the controversy, leads Yorick to an attack on polemic divines: "I wish there was not a polemic divine . . . in the kingdom;—one ounce of practical divinity—is worth a painted ship load of all their reverences have imported these fifty years" (*TS* 5.28.462); and in the next chapter, he reads Rabelais's description of Gymnast and Tripet's riding competition (another document!—and one that Yorick keeps in his coat pocket),[25] which serves to pin down in all our minds, exactly and definitely and determinately, Yorick's attitude toward the cavortings of the intellectual community. Yet Yorick's "familiarity" with Spencer suggests as well his community with that world of books and words. Significantly, it is the same community that Walter looks for when he seeks in *De Legibus* a consolation for the maiming of Tristram:

26 · Textual and Critical Intersections

> Nay, said he, mentioning the name of a different great nation
> upon every step as he set his foot upon it—if the EGYPTIANS,—
> the SYRIANS,—the PHOENICIANS,—the ARABIANS,—the
> CAPADOCIANS,——if the COLCHI, and TROGLODYTES
> did it——if SOLON and PYTHAGORAS submitted,—what is
> TRISTRAM?——Who am I, that I should fret or fume one moment
> about the matter? (*TS* 5.27.460)

Whether it is the link that Sterne forges with Rabelais at the end of this scene, the link with Shakespeare inherent in the naming of Yorick, or the link with a world of past scholars and churchmen, and the lost cultures of the past (and we must remember that volume 5 opens with a somewhat parallel passage, again an interpolated document, Cicero's consolatory letter to Sulpicius, by way of Burton's *Anatomy of Melancholy* [*TS*, Notes 348–50]),[26] one has here, I suggest, an answer to the question posed earlier: why do we continue to talk and write and exercise our language in the pursuit of knowledge, definition, unattainable clarity, and wisdom?

The real community of *Tristram Shandy* is not, as is so often said, simply that of the Shandy brothers; rather, it is represented by all the authors and books, all their documents and cultures and artifacts, all that illustrates to us what it means to live in a world written by God, and hence always approximated by the same human endeavor. At times the documents are necessarily ludicrous, as is so much human effort in the face of the infinite, but at other times they are useful and perhaps even profound, as human effort can also be. Sterne keeps us aware of both possibilities, and aware above all that while every attempt to create a world of certainty and truth will fail, the attempt is what ties us to the community of humanity, what offers us the equivalent of communion with our legacy, and, in the end, allows us to create, if not God's world, then our own world in imitation of His. Writing seems to have been an activity Sterne delighted in, not as an epistemological experience, but as an ontological one. Sterne's "documents" suggest to me that the present emphasis in narrative theory on the epistemology of indeterminacy is a tendency he might have predicted but never have succumbed to. Sterne's fiction arises, to the contrary, in the ontology of the human urge to speak the truth.

That that urge so often takes the shape of fiction and folly is nothing that was not explained to him by his faith and redeemed by it as well.

Nietzsche is one of his few readers who seems fully to appreciate Sterne's ontological bent: "his antipathy to seriousness is united with a tendency to be unable to regard anything merely superficially. Thus he produces in the right reader a feeling of uncertainty as to whether one is walking, standing or lying: a feeling, that is, close to floating."[27] Classical skepticism might call it hovering among all possibilities, but I suspect Nietzsche, Sterne, and Sextus Empiricus each had a nicely muddled idea (*clarity* would not suffice) of approximately the same thing.

Originally published in *Eighteenth-Century Fiction* 4, no. 4 (1992).

Notes

1 "Obviously a god is hidden in *Tristram Shandy* and his name is Muddle, and some readers cannot accept him." E. M. Forster, *Aspects of the Novel* (New York: Harcourt, 1927), 146.

2 See, e.g., J. Hillis Miller, "Narrative Middles: A Preliminary Outline," *Genre* 11 (1978): 375–87; Ralph Flores, "Changeling Fathering: *Tristram Shandy*," in *The Rhetoric of Doubtful Authority: Deconstructive Readings of Self-Questioning Narratives, St. Augustine to Faulkner* (Ithaca, NY: Cornell University Press, 1984), 116–44; and Jonathan Lamb, *Sterne's Fiction and the Double Principle* (Cambridge: Cambridge University Press, 1989).

3 The most glaring instance is Wolfgang Iser's *Laurence Sterne: Tristram Shandy* (Cambridge: Cambridge University Press, 1988), where the reading of *Tristram* as an indeterminate text turns Sterne into both a forerunner and a strict proponent of Iser's own critical theories. See also Robert Markley, "*Tristram Shandy* and 'Narrative Middles': Hillis Miller and the Style of Deconstructive Criticism," *Genre* 17 (1984): 179–90, an attempt to justify Miller's obfuscations while at the same time "translating" them into what might pass for a transparent (i.e., a *clear*) expository prose.

4 This structure of borrowings is apparent on almost every page of *TS*, Notes. One need only compare these notes with those required for Fielding's or Smollett's fictions (excepting *The History and Adventures of an Atom*) in the Wesleyan and Georgia editions, respectively, to realize a fundamental difference between Sterne and the novelists with whom he is most often grouped.

5 See the very fine essay by Donald R. Wehrs, "Sterne, Cervantes, Montaigne: Fideistic Skepticism and the Rhetoric of Desire," *Comparative Literature Studies* 25 (1988): 127–51.

28 · Textual and Critical Intersections

6 See David Hume, *An Enquiry concerning Human Understanding*, 1748, ed. Antony Flew (La Salle, IL: Open Court, 1988), 189–90 (section 12, part 2):

> For as, in common life, we reason every moment concerning fact and existence, and cannot possibly subsist, without continually employing this species of argument, any popular objections, derived from thence, must be insufficient to destroy that evidence. The great subverter of *Pyrrhonism* or the excessive principles of scepticism is action, and employment, and the occupations of common life. These principles may flourish and triumph in the schools; where it is, indeed, difficult, if not impossible, to refute them. But as soon as they leave the shade, and by the presence of the real objects, which actuate our passions and sentiments, are put in opposition to the more powerful principles of our nature, they vanish like smoke, and leave the most determined sceptic in the same condition as other mortals.

Cf. the essays by M. F. Burnyeat ("Can the Skeptic Live His Skepticism?") and Robert J. Fogelin ("The Tendency of Hume's Skepticism") in *The Skeptical Tradition*, ed. Myles Burnyeat (Berkeley: University of California Press, 1983), 117–48 (esp. 118–21) and 397–412 (esp. 398–404), respectively.

7 Terence Penelhum, *God and Skepticism: A Study in Skepticism and Fideism* (Dordrecht: D. Reidel, 1983), 124.

8 Sterne uses the phrase "riddles and mysteries" twice in *Tristram Shandy* and twice in his sermons. See *TS* 4.17.350 and 9.22.776; see also *TS*, Notes 313, n. to 350.11–19. Despite this religious context, critics have tended to follow Martin Battestin in asserting that the phrase indicates a secular world view: the Shandy world is "inexplicable even when it appears most obvious, overwhelming in its multiplicity, unpredictable in its contingencies, it bewilders and eludes them all." Battestin, *The Providence of Wit: Aspects of Form in Augustan Literature and the Arts* (Oxford: Clarendon Press, 1974), 245. As Donald R. Wehrs points out, however, a fideistic Christian defines the mundane world in exactly the same fashion, human helplessness leading *to* faith and not *away* from it, as Battestin insists. See Wehrs, "Sterne, Cervantes, Montaigne," esp. 145–46. That Sterne also has Locke in mind when using the phrase "riddles and mysteries" (see "Scholia," *Scriblerian* 19 [1986]: 92–93) in no way negates this linkage between skepticism and faith; indeed, it helps explain Locke's own significant commitment to orthodoxy despite what Battestin (245) calls "a distinctly 'modern' view of man based on Lockean epistemology."

9 Melvyn New, "'At the backside of the door of purgatory': A Note on Annotating *Tristram Shandy*," in *Laurence Sterne: Riddles and Mysteries*, ed. Valerie Grosvenor Meyer (London: Vision Press, 1984), 17.

10 The title of Lamb's book, *Sterne's Fiction and the Double Principle* (Cambridge: Cambridge University Press, 1989), contains its own statement of the problem I am exploring, namely, the human inability to confront "doubleness" without reducing it to a "principle"—to oneness. Only once, to my mind, does Lamb come close to recognizing this paradox (104): "The lesson for the reader, you or me, comes unsettlingly close." Far more telling is the fact that not only Sterne, but Cervantes and Montaigne as well are found to conform to Lamb's "double principle." Reductiveness, even in the pursuit of indeterminacy, is no virtue.

11 Lamb, 3.

12 Walker was the author of *Of Education* (1673; 6th ed., 1699), from which Sterne borrowed, verbatim in many instances, his discussion of auxiliary verbs at the end of volume 5; see *TS*, Notes 392–94, n. to 484.11ff.

13 See Melvyn New, "Sterne, Warburton, and the Burden of Exuberant Wit," *Eighteenth-Century Studies* 15 (1982): 245–74, for a full discussion not only of Sterne's borrowings from Warburton, but of his mixed response to Warburton's great (if hobby-horsical) learning.

14 John Keats, letter to his brothers, December 21, 1817. Herbert Read, an astute reader of Sterne, was perhaps the first to connect Sterne and Keats: "We know that Keats was familiar with *Tristram Shandy*, and it may be that his notion of *Negative Capability* ('which Shakespeare possessed so enormously') owes something to Sterne's character of Yorick—in any case, Sterne was certainly also 'a man . . . capable of being in uncertainties, Mysteries, doubts.'" Read, *The Contrary Experience* (London: Faber and Faber, 1963), 330.

15 *TS* 3.12.214: "Of all the cants which are canted in this canting world,——though the cant of hypocrites may be the worst,—the cant of criticism is the most tormenting!"

16 See, e.g., *TS* 2.11.125: "The truest respect which you can pay to the reader's understanding, is to halve this matter amicably, and leave him something to imagine, in his turn, as well as yourself." Perhaps the favorite incident for those critics who take such comments literally as the shaping spirit of the work is Tristram's invitation in volume 6, chapter 38, to draw the Widow Wadman in the blank page provided for our fancy. Yet surely, even here, Sterne's point is far more determinate than indeterminate, since his work depends not at all on the reader actually taking pen and ink in hand (and I have never found a single copy of *Tristram Shandy* in which the offer was accepted), but on grasping the humor of Tristram's distinction between wife and mistress. That women might not find the passage humorous at all indicates precisely how overdetermined Sterne's joke is at this point. [Subsequently, I have been informed of

30 · Textual and Critical Intersections

several copies located where someone provided a sketch—whether of a mistress or not has remained indeterminate.]

17 Interesting recent discussions of Sterne and Shaftesburian sensibility include Robert Markley, "Sentimentality as Performance: Shaftesbury, Sterne, and the Theatrics of Virtue," in *The New Eighteenth Century: Theory, Politics, English Literature*, ed. Felicity Nussbaum and Laura Brown (New York: Methuen, 1987), 210–30; and John Mullan, *The Language of Feeling in the Eighteenth Century* (Oxford: Clarendon, 1988), 147–200. See also *TS*, Notes 180–81, n. to 157.14ff.

18 Montaigne's own embrace of Pyrrhonic skepticism, most especially in the "Apology for Raimond de Sebonde," leads I think to his often stated love of self-exploration. See, for example, "Of the Resemblance of Children to their Fathers":

> I do not hate Opinions contrary to my own. I am so far from being angry to see a Disagreement betwixt mine and other Men's Judgments . . . that on the contrary . . . I find it much more rare to see our Humours and Designs jump and agree. And there never was in the World two Opinions alike, no more than two Hairs, or two Grains. The most universal Quality, is *Diversity*.

And "Of Repentance":

> Could my Soul once take footing, I would not essay, but resolve; but it is always learning and making trial. Every Man carries the entire Form of [the] human Condition.

Michel de Montaigne, *Essays*, trans. Charles Cotton, 6th ed. (London, 1753), 2:521, 3:20.

In September 1760 Sterne confirmed a correspondent's guess that Montaigne was a favorite author: "'for my conning Montaigne as much as my pray'r book'—there you are right again" (*Letters* 168).

19 I explore this aspect of *Tristram Shandy* in "Swift and Sterne: Two Tales, Several Sermons, and a Relationship Revisited," in *Critical Essays on Jonathan Swift*, ed. Frank Palmeri (New York: G. K. Hall, 1993), 164–86.

20 An interesting confluence of Sterne's interest in the learned community and his life as an Anglican clergyman may be seen in a popular clerical manual like John Wilkins's *Ecclesiastes, or A Discourse concerning the Gift of Preaching*, which reached its ninth edition by 1718. Wilkins's efforts are primarily bibliographical, pages upon pages listing works to consult on such topics as "Scripture-Philosophy," "Scripture-Geography," and "Scripture-Measures and Weights," then on individual books of the Bible, usually at least twenty

sources for each, and finally on topics such as "Independency" or "Communion and Schism," each list divided into "pro" and "con." This vast accumulation of learning, when thus cataloged, is at once an impressive commentary on human endeavor and human folly; perhaps Wilkins sensed the ambiguity when he warns the clergy in his introduction to "beware of that vain affectation of finding something new and strange in every text, though never so plain. It will not so much shew our *parts* . . . as our *pride* and wantonness of wit" (16).

21 See, e.g., Isabel Rivers, *Reason, Grace, and Sentiment: A Study of the Language of Religion and Ethics in England, 1600–1780* (Cambridge: Cambridge University Press, 1991), 70–88. [The validity of this discussion is suggested by my offering a "solution" to "*hooks and eyes*" thirty years after this essay appeared; see below, p. 329, in my essay on Sterne and Joyce.]

22 There is good evidence, indeed, that Sterne wanted to pass as more learned than he really was; see my "Sterne, Warburton" for one possible explanation. The single instance where he most successfully achieved an unearned reputation may be his borrowings from Locke; twentieth-century critics have often discovered in Sterne a profound commentator on *An Essay concerning Human Understanding*, although they remain undecided as to whether Sterne supports or criticizes Locke. In fact, Sterne's citations of Locke repeat the most common notions associated with him and might easily derive from popular sources, e.g., Chambers's *Cyclopædia*.

23 Sterne gives ample indication that Burton's *Anatomy of Melancholy* is on his mind, from the two mottoes on the title page of the first edition of volume 5 to borrowings from Burton in both the Whiskers episode (see *TS*, Notes 342, n. to 412.5ff.) and Walter's funeral oration (345, n. to 418.8–12).

24 Spencer's *De Legibus Hebræorum Ritualibus* appears twice (items 303 and 810) in *A Facsimile Reproduction of a Unique Catalogue of Laurence Sterne's Library* (London: James Tregaskis, 1930); Rubenius appears as item 828. The catalog is not an accurate representation of Sterne's library (other libraries were grouped in the sale), but the appearance of Rubenius and Spencer in a 1768 sale catalog of private libraries helps make one essential point of this essay: there was a community of learned lay readers (with a capacity for Latin, to be sure) in mid-eighteenth-century England whose libraries were well stocked with arcane learning from the seventeenth century.

25 Sterne borrows the entire description from Rabelais. See *The Works of Francis Rabelais, M.D.*, trans. Thomas Urquhart and Peter Motteux, with notes by John Ozell, 5 vols (1750), 1:35; see also *TS*, Notes 376–78, n. to 463.1ff.

26 That Warburton had used a similar parody of the letter by Scarron to attack the "wits" of the age (see the "Dedication to Free Thinkers" in his *Divine*

Legation of Moses) was almost certainly on Sterne's mind; and perhaps, as well, a parody of Cicero's letter by Swift. To suggest that such a text, then, is somehow open and indeterminate, and that the annotator who directs attention to these relationships limits the reader's freedom, strikes me as absurd; indeed, I might suggest instead, that the reader who does not hear Cicero, Burton, Scarron, Swift, and Warburton in this passage is exiled from the community of *Tristram Shandy*, much as Toby "frees" himself by this literal interpretation: "My uncle *Toby* had but two things for it; either to suppose his brother to be the wandering *Jew*, or that his misfortunes had disordered his brain" (*TS* 5.3.423). Toby is at this point a very poor reader of his brother's text.

27 Friedrich Nietzsche, *Human, All Too Human*, trans. R. J. Hollingdale (Cambridge: Cambridge University Press, 1986), 239.

2

The Odd Couple

Laurence Sterne and John Norris of Bemerton

In Sterne's entire canon, John Norris is named only once, and on that occasion he is "under erasure"—literally. In the "Rabelaisian Fragment," Sterne's aborted creative effort between the *Political Romance* and volumes 1 and 2 of *Tristram Shandy,* he portrays a sermon writer, Homenas, pilfering from another cleric, John Rogers: Homenas "was all this while Rogering at it as hard as He could." For those who believe Sterne had no decorum at all, it should be noted that he lined over this outrageous pun and subsequently substituted the name "Norris" where "Rogers" could be expected; and then, since third thoughts are even cleaner than second thoughts, he lined out "Norris" and wrote in "Clark" (*MW* 159). In this essay, I will offer evidence that throughout his career Sterne "was Norrising at it" more than anyone has previously suspected; and, to satisfy those who believe identifying an author's sources is wasted energy until one assigns interpretative significance, I will also reluctantly indicate some possible paths for future critical readings. I say reluctantly, because I think the roles of annotator and interpreter are essentially different: the annotator complicates the text by entwining it with a source; the interpreter simplifies the text by offering a solution as to how that complication might be untangled.

John Norris is twice again referred to in Sterne's canon, but not by name. In sermon 29, "Our conversation in heaven," he is labeled "a very able divine in our church" (*Sermons* 280), and in sermon 39, "Eternal advantages of religion," "an able enquirer" (372).[1] In both instances we know it is Norris because Sterne is in the middle of long verbatim borrowings, the first of which was noted by Lansing Hammond, the second not.[2] I believe Tillotson is the only other figure complimented in this anonymous way in the sermons.

34 · Textual and Critical Intersections

The scant attention given John Norris (1657–1711) today is almost solely directed toward his role as the "last" of the Cambridge Platonists. His major philosophical work, *An Essay towards the Theory of the Ideal or Intelligible World* (1701–4), which attracted the parodic attentions of Tom D'Urfey, seems of interest primarily because in it Norris pays homage to Descartes and Malebranche rather than to English philosophy. Indeed, Norris was the first, in 1690, to publish a criticism of Locke's *Essay concerning Human Understanding,* shortly after it appeared, a forty-four-page pamphlet, often reprinted. Locke wrote a brief and rather angry response against Norris, and a longer response, covering much the same ground, against Malebranche, but published neither himself.[3]

But Norris was also—and perhaps foremost—a religious writer, and when, in *Christian Blessedness,* he suggests we may be surprised to see him "*again so soon*" in print, we might be tempted not to accept his excuse that "*considering the shortness and uncertainty of Life . . . a Man can never live too fast . . . nor make too much haste to do good.*"[4] Norris's life was one of retirement, reading, and *religious* writing; the fruits include, among his many titles, *An Idea of Happiness* (1683), *The Theory and Regulation of Love* (1688), *Reason and Religion* (1689), *Christian Blessedness* (1690), three separate volumes of *Practical Discourses* (1691, 1693, 1699), *Letters concerning the Love of God* (with Mary Astell, 1695), *An Account of Reason and Faith* (1697), *Concerning Humility* (1707), and his final work, *Concerning Christian Prudence* (1710).

Moreover, Norris's work remained popular; the *Theory and Regulation of Love* and *Reason and Religion* both reached seventh editions, in 1723 and 1724, respectively. His exchange with Astell was published as late as 1730, and *An Account of Reason and Faith* had a thirteenth edition in 1740. His *Miscellanies* had five editions during his lifetime and a ninth edition by 1730. *Christian Prudence* reached its seventh edition in 1722 and was extracted by Wesley in 1742. And his *Practical Discourses upon the Beatitudes* reached its fifteenth edition by 1728. These reprintings tell us much about the eighteenth century and its reading tastes.

The first to uncover Sterne's debt to Norris was an anonymous contributor to the *Gentleman's Magazine* in 1800: "I was astonished to find, on looking into Sterne's Sermons the other day, whole passages copied from those of John Norris."[5] A century and a half later, Hammond echoes this astonishment: "That Norris' name should appear at all in the list of predecessors to whom Yorick was indebted is surprising, for the two men could have had little in common; this acquaintance with the mystic, Platonist, and poet of Bemerton stands as another illustration of how impossible it is to predict from whom Yorick was likely to borrow."[6] Hammond goes on to note, astutely I think, that Norris's writings were filled "with just that sort of quotation Sterne had found so much to his liking elsewhere," but finding no further borrowings, he decides, finally, that Sterne's "acquaintance with Norris's writings may have been limited strictly to those three or four sermons which he had ransacked," and suggests that Sterne found them in some "collection of miscellaneous sermons."[7]

Let me suggest that neither Hammond nor I have yet identified all the borrowings from Norris in Sterne. In at least one instance, for example, Hammond caught a borrowing from one page of Norris and missed a second verbatim borrowing a few pages later; my own survey will prove equally flawed. The attempt to preach "practical divinity" in a "practical style" is the hallmark of Anglican centrism throughout the century, and it is often impossible to distinguish (or recall) Sterne's own "practical" voice in the sermons from verbatim borrowings of authors seventy or eighty years earlier. That Norris published four volumes of sermons under the title "Practical Discourses" is telling, all the more so given his quite different prose style in his philosophical writings, a difference one notes in Samuel Clarke as well.[8] Hence, while I have added to Hammond's list of borrowings in my edition of Sterne's *Sermons* (*Sermons,* Notes 218–19, 247–48, 254–57, 305–6, 310–11, 316–19, 433–34, etc.), I know I have not been able to catch every echo. As with Sterne's borrowings from his favorite authors, Rabelais, Montaigne, Cervantes, and—in the sermons—Tillotson, his debt is a question of both specific passages and more generalized dependencies; hence, rather than offering here a definitive catalog of the relationship, I will argue only that Norris's canon may warrant as much attention when reading Sterne as we have given to his known favorites—as much, to be sure, as has been afforded to Locke.[9]

Gardner Stout, in his edition of *A Sentimental Journey,* calls attention to a borrowing from Norris, noted by Hammond, in order to annotate that passage in which Yorick asserts that Smelfungus and Mundungus will be unhappy in Heaven, because "they have brought up no faculties for this work; and was the happiest mansion in heaven to be allotted to [them], they would be so far from being happy, that the[ir] souls . . . would do penance there to all eternity."[10] Significantly, as well as pointing to Norris, and Sterne's verbatim borrowing in "Our conversation in heaven," Stout's annotation brings to bear on the passage one of the most famous sentences in *Tristram Shandy* (*TS* 7.13.593): "REASON, is half of it, SENSE; and the measure of heaven itself is but the measure of our present appetites and concoctions——." He might have pointed as well to a sentence a few chapters further on:

> ——Alas! Madam, had [my story of the nuns of Andoüillets] been upon some melancholy lecture of the cross—the peace of meekness, or the contentment of resignation——I had not been incommoded: or had I thought of writing it upon the purer abstractions of the soul, and that food of wisdom, and holiness, and contemplation, upon which the spirit of man (when separated from the body) is to subsist for ever——You would have come with a better appetite from it——. (*TS* 7.26.615)

The sentences in "Our conversation in heaven" underlying both passages are these:

> The apostle tells us, that without holiness no man shall see God;—by which no doubt he means, that a virtuous life is the only medium of happiness and terms of salvation,—which can only give us admission into heaven.—But some of our divines carry the assertion further, that without holiness,—without some previous similitude wrought in the faculties of the mind, corresponding with the nature of the purest of beings . . . that it is not morally only, but physically impossible for it to be happy,—and that an impure and polluted soul, is not only unworthy of so pure a presence as the spirit of God, but even incapable of enjoying it, could it be admitted. (*Sermons* 278)

The idea of a moral preparation for the afterlife is commonplace in Anglican sermonizing (and, indeed, Hammond suggests a borrowing from Tillotson at this point),[11] especially on the occasion of All Saints' Day, but the necessity of an earthly, sensate preparation for Heaven is a particular emphasis of Norris, almost certainly derived from the Cambridge Platonist with whom he corresponded, Henry More; and Norris comes very close to Sterne in a passage immediately preceding the long passage Sterne definitely borrows for the remainder of his discussion:

> And first, the Holy Spirit will not enter but into a pure and clean Heart. . . . [The Holy Spirit] does not come in . . . till the Man has well attended to, and complied with those his antecedent Motions and Suggestions, till he has swept and made clean the inner Room of his Heart: So that Purity of Heart is absolutely necessary . . . for the residence and in-dwelling of the Holy Spirit.[12]

Later in the same volume, Norris comes even closer:

> there are some certain Dispositions of Soul necessary to relish and enjoy the Happiness of Heaven. This I think is a Supposition that need not be disputed, since even to the enjoyment of sensible good there is requisite a proportion of Sense. . . . There is greater reason to think that the Delights of Heaven . . . cannot be tasted but by a suitable Disposition of Soul.[13]

At this point in his sermon, Sterne offers the long verbatim borrowing from Norris, the gist of which is the same: there must be a reformation of sensual pleasures *here* in order to enjoy Heaven *hereafter:*

> The consideration of this has led some writers so far, as to say, with some degree of irreverence in the expression,—that it was not in the power of God to make a wicked man happy, if the soul was separated from the body, with all its vicious habits and inclinations unreformed;—which thought, a very able divine in our church has pursued so far, as to declare his belief,—that could the happiest mansion in heaven be supposed to be allotted to a gross and polluted spirit, it would be so far from being happy in it, that it would do penance there to all eternity:—by which he meant, it would carry such appetites along with it, for which there could be found no suitable objects. (*Sermons* 280)[14]

For Stout, the passage indicates that "man knows and enjoys God, the Supreme Good, primarily by virtue of a faculty which participates in and is essentially of the same nature as its divine object"—a "characteristically Latitudinarian" principle, he argues, tending as it does to "deëmphasize grace, which is seen by the Latitudinarians primarily as coöperating with the man who has already chosen the good."[15] Read in the light of Norris's whole sermon, however, the hint of scandal in Stout's description is nowhere apparent. Rather, Norris is making a rather fundamental and certainly orthodox point, one that Sterne fully endorses as his own sermon continues: how can we hope for Heaven unless we *transform* ourselves into the "likeness of what we hope to be hereafter.—How can we expect the inheritance of the saints of light, upon other terms than what they themselves obtained it?—" (*Sermons* 281); and Sterne continues for another two pages, outlining the evils we must leave behind, impure desire, anger, rage, envy, lust, wicked imaginations, drunkenness and gluttony, craft, avarice, deceit, fraud and treachery, ambition, discord, cursing and bitterness, backbiting and slander, theft, rapine, violence, and extortion. Philippians 3:20, whether in Norris's hands or in Sterne's, is not an assertion of parity with the Divine, but rather an assertion of an ethic of otherworldliness, the need for "forgetting this world,—disengaging our thoughts and affections from it" (*Sermons* 281) so that, at the Last Judgment, we can be found worthy of the Communion of Saints—hence the All Saints' Day occasion of the sermon is particularly relevant to its subject.

With this in mind, we can return to that passage in *Tristram Shandy* cited by Stout, "REASON, is half of it, SENSE; and the measure of heaven itself is but the measure of our present appetites and concoctions," and note that it is the concluding sentence of a short paragraph that begins:

> I love the Pythagoreans (much more than ever I dare tell my dear Jenny) for their "χωρισμὸν ἀ πὸ τοῦ Σώματος εἰς το Καλῶς Φιλοσοφεῖν"—[their] *"getting out of the body, in order to think well."* No man thinks right whilst he is in it; blinded as he must be, with his congenial humours, and drawn differently aside . . . with too lax or too tense a fibre——REASON, is, etc. (*TS* 7.13.593)

Sterne's Greek text sent the Florida editors to the Pythagorean fragments, where they came up empty; they had better have gone to John Norris, for both the Greek and the English, in the first volume of *Practical Discourses* (1691), his sermon on righteous and unrighteous judgment:

> But the *Pythagoreans* went higher, and taught their Disciples, χωρισμὸν ἀ πὸ τοῦ Σώματος εἰς το Καλῶς Φιλοσοφεῖν, that they must separate and unwind themselves even from their very Bodies, if they

would be good Philosophers. This in a Qualified and Corrected Sense is true, for the Body is the great Impediment and Disadvantage of the Soul, and therefore all Bodily Passions and Inclinations, as well as Intellectual Habits and Appetites must be put to *Silence,* in the still and Attentive Search and Inquiry after Truth.[16]

I do not think this concurrent appearance of Norris in *A Sentimental Journey, Tristram Shandy,* and the sermons is accidental. Rather, it bespeaks Sterne's grasp of a fundamental argument in Norris, repeated many times in many places, an emphasis steeped in Norris's Neoplatonism and yet carefully integrated (note his "Qualified and Corrected Sense" in the passage just quoted) into a traditional and thoroughly orthodox Christian scheme. Whatever its modifications within a variety of ongoing debates, we may take this for Norris's fundamental truth about being human:

> 'Tis the grand disadvantage of our Mortal condition, to have our Soul consorted with a *disproportionate* and *uncompliant Vehicle,* and to have her aspiring Wings pinn'd down to the ground. We have a mixt constitution, made up of two vastly different substances, with Appetites and Inclinations to different Objects, serving to contrary Interests, and steering to opposite Points. A compound of Flesh and Spirit, a thing between an *Angel* and a *Beast.* We lug about with us a *Body* of sin. . . . We have, 'tis true, a Law in our *Minds,* but then we have also another in our *Members,* which *wars always,* and *most times prevails* against that of our *Mind.*[17]

The passage seems to me, traditional as it is, as good a gloss on Sterne's fictions as we are likely to possess. More to the point, this echo of Norris in that volume of *Tristram Shandy* occupied with Tristram's flight from death into a world of dead saints (in Auxerre), and in a chapter preceding a discussion of the dimensions of Hell (lifted from Burton's *Anatomy of Melancholy*), might suggest that Sterne, himself fleeing from England with death's hand upon him,[18] is preoccupied with his own ultimate destiny ("*de vanitate mundi et fugâ sæculi*") as he writes; and that in *A Sentimental Journey,* published one short month before his long-anticipated death, he may again have had Death, Judgment, Heaven, and Hell—the four last things, about which he had so often preached—uppermost in his mind.

40 · Textual and Critical Intersections

But the borrowing from Norris also opens to us the possibility of understanding better than heretofore the determinate ideas annexed to those vexed concepts of "reason" and "sense" in Sterne's writings. *Christian Blessedness* offers many clues to Sterne's absorption of Norris's thinking on these two subjects. For example, in explicating the sixth beatitude, "Blessed are the pure in heart; for they shall see God," Norris constructs an entity neither reasonable nor sensible, yet clearly related to both, what he calls "the Intellectual Heart" or "Spirit of our Minds," or "Flower and Essence of our Soul," and defines in this manner:

> This is that which sees in the eyes, and hears in the ears. This is that which understands and wills, loves and hates. Here are all the Springs and Powers of Life and Motion, here is the last resort of all outward Impressions, and from this *Central Point* are derived all the Lines of Action and Motion, even as all the Arteries and Veins are from the Natural Heart, which it diffuses and disperses throughout the Body, and has its Pulses in every part. . . .
>
> This Heart is always *Beating,* the Pulses of it never rest, Thought rises upon Thought, and Desire succeeds Desire. The Motion is perpetual, constant and vehement. . . . Now what a dangerous thing is such a Motion as this, if not rightly determin'd? Of what vast heights in goodness is it capable! And to what vast heights of wickedness may it rise, if not well-govern'd.[19]

These observations occur just a few pages prior to the passages discussed earlier that Sterne quotes verbatim in his All Saints' Day sermon (29); it is noteworthy that the Beatitudes are the Gospel reading for the Anglican service on that day.[20]

This "Intellectual Heart," we soon discover, is not distinguishable from God, defined as "the Immediate *Place* of *Spirits* and *Souls,* who all live, move, and have their being in him, and are joyn'd to him by a *Central Touch,* as the great Plotinus speaks." But we are also informed, as Norris moves toward his point concerning the preparation of the senses for Heaven, that while we dwell in God "Essentially and Totally," God dwells in us only as a "special Presence, by the Spirit of Grace and Benediction," which does not enter but into a purified and cleansed heart.[21] Hence, Norris concludes, we do not see God now because of the "grossness of this Tabernacle wherein the Soul is incased. This is that *Glass* through which we now see so Darkly, and which makes us do so. This is that black Skreen that parts the *Material* from the *Intelligible* World. The more abstract therefore we are from the Body, and from the Bodily Life, the more fit we shall be both to *behold,* and to *indure* the Rays of the Divine Light."[22]

Norris covers this ground again and again in his theological writings, but perhaps nowhere more clearly than in his *Practical Treatise concerning Humility* (1707): "The great and ultimate foundation of Humility, as of every other good thing that is in us, is no doubt the Grace of God, who is that Father of Lights from whom every good and perfect Gift descends, that living Spring and Fountain, who like the Sun, sends forth the Rays of his Goodness and Perfection upon us."[23] Stout's notion, that Norris, or the Cambridge Platonists, or the latitudinarians discounted Grace, could not be more erroneous; it would suggest, among other things, that Christianity could ignore the crucifixion, but as Norris notes: "[we are] Creatures whose Nature is Corrupted, and the Powers and Faculties of it in a Disorder, the Spirit being subject to the Body, and the Law in the Members Warring against the Law of the Mind, whereby we are alienated from the Life of God, strongly inclined to the Pleasures of Sense . . . so as not to be restored to it without an Infinite Grace of God." The manifestation of "Infinite Grace" is Christ, who was, as Norris notes, called on to make a "Sacrifice of an Infinite Value, because our Sins were of an Infinite Demerit." Norris never wavers from this view, returning to it one hundred pages later: "I look upon Grace as the Suppletory of corrupt Nature, and a Remedy against Original Sin, and a Counterpoise to the weight of that evil Concupiscence which dwells in us, and so to bear date since the fall, as being the Purchase and Procurement of the Mediatour."[24]

Significantly, perhaps, Norris joins this discussion to a restatement of the Pythagorean adage Sterne had borrowed in *Tristram Shandy* (7.13), this time attributing the idea to Plato, who

very elegantly represents how the Soul is deceived and abused by the Body in her Philosophical Perceptions, and how necessary it is that she should withdraw her self from it. . . . And accordingly he tells us, that they that Philosophize rightly, are the only Persons that always study to loosen the Soul from the Body. . . . The great Business,

Study, and Exercise of a Philosopher is to withdraw his Soul from his Body.[25]

We have been tempted to believe that Sterne, modernist that he has seemed to us to be, rejects this heavy Cartesian or Augustinian dualism, and uses the occasion of his fictions to mock it. I myself can make a case from this perspective, citing, for example, Walter's parodic letter to Toby on Plato's two loves (*TS* 6.36) or the concluding discussion of *Tristram Shandy,* borrowed from Montaigne by way of Pierre Charron's *Of Wisdome,* where the shame attached to human sexuality is held up to ridicule (*TS* 9.33). Sterne's borrowing from Norris in sermon 29, however, certainly does not suggest parody; the subject, salvation, is one of utmost importance to the Christian—indeed, there is no issue of greater concern, as Norris and Sterne make clear in sermon after sermon. In facing this question for himself, however, rather than for his congregation, did Sterne reject his hope of Heaven in favor of a jest? Or is the presence of Norris an indicator that we must read Sterne another way, and that when, in the very next chapter of volume 7, Tristram discusses Hell, the demise of the Christian faith within fifty years (when it and our souls will have "worn out together"), and, finally, the triumphant reign of Priapus (*TS* 7.14.594–95), that all this has nothing to do with the prior chapter, over which Norris hovers as guardian angel? Borrowed materials do not necessarily simplify or explicate passages, but often becloud them. The purpose of recovering borrowings, then, ought not be taken as some dimwitted effort to "determine" the text before us, but quite the contrary, to make it available in all its complexities, including complications hidden from sight until we have recovered its sources.

Norris's *Theory and Regulation of Love* (1688) and, with Mary Astell, *Letters concerning the Love of God* (1695) are just two of many places in which he discusses physical desire (the basis of *all* love) in ways that may have attracted Sterne's attention. It is important to recall that Sterne's concern with last things would almost certainly have involved the nature of human sexuality, that area of his own moral conduct in which he perhaps felt most vulnerable. Adultery and promiscuity are rarely discussed in his sermons; one notes, for example, the absence of either in the long list of vices to be overcome quoted above from sermon 29. Norris, on the other hand, joins his theology to his philosophy precisely on the question of "love," or "desire":

> I consider, that every man has a restless Principle of Love implanted in his Nature, a certain *Magnetism* of Passion, whereby (according to the *Platonic* and true notion of Love) he continually aspires to something more excellent than himself, either really or apparently, with a design and inclination to perfect his Being. This affection and disposition of Mind *all* Men have, and at *all* times. Our other Passions ebb and flow like the Tide.... But this of Love is as constant as our *Radical* heat, as inseparable as *thought,* as even and equal as the Motions of Time.... Now this *Amorous* Principle which every man receives with his Soul ... must necessarily have an object.[26]

Uncle Toby is awakened to the Widow Wadman when his "passion" for his bowling green is quieted by the Treaty of Utrecht; and one might well glimpse the presence of Norris in Tristram's reaction, namely, his desire to write "the most compleat systems, both of the elementary and practical part of love and love-making, that ever was addressed to the world," an account that would involve him with Plato and Plotinus, devils and Ficino, and ultimately, the question of whether love is something one "falls into" and hence is "*below a man*" (Plato's "damnable and heretical" thinking), or, conversely, whether love should be whatever one finds in the concupiscible eyes of the Widow Wadman (*TS* 6.36–37).

When Walter Shandy returns to the subject in volume 8, the authority is again Plato: "I wish, Yorick, said my father, you had read Plato; for there you would have learnt that there are two LOVES," a theory again supported by citing Ficino (*TS* 8.33.720). For Norris, "there is not a finer or more Sublime piece of Speculation in all *Plato's Philosophy,* than that of his *Ideas* and that of his *Love....* *Platonic Love* is a thing in every bodies Mouth, but I find scarce any that think or speak accurately of it"; Norris, of course, believes he has understood Plato, reduced to a pair of dichotomies:

> That Love may be consider'd either bar[e]ly as a *Tendency* toward *good,* or as a *willing* this *good* to something capable of it. If Love be taken in the first Sense, 'tis what we call *Desire;* if in the second, 'tis what we call *Charity,* or *Benevolence.*

> There is either an Intellectual or a Sensual desire [based on its object]. . . . And this is that which *Plato* meant by his two *Cupids*. The latter of these is what we call Lust.
>
> The *Ordinary* Passion of Love, that which we mean when we say, such a Man, or such a Woman is in *Love*, is no other than plain Lust.[27]

These principles are so deeply embedded in Norris that one could cite such passages for a very long time. In this regard, it is perhaps not accidental that when we hear echoes in *Tristram Shandy* of Norris on love (*TS* 6.36, 7.13–14, 8.33, 9.33), they occur juxtaposed with borrowings from Burton's *Anatomy of Melancholy* and Charron's *Of Wisdome*—indeed, the specific mentions of Plato are lifted from Burton, rather than from Platonic sources (*TS*, Notes 437–41, 462–63, 523–24, 549–50). Sterne's purposes in these chapters toward the end of his work seem to take on additional meaning when we also hear Norris in them; if Burton and Charron (Montaigne's student and erstwhile "organizer") represent a skeptical approach to life, and particularly to the mysteries of human physicality and human love (Sterne's favorite chapter in the *Anatomy* is the one treating "love-melancholy"), Norris serves to balance the scale with an idealism that prevents either viewpoint from totally exonerating itself.

The first two sermons Sterne himself selected for publication, "Inquiry after happiness" and "The house of feasting and the house of mourning described," read under the sign of Norris, can perhaps take us a bit further toward understanding Sterne's purpose in refusing to choose between positions, to be instead, as Thomas Mann might phrase it, a "master of counterpositions." For example, the second sermon argues, as one expects from the pulpit, that it is best to dwell in the house of mourning, because it prepares us for Heaven far better than the house of feasting. It is a traditional argument, and Sterne certainly did not need Norris to make it. Nonetheless, in *Christian Blessedness,* when discoursing on the second Beatitude, "Blessed are they that mourn: for they shall be comforted," Norris does make exactly the same point as Sterne—and in somewhat the same spirit, for his first emphasis is to ensure that we recognize religion is not a gloomy affair: "It is indeed most certain, that Religion has its Joys and Pleasures, and that the Christian Religion has the most of any . . . ; that the Best Life is also the most Pleasant Life, and that 'tis worth while to live well, if 'twere only for the meer pleasure of doing so." In fact, says Norris, we are "*commanded*" to be joyful and cheerful, and he offers some half-dozen scriptural verses to support this argument.[28] Yet, given the uncertainty of salvation, he argues that we are also justified in bearing ourselves with gravity, seriousness, and sobriety; if not for this uncertainty, "why should not a Man give himself up to the utmost Gaity and Jollity, and express it in all manner of odd Postures and Gestures up to the height of an *Antick Dissoluteness?*" "Why not *Shandy* it," we might paraphrase Norris's rhetorical question, for which he provides an immediate answer: because we are going to die and be judged, a man must "temper and correct the Luxuriancy of his Spirit, with some Grains of Sadness and Pensiveness, and beware of laughing too much here, lest it should be his Turn to weep and mourn hereafter."[29] Sterne's own conclusion is the same: we favor the house of mourning "not for its own sake, but as it is fruitful in virtue, and becomes the occasion of so much good. Without this end, sorrow I own has no use, but to shorten a man's days—nor can gravity, with all its studied solemnity of look and carriage, serve any end but to make one half of the world merry, and impose upon the other" (*Sermons* 20). We hear, of course, an echo here of Yorick and his stance early in volume 1 of *Tristram Shandy,* but if we also hear the echo of Norris (and of the Anglican response to the text more generally), we have, I believe, a more balanced view of much that happens in Sterne's fictions, a useful way of looking at Sterne's play between gravity and joy ("When the affections so kindly break loose, Joy, is another name for Religion" [sermon 20, "The prodigal son," *Sermons* 190]) as possibly more complicated than we thought: the enjoyment of this world, pleasant though it is, is not the "en*joy*ment" to which the promise of Heaven and its joys is given.

Similarly, Sterne's emphasis in the opening sermon of the first volume, published just a few months after *Tristram Shandy* took London by storm, is to draw a sharp distinction between true and deceptive happiness. Again, the measure is otherworldly consideration; and Sterne's opening sentence finds many echoes in Norris: "THE great pursuit of man is after happiness: it is the first and strongest desire of his nature" (*Sermons* 3), Sterne writes. Norris agrees: "the great and general Center of Human Nature, whither all the Lines of Appetite tend, and where they all meet, is *Happiness:* The desire of Happiness is the First and *Master-Spring* of the *Soul* . . .

that which sets all the Wheels on work, and governs all the *under-motions* of the Man. . . . 'Tis indeed the strongest and most radical Appetite that we have."[30] For Norris, the observation is ultimately a philosophical one—we can only "desire" what appears good to us, what makes us happy; we can never love evil, in other words, because what we are attracted to is, by definition, what we think is good. From Norris's perspective, and the idea seems incredibly important for understanding Sterne, the senses and the passions, in themselves, are good; only errors in understanding and judgment, the desire after the wrong objects, make them seem otherwise.[31] They are not to be suppressed but directed, not contained but educated. That reason is, half of it, sense, is to be seen as God's gift, but only if our vision of perfection in Heaven is not shaped by the imperfect sensations of this world.[32] And for Norris and Sterne, this true vision is provided by only one light, as Sterne argues in "Inquiry after happiness":

> LORD! says the psalmist, Lift up the light of thy countenance upon us. Send us some rays of thy grace and heavenly wisdom, in this benighted search after happiness, to direct us safely to it. . . . And make us know the joy and satisfaction of living in the true faith and fear of Thee, which only can carry us to this haven of rest where we would be—that sure haven, where true joys are to be found, which will at length not only answer all our expectations—but satisfy the most unbounded of our wishes for ever and ever. (*Sermons* 5)

Few if any recent paths exploring Sterne's work have led to Heaven, but with Norris as a guide, we seem to arrive there from any number of different starting points. Indeed, if we were pressed to reduce John Norris's theology to one principle, it might be that wherever he begins his examination of the human qualities of sense and reason, he ends, logically and coherently—to his own satisfaction, at any rate—with God in his Heaven, even if much is wrong with the world. For Sterne, also, the thoughts borrowed from Norris seem to tend in one direction; whether in the sermons or the fiction, there is a sense that for Sterne the mystic theologian represented a path through human error and failure to divine enjoyment, Sterne's final goal in a world still very much governed by a teleological outlook. The boundaries of that path, determined as much by theology as by Norris's philosophical bent, are defined, on the one hand, by a surprising celebration of sensibility (that is, sense perception), and, on the other hand, by a pervasive assault on the human reason. I cannot do justice to the depth of his arguments on either subject, but merely want to indicate certain ideas that would have served to intrigue the Sterne we believe we know from his fictions.

It is Norris's theory of the natural goodness of our senses and passions that seems at first glance most at odds with orthodox Christian thought—and, at the same time, closest to some of Sterne's most cherished notions, particularly in *A Sentimental Journey*. A closer examination of Norris's writings, however, reveals the traditional theological underpinnings of this theory, not only in Neoplatonic idealism, but in Augustine and Aquinas as well. Most importantly, Norris *never* abandons the notion of a severe and permanent Original Sin: "That Man is deeply lapsed and degenerated from a state of Excellency and Perfection, is evident from the Ruins of his Nature, which is now too faulty and defective to be the first and original workmanship of God."[33] Through Christ (the Logos, Truth), however, the senses and passions, originally designed to make possible our interaction with both the Good and God (and they are one and the same for Norris), can be redeemed: "our Saviour by assuming our intire Nature, justify'd the innocency of *all* our Natural Passions."[34] This is why, for Norris, those "passions" most "resembling" God and most fit for the human condition, namely pity and compassion, are the hallmarks of Jesus's early existence and the essential pattern for us to adhere to in our own lives. Put another way, "sentimentalism" has a very strong theological dimension, but not because Christianity was liberalized or liberated by the Cambridge Platonists and latitudinarians (Norris is unrelentingly hostile to Roman Catholics, dissenters and enthusiasts, Quakers, and the existence of such labels as High and Low Churchmen),[35] but because Christ himself formed the model for the "man of feeling": "the *Best-natured* and most tenderly compassionate Soul in the World."[36]

In this regard, we also need to explore Norris's exchange with Mary Astell about God's love (*Letters concerning the Love of God*), along with his own *Theory and Regulation of Love;* when we find Norris, a bit too enthusiastically perhaps, praising "even the grossest Pleasure of Sense" as a "Ray and Emanation of the universal good" and arguing "that in the Human frame God has prepared Organs and Instruments for the use of Sensual

48 · Textual and Critical Intersections

Pleasure, and that he has also given us Natural Appetites and Inclinations to it,"[37] we may surely hear some Sternean echoes. Norris's concerns in this work, consisting of an exchange of letters between himself and Henry More, may be summarized in two questions: first, why sensuality, by which he seems here to mean sexuality (but "not of such species of it as are complicated and accompany'd with *civil incommodotyes* such as *Adultery, Fornication,* &c. . . . but in Sensuality as such"), is to be condemned, even though it has been a "Continual Topic for Invectives . . . to the *Platonists* and *Stoicks*"; and second, whether masturbation is also to be condemned, since it cannot be said to "disturb" society?[38] Norris is extremely reluctant to condemn either, but finally acquiesces to More's chaste reasoning on both, namely, that shame indicates human beings were "designed for an *Angelical life,* where *they neither marry, nor are given in marriage,*" and that the purpose of sexual intercourse is the production of children.[39] Much of the discussion seems directly apropos of the closing pages of *Tristram Shandy,* wherein Sterne questions, by means of a long verbatim quotation from Pierre Charron, precisely as Norris had done, why sexual appetite, which "in itself, and simply taken—like hunger, or thirst, or sleep—[is] an affair neither good or bad—or shameful or otherwise," was nonetheless condemned by "the delicacy of *Diogenes* and *Plato*"; and why "the preparations—the instruments, and whatever serves thereto, are so held as to be conveyed to a cleanly mind by no language, translation, or periphrasis whatever?" (*TS* 9.33.806).

For Norris, such a view toward the senses must follow from his core philosophical assumption that matter cannot think; it therefore follows that "since all Sensation . . . is a kind of Thought, we may . . . conclude that 'tis the Soul and not the Body that is the true Subject of it. That 'tis the Soul that sees and not the Eye. . . . And that tho' we talk of intellectual and sensual, spiritual or corporeal Pleasures, yet that 'tis not the Body but the Soul only that is the proper Subject of them."[40] Sterne's version of this argument appears most forcefully in *A Sentimental Journey,* when Yorick encounters the reader's sexual prudery after the "affair" with the fille de chambre:

> YES——and then—Ye whose clay-cold heads and luke-warm hearts can argue down or mask your passions—tell me, what trespass

The Odd Couple: Laurence Sterne and John Norris of Bemerton · 49

is it that man should have them? or how his spirit stands answerable, to the father of spirits, but for his conduct under them?

If nature has so wove her web of kindness, that some threads of love and desire are entangled with the piece—must the whole web be rent in drawing them out?—Whip me such stoics, great governor of nature! (*SJ* 124)

Like Norris, Sterne does not see himself as liberating the senses or sentiments in some romantic flight of freedom or fancy; to the contrary, his language here echoes a passage from sermon 18 ("The Levite and his concubine"): "Let the torpid Monk seek heaven comfortless and alone—— GOD speed him! For my own part, I fear, I should never so find the way: let me be wise and religious——but let me be M A N: wherever thy Providence places me, or whatever be the road I take to get to thee [the teleological thrust of this is noteworthy]——give me some companion in my journey, be it only to remark to, How our shadows lengthen as the sun goes down" (*Sermons* 170). And to complete the passage in the *Journey,* Sterne invokes Psalm 100:3: "let me feel the movements which rise out of it ['my situation'], and which belong to me as a man—and if I govern them as a good one—I will trust the issues to thy justice, for thou hast made us—and not we ourselves" (*SJ* 124).

Behind the psalmist's insistence that we are not self-made is the all-encompassing scriptural observation demarcating the limitations of human knowledge in Isaiah 55:8: "For my thoughts are not your thoughts, neither are your ways my ways, saith the Lord." If there is any theme in Norris more pervasive than his Platonizing curiosity about the "ideal" world, it is his scripturalizing skepticism about the possibility of knowledge. Many, many writers have, of course, expressed this skepticism, but when Sterne does so in sermon 19, "Felix's behaviour towards Paul," he will again turn to Norris. The passage is very familiar to readers of *Tristram Shandy* because it has served as the basis for recent readings that find Sterne the precursor of postmodern indeterminacy:

That in many dark and abstracted questions of mere speculation, we should err——is not strange: we live amongst mysteries and riddles, and almost every thing which comes in our way, in one light or other, may be said to baffle our understandings,——yet seldom, so as to

50 · Textual and Critical Intersections

mistake in extremities, and take one contrary for another;—'tis very rare, for instance, that we take the virtue of a plant to be hot, when it is extremely cold,—or, that we try the experiment of opium to keep us waking:——yet, this [taking the wrong path to happiness] we are continually attempting in the conduct of life, as well as in the great ends and measures of it. (*Sermons* 182)

While the sentiment has roots in Locke's *Essay concerning Human Understanding,* it is actually a verbatim borrowing from Norris's *Practical Discourses* (1691), excepting only Sterne's substitution of opium (which, interestingly enough, is also in Locke) for Norris's "very mean *Botanic* now, that shall gather Poison instead of Pot-herbs."[41]

The passage has, of course, two well-known echoes in *Tristram Shandy,* the first occurring in volume 4, Tristram's explanation of why his father retires to the fish pond on hearing that his son has been christened Tristram:

But mark, madam, we live amongst riddles and mysteries—the most obvious things, which come in our way, have dark sides, which the quickest sight cannot penetrate into; and even the clearest and most exalted understandings amongst us find ourselves puzzled and at a loss in almost every cranny of nature's works; so that this, like a thousand other things, falls out for us in a way, which tho' we cannot reason upon it,—yet we find the good of it . . . and that's enough for us. (*TS* 4.17.350)

The second passage is in volume 9, where Sterne begins with the observation that "we live in a world beset on all sides with mysteries and riddles" (*TS* 9.22.776), the greatest of which is why nature, which usually makes means to suit its ends, always fails in the making of a husband. The phrase "mysteries and riddles" has been to postmodernists what the three journeys to Auxerre were to the preceding generation of formalists, the clue to unravel the whole of *Tristram Shandy.* In many such readings, the phrase is taken as Sterne's commitment to an indeterminate, undecidable, equivocal, uncertain, and ambiguous world; yet for Norris (as, indeed, for Locke) and Sterne, the phrase simply restates a most fundamental Christian text, 1 Corinthians 13:12, "For now we see through a glass darkly; but then face to face," wherein, as the commentators note, the Greek *ainigma* means "in a riddle" (*Sermons,* Notes 219–20). Norris, to be sure, cites another text in this instance, Wisdom 9:16, but in his frequent return to the idea throughout his writings, 1 Corinthians 13:12 is clearly the text he has in mind. For example, in his most specific examination of knowledge, *Reflections upon the Conduct of Human Life: With Reference to the Study of Learning and Knowledge* (1690), he concludes:

> the utmost Pitch of Knowledge man by his utmost endeavours can arrive to in this world is very inconsiderable. . . . What we know of God is but *little,* for as the Apostle says, *we see through a Glass, darkly;* what we know of our selves perhaps is *Less,* and what we know of the world about us *is not much.* . . . There is not *one* thing from the greatest to the *least,* which we do or can understand *thoroughly.* Those that apply their whole study to any one thing, can never come to the End of that one thing, for not only every *Science* but every *particular* of it has its unmeasurable depths and recesses.[42]

Needless to say, the observation forms the basis for several aspects of Christianity's moral structure, including the depraved nature of human reason after the Fall, the sins of pride and discontent, the vanity of mundane knowledge, and the like. In their sermons, Norris and Sterne amply cover these subjects, but in that instance where Sterne once again borrows his language from Norris, the turn applied to 1 Corinthians 13:12 returns us to the Heavenward path encountered throughout this exploration. For although our knowledge is limited, both authors agree that it is sufficient to the only meaningful purpose of human life, the quest for Heaven, where, indeed, all our questions will be answered, and God (Truth) fully revealed to those who have sufficiently prepared themselves for oneness with the divine. "Practical divinity" in this light is religious instruction in gaining Heaven, a task toward which all human life should—but does not—direct its energies. In this preoccupation, Norris shares a most fundamental notion of the earlier Cambridge Platonists, whose Heaven-centered theology is one powerful indicator of just how astray R. S. Crane wandered in tying More, Cudworth, and their followers to a secular morality.

In *Reflections,* we can find Norris moving effortlessly from human darkness to the wrong uses we make of what little light we have, considering the end we should always keep in view: "I consider, that as we can here know but Little, so even that very little which we do, serves more to our Trouble and Disquiet, than to our Pleasure and Satisfaction."[43] And again, he fol-

52 · Textual and Critical Intersections

lows the "mysteries and riddles" passage in *Practical Discourses* (1691), with a very similar observation:

> The generality of Men place their Wisdom in that which is directly their Folly, and their greatest Wisdom in their greatest Folly; they lay deep Plots for shallow Interests, and are very slight and superficial in their Contrivances about things of real Moment and Consequence; they work out a frame of little Designs, with as much industry, art and wariness, as the laborious Spider weaves her fine-wrought Web, and to as much purpose, to catch a *Fly,* to bring about a *Trifle,* when the same, perhaps half the labour and thoughtfulness would have served for the securing a weighty and substantial Interest.[44]

Lurking behind both passages is Psalm 39:6 (quoted from the Psalter version): "For Man walketh in a vain shadow, and disquieteth himself in vain," and Norris gives the notion yet another statement in his next installment of *Practical Discourses* (1693):

> Do [men] not disquiet themselves about Phantastick and Imaginary Goods; which many *Happy* Men never have, and some . . . never desire, I mean Greatness, Dignity and Honour, which add as much to a Man's Happiness, or real Worth, as a high Shoe . . . to his Natural Stature, and no more. Are they not uneasie and full of Concern about Fame and Glory, about their Titles and their Coats of Arms. . . . There is no Man but who vainly disquiets *himself.*
>
> Poor unhappy Creature that he should do so! Are there not necessary and unavoidable Causes of Trouble sufficient, but he must needs add Voluntary Afflictions to his heap of Misery, impose supernumerary Penances, disquiet himself, and that too in Vain, without Reason, and without Measure.[45]

In sermon 22 ("The history of Jacob"), Sterne seems, once again, to have had Norris open before him:

> If there is an evil in this world, 'tis sorrow and heaviness of heart.—— The loss of goods,——of health,——of coronets and mitres, are only evil, as they occasion sorrow;——take that out——the rest is fancy, and dwelleth only in the head of man.
>
> Poor unfortunate creature that he is! as if the causes of anguish in

the heart were not enow——but he must fill up the measure, with those of caprice; and not only walk in a vain shadow,——but disquiet himself in vain too. (*Sermons* 212–13)

In volume 3 of *Tristram Shandy,* this becomes a heartfelt lament over Walter's failure to oil the door hinges:

——Inconsistent soul that man is!—languishing under wounds, which he has the power to heal!—his whole life a contradiction to his knowledge!—his reason, that precious gift of God to him— (instead of pouring in oyl) serving but to sharpen his sensibilities, ——to multiply his pains and render him more melancholy and uneasy under them!—poor unhappy creature, that he should do so! ——are not the necessary causes of misery in this life enow, but he must add voluntary ones to his stock of sorrow;——struggle against evils which cannot be avoided, and submit to others, which a tenth part of the trouble they create him, would remove from his heart for ever? (*TS* 3.21.239)

With Norris in mind, we may first note in this passage the same play of reason and sense (sensibilities) that we have discussed; but above all else, we will want to understand the passage in terms of the need to establish the right priorities and values in our conduct in this world as the secret of happiness both here and hereafter. Conversely, the failure properly to evaluate the events of this world—and the part we are playing in those events—leads to both unhappiness here and, it is clearly implied, unhappiness in eternity—the "weighty and substantial interest" of all human beings. This is to say not that this world cannot be enjoyed, but rather that its "true" enjoyment, its proper and rational enjoyment, will turn out to be that which smooths the path to Heaven. Religion is not a hindrance to pleasure but a guide; and all those uses to which we put our senses and desires, all those uses which prove vain and futile (and "disquieting") in that they fail to produce the pleasure or happiness we universally seek, are the misdirections of error and irreligion.

Norris, the belated Cambridge Platonist, and Sterne, the author for whom the aposiopesis was the most characteristic gesture, coincide in their Christian vision of the end of life and in their hope for "peace at last." That is certainly the conclusion of Sterne's sermon 28, "Temporal advantages of

54 · Textual and Critical Intersections

religion," in which he first acknowledges the joys of a religious life in this world, only to turn at the last to the "certainty of a future life, which christianity has brought to light":

> virtue is not even destitute of a present reward,—but carries in her hand a sufficient recompence for all the self-denials she may occasion:—she is pleasant in the way,—as well as in the end;—her way being ways of pleasantness, and all her paths peace.—But it is her greatest and most distinguished glory,—that she befriends us hereafter, and brings us peace at the last;—and this is a portion she can never be disinherited of. (*Sermons* 275)

It ought not surprise us that the entire passage is taken, almost verbatim, from Norris's *Practical Discourses* (1691):

> the Practice of . . . Vertue . . . is not destitute even of a *Present* Reward, but carries in hand a sufficient Recompence for all the trouble she occasions. She is pleasant in the *Way* as well as in the *End,* for even her very Ways are Ways of Pleasantness, and all her Paths are Peace. But 'tis her greatest and most distinguishing Glory and Commendation, that she befriends us *Hereafter,* and brings us Peace at the last. And this is a Portion she can never be dis-inherited of.[46]

Our conversation is, indeed, in Heaven, and the mystic of Bemerton and the madcap of Shandy Hall never lost sight of that Christian faith, no matter how profoundly the one lost himself in Platonic mazes, how comically the other in labyrinths of his own making. What John Norris helps us best to understand about Laurence Sterne is that however much of a piece his fictions may seem with our own time, they re-create a world in which Divine Judgment was still the very real human end, and hence a world enormously different from our own, a world separated from ours by a gulf as wide as Heaven itself.

Originally published in *Philological Quarterly* 75 (1996).

Notes

1 In the sentence immediately preceding this allusion to Norris, Sterne had quoted the Latin tag "de contemptu mundi & fugâ sæculi" (372) that he would later assign to Yorick (*TS* 1.10.20), who sits on his broken-winded horse meditating "delightfully *de vanitate mundi et fugâ sæculi*, as with the advantage of a death's head before him."

2 Lansing van der Heyden Hammond, *Laurence Sterne's "Sermons of Mr. Yorick"* (New Haven, CT: Yale University Press, 1948), 142; see also *Sermons*, Notes 318–19, 400–401.

3 See John Norris, *Cursory Reflections upon a Book Call'd "An Essay concerning Human Understanding"* (1690), reprinted by the Augustan Reprint Society, no. 93, ed. Gilbert D. McEwen (Los Angeles: Clark Library, 1961). [For a modern scholarly edition, see Mary Astell and John Norris, *Letters concerning the Love of God*, ed. E. Derek Taylor and Melvyn New (Burlington, VT: Ashgate, 2005), 184–220]. Norris's primary objection is Locke's dismissal of innate ideas, and the concomitant notion that "Ideas" are corporeal; when Locke responds, he takes a skeptical position, arguing that Malebranche (and hence Norris) treads where he refuses to follow, that is, into the "manner" by which impressions are made into ideas: "This I can resolve only into the good pleasure of God, whose ways are past finding out." John Locke, "An Examination of P. Malebranche's Opinion of Seeing All Things in God," in *The Works of John Locke* (London: Thomas Tegg et al., 1823), 9:217. See also his "Remarks upon some of Mr. Norris's Books, wherein he asserts P. Malebranche's Opinion of seeing all Things in God," *Works*, 9:10.

4 John Norris, *Christian Blessedness, or Discourses upon the Beatitudes of Our Lord and Saviour Jesus Christ* (1690), "To the Reader."

5 *Gentleman's Magazine* 70 (1800): 741, as cited by Hammond, *Laurence Sterne's*, 85–86.

6 Hammond, *Laurence Sterne's*, 70.

7 Hammond's parallels are gathered in three pages in his appendix, 142–44.

8 Cf. Norris's advice on sermon-writing in a sermon preached at Bath in 1689: "we should not trouble our Unlearned Auditories, either with Thorny Questions and Knotty Controversies which in themselves have no Practical use, or with more refined Theories and School Niceties, which to them are as useless and unpractical as the other.... Nor is it enough that the Truths we Preach be *Useful* and *Plain*, unless ... they be deliver'd in a Plain and Intelligible *Manner*." John Norris, *Reflections upon the Conduct of Human Life ... To which is annex'd, a Visitation Sermon* (1690), 188. Nor does Norris contradict this tradition when he suggests that plain truths should be delivered with "some

56 · Textual and Critical Intersections

degrees of *Warmth* and *Concernedness*" (189), although "some degrees" reflects, obviously, the undefined boundary of a nonenthusiastic "warmth." Cf. Sterne's very similar comments on sermon-writing, *TS* 4.26.376–77.

9 J. T. Parnell, who embraced my suggestion to read Norris, uncovered a quite probable borrowing in Le Fever's death scene (*TS* 6.10.511–13) that I had failed to spot; see "Scholia," *Scriblerian* 29, no. 2–30, no. 1 (1997): 295–96. In his unpublished doctoral dissertation, "*Tristram Shandy*'s Contexts" (University of London, Goldsmiths College, 1996), Parnell uses the Norris-Sterne connection to situate Sterne's sentimentalism within an "affective" Anglicanism created by Norris's subtle blending of Platonism and mainstream theology. One cannot, of course, attribute this "blend" to Norris alone, but his command of the relationship is remarkable among Anglicans for both its clarity and its lack of apology (see, e.g., the first sermon in *Christian Blessedness*). Among the rewards of a reexamination of Norris's writings would be the correction of R. S. Crane's dubious linkage of the Cambridge Platonists with a secularized "man of feeling" ("Suggestions toward a Genealogy of the 'Man of Feeling,'" *ELH* 1 [1934]: 205–30), a linkage at the heart of much that has been written about Sterne's sentimentalism.

10 Laurence Sterne, *A Sentimental Journey*, ed. Gardner D. Stout (Berkeley: University of California Press, 1967), 120.

11 Hammond, *Laurence Sterne's*, 159–60. Hammond is following Wilbur Cross, who believed the sermon was "worked over from Tillotson"; in a footnote (159), however, he acknowledges that "closer similarities" are found in Norris.

12 Norris, *Christian Blessedness*, 133–34. Cf. the extensive discussion of the same argument in John Norris, *A Treatise of Christian Prudence* (1710), 172–83.

13 Norris, *Christian Blessedness*, 171–72.

14 Cf. John Norris, *Practical Discourses upon Several Divine Subjects* (1691), discourse 6 ("Heavenly-mindedness"), which makes the same point (esp. 196–97). Earlier in this discourse, Norris had established his orthodoxy concerning Original Sin: "That man is deeply lapsed and degenerated from a state of Excellency and Perfection, is evident from the Ruins of his Nature, which is now too faulty and defective to be the first and original workmanship of God" (169). Significantly, his text for this sermon is the same as Sterne's for sermon 29, that is, Philippians 3:20, "For our conversation is in heaven." That Norris's notion of "heavenly-mindedness" is derived from his mentor, Malebranche, is argued in Mason I. Lowance's analysis of their combined influence on Jonathan Edwards, "Jonathan Edwards and the Platonists: Edwardsean Epistemology and the Influence of Malebranche and Norris," *Studies in Puritan American Spirituality* 2 (1992): 129–52. The role of More is equally essential, I believe, and chronologically prior to Malebranche's influence; the best study

of this aspect of More's theology remains, I believe, Aharon Lichtenstein, *Henry More: The Rational Theology of a Cambridge Platonist* (Cambridge, MA: Harvard University Press, 1962).

15 Sterne, *A Sentimental Journey*, 341.

16 Norris, *Practical Discourses* (1691), 41–42.

17 John Norris, *Treatises upon Several Subjects* (1698), reprint ed. (New York: Garland, 1978), 150. The particular treatise was originally published in 1689 as *Reason and Religion*; the passage is from part 2, contemplation 4, "Man consider'd as an Irregular Lover."

18 For Sterne's long struggle against his ill health, see Arthur H. Cash, *Laurence Sterne: The Later Years* (London: Methuen, 1986), 104–5, 119–21, and passim.

19 Norris, *Christian Blessedness*, 156–58. In *Theory and Regulation of Love: A Moral Essay* (1688), Norris gives this notion physical and physiological touches that suggest, if nothing else, the difficulty of tracing Sterne's sources to strictly "scientific" writings in an age when science and religion were mutually serving one another, even while competing for primacy. Hence, God or the good is seen as a *"great Magnet"* that draws us with as "much necessity as a stone falls downwards"; the heart is "the great Wheel of the Humane Machine, the Spring of all Animal and vital Motion," while love is "the great wheel of the *Intellectual* frame"; and, a final example, "as by the *Pulsation* of the *Heart* the Arterial blood is transmitted to the Brain, whereby are generated those Animal Spirits which are the Instruments of Motion throughout the Body . . . assist[ing] the Motion of the Heart by Contracting its Muscular Fibres, and so straitning its Ventricles to expel the blood . . . ; the same Reciprocation may we observe in the Motion of Love" (20, 24, 26). One wants to associate such passages with Yorick's taking of the fair grisset's pulse in *A Sentimental Journey*, but even more important, I think, is to keep them in mind when reading accounts of Sterne's sentimentalism that derive it solely from physiological or "psychological" antecedents; see, e.g., James Rodgers, "Sensibility, Sympathy, Benevolence: Physiology and Moral Philosophy in *Tristram Shandy*," in *Languages of Nature: Critical Essays on Science and Literature*, ed. L. J. Jordanova (New Brunswick, NJ: Rutgers University Press, 1986), 117–58; and John A. Dussinger, "Yorick and the 'Eternal Fountain of Our Feelings,'" in *Psychology and Literature in the Eighteenth Century*, ed. Christopher Fox (New York: AMS Press, 1987), 259–76.

20 It is immensely important—and often overlooked—when discussing sermon literature to pay attention to the occasion of the sermon and the role of its text, if any, in the church calendar; see my comments in *Sermons*, Notes 8–9, 75–76, 94–98, 118–19, and passim.

21 Norris, *Christian Blessedness*, 158–59.

58 · Textual and Critical Intersections

22 Norris, 169–70. Cf. Norris, *Reflections upon the Conduct of Human Life*, where he makes the same point with a Shandean interest in the anatomy: chastity and temperance, we are told, clarify the medium (the body) through which the soul views the world, by composing the *Passions*: "For the Motion of the Passions Ferments the Spirits, and the Fermentation of the Spirits agitates the Blood, and by agitation raises all the feculent and drossy parts of it." Moreover, the passions "also *divide* and *disperse* the *Faculty*," and "the more things" a man "thinks upon at once, the more Languid and Confuse will his Conception be" (85–86, 88). The opening chapter of *Tristram Shandy* surely comes to mind.

23 Norris, *A Practical Treatise concerning Humility* (1707), 40.

24 Norris, 51, 52, 162.

25 Norris, 108–9. That Norris held this idea throughout his career is suggested by its clear appearance in one of his earliest works, *An Idea of Happiness in a Letter to a Friend* (1683):

> Plato defines *Contemplation* to be . . . a Solution and a Separation of the Soul from the Body. And some of the severer *Platonists* have been of Opinion that 'tis possible for a Man by mere *intention* of thought not only to withdraw the Soul from all commerce with the Senses, but even really to separate it from the Body, to *untwist* the Ligaments of his Frame, and by degrees to *resolve* himself into the State of the Dead. (31–32)

26 John Norris, "A Discourse concerning Heroic Piety," in *A Collection of Miscellanies*, 2nd ed. (1692), 286–87. In the essay following, "Contemplation and Love," Norris returns to the "*Amorous* Principle," informing us that "'tis the peculiar Glory of Man to be an *Amorous*, as well as a *Rational* Being," amorousness being the means by which he "relieves his *domestic* poverty by *foreign negotiation*." Hence, although the "*Pathetic* part of Man" (one of the "noblest perfections" he has) is "condemn'd by a whole order of Men as inconsistent with the Character of Wisdom," Norris argues that "our Passions were given us to perfect and accomplish our Natures" (325–26). One has here a recipe for *A Sentimental Journey*.

27 Norris, *A Collection of Miscellanies*, 436, 441, 446–47. The first passage is from "Another Letter . . . concerning the true Notion of Plato's Ideas, and of Platonic Love," the second from "A Letter concerning Love and Music." Norris's introduction of "benevolence" at this point in his discourse is echoed many times in his theological writings, as one might expect from a Christian author; whether Sterne's own thoughts on benevolence were influenced by Norris is difficult to ascertain, precisely because Norris blends in so seamlessly with mainstream sermonizing on the subject. It is also significant that in the earlier *Theory and Regulation of Love*, Norris attributes the two modes of love to Au-

gustine (3–4), a common strategy in all his writings. In many respects, there is no easier intellectual exercise than Platonizing Christianity—or Christianizing Plato.

28 Norris, *Christian Blessedness*, 35 (qtd.), 36–37.

29 Norris, 51.

30 Norris, *Practical Discourses* (1691), 204–5. Norris's usurpation of mechanistic language is a commonplace in his writing, and warns us to beware of carelessly associating that mode of discourse exclusively with scientific or secular developments in the eighteenth century. Following Descartes and Malebranche, Norris is often at pains to show that the mechanical body is proof of the "enspiriting" existence of God; see above, n. 19.

31 Norris is also quite Sternean in his awareness of the strength of our senses in determining our actions: "A Sensible Representation," he writes in *Practical Discourses* (1691), "is the strongest of all Representations; a Sensible Representation even of the *Vanity* of the World, would work more with us, than the Discourse of an Angel about it" (26). Cf. Sterne's praise of Trim's dropping his hat at the precise moment he intones "Are we not here now . . . and are we not . . . gone! in a moment!" to begin his funeral oration for Bobby (*TS* 5.7.431–32). For more on the "strict union of Soul and Body" see Norris, *A Collection of Miscellanies*, 447–48.

32 A consistent theme in Norris is the linking of sin and folly, sinner and fool (see, e.g., *Practical Discourses* [1691], 243–45, 253), but this call to avoid sin by studying ourselves and the world better than we do, runs alongside the equally consistent theme of the intellectual darkness of our present state. We need all the knowledge we can muster to avoid sin, but without revelation and grace very little knowledge is available to us: this is a fundamental Christian paradox rather than an inconsistency or incoherence—and for the Anglican community, its uneasy resolution inheres in the concept of "sufficient knowledge."

33 Norris, *Practical Discourses* (1691), 169.

34 Norris, *Christian Blessedness*, 123.

35 Norris rarely discusses clerical politics, but when he does he sheds interesting light on a distinction that clearly has meant more to us than to him. In *Concerning Christian Prudence* (1710; 7th ed., 1722), he first dismisses "high" and "low" by saying he cannot find the distinction in Scripture (291). Later in the same treatise he argues that the label "high" means being "heartily and sincerely well affected to the Constitution of the Church of *ENGLAND* as by Law Establish'd" and nothing more—so that a High Churchman is "no more than a *Church-Man*, since every true Church-Man ought to be so affected" (395). Norris seems to be responding here to a charge that he was "high Church," an interesting label for a platonic mystic and follower of Henry More; I suspect

60 · Textual and Critical Intersections

"high" and "low" have the same explanatory value for the theology (as opposed to the politics) of Anglicanism as "liberal" and "conservative" have for understanding American political theory (as opposed to campaigning).

36 Norris, *Christian Blessedness*, 134.

37 Norris, *Theory and Regulation of Love*, 99–100.

38 Norris, 162–63, 165.

39 Norris, 172–73 (qtd.), 224–25.

40 John Norris, *An Essay towards the Theory of the Ideal or Intelligible World* (1701–4), part 2, 56. Significantly, Norris cites Augustine to support his argument at this point, rather than Descartes or Malebranche. His conscious effort to reconcile the "modern" philosophy with Scripture (and the received commentary) is nowhere more apparent than in these sentences from the *Essay*: "The World is a great *Machine*, and goes like a Watch, and the several Bodies that compose its System are . . . mechanically made and laid together, and must be in like manner resolv'd and accounted for. . . . This you may call, if you please, *New Philosophy*, but 'tis what should have been the *Old*" (87–88). Norris's point is that only God can account for both the creation and the "life" of the mechanism, for all its sensations and all its sentiments, insofar as a mechanism is without consciousness, while the human "mechanism" is conscious of itself. The argument seems obviously Cartesian, but Norris points to Scripture instead: "For the earth bringeth forth fruit of herself; first the blade, then the ear, after that the full corn in the ear" (Mark 4:28). One is reminded of Ruskin's citing of Psalm 104 as "scientific" evidence.

41 Norris, *Practical Discourses* (1691), 238. Norris quotes Wisdom 9:16, "hardly do we guess aright at the things that are upon Earth, and with labour do we find the things that are before us," as the scriptural text underlying his own. The relevant passage in Locke is from *An Essay concerning Human Understanding* (1690), 4.3.22; see *Sermons*, Notes 218, n. to 182.21–30. Significantly, Sterne quotes Wisdom 9:16 in sermon 27, "Abuses of conscience considered," the sermon that reappears in *Tristram Shandy*; here, too, his point is that despite our general ignorance, we would have sufficient knowledge of our own conscience were we not betrayed by "biases" of judgment.

42 Norris, *Reflections upon the Conduct of Human Life* (1690), 104–5.

43 Norris, 109.

44 Norris, *Practical Discourses* (1691), 239.

45 Norris, *Practical Discourses* (1693), 110–13. Cf. a similar statement a few pages earlier: "Strange kind of Inchantment, that Men should be thus condemn'd to hunt after Shadows, and embrace Dreams, to seek continually after Happiness where it is not to be found, and where they know it is not to be found, by all the Reason and Proportion of Things, by the express Declarations of God in

The Odd Couple: Laurence Sterne and John Norris of Bemerton · 61

Scripture, and by all the Experience of Mankind" (103). Norris's concluding triplet neatly lays out the three authorities of Anglicanism: reason, revelation, and religion (i.e., the historical church, the "Experience of Mankind").

46 Norris, *Practical Discourses* (1691), 141. In what might be considered a companion piece to sermon 28, Sterne's "Eternal advantages of religion" (sermon 39) again turns to Norris's *Practical Discourses* (1691) for an extensive borrowing, beginning with this telling observation: "one would think it next to impossible, that a Man who thinks at all, should not consider frequently and thoroughly the vanity and emptiness of all Worldly Good, the shortness and uncertainty of Life, the certainty of Dying, and the uncertainty of the Time when; the Immortality of the Soul, the doubtful and momentous Issues of Eternity, the Terrours of Damnation, and the Glorious things which are spoken, and which cannot be uttered of the City of God" (Norris, 9–11); cf. *Sermons* 372–73. Any reading of Sterne that fails to account for these considerations elides, I believe, a most fundamental fact about the world Sterne's fictions bring into being.

3

Laurence Sterne's Sermons
and *The Pulpit-Fool*

It is worth recalling that Laurence Sterne's career as a fiction writer began with two church-related satires, *A Political Romance* and the so-called Rabelaisian Fragment. The first reduces a squabble over perquisites among the dignitaries of the York establishment, the most important diocese in the Anglican communion next to Canterbury, to the dimensions of a rural parish; it was published at the end of 1758 and quickly suppressed by those same dignitaries, a certain sign of the effectiveness of Sterne's barbs.[1] The second consists of two chapters of an aborted Kerukopædia, or "Art of Sermon Writing," clearly modeled after Pope's *Peri Bathous* (*MW* 152–75). Sterne was just getting under way when he seems to have discovered the possibilities of *Tristram Shandy,* and while some passages from the "Fragment" are worked into the subsequent fiction, Sterne's normative notions of good sermon-writing must be garnered from other sources.

When we ask about the sources and analogues for these two works, it is almost self-evident that Rabelais, Pope, Swift, and Cervantes will come to the forefront. At times, however, when authors are prompted by a particular situation, their minds might well return to works which had confronted a similar situation. Thus, as Sterne observed the various high-ranking churchmen of York engaging in a pamphlet war over pelf and privilege (and he was aiding and abetting the dean of York, John Fountayne, in this exchange), he may have recalled some very pointed verse written about similarly venal clerics. Indeed, if that was the case, that poem would have also opened to him the entire subject of good sermon-writing, since that is, indeed, the primary subject of both *The Pulpit-Fool. A Satyr* and its continuation, *The Second Part of the Pulpit-Fool. A Satyr. Containing a Distinct Character of the Most Noted Clergy-Men ... both Church-men and Dissenters* (hereafter referred to as parts 1 and 2 of *Pulpit-Fool*). At the risk of being accused of a bit too much coyness, I would like to suspend identification of the author and date of this work for a few more paragraphs, in order to emphasize the point of my essay: Sterne's Anglican theology is not a version of mid- or late eighteenth-century secularism or sentimentalism, but something quite different, a theology that finds a strong echo, for example, in this advice on pulpit oratory from the preface to part 1 of the *Pulpit-Fool:* "The Wise Preacher commands attention only by the seriousness of his Discourses, which are always confin'd to what we ought to believe or Practice, without wandering into unnecessary Disputes or Impertinent Digressions; and for that Reason he never Rails in the Pulpit at such who only differ from him in a few Ceremonies, which he calls indifferent."[2]

What is of particular interest in this lengthy satire of almost four thousand iambic pentameter lines, primarily in couplets but with frequent triplets as well, in addition to its harsh abuse of the supposed venality of named clerics, is its mirroring of Sterne's own formulations for good preaching, and, indeed, of the sentiments he puts into the mouth of his alter ego, the cleric Yorick, in *Tristram Shandy:*

> I was delivered of [the sermon he has been using to light his pipe] at the wrong end of me—it came from my head instead of my heart— and it is for the pain it gave me, both in the writing and preaching of it, that I revenge myself of it, in this manner.—To preach, to shew the extent of our reading, or the subtleties of our wit—to parade it in the eyes of the vulgar with the beggarly accounts of a little learning, tinseled over with a few words which glitter, but convey little light and less warmth—is a dishonest use of the poor single half hour in a week which is put into our hands—'Tis not preaching the gospel—but ourselves—For my own part, continued *Yorick,* I had rather direct five words point blank to the heart. (*TS* 4.26.376)

Pulpit-Fool also appeals precisely to the heart on numerous occasions:

> Speak from the Heart, and then the Heart you'll touch
> Don't say too little, nor yet over-much.

Or again:

> In all your Drafts, let Nature copied be,
> *That we the Heart may through the Picture see.*

And another time:

All this is Fool; 'tis not a Preacher's part

To please the Mind, unless he strike the Heart.[3]

It is a theme the poet reiterates throughout the two parts of his poem, elaborating by referring to prose authorities giving the same advice, describing at length the bad preachers who do not move their congregations, and the good preachers who do. Significantly, his argument is for inclusiveness, and so he draws both good and bad examples from all the Christian persuasions of his day—the Anglican communion, nonjurors, Dissenters (including Quakers and Baptists), even some Roman Catholics. His primary targets are those preaching exclusion, and those who have demonstrated greed and lust; he is particularly rabid against those who are "sinners" in their private chambers and exclusionists in their public pulpits.

Indeed, the poet begins part 2 with a statement of purpose that might well have caught a Sternean eye, invoking a word that will soon become associated with a quite different connotation: "If I shou'd Write on MODERATION's side, / They'd cry——*He Trims, is true to neither side.*"[4] Corporal *Trim* is, of course, commonly thought of as Toby's faithful servant, neat and "trim" as befits his duties, and certainly a good person; we perhaps need to recall, however, that the comic "villain" of *A Political Romance* is the sexton and dog-whipper, also named *Trim.*[5] Nonetheless, we may still want to suggest that the poet and Sterne share a moderate, rationalized, and hence lukewarm religious faith, in keeping with an age increasingly secular and, influenced by Shaftesbury and Hume, increasingly sentimental. And we may further want to suggest that both the poem and Sterne's advice to sermon writers promote a theology of the heart rather than the soul, of sense rather than spirit, a preaching quite distinct from the "real" theology we would encounter at the opening of the century, when religion was still a "living force." Now, it would seem, both poet and Sterne revel in nontheological preaching—both argue for moral essays replete with rhetorical devices directed "point blank" to the heart, capable of moving their audience (hardly a congregation by this time) with moral lessons in keeping with an age being shaped by deists and unbelievers, and perhaps best understood in the light of Cardinal Newman's and Leslie Stephen's nineteenth-century denigration of the Anglican communion that, in their eyes, had lost all its intensity and most of its faith. This, in short, is the author of those existential, phenomenological, structural, and deconstructionist fictions entitled *Tristram Shandy* and *A Sentimental Journey*, products of an intellect at home with modernity because his own age (witness the poet of *Pulpit-Fool*) was already leaving behind its outmoded Christian heritage.[6]

Or perhaps not. The poet in question is the bookseller John Dunton (1659–1732), who published *Pulpit-Fool* in 1707, six years before Sterne was born. Dunton is familiar to readers of Sterne as a fictional precursor; his *Voyage Round the World* (1693) seemed so Shandean, in fact, that one of the early "imitations" of Sterne, *The Life, Travels, and Adventures of Christopher Wagstaff, Gentleman, Grandfather to Tristram Shandy* (1762), simply reprinted Dunton's work under the new title.[7] But never before, to my knowledge, has he been suggested as a model for Sterne's theology. Yet, as one reads *Pulpit-Fool*, two realizations emerge: first, Dunton is simply codifying, in his rambling poem, the arguments of latitudinarian preaching from the Restoration onward; and second, it is a mistake to suggest that either "moderation" or preaching "to the heart" is a mark of a midcentury slide toward secular thought, much less toward heresy, deism, atheism, hypocrisy, indifference, or modernism in its many guises, all of which have entered into recent accounts of Sterne's religion or, rather, his lack of it.

To be sure, the only extensive study of Dunton in the early twentieth century, C. A. Moore's "John Dunton: Pietist and Imposter," exhibits many of the attitudes that have made the study of religious belief so difficult for modern scholars.[8] The second sentence alone speaks volumes: "That he eventually went mad—as did his more illustrious contemporaries Defoe, Pope, and Swift—we should at least surmise from his later works . . . if we had no more explicit testimony." Moore is primarily concerned with Dunton's concentration at the beginning of his publishing career on books about death, some from his own hand, others collected from the available literature. Moore is at best aloof, at worst scornful, as his diction reveals: "As a purveyor of religious sentiment and a restorer of the melancholy decencies, Dunton was one of the most important figures in the transition [from earlier meditations on death to the graveyard school], . . . for, puerile as some of his disquisitions are, he made an effort to foster a literary, as well as a religious, conscience."[9] My own inclination might be to look at Dunton's publications on death in the light of an author for whom death

66 · Textual and Critical Intersections

was a pervasive subject in everything he wrote, Laurence Sterne. Thus, one of Dunton's first enterprises was the publication of his father's collection of "funeral discourses . . . to remind us of our mortality and fading state," under the title *The House of Weeping* (1682); the second sermon in the first volume of Sterne's collected sermons is "The House of Feasting and the House of Mourning Described" (1760).[10]

Dunton's poem is not good poetry, but it can nevertheless help us greatly toward a better understanding of Sterne as a sermon writer and midcentury Anglican cleric. Most important, perhaps, it directs us toward sermon writers approved by Dunton precisely because they wrote from and to the heart, eschewing controversy and polemical divinity (as Sterne labels it) for practical and peaceful oratory, yet preaching with warmth and piety.[11] Hence, in part 2 of *Pulpit-Fool* there is a long normative section in which Dunton praises some of the preachers of the prior sixty years:

> *Pious, Learned, Mild,*
> Free from all Tricking and affected Stile;
> . . . .
> *Now Pulpit Fools*——repent and learn of these,
> How you shou'd *Preach,* and how your Credit raise,
> 'Tis not by RAILING, but by preaching Peace.[12]

Then follows a short list of names of those who do just that, Doolittle, Comber, Mead, Patrick, Alsop, Stillingfleet, Horneck, and Annesley. Some of the names will be familiar to those having an acquaintance with seventeenth-century theology, others will need to be researched, but of their collective pulpit oratory, Dunton speaks most favorably:

> *All, All is Peace,* all prejudice forgot;
> . . . .
> Would you below, be blest like them above?
> *Preach* Peace like them, and learn from them to love.
> If PEACE be Heav'n to ev'ry Saint that dies,
> *No Pulpit Quarrel can be counted Wise.*[13]

Dunton continues this theme for another hundred lines, entwining an insistence on peacefulness with directions to employ a language of the heart, not only in the couplet quoted earlier—"Speak from the Heart, and then the Heart you'll touch," but again, some twenty lines later: "And 'tho' he strives with Warmth drawn up by Art, / Seems Ice to me, and cannot warm my Heart"; and yet again: "learn your Art, / For there is many an honest Christian Heart / Which may be touch'd, if the Preacher does his Part."[14] At the very least, we might want to suggest that an understanding of Sterne's pulpit rhetoric, the tradition in which he found himself and to which he may have contributed innovations, can only be evaluated after we have read sermons by the dissenting Thomas Doolittle (1630?–1707), whose *Concerning the Lord's Supper* (1667) went through twenty-seven editions, and those by Thomas Comber (1645–99), dean of Durham, whose entry in the *Oxford Dictionary of National Biography* (*ODNB*) clearly illustrates how difficult it was for anyone in the period to steer a moderating course.[15] We should add, of course, the other half-dozen preachers Dunton found conforming to his two basic standards: preaching toleration and preaching from and to the heart. Few readers of Sterne's sermons have wanted to take that route to further knowledge; rather, we find assertions of his unique use of standard rhetorical figures, like personification or interrogation, based solely on reading his sermons—we are left quite in the dark as to whether or not Doolittle, or Comber, or any of the other six totally eschewed such figured language, whether they also appealed to the emotions of their congregation, or only to their reason.

Among the many descriptions of favored sermonists, the portrait of Thomas Rosewell (1630–92) is particularly instructive. Rosewell, a Presbyterian, was tried for high treason in 1684, found guilty, but then released, perhaps because of strong support from Anglican clergy.[16] Dunton emphasizes the extemporaneous and emotional nature of his preaching, although he was a cleric equally renowned for his learning and scholarly nature:

> But *Roswel* shuts his Book, can't use a Note,
> What's wrought i' th' Heart, flows from the Preacher's Throat.
> . . . .
> He prov'd our *Tears* so much our Joy and Treasure,
> That now our *Pennance* is our greatest Pleasure.
> He painted *Death* to th' Life, has Eyes to see
> How Spirits Act, and what they do, and be.[17]

Like Sterne two generations later, the ideal preacher is said to speak to the heart, to move his congregation to tears, which are a treasured joy, and,

68 · Textual and Critical Intersections

finally, to "paint" a picture in order to embody the abstract. Quite possibly, sentimentalism, the "man of feeling," originates not in Shaftesbury and Hume, Rousseau and Diderot, but rather in the British seventeenth-century pulpit, and most particularly, in its account of the life and mission of Jesus.

Dunton is not selecting a few odd voices in the wilderness. Indeed, just before the passage citing Doolittle and Comber he had listed more than 170 (!) other good preachers by name, offering them to the pulpit-fools who, he maintains, can benefit from their example. They should, he proclaims, shape their sermons after those who preach peace: to repeat, "*Now Pulpit Fools*——repent and learn of these, / How you shou'd *Preach,* and how your Credit raise."[18] Most of the names will be unfamiliar to all but the most assiduous of scholars of the period, although others are those one would probably recognize, with South and Tillotson leading the list. "Dr. Stearn" appears, Laurence's great-grandfather Richard (1595/96–1683), archbishop of York from 1664 until his death; if Sterne did indeed know about the poem, surely this triplet would have caught his eye:

> *Foy, Clogher, Pooly, Francis,* Dr. *Stearn,*
> *Row, Fisher, Jones, Weld, Phraser,* aged *Mearn*
> With *Marsh, King, Sinclare, Smith,* and Polish'd *Fearn.*[19]

My point is not that we need uncover the identities and careers of all these sermon writers, much less that we should read them all in order to comment perceptively and validly about Sterne's sermons. We do, however, need to read *some* of them; we do need to realize that his writing is embedded in a vast body of available literature and that newcomers to the profession were encouraged to imitate that tradition—to plagiarize, if you will—rather than to innovate from the pulpit. Did some of those 170 writers Dunton praised use metaphors and strong visual imagery? Did some encourage their congregants to think along with them? Did some offer personal observations? Did some use interrogation, generally considered a rather effective didactic tool? Recent critics have cited all these characteristics as marking the uniqueness of Sterne as a sermon writer, but unless they can show that such devices never or rarely appeared in the sermons of the 170 preachers Dunton offers for imitation, such claims lack the necessary evidence for scholarly conviction. And because Bishop Joseph Hall's name is one of the 170, I would, indeed, suggest that the journey begin by reading him, since there is not a single rhetorical gambit offered by Sterne that had not already appeared in the extensive prose writings of Hall.[20]

A second lesson we might take away from Dunton's poem is that the religious intensity of sermon-writing in the seventeenth century was deliberately tamped down from the very beginning of the eighteenth in direct causal and self-conscious reaction to that intensity. The "coolness" of sermons in midcentury, therefore, cannot be attributed simply to an evolving century-long slide toward the secular and the sentimental. Dunton's many quarrels in his later life have led those few who talk about him at all to suggest madness, and indeed there is an irrationality at the heart of *Pulpit-Fool* that might support such a diagnosis.[21] Part 1 of this poem about religious toleration is devoted almost solely to attacking his enemies; as with Pope's final version of the *Dunciad,* some pages exhibit a trickle of verse riding above an ocean of vituperative prose (his own and others), explaining in detail the vices and venalities of his enemies. Part 2 contains more passages exhibiting his normative values, but it too is packed with personal complaints, biting hostilities, and insults almost worthy of Pope himself, although part 1 is far richer in such moments, for instance, "He'll Cant, he'll Plot, Unsay, Protest and Rave, / *Amphibious Animal, half Fool, half K[nave]*"; and "How dare you PREACH and Whore too, Aged Dust? / Why do'st provoke the Ashes of thy Lust!"; and, from part 2: "Whate'er he does is always in Extreams, / Sometimes *the Whig,* sometimes *the Tory,* damns, / *And thinks to enter Heav'n by Pulpit-shams.*"[22]

However, I think that the poem quite forcefully reflects as well the ugliness of the religious turmoil from which Britain was slowly emerging during Dunton's lifetime, giving us, instead of historical accounts of battles and executions, martyrdoms and exiles, the felt experience, the raw feelings that remained after "peace" seemed to have been restored with Charles II. The pulpit was still on fire in places, and Dunton's poem captures that intensity quite well, not only with its barbed observations, but even more with its blunt excesses. In the very act of damning these firebrands, the poet reenacts their sins, not ironically as a distanced persona, but quite deliberately as a Presbyterian often enraged by the established church, and as a private citizen cozened in several financial dealings by at least one member of the clergy.[23] At the same time, like the age itself, he longs for peace and reconciliation, and hence presents to his readers the image of an insanely bifurcated personality, an embodiment of the very rage he wishes to extinguish. There is in this dilemma, I believe, the core struggle of a Christian faith torn apart by its own inherently conflicting message: a religion of Peace, on the one hand, of Truth, on the other. It is a conflict as old as Jesus's first preaching against the Pharisees, and it continues to be played out in the faith throughout the entire eighteenth century; indeed, it may be the defining quality of all Christian belief, irenic in intent, militant in its grasp on truth.[24] For Sterne, for Dunton, for the 170 model preachers, it turns out to be the paradox at the core of their systems of belief: preach truth, and offend those holding another truth; preach peace, and offend those who want the truth. As for preaching the truthfulness of peace and the peacefulness of truth, that will please no one.

This takes us to the final instruction we may garner for a better reading of Sterne's sermons through the verses of John Dunton. The attempt to bring peace to the Christian communion in the eighteenth century required an enormous amount of rhetorical skill, by which I mean an overwhelming persuasiveness addressed both to forgetting the past and to creating a vastly different atmosphere, one in which truth and peace might coexist despite their fundamental allergic reaction to one another. Dunton, hardly a profound thinker, much less a learned theologian, nevertheless takes us to the heart of this enterprise precisely because his vision is so single-minded, perhaps even simpleminded: excesses are so readily apparent on all sides of any question, all one needs to do is define one's position as that of a mediator among them. Dunton is quite good, whether driven by his madness or simply by the will to imitate, at reproducing the vituperation still being offered by those clerics he collectively labels "pulpit-fools." He is less effective, as perhaps all satirists tend to be, at describing for us the normative values behind his response to this abuse of the peace of Christianity, but these values are, nonetheless, sufficiently clear. In the clergy of every sect, from Quakers to Roman Catholics, from Presbyterians to Anglicans, he looks for examples of this peaceful preaching, for a rhetorical and intellectual (theological) simplicity directed to the heart (beautifully summed up by Sterne as practical versus polemical divinity). He finds examples in all communions, and distributes praise among them, not equally, to be sure, but sufficiently to indicate his reliance on a tolerance that was not the invention of secularism and sentimentalism in the midcentury but came about some ninety years earlier. His faith in heartfelt discourse is perhaps influenced by Locke's sense perception, but just as likely by the simple observation of rhetorical theory, in its classical form, that human beings are persuaded more easily and fully by pathos than by logic.

Perhaps Dunton was all too aware of what had happened when the Walter Shandys of the previous era had become convinced of the truth of their ideas; perhaps he was also swayed by his exhaustion with the crosscurrents of doctrinal dispute that ebbed and flowed during the reigns of William and Anne. As he searches for peacefulness, his religion turns toward an emotional rather than rational appeal, an insight I think he shares with Sterne. The demilitarization of the world begins with disarming our ideas (or "opinions," as Sterne would call them) of their insistence on truth and maintaining an openness to divesting the self of self as a likely path toward whatever intelligible world lies beyond our present reality.

I invoke the "intelligible world" to help account for the most mysterious aspect of Dunton's *Pulpit-Fool*, a mystery parallel to one I raised some twenty years ago concerning Sterne: in Sterne's writings, the sermons and fictions, as in Dunton's poem, special recognition is given to a most unlikely candidate, the last of the Cambridge Platonists (although a graduate of Oxford), John Norris of Bemerton (1657–1712).[25] As with Sterne, the wonderment comes from trying to reconcile practical divinity with Norris's acute intellectualism on the one hand, and his Platonic mysticism on the other. Norris's most extensive philosophical work is his two-volume *An Essay towards the Theory of the Ideal or Intelligible World* (1701–4), humorously parodied by Dunton's contemporary, Thomas D'Urfey, as *An Essay towards the theory of the Intelligible World. Intuitively Considered. Designed for Forty-Nine Parts* (1705?, but dated 1700, obviously part of D'Urfey's humor). We should also note Norris's critical response to Locke's *Essay concerning Human Understanding;* he was the first philosopher to respond in print to Locke, and he continued to oppose him throughout his career.[26] However, what has perhaps been overlooked is that on four separate occasions Norris published his sermons under the title *Practical Discourses* (1691, 1693, 1694, and 1698).[27] The notion that Sterne's use of "practical" points to moral rather than theological discourses, akin to the essays in the *Spectator* rather than sermon literature in the wake of Tillotson, needs to be weighed against a thorough reading of Norris's four volumes of "practical discourses"; to paraphrase Johnson, "If they are not sermons, where are sermons to be found?"

I have not come across any mention of Dunton's poem in the literature on Norris, all the more deplorable because Dunton is wonderfully perceptive about his many stylistic faces, the blending of poet, philosopher, and theologian.[28] He opens his encomium, for example, with an allusion first to the fact that Norris was the primary exponent of Malebranche's philosophy in England, but in the next breath, he invokes Norris's treatise *Concerning Humility* (1707), published in the same year as *Pulpit-Fool,* a practical conduct book, yet steeped in the pacific lessons of Christian belief:

> With him [Bishop Benjamin Hoadly] let *Norris* be forever joyn'd,
> Alike in Metaphysicks, and in Mind,
> He searcht *Malbranch,* and now the *Rabbi* knows,
> The secret Springs whence TRUTH and Errour flows.
> . . . .
> Or if all Graces you wou'd see in one,
> View his HUMILITY for there 'tis found;
> Then Pulpit-Fools to *Norris all submit,*
> For here, or no where you will meet with Wit.[29]

That Dunton juxtaposes "TRUTH" with "HUMILITY" in this passage suggests the relationship developed earlier in this essay between truth and peace; one might recall, for example, Walter Shandy's very negative attitude toward this Christian virtue: "As for the theological virtues of faith and hope, they give [the soul] courage; but then that sniveling virtue of Meekness (as my father would always call it) takes it quite away again" (*TS* 9.12.762).

Interestingly, it is Norris's poetry that receives the highest praise. In this, Dunton's statements are hyperbolic, but not at all eccentric; Norris's very high reputation as a poet survived into the nineteenth century. The passage I am about to quote is keyed by a footnote: "He printed a Volume of Divine Poems, that will spread his Fame to the End of Time":

> *Norris* can never die, of Life secure,
> As long as Fame or Aged Time endure.
> . . . .

Mysteriously the bounteous Gods were kind,
And in his Favour Contradictions joyn'd;
Honest, and Just, yet courted by the Great;
A *POET,* yet a plentiful Estate;
Witty, yet Wise; unenvy'd, and yet prais'd
And shews the Age can be with Merit pleased.[30]

As far as Norris's biographers have ascertained, Dunton exaggerates greatly here, Norris being neither of a large estate nor courted by anyone of note; still, that is all slight praise, even if inappropriate, compared to what follows:

Press on *bright Saint,* and nobly climb the Sphere,
You yet at your Meridian don't appear;
Still soar, and nearer still to Heaven retire,
Be high that we may leisurely admire.

. . . .

We boast our Laurel to the Gown ally'd:
Let future Chronicles then, silent lie.[31]

Dunton, unlike some modern writers on Sterne, seems to have no problem weighing the poet as theologian, the theologian as philosopher, the philosopher as poet; the important point for him is the model Norris provides to future writers of both practical conduct and soaring wisdom: "Oh may his Verse of Learned *Norris* taste! / And mend the coming Age, as he the last."[32]

There is sufficient hyperbole here to make one uneasy about the reasons for Dunton's praise of Norris, but I would like to suggest that he found in Norris many of the same qualities that so attracted Sterne. Above all, Norris offers a means by which the truth of an idealistic theology can be set in proximity (I would not want to say reconciled) with the peace of a practical, one might say, social, religion. Dunton's glimpse of this value is manifested in the hundred lines he devotes to Norris, but the poem itself is unable to sustain such a vision and remains an unhappy witness to the factiousness and sectarianism of his own day. Sterne, I believe, had the same understanding of Norris as did Dunton, but was able to incorporate Norris's multivalences into his own work, into sermons that are both orthodox and directed to the heart, and into fictions, unorthodox and directed to the head (anyone seeking in Sterne for an unmixed sentimental or emotional jolt had better look to gothic fiction or Richardson). Readers who disagree with this factious if not fatuous assessment of Sterne's fictions know full well, of course, how to correct it: read Sterne against the fiction writers of his age and show how brilliantly and pervasively he uses sentiment and emotion in relation to them, on the one hand, or consider how all his fictional innovations are copied from his contemporaries, on the other. And readers who disagree with my description of his sermons—"both orthodox and directed to the heart"—need to establish a similar contextual framework for demonstrating their counterjudgments: I would suggest beginning with the four thousand lines of Dunton's *Pulpit-Fool,* followed by studying the content and rhetoric of Sterne's sermons within the context provided, say, by just one-tenth of the sermon writers Dunton praises, not, unfortunately, a single sermon by each, but multiple sermons, spanning different occasions, so that one can acknowledge the difference between, for example, a charity sermon and one preparatory to the taking of Holy Communion.[33]

Walter Shandy, we may recall, offers a "North west passage to the intellectual world" (perhaps another, heretofore unnoticed, allusion to Norris's "intelligible world"), by way of auxiliary verbs, which would enable "a young gentleman to discourse with plausibility upon any subject, *pro* and *con,* and to say and write all that could be spoken or written concerning it, without blotting a word, to the admiration of all who beheld him" (*TS* 5.42.484–85). I fear, however, that no easy passage can be found for reading sermons, but only a very tedious slog through the vast territory of sermon literature. For those unwilling to seek truth in this manner, I suppose one can only recommend peace, or, to find my concluding words yet again in *Tristram Shandy:* "I have no abhorrence whatever, nor do I detest and abjure either great wigs or long beards,——any further than when I see they are bespoke and let grow on purpose to carry on this selfsame imposture——for any purpose,—peace be with them;—☛ mark only,—I write not for them" (*TS* 3.20.238).

Originally published in *Eighteenth-Century Life* 35, no. 2 (2011).

Notes

1 See Arthur H. Cash, *Laurence Sterne: The Early and Middle Years* (London: Methuen, 1975), 269–77. In the very first sentence of *A Political Romance* (York, 1759), Sterne writes of the "World of *Fending and Proving* we have had of late" among the quarreling churchmen (*MW* 96). This is a commonplace phrase, but one does find it in a context pertinent to this essay, in part 2 of *Pulpit-Fool* (London, 1707):

> All Pulpit-Fools are Enemies to Love,
> If e'er they think, 'tis how to *Fend and Prove*:
> Then if you'd drop the Fool, and wisely Preach,
> Practice that Doctrine which you Weekly teach,
> And let your MOTIVES still be Love and Peace. (22, emphasis added)

Pulpit-Fool is cited hereafter by part and page number (the lines are unnumbered).

2 *Pulpit-Fool*, 1.iii. The author of *Pulpit-Fool* also praises those who "*Promote a Union of Hearts and Affections, &c.*" (1.iii). And this terse summary embodies the entire work: "*All serious Preaching must come from the Heart*" (1.6).

3 *Pulpit-Fool*, 2.23, 1.7, 1.12.

4 *Pulpit-Fool*, 2.4.

5 Sterne rises (or falls) to the level of the poem's invective late in the work, when he renders his final verdict on Trim: "the pimping, dirty, pettyfogging Character" (*MW* 99). For some of the poet's most vituperative language, see part 1, where he describes a "*Leud Pulpiteer*": "Is there a skipping Whore about the Town, / Or private Nanny-house to him unknown? / Here for a *S[tallio] n* there for Pimp he went, / To do both Drudgeries, alike Content" (1.53–54). There are many such passages, particularly in the final pages of part 1. (I thank Robert G. Walker for suggesting *Stallion* for the poet's "*S———n*," and, a few lines earlier, "*St———n.*")

6 For the most recent examples of this mode of reading Sterne's Anglicanism, see Judith Hawley, "Yorick in the Pulpit," *Essays in Criticism* 48 (1998): 80–88; Ian Campbell Ross, *Laurence Sterne: A Life* (Oxford: Oxford University Press, 2001), 226–45 and passim; Paul Goring, "Thomas Weales's *The Christian Orator Delineated* (1778) and the Early Reception of Sterne's Sermons," *Shandean* 13 (2002): 87–97; Duncan Patrick, "Unorthodox Theology in Two Short Works by Sterne," *Review of English Studies* 56 (2005): 49–58; Carol Stewart, "The Anglicanism of *Tristram Shandy*: Latitudinarianism at the Limits," *British Journal for Eighteenth-Century Studies* 28 (2005): 239–50; and James Gow,

"A Brief Account of Sterne's Homiletic Piracy," in *Divine Rhetoric: Essays on the Sermons of Laurence Sterne*, ed. W. B. Gerard (Newark: University of Delaware Press, 2010), 123–48. For a balanced account of the differing views of the sermons that have developed in the past quarter century, see Tim Parnell, "Laurence Sterne and the Problem of Belief," *Shandean* 17 (2006): 121–39; and 19 (2008): 9–26. One aim of the present essay is to restore *imbalance* to our readings of the sermons by suggesting—not for the first time—that one needs to read many other sermon writers before being able to evaluate the nature of Sterne's belief. The preponderance of the essays in *Divine Rhetoric* seems to support this view, as does the fine introduction by Gerard.

7 See René Bosch, *Labyrinth of Digressions: "Tristram Shandy" as Perceived and Influenced by Sterne's Early Imitators* (Amsterdam: Rodopi, 2007), 58–59. While Dunton's digressive style may have been a model for Sterne, so many other candidates offer themselves that in the absence of specific borrowings, the general consensus has been that the work was not a necessary influence; however, see *TS*, Notes 79, 89, 117, etc., for suggestions of echoes and analogues. In many ways, Dunton's autobiography, *The Life and Errors of John Dunton . . . written by himself* (1705), may have had more influence on Sterne. As with Colley Cibber's *Apology* (1740), the unreliable narrator of Dunton's *Life* may have served as a model for Tristram; in both instances, the Scriblerians found ample grounds for satirizing these works. See also Gary Sherbert, *Menippean Satire and the Poetics of Wit: Ideologies of Self-Consciousness in Dunton, D'Urfey, and Sterne* (New York: Lang, 1996).

8 C. A. Moore, "John Dunton: Pietist and Imposter," *Studies in Philology* 22 (1925): 467–99.

9 Moore, 467, 474.

10 See *Sermons* 12–20; and *Sermons*, Notes vii–xx, which uses this sermon as an entry into all forty-five of Sterne's published sermons. See also Margaret Anne Doody, *A Natural Passion: A Study of the Novels of Samuel Richardson* (Oxford: Clarendon, 1974), 151–87 (chapter 7), where Dunton's role in publishing *The Second Spira* (1693), a work central to the chapter, would be an initial point of contact between the two bookmen turned authors.

11 See *TS* 5.28.462 for another well-known statement of Sterne's sermon-writing practice: "I wish there was not a polemic divine, said *Yorick*, in the kingdom;—one ounce of practical divinity—is worth a painted ship load of all their reverences have imported these fifty years."

12 *Pulpit-Fool*, 2.21.

13 *Pulpit-Fool*, 2.21.

14 *Pulpit-Fool*, 2.23–24.

15 Andrew M. Coleby, "Comber, Thomas (1645–1699), Dean of Durham and Liturgist," *ODNB*, 2004.

16 Jim Benedict, "Rosewell, Thomas (1630–1692), Clergyman and Ejected Minister," *ODNB*, 2004.

17 *Pulpit-Fool*, 2.33.

18 *Pulpit-Fool*, 2.21.

19 *Pulpit-Fool*, 2.20.

20 For Hall's extensive influence in the sermons, see *Sermons*, Notes 25–26 and index.

21 The primary source of information on Dunton remains Stephen Parks, *John Dunton and the English Book Trade: A Study of His Career with a Checklist of His Publications* (New York: Garland, 1976). Parks notes about Dunton's "voluminous and discursive writings" after 1700 that "few met with success, and most served only to convince his contemporaries of his growing madness" (149). Of *Pulpit-Fool*, he says only that it "satirized in verse a number of the clergy" (162). More important, perhaps, in view of Sterne's publication of bawdry and sermons almost in tandem, we might note that in 1707 Dunton also published *Bumography, or A Touch at the Ladies Tails*, and *The He-Strumpets*, "a satyr on the 'Sodomite-Club.'"

Part 2 of *Pulpit-Fool* is cataloged as item 344 in Parks's checklist. It includes the legend from the title page: "Printed for *B. Bragge* . . . of whom is to be had *the First Part* . . . which (together with the *Second Part*) comprehends a *general History of the Clergy in Verse*; but more especially of such as are Heterodox, Leud, and Noted *for Railing at Protestant Dissenters*." And Parks quotes Thomas Hearne's reaction: "There is just publish'd the IId Part of The Pulpit Fool, by John Dunton a poor craz'd silly Fellow. In it he gives Characters of ye chief & most Learned (as he calls 'em) of ye Low Clergy Dissenters as well as others" (349–50). Ironically, Sterne's one contact with Hearne, who obviously has trouble accepting the irenic message of *Pulpit-Fool*, is that Walter Shandy almost certainly found his Latin version of "Ernulphus's Curse" in Hearne's *Textus Roffensis* (Oxford, 1720), the version he hands to Dr. Slop to read (*TS* 3.11.202–11). It is an example of precisely the sort of fiery religious rhetoric that is Dunton's primary target.

The *ODNB* entry for Dunton fails to mention *Pulpit-Fool*, although it is perhaps included in this statement: "[After 1704] he ruined what remained of his reputation, however, with scurrilous, 'abusive scribblings,' and public attacks centring upon his personal grievances, such as his *Whipping-Post, or, A Satyr upon Every Body* (1706)." See Helen Berry, "Dunton, John (1659–1732), Bookseller," *ODNB*, 2004. While there are quite a few "personal grievances" aired in *Pulpit-Fool*, the same could certainly be said of Pope's *Dunciad* as well.

78 · Textual and Critical Intersections

22 *Pulpit-Fool,* 1.58, 1.64, 2.18.

23 And yet, quite often in the poem Dunton will return to the concept of "indifferent Things" in his attempt to declare peace between Anglicans and Presbyterians:

> I am not such a Foolish Rhiming Sot,
> To mark my own Religion with a blot,
> My own: For CHURCH and *Presbyterians* are the same;
> *Or if we differ, 'tis but just in Name.*
> Our CHURCH and *Presbyterians* sure might close,
> For meer indiff'rent Things have made them Foes,
> *Indiff'rent things can never warrant Blows.* (1.63)

Much of this is directed toward the differing rituals and ceremonies among the various communions, but it indicates a major step in the direction of tolerance usually associated with a waning of faith; Dunton offers us an alternative way to evaluate Sterne's apparent lack of interest in polemical divinity.

24 Dunton often chastises the church militant of all shades and sects, e.g., "I hate such *Pulpit Soldiers,* and shall call, / His Bant'ring of our *Rites, an Omen of his Fall*; / We pray for *Peace, the Physick of our Nation,* / Not sprung from *War,* but from *Accommodation*" (1.34).

25 See Melvyn New, "The Odd Couple: Laurence Sterne and John Norris of Bemerton" (1996), reprinted as chapter 2 in this volume. Several scholars have since pursued this mystery, including J. T. Parnell, "A Story Painted to the Heart? *Tristram Shandy* and Sentimentalism Reconsidered," *Shandean* 9 (1997): 122–35; and Geoff Newton, "The Sermons of Laurence Sterne, Neoplatonism, and Two Short Works," in Gerard, *Divine Rhetoric,* 149–63. Norris has been attracting more and more attention, including a book-length study by W. J. Mander, *The Philosophy of John Norris* (Oxford: Oxford University Press, 2008), and a persuasive reading of Richardson's *Clarissa* based on Norris's theology, by E. Derek Taylor, *Reason and Religion in "Clarissa": Samuel Richardson and "The Famous Mr. Norris, of Bemerton"* (Burlington, VT: Ashgate, 2009). To my knowledge, Dunton's praise of Norris has never before been called to our attention.

26 *Cursory Reflections upon a Book Call'd "An Essay on Human Understanding"* first appeared in 1690, appended to Norris's first collection of sermons, *Christian Blessedness, or Discourses upon the Beatitudes of Our Lord and Saviour Jesus Christ.* For a modern annotated edition of *Cursory Reflections,* see Mary Astell and John Norris, *Letters concerning the Love of God,* ed. E. Derek Taylor and Melvyn New (Burlington, VT: Ashgate, 2005), 184–220.

27 *Christian Blessedness* was retitled *Practical Discourses upon the Beatitudes* when reprinted in 1694. In 1691, 1693, and 1698, Norris published *Practical Discourses*, enumerating them as volumes 2, 3, and 4, respectively.

28 I tried to illustrate the interconnection between Norris's philosophy and theology in my entry "Norris," in *British Philosophers, 1500–1799*, ed. Philip B. Dematteis and Peter S. Fosl (Detroit, MI: Gale, 2002), 291–98. W. J. Mander, in *The Philosophy of John Norris*, tends to separate them; hence, he has chapters titled "Metaphysics" and "Knowledge," and then "Faith and Reason" and "Love." As with Sterne, probably even with Dunton, I believe the interconnection of Norris's philosophy and creative work (poetry) with his faith is so profound that we must adjust our modern categories quite severely in order to deal with one or the other. Similarly, while I would never argue that we read Sterne's sermons without knowing him also as the author of *Tristram Shandy* and *A Sentimental Journey*, precisely the reverse is also true, that we cannot read the fictions sufficiently without knowing Sterne the sermon writer. The important point is not to read one or the other exclusively, but to negotiate the very different relationship among philosophy, theology, and literature in the eighteenth century and in the modern era.

29 *Pulpit-Fool*, 2.28. Perhaps not coincidentally, Dunton had published Richard Sault's translation of Malebranche's *Search after Truth*, the first volume in 1694, the second in 1695. A companion volume to the volume on humility is Norris's last work, *A Treatise concerning Christian Prudence, or The Principles of Practical Wisdom: Fitted to Use of Human Life, and Design'd for the Better Regulation of It* (1710). One might be tempted to suggest that Norris's work needs to be read not only by Richardson and Sterne scholars, but by Fielding and Burney and Austen scholars as well; Norris is a veritable fount for a practical *and* Christian ethical tradition, alive and well (and still quite popular) to the very end of the century.

Dunton's linking of Norris with Hoadly, the central figure in the Bangorian controversy, suggests how difficult it remained to seek truth and peace simultaneously; Hoadly's most provoking sermon, however, was delivered a decade after *Pulpit-Fool* was published; indeed, here Dunton refers specifically to a recently published sermon by Hoadly on "Moderation."

30 *Pulpit-Fool*, 2.28–29.

31 *Pulpit-Fool*, 2.29.

32 *Pulpit-Fool*, 2.29.

33 See Melvyn New, "Reading the Occasion: Understanding Sterne's Sermons," in Gerard, *Divine Rhetoric*, 101–19.

4

"The Unknown World"

The Poem Laurence Sterne Did Not Write

The evidence for Laurence Sterne's authorship of "The Unknown World" is, first and foremost, the appearance of the poem in the July 1743 issue of the *Gentleman's Magazine* (*GM*), where it is said to have been written "*By the Rev. Mr* ST—N" (figures 1–2). Needless to say, there might have been other clerics in England whose name would have been so abbreviated, and at least one other has been put forward as the poem's author, the Reverend Hubert Stogdon (1692–1728), to whom I shall return.[1] Sterne never claimed the poem for himself, as far as we can ascertain, and in the various collections of his work published following his death it was not included. Indeed, it was only in 1852 that the first claim for Sterne's authorship was offered, in Thomas Gill's *Vallis Eboracensis,* where Gill reprints a version of the poem "handed down in succession from the composer [that is, Sterne], to the Rev. gentlemen who have succeeded him in the living of Coxwold, and through the kindness of the Rev. George Scott, is now presented to the public" (figures 3–4).[2] Nothing else is said about the poem's history; Gill and Scott seem not to have known about the printing of the poem in the *Gentleman's Magazine* or anywhere else.

When Percy Fitzgerald published his two-volume biography of Sterne in 1864, he included a full text of the poem as a "characteristic specimen of [Sterne's] powers as a poet, . . . carefully handed down at Coxwould, from curate to curate in succession," and he adds the further information that "Mr. Scott, the present incumbent of Coxwould, has kindly favoured me with a copy of these lines."[3] As in Gill's account, the word *manuscript* does not appear. Possibly Gill saw the original manuscript and Fitzgerald a copy of it, possibly both saw the same copy; but Fitzgerald, as we know

The UNKNOWN WORLD.
Verses occasioned by hearing a Pass-Bell.

By *the* Rev. *Mr* ST——N.

But what's beyond Death?———*Who shall draw that Veil?* Hughes *Siege of* Damascus.

Hark, my gay friend, that solemn toll
Speaks the departure of a soul;
'Tis gone, that's all, we know——not where
Or how th' unbody'd soul does fare.

In that mysterious world none knows,
But God alone to whom it goes;
To whom departed souls return
To take their doom, to smile or mourn.

Oh! by what glimm'ring light we view
The unknown world we're hast'ning to!
God has lock'd up the mystick page,
And curtain'd darkness round the stage!

Wise heav'n to render search perplext,
Has drawn 'twixt this world and the next
A dark impenetrable screen,
All behind which is yet unseen!

We talk of heav'n, we talk of hell;
But what they mean no tongue can tell!
Heav'n is the realm where angels are,
And hell the *Chaos* of despair!

But what these awful words imply,
None of us know before we die!
Whether we will or no, we must
Take the succeeding world on trust.

This hour perhaps our friend is well;
Death-struck the next he cries, *farewell!*
I die!——and then for ought we see,
Ceases at once to breathe and be.

Figure 1. "The Unknown World," from the *Gentleman's Magazine* 13 (July 1743): 376.

Thus launch'd from life's ambiguous shore
Ingulph'd in death, appears no more,
Then undirected to repair
To diftant worlds we know not where.
　　Swift flies the foul, perhaps 'tis gone
A thoufand leagues beyond the fun ;
Or twice ten thoufand more thrice told,
Ere the forfaken clay is cold !
　　And yet who knows, if friends we lov'd,
Tho' dead, may be fo far remov'd ;
Only this veil of flesh between,
Perhaps they watch us, tho' unfeen.
　　Whilft we, their lofs lamenting, fay,
They're out of hearing, far away :
Guardians to us perhaps they're near
Conceal'd in vehicles of air.
　　And yet no notices they give,
Nor tell us where, nor how they live ;
Tho' confcious whilft with us below,
How much themfelves defir'd to know ;
　　As if bound up by folemn fate
To keep this *secret* of their *ftate*,
To tell their joys or pains to none,
That man might live by *Faith* alone,
　　Well, let my fovereign, f he pleafe,
Lock up his marvellous decrees ;
Why fhould I wifh him to reveal
What he thinks proper to conceal ?
　　It is enough that I believe,
Heav'n's brighter than I can conceive :
And he that makes it all his care
To ferve God here, fhall fee him there !
　　But oh ! what worlds fhall I furvey,
The moment that I leave this clay ?
How fudden the furprize, how new !
Let it, my God, be happy too.

Figure 2. "The Unknown World," from the *Gentleman's Magazine* 13 (July 1743): 376.

THE UNKNOWN ☉

Verses occasion'd by hearing a Pass-Bell,

By⁰ yᵉ Revᵈ Mʳ St—n.

Hark⁰ my gay Frᵈ yᵗ solemn Toll
Speaks yᵉ departure of a soul;
'Tis gone, yᵗ all we know—not where
Or how yᵉ the unbody'd soul do's fare.

In yᵗ mysterious ☉ none knows,
But ♄ alone to wᵐ it goes;
To whom departed souls return
To take yʳ Doom, to smile or mourn.

Oh! by wᵗ glimm'ring light we view
The unknown ☉ we're hast'ning to!
God has lock'd up yᵉ mystic Page,
And curtain'd darkness round yᵉ stage!

Wise ♅ to render search perplext,
Has drawn 'twixt yˢ ☉ & yᵉ next
A dark impenetrable screen
All behind wᶜʰ is yet unseen!

We talk of ♅ we talk of Hell;
But wᵗ yy. mean no tongue can tell!
Heaven is yᵉ realm where angels are
And Hell yᵉ chaos of despair.

But wᵗ yᵉˢᵉ awful truths imply,
None of us know before we die!
Whethᵉʳ we will or no, we must
Take yᵉ succeeding ☉ on trust.

This hour perhaps oʳ Frᵈ is well
Death-struck yᵉ next he cries, Farewell!
I die!—& yᵉᵗ for ought we see,
Ceases at once to breath & be.

Thuˢ launch'd fᵐ life's ambiguous shore
Ingulph'd in Death appears no more,
Then undirected to repair,
To distant ☉ˢ we know not where.

Swift flies yᵉ ♃, perhaps 'tis gone,
A thousand leagues beyond yᵉ sun;
Or 2ᶜᵉ 10 thousand more 3ᶜᵉ told,
Ere yᵉ forsaken clay is cold!

Figure 3. "The Unknown ☉," from Thomas Gill, *Vallis Eboracensis* (London, 1852), 199–200.

And yet who knows if Fr^nds^ we lov'd
Tho' dead, may be so far remov'd;
Only ye vail of flesh between,
Perhaps yy. watch us though unseen.
Whilst we, y^ir^ loss lamenting, say,
They're out of hearing far away;
Guardians to us perhaps they're near
Conceal'd in Vehicles of air.
And yet no notices yy. give,
Nor tell us where, nor how yy. live;
Tho' conscious whilst with us below,
How much y^ms^ desired to know.
As if bound up by solemn Fate
To keep ye secret of y^ir^ state,
To tell y^ir^ joys or pains to none,
That man might live by Faith alone.
Well, let my sovereign, if he please,
Lock up his marvellous decrees;
Why sh^d^ I wish him to reveal,
W^t^ he thinks proper to conceal?
It is enough y^t^ I believe
Heaven's bright^r^ y^n^ I can conceive:
And he y^t^ makes it all his care
To serve God here shall see him there!
But oh! w^t^ ☉^s^ shall I survey
The moment y^t^ I leave y^s^ clay?
How sudden ye surprize, how new!
Let it, my God, be happy too.[4]

[4] Explanation of the above, ☉ world, Þ He, ♉ heaven, ♃ soul, y^ms^ themselves, y stands throughout for th followed by a vowel, thus yy. is they, y^ir^ their, y^m^ them, &c.

Figure 4. "The Unknown ☉," from Thomas Gill, *Vallis Eboracensis* (London, 1852), 199–200.

from his transcriptions of several other documents, was a careless copier.[4] At any rate, the two versions differ in many accidentals and especially in those instances where rather eccentric abbreviated superscriptions appear. Fitzgerald, too, seems to have been unaware of the publication in the *Gentleman's Magazine.*

When Fitzgerald revised his biography for Wilbur Cross's 1904 edition of Sterne's *Complete Works and Life,* he repeated what he had said forty years earlier, but now tied the poem to the "Plurality of Worlds," the so-called Stapfer fragment that had been brought to his attention in the intervening years. He suggests in a footnote that the handwriting of the manuscript in Stapfer's possession left "no doubt of its authenticity," and then adds that "Sterne's handwriting is unmistakable, and can be recognised at once by anyone familiar with autographs; and this piece was duly compared with specimens of Sterne's handwriting, and was admitted by all to be his."[5] What is interesting in this account is Fitzgerald's failure to mention the "autograph" of "The Unknown World," given the opportune context for doing so—that is, it would have been natural for him at this point to suggest that both "found" manuscripts were in the same hand. But perhaps in 1904 he no longer recalled what he had been shown in 1864— and, as I explain below, whatever had been shown to Gill and to him was now lost.

The story becomes more elaborate but not more substantive in Cross's *Life and Times of Laurence Sterne* (1909). Picking up the clue from Fitzgerald, Cross discusses the poem as a thematic adjunct of "Plurality of Worlds." Sterne, we are told, "liked the poem so well that he took it away with him to Coxwold, where it was carefully guarded by his successors for a century; one of whom—the Reverend George Scott—permitted Thomas Gill . . . to print it. . . . Spirited away from Coxwold, the manuscript is now possessed by a member of the Scott family."[6] Again, we may note some very careful (or careless?) wording: the manuscript is "spirited away," but whether Gill saw it or a copy is not made clear. Cross does astutely observe that if the poem ended up in Coxwold, Sterne must have carried it there, because when the poem was published in 1743, he was living in Sutton-on-the-Forest, and would do so for another seventeen years. It is a little surprising that a document of so much importance to him would not be included in the careful preparations he made for posthumous publication—or that his

86 · Textual and Critical Intersections

daughter, Lydia, his posthumous editor, seems to have been totally ignorant of her father's authorship of a work he had treasured during his entire adult life (see *Letters* 214–19, letter 77).[7]

What seems to me especially significant thus far is that neither Gill nor Fitzgerald nor Cross knew about the version in the *Gentleman's Magazine.* Only in 1925, in Cross's second edition, is this fact addressed (information that is repeated in the third edition, of 1929), and in a most awkward manner, suggestive of some discomfort with the discovery. Cross begins as he had in 1909, connecting the poem to "Plurality of Worlds," but then adds, "The poem, perhaps copied from a newspaper, appeared in the *Gentleman's Magazine* for July 1743"; he notes the attribution line and, what was missing from the Coxwold version, the epigraph from *Siege of Damascus.* And then Cross repeats what he had said in 1909: "Sterne liked the verses so well that he took the manuscript with him to Coxwold," but now adds a qualification: "the manuscript is now possessed, it is said, by a member of the Scott family."[8] It seems likely that Cross sought the "manuscript" from the family at this time and was rebuffed. More important, Cross does not think through the authorship problem: surely the discovery of a printed version of the poem attributed to "the Rev. Mr. St—n" would seem to validate the story of a poem written by Sterne, the manuscript of which is found to be in the continuous possession of the vicars of Coxwold from his death to the middle of the nineteenth century. Still, several further questions now emerge: Did Sterne send the poem directly to the *GM* or first to a newspaper—a York paper, perhaps? Did the author send the Gill/Fitzgerald version, with its unique esoteric symbols and erratic abbreviations, or did he send the version printed by the *GM?* Most pertinent, was the manuscript held *in camera* by the Scott family in Sterne's hand or in someone else's? Was it made before the *GM* version or after it?

The apparent answer to all these questions is that Sterne wrote the Coxwold manuscript first published by Gill in 1852, and that the *GM* version, uncovered by Cross some seven decades afterward, offers solid validation for attributing the poem to Sterne. Thus, it does seem that the appearance of the poem in the *GM,* with its author "almost" identified, added to the existence of a Coxwold version of the poem, established Sterne's authorship of "The Unknown World." What is far less clear, however, is the relationship of the Coxwold version to the *GM* version.

"The Unknown World": The Poem Laurence Sterne Did Not Write · 87

A few additional directions and misdirections can be garnered from the poem's subsequent history in the hands of the biographers. In the bibliography attached to his 1929 edition, Cross offers an assertion we have not seen before—namely, that Gill "published the poem from manuscript." He offers no supporting evidence, however, although he does locate two additional magazine publications, the *Scots Magazine,* also in July 1743, and the *Ladies Magazine* (1751). He concludes, rather cryptically, "Sterne's authorship hitherto regarded as doubtful."[9]

Arthur Cash's account adds no further clarification; he adopts the hint of a possible Yorkshire newspaper printing ("the *Magazine* often picked up pieces from provincial papers") and then treats as fact what can only be supposition: "In the original manuscript, quite different from the *Gentleman's Magazine* printing, Sterne had used symbols for four key words." The guesswork is then compounded: "At the age of twenty-nine Sterne was already an experimenter in semiotics."[10] It is important to recall that whatever manuscript Reverend Scott had in his possession, we were never actually informed whether Gill was shown a manuscript, whether it was in Sterne's hand or in another hand, or whether it was only a copy of the manuscript (as seems to have been the case with Fitzgerald). Nonetheless, Ian Campbell Ross embroiders on the legend without reexamining the evidence:

> "The Unknown World" is not distinguished, but it is competent and in one respect at least curious—for Sterne's eccentrically employed four symbols . . . in the manuscript. The purpose of these symbols is far from clear and was evidently not so at the time of writing either, for the *Gentleman's Magazine* understandably dispensed with them when it published the poem. . . . If Sterne's leaning towards the curious led him to submit the poem to the *Gentleman's Magazine* in this form, he was soon made aware that the polite magazine readers of the 1740s did not share his taste. The magazine printed the poem, but in conventional typography.[11]

Ross goes on to the most elaborate discussion of the poem yet undertaken, finding that it offers a "unique insight . . . into Sterne's earliest literary influences" and confirmation "of the extent to which, even as a young man with a reputation for gaiety, Sterne was preoccupied by death."[12]

88 · Textual and Critical Intersections

Much of this is unfounded supposition, as any equally unsubstantiated countersupposition makes evident. Let us suppose that Sterne did indeed write and submit the version of "The Unknown World" that was printed by the *GM,* a manuscript now lost but quite conventional in all ways. Sometime thereafter, he (or someone else) copied the *GM* version but altered it with the odd symbols and abbreviations of the Coxwold version, either as an exercise (perhaps even a child's game of rebuses—I can, as a supposing biographer, envision Laurence setting Lydia the task)—or, a more sinister hypothesis, as a device to render the manuscript "antique" in appearance.

The latter scenario might implicate the Reverend George Scott. Is it probable that Sterne would save a manuscript of his poem, but not its printed version, his first London foray? So let us suppose that Sterne or Lydia or Reverend Scott had access to a printed version. In many ways, Sterne's motivation for rewriting the poem using symbols and abbreviations he never employed elsewhere in his writings, and used here quite inconsistently and erratically, seems least substantial. That Lydia played a game with her father's poem, copying the printed version and trying to substitute symbols with consistency, but, as a child, failing with some frequency, appears to me more likely. And, returning to another possible but less plausible scenario, one of Sterne's successors might have found the original printing by "the Rev. Mr St—n," created a "manuscript," one enhanced in value both by suppressing the *GM* version and by adding the oddities as "signs" of Sterne's presence.[13] This eventually would have made its way into Gill's hand, at a time and place—mid-nineteenth-century England—with a particular penchant for literary forgery and disappearing manuscripts.

Biographers construct their "lives and adventures" on just such a necessary combination of facts and suppositions, but at some point, when the facts peter out or are no longer sought, what started as educated and careful guesswork becomes simply a fictional narrative, loosely based on information collected by others. However, to be fair to Sterne's biographers, scholarly or otherwise, for 150 years the critical consensus has been that "The Unknown World" is Sterne's work, both the *GM* version and the Coxwold version, with all those well-known Shandean "oddities."

In "Sterne's Verse," which appeared in the *Shandean* in 2003, W. G. Day offers the most thorough examination of the poem and Sterne's authorship to date. He notes the attribution to St—n and the "more powerful piece of evidence," the "manuscript" ("Sadly . . . no longer extant") given to Gill, who was, he maintains, a "reputable historian, [who] would have had experience of Sterne's handwriting from the parish registers he consulted, and gives us no reason to suppose that his identification of the writer of the MS was anything other than correct." For the first time in discussions of the poem, Day notes that it was turned into "a song without any acknowledgment of the authorship of Sterne, and was reprinted a number of times in the 1760s and 1770s." Perhaps his most interesting discovery is of a "manuscript copy" housed in the Bodleian, which he found "of no apparent textual importance." The fact that the poem was copied by someone, sometime, into a commonplace book in the second half of the century does indicate one typical way in which readers in the eighteenth century reacted to literature that pleased or spoke to them: they copied it. Day, unlike Ross, spins no further suppositions from the poem, and we may take his bibliographical assertion as fully indicative of the consensus on the question of the authorship of "The Unknown World" 151 years after the Coxwold version first appeared in Thomas Gill's *Vallis Eboracensis:* Day agrees with the biographers that "the attribution to Sterne is secure."[14]

We can now be quite certain that Sterne was not the author of "The Unknown World." In 1809, the *Monthly Repository of Theology and General Literature* published a long memorial notice of the Baptist minister, the Reverend Hubert Stogdon (spread over the February and March issues), who had died almost a century earlier, in 1728. The account prompted in the next year's volume the submission of a poem thought to be written by him: "The Unknown World." The carefully worded presentation by the contributing correspondent is worth recording: "The following verses were taken nearly thirty years ago, from an old Magazine. They were there ascribed to the Rev. Mr Stogden; but I know not whether the same with him of whom you have given us so interesting and instructive an account, or not. If you think them worthy of insertion, they are at your service."[15] We now know that the first printing of the poem in the *GM* occurred almost seventy years earlier, but the correspondent's "thirty years" reminds us that the poem was often reprinted after that—those instances uncovered by Cross and Day prove to be the tip of the iceberg, because "The Unknown World" was incorporated into numerous hymnals in both Britain and the United States, in interdenominational and evangelical hymnals as well as Anglican ones; it would continue to appear throughout the nineteenth century.[16] This popularity may play a role in explaining the Coxwold version.

Stogdon had been dead fifteen years by 1743, so we must certainly have more cause than the appearance in the *Monthly Repository* to attribute the poem to him. The necessary evidence comes with the discovery that a version of the poem appeared in 1739 in the second volume of the posthumously published *Miscellaneous Works in Prose and Verse of Mrs. Elizabeth Rowe.*[17] Here is the complete poem, as printed there:

> *Hark! my gay friend, that solemn toll*
> *Speaks the departure of a soul;*
> *'Tis gone——that's all we know; but where,*
> *Or how th' unbody'd soul does fare,*
>
> *In that mysterious world, God knows,*
> *And God alone, to whom it goes;*
> *To whom departed souls return,*
> *To know their doom, to shine, or burn.*
>
> *Ah! By what glimm'ring light we view*
> *The unknown world we're hast'ning to:*
> *Heav'n has lock'd out the future age,*
> *And planted darkness round the stage.*
>
> *This hour perhaps our friend is well,*
> *Death-struck the next, cries out, Farewel,*
> *I die! And then, for ought we see,*
> *Ceases at once to breathe and be.*
>
> *Then launch'd from life's ambiguous shore,*
> *Ingulph'd in death appears no more;*
> *T'immerge where unseen ghosts repair,*
> *In distant worlds, we know not where.*
>
> *Spirits fly swift; perhaps 'tis gone*
> *A thousand leagues beyond the sun,*
> *Or twice ten thousand more twice told;*
> *Ere the forsaken clay is cold.*

And yet who knows, the friends we lov'd,
They may not be so far remov'd;
Only the veil of flesh between,
May oft glide by us tho' unseen.

While we (their loss lamenting) say
They're out of hearing, far away;
Guardians to us perhaps they're near,
Conceal'd in vehicles of air.[18]

The undated letter in which this poem appears is addressed to Lady Frances Hertford, Rowe's longtime friend, and appears in a sequence of more than one hundred letters to her, arranged, it would seem, in chronological order. Internal allusions in preceding and following letters allow us to date the letter almost definitely in 1729. Thus, when Rowe informs Lady Hertford that the verses "were writ by a man of good sense, who since he wrote them is gone to make the important discovery in the invisible world,"[19] we have a very strong indication of the author's recent death. Stogdon, we recall, died in 1728. While there are many differences between this version and that in the *GM,* we would have to accuse Sterne of plagiarism to assign the *GM* poem to him, given this version in Rowe—or to assume that he wrote it when he was sixteen years old, put it into Rowe's hands, and that Rowe told an untruth in saying the author was dead. Far, far more likely, Rowe received the poem from Stogdon. They were certainly more likely to have mutual interests, given their shared devotional piety, and, indeed, "The Unknown World" seems very much an amateur poet's efforts to imitate Rowe's own poetry and spiritual musings.[20]

There is, of course, the difference between Rowe's version of the poem and the version that was attributed to Stogdon (or Sterne) to account for; and a second difficulty, the poem's appearance in the *GM* in 1743, long after Stogdon and Rowe had died. Here I am afraid I can only raise possibilities. The different texts might suggest, for example, that Rowe, a far better poet than the author of these verses, attempted to refine them in her letter. Certainly her version is almost always an improvement in rhythm and diction. Had Stogdon sent her the verses for her approbation or correction? We do know that he wrote copiously.[21] Or, since Rowe's letter was written shortly after his death, did a member of the Stogdon family send it to her, perhaps because it was so similar to her own published poetry?

92 · Textual and Critical Intersections

Equally suppositional must be our attempts to explain the poem's appearance in the *GM*. The most likely account—that it was published in a newspaper before 1743 and picked up by the *GM*—must again be entertained, this time to justify not Sterne's authorship, but Stogdon's; a search through the online Burney Collection reveals only one newspaper printing, and that one anonymous, in 1757.[22] It is also possible that Elizabeth Rowe's executors found the manuscript among her papers and sent it off to the *GM,* part of settling her estate. These are events we cannot, without additional evidence, chronicle with any certainty. What we can suggest, however, is that every scenario in which Stogdon now plays a part as the author of "The Unknown World" makes far better sense than trying to find a link between Rowe and Laurence Sterne, in order to explain her quoting a version of the poem at a time when he was still a schoolboy.

What can we now say about the Coxwold manuscript itself? I will return to my more generous guess, namely, that Lydia (or someone else) made a game of rebuses with a version of the poem that came into her possession, sometime between its original appearance, which may have been in 1743 but possibly before then, and 1852, when the Coxwold version was turned over to Gill, by which time numerous reprintings had occurred, both in magazines and in hymnals, any one of which might have found its way to the Coxwold vicarage. I prefer that suppositional account to the more sinister one, that a manuscript of the poem was created from a printed version, one that might look like an oddity from the pen of the oddest cleric surely who ever resided in the village.[23]

Finally, what is an editor of Sterne's *Miscellanies* to do? I believe there is no longer any sufficient cause to consider "The Unknown World" as Sterne's, and there is quite substantial, if not definitive, evidence to assign the poem to Hubert Stogdon. I would not include it among Sterne's miscellaneous writings at all, or, perhaps, only as a "de-attribution," but since the poem has had little presence in the critical commentary on Sterne, I do not believe even that is necessary.[24] Suffice it to say, future biographers will have to reexamine the evidence here presented if they wish to restore "The Unknown World" to Sterne's canon.

Originally published in *Huntington Library Quarterly* 74, no. 1 (2011).

Notes

1 In attributing unsigned work, one tends to jump to conclusions when confronting abbreviated names that confirm one's preconceptions; hence Rev. Mr St—n, despite the missing *e*, must surely be Sterne. Or, it might turn out, the Rev. Mr. Stogdon (at times, Stogden); or, we might even suggest, the Rev. Mr. Joseph Standen (1673–1749), vicar of Speen (1726–49). As we shall see, Standen had a connection to Elizabeth Rowe, who will play an important role in this account of "The Unknown World," and he also seems to have had a reputation much like Sterne's. Standen was a sometime poet, "a man of talent but of some eccentricity of manner; he possessed no small share of wit and humour, the latter sometimes bordering almost on the ludicrous, in which he would occasionally indulge, even in the pulpit. His farewell sermon to his dissenting congregation was from Acts 13:46, 'Lo! I turn to the Gentiles.'" See *The History and Antiquities of Newbury and Its Environs*, ed. Edward William Gray (Speenhamland, UK, 1839), 123.

2 Thomas Gill, *Vallis Eboracensis* (Easingwold, UK, 1852), 199. I have reproduced both the Coxwold and *GM* versions in this essay (figures 1–4). Both have often been reprinted, primarily in the biographies of Sterne.

3 Percy Fitzgerald, *The Life of Laurence Sterne* (London: Chapman and Hall, 1864), vol. 1, 197. Fitzgerald finds a "charming simplicity and quaintness in these lines which makes us wish their author had written more," as well as an "earnestness, and a genuine pathos, which no ordained Tartuffe, or whining sentimentalist, could have given utterance to" (199). This is the first of several appraisals reflecting familiarity with Sterne's works rather than a close look at the poem itself.

4 The editors of Sterne's *Letters* were reminded of this yet again when the holograph of a letter recently resurfaced for which they had relied on Fitzgerald's transcription; see Melvyn New, "A Sterne Holograph," *Shandean* 21 (2010): 81–83.

5 Percy Fitzgerald, *The Life of Laurence Sterne*, intro. Wilbur L. Cross, in *Complete Works and Life of Laurence Sterne*, ed. Wilbur L. Cross (New York: J. F. Taylor, 1904), vol. 1, 64. See n. 23, below, for further discussion of Sterne's hand.

6 Wilbur L. Cross, *The Life and Times of Laurence Sterne* (New York: Macmillan, 1909), 149. Cross suggests that Sterne heard the "knell for the death of some parishioner at Sutton or some citizen of York," that it is "quite original in its details" (although owing something to Pope's "Dying Christian to His Soul"), that Sterne took the symbols from Burton's *Anatomy of Melancholy*

94 · Textual and Critical Intersections

(149), and, finally, that it is "but one of many poems that Sterne scribbled off for the entertainment of himself and his friends" (151).

7 Lydia Sterne edited the posthumous collection of sermons in three volumes in 1769, and his letters, again in three volumes, in 1775, in the third volume of which she included two miscellaneous works, the "Rabelaisian Fragment" (for which a holograph exists) and "The Impromptu," included in *MW* 213–19, with the caveat by the editors: "we would not be surprised if a more complete datebase eventually uncovers a version assigned to a different author" (214).

8 Wilbur L. Cross, *The Life and Times of Laurence Sterne*, new ed. (New Haven, CT: Yale University Press, 1925), vol. 1, 146. The motto from John Hughes (1678–1720), *The Siege of Damascus* (1720), suggests another link, interestingly enough, to Elizabeth Rowe; Hughes and Rowe moved in similar literary circles, and Rowe was supportive of efforts to collect his writings; see *Miscellaneous Works in Prose and Verse of Mrs. Elizabeth Rowe* (London, 1739), vol. 2, 168.

9 Wilbur L. Cross, *The Life and Times of Laurence Sterne*, 3rd ed. (New Haven, CT: Yale University Press, 1929), 597. There were many other reprintings overlooked by Cross, and especially the poem's afterlife as a "hymn," both in Britain and America, in Anglican and other congregations. The first such appearance I have located is in *The Seraph: A Collection of Divine Hymns and Poems* (Edinburgh, 1754), 265. It was also reprinted in *Schofield's Middlewich Journal or Cheshire Advertiser* (Tuesday, May 17, 1757), and again in William Dodd's *An Account of the Rise, Progress and Present State of the Magdalen Charity* (1761), which included a section, "Hymns and Sacred Poems for the Use of the Magdalens." Dodd's work and the Magdalen music book were often reprinted, the latter well into the nineteenth century; the website Hymnary.org lists seven appearances from 1774 to 1842 of "The Unknown World" in hymnals for Baptist, Episcopal, and "Christians of All Denominations" in America. See also W. G. Day, "Sterne's Verse," *Shandean* 14 (2003): 10–11, where he discusses some of the Magdalen reprintings; I discuss Day's contribution further below.

10 Arthur Cash, *Laurence Sterne: The Early and Middle Years* (London: Methuen, 1975), 152. Cash distinguishes the poem as "the most lugubrious piece he is known to have written."

11 Ian Campbell Ross, *Laurence Sterne: A Life* (Oxford: Oxford University Press, 2001), 110–11.

12 Ross, 112.

13 As Cross (see n. 6, above) and others have noted, the symbols, from astrology, appear on the famous title page of Burton's *Anatomy of Melancholy* and in the text as well. When we believed Sterne the author of the poem this had some significance, since we know that Burton was a favorite author. Whether

the symbols evolved to some deeper spiritual significance over the next two centuries has not been discovered; Masonic and Rosicrucian possibilities have been examined without useful results, as have attempts to find any substantial meaning in Burton's use; see E. Patricia Vicari, *The View from Minerva's Tower: Learning and Imagination in "The Anatomy of Melancholy"* (Toronto: University of Toronto Press, 1989), 209–12; she seems to suggest that Burton's purpose was decorative.

14 Quotations from Day, "Sterne's Verse," in this paragraph appear on pages 9–10. Day reprints the Gill version and the version in the *Scots Magazine*, believing it is pointed "with a great deal more sympathetic understanding of the sense of the poem" than the *GM* version (9).

15 *Monthly Repository of Theology and General Literature* 5, no. 51 (March 1810): 147. The two articles composing the biography of Stogdon appeared in vol. 4, no. 38 (February 1809): 57–62, and vol. 4, no. 39 (March 1809): 121–25. The editors obviously agreed that the Reverend Stogdon they had memorialized was indeed the author of "The Unknown World" and reprinted it in full with "By the Rev. Mr Stogden" as its attribution. I have not been able to locate the copy of the poem with Stogdon's name attached some "thirty years earlier"—indeed, in none of the appearances cited in n. 9 does his name or Sterne's appear. Of course, the wording of the contributor here may mean that what he offered to the *Monthly Repository* was a copy made thirty years earlier from a magazine of a much older date; as mentioned earlier, copying poems, especially devotional poems, was a common act of both approbation and piety throughout the eighteenth (and nineteenth) centuries.

16 See n. 9, above, for more on this point.

17 Elizabeth Singer Rowe (1674–1737) was a talented poet and writer of religious prose, praised by such well-known figures as Pope, Prior, Richardson, and Johnson. This posthumous collection in two volumes contains a lengthy biographical introduction and several poems celebrating her by, among others, Isaac Watts, Thomas Amory, and Elizabeth Carter; one by Joseph Standen (vol. 1, ci–civ), written in 1712, addresses her recovery from smallpox. Between these two *St—n*s, however, *Standen* and *Stogdon*, it will become clear why the latter is the only viable candidate for the authorship of "The Unknown World." Rowe's *Miscellaneous Works* went through five editions before the end of the century.

18 Rowe, *Miscellaneous Works*, vol. 2, 122–23.

19 Rowe, vol. 2, 122.

20 See, e.g., the poems in her *Collection of Divine Hymns and Poems* (1709). "The Unknown World" has several times been compared to Pope's "The Dying Christian to His Soul," and indeed both poems are in a hoary tradition. Thus

the fact that Rowe is said to have recited Pope's poem when near death, "with an air of such intense pleasure, as evidenced that she really felt all the elevated sentiments of pious ecstasy and triumph, which breathe in that exquisite piece of sacred poetry" (Rowe, *Miscellaneous Works*, vol. 1, xxxvii), may help explain why she was taken with Stogdon's less skillful effort. And, indeed, she seems to have kept the poem—or at least its most traditional sentiments—in mind, for in a letter written close to the time of her death she writes: "I am going to act the last and most important part of human life; in a little time I shall land on the immortal coasts, where all is new, amazing, and unknown" (vol. 1, xlvii). It is indeed a consistent theme in the letters of her final year. To the modern sensibility, Rowe might seem lugubrious in her preoccupation with death; Johnson, also, to the shame of modern sensibility, has been called lugubrious.

21 "It was Mr. Stogdon's custom to keep a diary, in which he entered, for his private use, the various instances of the conduct of providence which he had experienced, and reflexions on the review of his own temper and behaviour, or his moral and religious decays, neglects or improvements. He used to fill one book in a year." *Monthly Repository* 4, no. 38 (February 1809): 61. All these he is said to have burned a few days before his death—perhaps, however, he instead sent "The Unknown World" to a person he believed would value it. Stogdon was also the author of several tracts of religious controversy.

22 Seventeenth and Eighteenth Century Burney Newspapers Collection, Gale, https://www.gale.com/c/seventeenth-and-eighteenth-century-burney-newspapers-collection. Burney does not contain the provincial Yorkshire papers, but of course they were of interest only when we believed Sterne to be the author; there would be no reason for Stogdon or Rowe or Rowe's executors to send the poem to the York area. See also n. 9, above.

23 I do not share Fitzgerald's assurance that Sterne's hand is particularly easy to identify (Fitzgerald, *Life of Sterne*, vol. 1, 64), but one advantage of the scenario of Lydia copying out the poem rather than another person is that her handwriting was rather similar to Sterne's; this might help explain why Gill was deceived, if he did in fact see a manuscript rather than a transcription.

24 Recent commentary, nonetheless, includes Duncan Patrick, "Unorthodox Theology in Two Short Works by Sterne," *Review of English Studies* 56 (2005): 49–58; and Geoff Newton, "The Sermons of Laurence Sterne, Neoplatonism, and Two Short Works," in *Divine Rhetoric: Essays on the Sermons of Laurence Sterne*, ed. W. B. Gerard (Newark: University of Delaware Press, 2010), 157–58. Patrick argues that the poem's expression of doubt about what happens after death is evidence of Sterne's deism, heresy, and so on. Newton compares "The Unknown World" to the writings of John Norris (surely a spiritual and poetic model for Rowe, whose writings often mirror his very popular

and often-reprinted works), and concludes that the poem "represents much thought of the seventeenth and eighteenth centuries that has been often—perhaps even tiresomely—expressed in poetry and sermons; in short, the poem projects commonplace orthodoxy to a fault" (158). By carefully reading the text rather than playing out preconceptions about Sterne, Newton comes far closer to accuracy than does Patrick's glaring misreading. [More than a decade after publishing this essay, it came to my attention that the poem had its first appearance in the posthumously published *Poems and Letters of the Late Reverend Mr. Hubert Stogdon, Collected from his original papers,* ed. Nicholas Billingsley (London, 1729), 10–13, and that Stogdon (1692–1728) has an entry in the *ODNB* (2004), oversights that illustrate my blindness as well as insight—following the byway of Elizabeth Rowe, I quite missed the highway of Stogdon's own brief career.]

Digressions in
the Manner of Sterne

5

Taking Care

A Slightly Levinasian Reading of *Dombey and Son*

Our quaint metaphysical opinions in an hour of anguish are like playthings
by the bedside of a child deathly sick.

Samuel Taylor Coleridge

In 1988, Arion Press of San Francisco published a fine-press edition of Laurence Sterne's *Life and Opinions of Tristram Shandy* (1759–67) with thirty-nine photo collage illustrations by John Baldessari, a California modernist whose trademark is a round colored disk pasted over faces in his photo collages. Baldessari has suggested that this device indicates his hatred of certain occupations—bankers, lawyers, businessmen—the Paul Dombeys of the world. One might suggest that these are the same holders of wealth who are willing and able to support his art, so that this particular *Tristram Shandy* appeared in a limited edition of four hundred copies at $900 per copy; an additional suite of five large-scale lithographic prints (selected from the original thirty-nine illustrations) was available for $4,800.[1] Well might little Paul Dombey inquire: "Papa! What's money?"[2]

Sterne had had, of course, other illustrators before Baldessari, including the famous William Hogarth, whom Sterne had solicited for illustrations for the first two installments, and the less well-known C. R. Leslie, whose painting of *Uncle Toby and the Widow Wadman*, completed in 1830, had achieved iconographic status by midcentury.[3] Careful readers of *Dombey and Son* will have seen this portrait on the wall overlooking the devils' dinner as portrayed by Phiz (Hablot Browne) for chapter 26; my label for the trio—Dombey, Carker, Bagstock—at their celebratory dinner takes its cue from the illustration's legend: "Joe B is sly Sir; devilish sly."[4]

A comparison between these earlier illustrators and Baldessari is instructive, and especially when informed by the writings of Emmanuel Levinas. Baldessari's justification for obliterating the faces of those who looked like "bank presidents opening a bank"—he "hated" them[5]—is, most obviously, a dubious usurpation of authority from the literary to the visual text, from the originary to the secondary; Baldessari's trademark would appear to be wholly interchangeable with any literary text, as opposed to the illustrations of Hogarth and Leslie, which move toward a transparency whereby the objective (and secondary) representation sacramentalizes the text, reaffirming rather than ignoring its real presence. But even more disturbing is the deplorable embrace of violence in Baldessari's comment. A decade ago, in writing about the Baldessari illustrations, I suggested this violence had "much to do . . . with living too comfortably with untruths."[6] And I invoked Levinas directly:

> Put as succinctly as possible, Baldessari and literary critics might profit from adding Emmanuel Levinas to their reading list, if they have not already done so. They might then be less inclined to efface the faces they meet, Baldessari among [his found images], theorists among the authors they have deauthorized; and more inclined, I would hope, to recognize the vital importance of the other (the face of the other) in determining our own presentness. Above all, we might come to recognize the unethicalness of the disk . . . which jealously, resentfully effaces the author he thought he was complementing.[7]

Throughout that essay Hogarth's illustrations were offered as an aesthetic and ethical alternative to Baldessari's, but the essay's conclusion turned to Leslie's *Uncle Toby and the Widow Wadman* and again to Levinas. One may look at the Leslie image (figure 5) or reread the wonderful chapters 24 and 25 of volume 8 of *Tristram Shandy* and discover in both an uncanny echo of one of Levinas's most beautiful insights:

> Signification is not added to the existent. . . . The symbolism of the sign already presupposes the signification of expression, the face. In the face the existent par excellence presents itself. . . . The primordial signifyingness of the existent, its presentation in person or its expression, its way of incessantly upsurging outside of its plastic image, is

produced concretely as a temptation to total negation, and as the infinite resistance to murder, in the other qua other, in the hard resistance of these eyes without protection—what is softest and most uncovered.[8]

Baldessari succumbs precisely to this temptation of total negation, of murder. The crucial difference, then, between the art of Hogarth and Leslie on the one hand, and Baldessari on the other, is *ethical;* his is an art that obliterates the face of the other, a commentary that obliterates the face in the text. I concluded my observations, perhaps melodramatically, with the famous final words of *1984:* "If you want a picture of the future, imagine a boot stamping on a human face—forever."[9]

We do not know for certain whether the inclusion of the Leslie painting in Phiz's illustration (figure 6) was Dickens's or Hablot Browne's idea,

Figure 5. *Uncle Toby and the Widow Wadman,* by Charles Robert Leslie, 1830 (1842). Photo: © Tate, London.

Figure 6. "Joe B is sly, Sir, devilishly sly," by Phiz (Hablot Browne), illustrating chapter 26 of *Dombey and Son*, 1848 (1874). Image scanned by Philip V. Allingham for *The Victorian Web*.

but Michael Steig, the best commentator on the relationship between the novelist and the illustrator, argues most convincingly that the inspiration was Browne's, and perhaps a commentary on sexual incapacity (certainly a central Sterneian theme): Dombey "is not able to command Edith's submission."[10] Of more importance to my present purpose, however, is Steig's notion of Phiz's independence: "But with Dickens and his illustrators we cannot, despite Dickens's practice of giving detailed instructions, assume . . . a single intention. Because the illustrations include elements which are specified by the author, but are not the author's own creations, and further because the artist introduces details of his own, we find that the illustrator is at once collaborator . . . interpreter . . . and perhaps even an *artist*, sometimes creating independently valuable works of art."[11] And again: "Perhaps the question can never be settled, but on the basis of the evidence it seems to me harder to present a convincing argument for Dickens's complete dominance over his artist than for Browne's independence in matters of iconography."[12] Assuming this independence, we can ask what it was that Browne read in the chapter that led him to Leslie.

The most pleasing answer from my perspective would draw the following equation: just as I was led from the violence of Baldessari to the faces of Leslie to the melodrama of the Orwellian boot, so was Browne drawn by the contrast in this chapter between these three men, whose existence is defined by their collective willingness to efface every face they meet, and the loving faces that Leslie found in Sterne's description of Toby's vulnerability to the vulnerable eye of the Widow Wadman. If this were indeed the case, perhaps Browne also had an insight into the *melodramatic* ending that Dickens provided for the chapter, so much insight that we might come to believe that the Browne illustration summons forth the real presence of the text, converting the melodramatic into a sacramental moment in which we understand, perhaps for the first time, the pervasive presence of demonic evil in the world of *Dombey and Son*. Uncannily, Dickens echoes Orwell: "There was a faint blur on the surface of the mirror in Mr. Carker's chamber, and its reflection was, perhaps, a false one. But it showed, that night, the image of a man, who saw, in his fancy, a crowd of people slumbering on the ground at his feet, like the poor Native at his master's door: who picked his way among them: looking down, maliciously enough: but trod upon no upturned face—as yet."[13]

It is noteworthy that in the opening of the next chapter, Dickens observes that Mr. Carker "had his face so perfectly under control, that few could say more, in distinct terms, of its expression, than that it smiled or that it pondered." What Browne's inclusion of the Leslie portrait has suggested is that a face under such control is already effaced; the desire to efface others turns on itself, and already the evil intentions celebrated at the dinner are ironically undercut by their toast to the "angelic Edith."[14] The devils' dinner turns, despite its participants, into the communion table, and the Leslie icon on the wall, framed by candles, reminds us that the privilege of real presence is to convert evil to good. Similarly, the privilege of both author and illustrator is to incarnate that conversion in words and images, to provide, in other words, a text the transparency of which makes meaning (Greek: logos) possible. Levinas would explain it thus: "expression defines culture; culture is art, and art or the celebration of being constitutes the original essence of incarnation. Language qua expression is, above all, the creative language of poetry. Art is then not a blissful wandering of man, who sets out to make something beautiful. Culture and artistic creation are part of the ontological order itself."[15] One need only add that for both Dickens and Levinas that order is ethical.

I have taken this circumambulating entry into the possibility of a Levinasian meditation on *Dombey and Son* in order to suggest an analogy that may help us explore what I am coming to believe is the great critical failing of our age, our naive and essentially unexamined practice of juxtaposing the theoretical with the aesthetic in order to *make* the work of art "speak to us." Levinas, with his privileging of the caress over the grasp, unknowingness over cognitive mastery, makes every such juxtaposition involving his own theoretical activity at best problematic, at worst, a usurpation. Yet, as he himself acknowledges in his own complex attempt to unravel art from criticism, "Reality and Its Shadow" ("La réalité et son ombre," 1948), without the critic, art's place in the world would be greatly reduced, if not irresponsible (unethical): "But all this is true for art separated from the criticism that integrates the inhuman work of the artist into the human world. Criticism already detaches it from its irresponsibility by envisaging its technique."[16]

Levinas's aim in "Reality and Its Shadow" would appear to be the revival of Plato's infamous denigration of art as twice or thrice removed from Truth, but now restored to its full significance by the critic qua philosopher. Fortunately, as is also true of Plato, Levinas is too much an artist himself—and too much a philosopher, as well—to allow himself or his readers fully to credit this assault on art. Significantly, precisely his comments on Dickens in this essay can, alongside my initial comments on the illustration of Hablot Browne, help us toward an understanding of how we might situate Levinas in proximity with *Dombey and Son,* not in order to "understand" the novel, but rather to incarnate the text's always absent meaning into that real presence by which art regains, despite Levinas's temporary displacement, its exalted position as "the supreme value of civilization."[17] Criticism, in this light, is the means by which art engages in its endless negotiation with the eternal.

Levinas invokes Dickens twice in "Reality and Its Shadow." In the first instance, he is in the midst of pursuing the notion—which he shares with Keats—that all art is a caricature of life because the work of art embodies "a quasi-eternal duration," afloat in "an eternally suspended future." The "life" within art is thus "a lifeless life, a derisory life which is not master of itself, a caricature of life"; and this leads Levinas to Dickens, among other artists: "*Every image is already a caricature.* But this caricature turns into something tragic. The same man is indeed a comic poet and a tragic poet, an ambiguity which constitutes the particular magic of poets like Gogol, Dickens, Tchekov—and Molière, Cervantes, and above all, Shakespeare."[18] Because all art is constituted as images of the objects of the real world, separated from that world by its completeness and its disengagement, Levinas seems ready to condemn art to irrelevancy, a futile attempt to "go beyond," toward the realm of Platonic notions; art is, then, failed philosophy. However, in his most typical gesture, Levinas immediately suggests, instead, the alternative of unknowingness as his new definition of art: "just this is the artwork, an event of darkening of being, parallel with its revelation, its truth."[19]

This suggestion, in turn, harks back to an earlier passage in the essay: "Does not the function of art lie in not understanding? Does not obscurity provide it with its very element and a completion sui generis, foreign to dialectics and the life of ideas? Will we then say that the artist knows and expresses the very obscurity of the real?"[20] Here we are on Levinas's most cherished ground, the importance of the obscure, the unknown, or, as Paul Celan writes: "Wahr spricht, wer Schatten spricht" (He speaks truly, who speaks the shade).[21] If knowledge is the condition of being, then art is somewhere else, "on the hither side" perhaps: "Does not the commerce with the obscure, as a totally independent ontological event, describe categories irreducible to those of cognition? We should like to show this event in art. Art does not know a particular type of reality; it contrasts with knowledge. It is the very event of obscuring, a descent of the night, an invasion of shadow."[22]

It is to be expected that Levinas would now seek a theological equivalent, and indeed he immediately moves in that direction. Art, he insists, is not revelation; nor, even more paradoxically, is it creation. Rather, given his argument that art substitutes images for objects, where images are precisely not concepts, ideas, or powers, we may conceive of the work of art as a "fundamental passivity," visible to sensation and connected to "ecstatic rites."[23] The connection is drawn to music, because, one suspects, of music's "inarticulateness": "An image is musical. Its passivity is directly visible in magic, song, music, and poetry. The exceptional structure of aesthetic existence invokes this singular term magic [we recall that Dickens was invoked as a poet of this 'particular magic'], which will enable us to make the somewhat worn-out notion of passivity precise and concrete."[24] And again, Levinas shepherds his argument toward theology:

> Here we have really an exteriority of the inward. It is surprising that phenomenological analysis never tried to apply this fundamental paradox of rhythm and dreams, which describes a sphere situated outside of the conscious and the unconscious, a sphere whose role in all ecstatic rites has been shown by ethnography. . . . A represented object, by the simple fact of becoming an image, is converted into a non-object; the image as such enters into categories proper to it which we would like to bring out here. The disincarnation of reality by an image is not equivalent to a simple diminution in degree. It belongs to an ontological dimension that does not extend between us and a reality to be captured, a dimension where commerce with reality is a rhythm.[25]

Or, we might suggest, returning to our discussion of illustrating a text, art is a dimension of the sacramental, the incarnation of the object by the liturgical.

So much has already been written about Paul's death, by both those who embrace its sentimentality and those who are appalled by it, that one would almost prefer to avoid additional commentary. But Levinas has led us, perhaps unexpectedly, to "What the Waves Were Always Saying," and, indeed, it is at this point in "Reality and Its Shadow" that he invokes Dickens for a second time. Expanding on his concept of art as rhythm, Levinas explores its novelistic manifestation in the sequence of events that Aristotle defines as "plot" and Levinas as "a *situation*—akin to a plastic ideal."[26] This plasticity, the "natural selection of facts and traits which are fixed in a rhythm, and transform time into images," may, in fact, be the goal of the "psychological novel." Levinas is challenging, it would appear, the far more traditional view that such novels must look inward; for him the opposite is the case. Returning to his investment in the obscurity of the image, he now singles out Dickens to support his belief:

> an exterior vision—of a total exteriority, like the exteriority in rhythm we have described above . . . is the true vision of the novelist.

Atmosphere is the very obscurity of images. The poetry of Dickens, who was surely a rudimentary psychologist, the atmosphere of those dusty boarding schools, the pale light of London offices with their clerks, the antique and second-hand clothing shops . . . only appear in an exterior vision set up as a method. There is no other method. Even the psychological novelist sees his inner life on the outside, not necessarily through the eyes of another, but as one participates in a rhythm or a dream. All the power of the contemporary novel, its art-magic, is perhaps due to this way of seeing inwardness from the outside.[27]

We can enumerate many scenes in Dickens that might have led Levinas to cite him as his primary exemplum, but surely the death of Paul would be a most likely candidate. And since Sterne has already imposed himself into *Dombey and Son,* via Browne's rendition of the Leslie painting, perhaps we can also invoke his own fictional deathbed scene, surely one of the most famous sentimental deathbed scenes prior to Dickens, the death of Le Fever in volume 6 of *Tristram Shandy.* The question for both artists, interestingly enough, seems to have been how to break the "rhythm" of the scene. Thus Sterne: "Nature instantly ebb'd again,——the film returned to its place,——the pulse fluttered——stopp'd——went on——throb'd ——stopp'd again——moved——stopp'd——shall I go on?——No" (*TS* 6.10.513).[28] Most criticism of Sterne has centered on the "No," the moment when it is felt Sterne yet again winks at his audience, shattering the rhythm of the event and letting us know that the sentimentalism demanded by his readers comes with a jester's cap.

With Dickens, too, criticism of the death scene has bypassed the moment of dying—the plastic event that can never be other than it is, fated to occur every time we encounter the book—to concentrate on Miss Tox's famous declaration that shatters the sentimental scene and returns us to the world: "that Dombey and Son should be a Daughter after all!"[29] Levinas's musings on rhythm and image may suggest, however, that we can profitably return to these scenes with a better sense of their artistic achievement (and in them both, Sterne and Dickens addressed their artistry to the senses rather than to the understanding) if we learn to read the play of rippling shadows on the wall as incarnating a truth other than the truth of dialectical reasoning. Whether by magic, by music, by incantation, the text

110 · Textual and Critical Intersections

demands a responsive criticism that is difficult to locate in an intellectual milieu where the most proscribed "ism" is "sentimentalism":

> Sister and brother wound their arms around each other, and the golden light came streaming in, and fell upon them, locked together.
> "How fast the river runs, between its green banks and the rushes, Floy! But it's very near the sea. I hear the waves! They always said so!"

Paul is almost gone now, already in sight of the nether shore, but he returns for one final observation: "Mama is like you, Floy. I know her by the face! But tell them that the print upon the stairs at school is not Divine enough."[30] At his ending, in his final words, Paul turns "critic," twice evaluating what Levinas would establish as the fundamental relationship of art, the resemblance between image and object.

In measuring Florence and the "print upon the stairs" by their resemblance to his mother, Paul concretizes Levinas's abstract discourse on the painterly image:

> The consciousness of the representation lies in knowing that the object is not there. . . . These elements [of plasticity] . . . in the absence of the object . . . do not force its presence, but by their presence insist on its absence. . . . They occupy its place fully to mark its removal, as though the represented object died, were degraded, were disincarnated in its own reflection. The painting then does not lead us beyond the given reality, but somehow to the hither side of it.[31]

At the moment of Paul's death, if we listen carefully enough, the rhythm of the waves tells us, as did the rhythmic breathing of Le Fever, that the work of art—in offering the image or shadow that is the always accompanying nether side of the objects of the world, and in thus refusing the dialectic knowingness by which those objects can be grasped and demystified—will always make its ultimate claim in the face of death, "the old, old fashion—Death!" Paul, as a critic of resemblance, of art, opens us to something other than death, other than reality: "Oh thank GOD, all who see it, for that older fashion yet, of Immortality! And look upon us, angels of young children, with regards not quite estranged, when the swift river bears us to the ocean!"[32]

It seems appropriate that Dickens here envisions a movement beyond time (the ungraspable aesthetic image of time, we might suggest, is always

Immortality), toward whatever is not time, the "being out of time" that is death itself, but as well the transcendence of time that is his own art when it is made the subject of critical observation. As Levinas suggests, "It is not that an artwork reproduced a time that has stopped: in the general economy of being, art is the falling movement on the hither side of time, into fate."[33] The death of Paul turns into the life of Florence, and much as did Browne's illustration, Paul's *critical* moment manifests that mode of commentary by which a work of art and "the hither side of the world which is fixed in art" are neither effaced nor denied by criticism, but instead reintroduced "into the intelligible world in which it [the work of art] stands, and which is the true homeland of the mind."[34]

We are now ready, I think, to offer the analogy promised earlier. If Browne the "illustrator" can be considered just one more critic of Dickens, does not the presence of Leslie (and thus Sterne) in his illustration suggest that criticism shares with art—despite Levinas's platonic feint at separating the two—its existence as an image or shadow of the object, unknowing even in its knowingness? Is it not possible, then, to rephrase Levinas's question—"does not the function of art lie in not understanding?"—to include the critic: "Does not the function of art—*and criticism*—lie in not understanding"?[35] The movement from death toward immortality is recapitulated every time the work of art escapes from the hands of the artist into the hands of a responsive critic, not because the critic "understands" the work, but because the work of true criticism, the true measuring of resemblance between the images of the artist and the images of the critic (can any reader doubt the "truth" of Paul's commentary on resemblance?), becomes always an image of the infinite, whereby the mind spills out beyond its capacity: "Is not to interpret Mallarmé to betray him? Is not to interpret his work faithfully to suppress it? To say clearly what he says obscurely is to reveal the vanity of his obscure speech."[36]

Obviously, this notion of criticism is an imaginary one, given that within the economy of the critical we can posit an entirely different mode, the Baldessari model, whereby the image is effaced, stomped on in the name of a dialectic certainty that manifests itself in self-confessed "hatred." If Paul turns critic on his deathbed in order to sanctify the face of Florence, can we not also suggest that Dombey, Carker, and the Major represent all that can and does go wrong when we read a text—or the world—as though the end of reading were dominance, interestedness, and empowerment?

Specifically, how can we offer a Levinasian reading of *Dombey and Son* that turns philosophy into art, into that image of itself which, in juxtaposition with the work of art, may perhaps startle us with its resemblance, or disturb us, as the print on the stairs, with its inadequacy, but which refuses domination of the text?

Criticism cannot avoid its intimate relationship with the work of art, but as with Sterne's presence in Leslie's print on the wall within Browne's illustration of Dickens's scene, this relationship is always itself a shadow. The good reader, conversant with a multitude of shadows, a host of images united only by their unwillingness to solidify into assertions, brings a selection of those images into passive proximity with the work of art. In those two words, *passive proximity,* we may find, perhaps, the image of Levinas as a "reader" of the work of art, and hence our own clue as to how he may best be brought into a helpful relationship with Dickens. What we seek, above all, is not to efface Dickens with Levinas, not to conduct a philosophical unraveling of the unknowingness of the artist, in which Levinas simply replaces, for the nonce, Freud or Lacan, Marx or Gramsci, Foucault or Habermas, as the boot on the face of the literary work. On the contrary, I would here attempt a commentary no more invasive—but just as telling—as the Browne illustration, a commentary guided by an overarching insistence that we do not, in the critical process, reduce otherness (the rhythms of the artist) to sameness (the thoughts of the critic).[37]

Jonathan Swift, whose *Tale of a Tub* (1704) is surely one of the most perceptive engagements with *artistic criticism,* with "reality and its shadow," in the English language, seems an unlikely precursor of the philosopher Levinas, yet both seem to twine themselves tightly around one similar concept; hence Swift:

> For what man in the natural state or course of thinking, did ever conceive it in his power to reduce the notions of all mankind exactly to the same length, and breadth, and height of his own? Yet this is the first humble and civil design of all innovators in the empire of reason.[38]

One can turn to almost any page of Levinas and find Swift's sentiment echoed, not merely philosophically but, as well, in images and shadows; I select this passage in particular because it contains one of Levinas's favorite invocations of literature:

Philosophy is produced as a form in which the refusal of engagement in the other . . . indifference with regard to others, the universal allergy of the early infancy of philosophers is manifest. Philosophy's itinerary remains that of Ulysses, whose adventure in the world was only a return to his native island—a complacency in the Same, an unrecognition of the other.[39]

To be sure, Levinas's entire project seems designed to find a way *not* to "renounce knowing and meanings in order to find sense,"[40] but by sanctifying the face of the Other, by journeying like Abraham into the unknown that refuses a return to the Same, Levinas imagines a philosophical thinker that may help us to read differently, to modify—if we cannot ever overcome— the almost irrepressible human urge to dominate with knowledge, to illuminate that which remains in the shadows. It is for this reason that I call a Levinasian approach to a literary text *ethical,* defined within an *ethical aesthetics* as the attempt to reorient criticism from the knowledge of the philosopher-critic to a responsiveness to the images that constitute the work of art; such reorientation would begin with the recognition that philosophy too cannot escape its own image.[41]

Levinas has been brought alongside *Dombey and Son* once before in the critical heritage, in a very fine but to my knowledge largely uncited essay by Henri Talon that appeared in the inaugural volume of the *Dickens Studies Annual,* in 1970. The title, "*Dombey and Son:* A Closer Look at the Text," is significant; the date even more so, for the essay appeared at about the same time that the critical profession en masse was beginning its long march toward empowerment, fueled above all by French theory, among its several seemingly diverse sources. Talon was, however, not an American looking for a stick with which to beat *Dombey and Son* into submission as a commentary on Vietnam and social injustice, but a French scholar of English literature; the catalog of images he could bring to Dickens was enormously impressive (born in 1909, Talon was toward the end of his career with this publication). He had written on D. H. Lawrence and D. G. Rossetti, on Thackeray and Forster; however, what particularly resonates to my ears, attuned as they are to eighteenth-century England, is that Talon had written books on John Bunyan and William Law. Surely the shadow of both figures is in two of his opening comments: "I should first like to make clear that the theme of this novel proceeds from moral, not political, certitude. . . .

Miracles are not exceptional occurrences in Dickens' fictional universe."[42] And before Levinas is cited, we recognize him in this acknowledgment, so often missing in Dickens criticism: "I suppose the readers who tax him with intellectual poverty can recognize 'ideas' only when conveyed by discourse, whereas in Dickens' fictions they are most often and most vividly suggested by pictures . . . an art of living which makes him, in Santayana's words, 'a good philosopher.' Philosophy, as Étienne Gilson reminded us recently, is not primary knowledge; philosophy is wisdom."[43]

In a series of topics derived from the novel, Talon brings Levinas into proximity with Dickens with a deftness that suggests to me an acute engagement with—and homage to—the philosopher's own most cherished images. Thus, for example, under the rubric *The House,* he is able to diminish much of the gender criticism that has since emerged on *Dombey and Son* simply by placing alongside a few lines from *Totality and Infinity*— "the empirical absence of the human being of 'feminine sex' in a dwelling nowise affects the dimension of femininity which remains open there, as the very welcome of the dwelling"[44]—the observation that "long before Freud some men had discovered this [feminine] principle within themselves. . . . It is found in Sol Gills and Captain Cuttle: thanks to them the Midshipman is a welcoming home for Walter, Florence, and Mr. Toots."[45]

Levinas is not mentioned again in the essay itself and only once again in the notes (and he fails to appear in the index to the volume), but that the next topical division is *The Meal* might again return to us the Levinasian presence, as in this sentence: "Indeed the meal is the symbol of the readiness to welcome even more than of the actual welcome. . . . In Dickens' anti-Malthusian universe there is always a 'vacant seat . . . at Nature's mighty feast' for anyone who is hungry. The starving man does not need to claim a 'right' to be fed, for there is always a Sol Gills or a Ned Cuttle or a Harriet Carker to beg him to come in and to lay the table in no time."[46] Few philosophers have vested more in the concept of hospitality than has Levinas, none among the moderns has argued more persuasively against the egotism of the *conatus,* that is, the Hobbesian-Malthusian universe: "'To leave men without food is a fault that no circumstance attenuates; the distinction between the voluntary and the involuntary does not apply here,' says Rabbi Yochanan. Before the hunger of men responsibility is measured only 'objectively'; it is irrecusable."[47]

The next division is even more overtly an embodiment of the Levinasian shadow, *The Hand and the Face.* Invoking Levinas's "face to face," Talon might almost be talking about Sterne's Uncle Toby and the Widow Wadman, one image invoking the other: "Words are often like screens between people, but the expression of the face opens the way to the heart. 'There was glory and delight within the Captain that spread itself over his whole visage, and made a perfect illumination there.'"[48] This glances, of course, at that magnificent chapter 49, in which Florence is cared for by Captain Cuttle, and Walter is returned from the sea. Certainly, one of those aspects of art that produces (or should produce) awe is the daring of an artist like Dickens, who manages time and again in this chapter to transcend the sentimental, not by eschewing sensibility, but by openly and happily embracing it. The image of Cuttle at the stove, "cooking with extraordinary skill, making hot gravy in a second little saucepan, boiling a handful of potatoes in a third, never forgetting the egg-sauce in the first,"[49] is an image of Levinas's finest reach of the ethical human being; small wonder that Dickens, that untrained philosopher of human experience, ends where Levinas would: "there was never such a radiant cook as the Captain looked, in the height and heat of these functions: it being impossible to say whether his face or his glazed hat shone the brighter."[50] And when Florence reciprocates his "care" and fills his pipe and makes a "perfect glass of grog for him, unasked, and set it at his elbow," how much richer is his response ("his ruddy nose turned pale, he felt himself so graced and honored")[51] than the critic's compulsion to efface the scene by discovering that the pipe is phallic, the perfect grog, an instance of feminine subjugation. Surely if Levinas in proximity to Dickens has any value at all, it will be to teach us how to admire, as does Talon, the skillfulness of Dickens's images of *caritas* and grace.

It is, however, in his concluding section, *Essence and Existence,* that Talon seems most Levinasian in his reading, echoing "Reality and Its Shadow," although he gives no indication of knowing it. I quote at length because I think the criticism is a model of good reading:

> Thus, in order to hold our attention, Dickens does not ask from us a willing suspension of disbelief in the same way as most great novelists do. When reading him we never forget for a moment that we

116 · Textual and Critical Intersections

have entered a world which is not ours. Not for a moment do we believe in the existence of Ned Cuttle, or Carker, or Florence, but this does not preclude us from feeling sympathy, or scorn, or pity: as Étienne Gilson has said, Dickens's characters do not exist, they *are*.

But this distinction between *esse* and *existere* is too subtle for many readers. "What pleasure can you take . . . in a caricatural world peopled with automatons?" Those who have read Santayana wonder how he could seriously write that Dickens does not exaggerate. . . . Of course Dickens exaggerates, and thus often gives relief to features that are familiar enough in the world, but that we are apt to forget. In this case exaggeration is the revealing agent of truth.[52]

Like Paul, this criticism seems to us today rather old-fashioned, lacking that ideological strength by which the author's failings can be brought to light. One might recall what Paul overhears—"or he dreamed it"—of the Apothecary's diagnosis, "that there was a want of vital power (what was that, Paul wondered!) and great constitutional weakness. . . . The little fellow had a fine mind, but was an old-fashioned boy."[53] The want of "power" in Talon's "closer look at the text" is perhaps the most admirable feature of his commentary; I would suggest that his writing about Dickens takes place in the shadows and through the images afforded by Levinas. Talon illuminates the text with his closer look, but is overpowered by what he reads, finding it at once transformational and incarnational of the reality that is the world prior to—and alongside—Dickens's world.

If any one particular chapter in *Dombey and Son* has challenged modern criticism's desire to subdue the text, to reduce it "exactly to the same length, and breadth, and height"[54] of our own world view, it would be chapter 59, "Retribution." It begins, as so often when Dickens is moving toward a conclusion, with the clearing away of evil, in this instance several remaining images of selfishness, Mrs. Pipchin and the Dombey household staff. They depart the house, now "a ruin, and the rats fly from it," a rhythm of repetition eventually replaced by the more sinister echo of a former motif, "Let him remember it in that room, years to come."[55] Dickens's portrayals of the abandoned Dombey domicile and of Mrs. Pipchin's dreams of once again gormandizing while her students wither with hunger ("there is a snaky gleam in her hard grey eye, as of anticipated rounds of buttered toast, relays of hot chops")[56] cohere to remind us that the "house" and "hospitality" are, in the economy of human relationship, works of sensibility not intentionality. Levinas comments on the Pipchins of the world, as well as on those who will replace them, many times in his writings, as in these sentences from his essay "Substitution": "The recurrence of the self in responsibility for others, a persecuting obsession, goes against intentionality, such that responsibility for others could never mean altruistic will, instinct of 'natural benevolence,' or love. It is in the passivity of obsession, or incarnated passivity, that an identity individuates itself as unique, without recourse to any system of references, in the impossibility of evading the assignation of the other without blame."[57]

Those representing the rage to save themselves, the "egoism of the *conatus*,"[58] are thus swept offstage and immediately replaced, in Dickens's typical contrapuntal rhythm, with Polly Toodle and Miss Tox. Mr. Toodle's unlearned understanding of Polly's ethical responsibilities is surely a shadow of Levinas's own image of goodness: "I shouldn't allow of your coming here, to be made dull-like, if it warn't for favours past. But favours past, Polly, is never to be forgot. To them which is in adversity, besides, your face is a cord'l. . . . You wish no better than to do a right act, I know; and my views is, that it's right and dutiful to do this."[59] Better than trying, as too many critics have done, to attribute this "sentimental masking" of the harsh realities of industrial England to some flaw in Dickens's artistry, economic knowledge, or social consciousness, might we not instead recognize that the passage is, rather, a profound *unmasking* of the pervasive implication in such criticism that the ethical no longer exists (if it ever was more than mere ideology) among human beings. Shrewdly enough, Dickens does not attach his image of human goodwill toward others to an artist, a critic, an intellectual, or an elite; it is no accident, I think, that the passage begins, in fact, with a reminder that Mr. Toodle is deeply implicated in the modern world, "Being, now, an ingein-driver [*sic*] and well to do in the world."[60] His goodness, Dickens would seem to be saying, is prior to this self-identification in the world's economy, so deeply embedded in him, so primal a response and responsibility to the needs of those around him that the Industrial Revolution has not touched it. It behooves criticism, I think, not to do more damage to Dickens's images of goodness than the collective reality in which he found them was able to do.[61]

Even more to the point is Dickens's portrayal of Miss Tox, one of his finest illustrations of the challenge he offers again and again in his fictions:

human virtue can be found in the unlikeliest vessels. For if Mr. Toodle is an unlikely enough shadow of Levinas's highly intellectualized appeal to an ethics based on responsibility, Miss Tox would seem almost the antithesis of whatever Levinas meant by his assertion that "the woman is the condition for recollection, the interiority of the Home, and inhabitation."[62] Her name in itself would seem to render her inhospitable to life, and from the first description of her, "a long lean figure, wearing such a faded air that she seemed . . . to have, by little and little, washed out," she is put in stark contrast with the life-giving Polly Toodle, "a plump rosy-cheeked wholesome apple-faced young woman."[63] Dickens could see, however, the image standing always alongside Miss Tox and the cruel, crushing realities of her existence. By juxtaposing her from the beginning with the truly despicable Louisa Chick (Mr. Chick's response to his wife's absurdities, the humming of tunes, probably has its roots in Uncle Toby's Lillibullero—thus does art build incessantly on its library of shadows) and later, more crucially, with the sadistic Bagstock, Dickens enables us to see that image as well.

Thus, by the time we reach the chapter "Retribution," we will have another way to read this early description, and Miss Tox's overwhelming passivity and self-abnegation will no longer seem the trap for an unwary Dombey that we may initially have supposed, nor a hypocritical masking of evil ambition and invidious intent. Rather, she is the essence of the ethical argument Dickens makes in *Dombey and Son:* although "washed out," Miss Tox, he writes at the very beginning, "might have been described as the very pink of general propitiation and politeness."[64] It will take us seven hundred more pages to give "propitiation" and "politeness" more ample meaning, and perhaps it takes Levinas to inform both words with significant philosophical depth. Even this early in the novel, however, her characteristic mode of "listening admiringly to everything that was said . . . and looking at speakers as if she were mentally engaged in taking off impressions of their images upon her soul, never to part with the same but with life,"[65] seems designed to establish her kinship with Paul, although it might detour some readers (as, I suspect, Dickens intended it should) down the path of scorn for a life so dependent on and attuned to others.

Both Paul and Miss Tox are artists, images of Dickens himself, for can we describe him—with our eye on Levinas's discussion of reality and image—any better than as an artist "taking off impressions" of the images of the people of his real world, "upon [his] soul, never to part with the same but with life"? And if her hands were constantly posed in a gesture of "involuntary admiration," and if she has the "softest voice that ever was heard" and an "invincible determination" never "to turn up [her nose] at anything,"[66] are we not in the presence of that image of the ethical that pervades so many pages of Levinas?

> Nothing is more passive than this being implicated prior to my freedom, this pre-original involvement, this frankness. The passivity of the vulnerable one is the condition (or uncondition) by which a being shows itself to be a creature.
>
> Frankness exposes—even to wounds. The active ego reverts to the passivity of a *self,* to the accusative form of the *oneself* [*se*] which does not derive from any nominative, from the accusation prior to any fault. But this exposedness is never passive enough: exposedness is exposed, sincerity denudes sincerity itself.[67]

Miss Tox, her frank interest in Dombey exposed to everyone except the utter block of wood that is Dombey himself, and ultimately rendered naked in Princess Place before the insidious spying of Bagstock and his telescope, is indeed a victim of the readers' initial scorn for the bad motives we assign to her.

Nonetheless, she emerges in the novel as a moral beacon, and on one occasion, in particular, when no one else is present who can direct us. In chapter 18, "Father and Daughter," immediately after Paul's death, Dombey locks himself away from everyone, and Mrs. Chick accuses Florence of not having tried hard enough (there is something positively Heideggerian in both Dombey and Mrs. Chick, as if Dickens could anticipate some of the worst moments of the twentieth century's most important philosopher). Into this physical and moral vacuum, Miss Tox moves toward Florence and her sorrow: "Miss Tox was of a tender nature, and there was something in this appeal that moved her very much. . . . For the moment she forgot the majesty of Mrs. Chick, and patting Florence hastily on the cheek, turned aside and suffered the tears to gush from her eyes, without waiting for a lead from that wise matron."[68] And then, as Dickens so often does, he immediately repeats the gesture so that the inattentive reader has a second chance to understand that virtue, our infinite care for the other person, is

120 · Textual and Critical Intersections

the shadow that tracks every human being; unable to convince Mrs. Chick to allow Florence entrance to her father in order to comfort him, to enter into a "sad community of love and grief,"[69] the girl sadly retreats upstairs:

> "Aunt," said Florence, "I will go and lie down on my bed."
> Mrs. Chick approved of this resolution, and dismissed her with a kiss. But Miss Tox, on a faint pretense of looking for the mislaid handkerchief, went up-stairs after her; and tried in a few stolen minutes to comfort her. . . . Her sympathy seemed genuine, and had at least the vantage-ground of disinterestedness.[70]

These hints are now fulfilled in chapter 59, when Miss Tox joins Polly Toodle in reoccupying the Dombey mansion:

> Miss Tox's sympathy is such that she can hardly speak. She is no chicken, but she has not grown tough with age and celibacy. Her heart is very tender, her compassion very genuine, her homage very real. Beneath the locket with the fishy eye in it, Miss Tox bears better qualities than many a less whimsical outside; such qualities as will outlive, by many courses of the sun, the best outsides and brightest husks that fall in the harvest of the great reaper.[71]

Dickens's insistence at this late point in the novel on separating the outside from the inside, the wheat from the chaff (and the scriptural passage "What is the chaff to the wheat? saith the Lord" is surely in Dickens's mind),[72] is noteworthy. The reality of Miss Tox is, I would suggest, in the image of her goodness, her return to the house of her abasement and exposure, carrying "morsels of cold meats, tongues of sheep, halves of fowls."[73] As such, she serves to anticipate, indeed to shadow, the most difficult moment in the novel, the return of Florence to the house of Dombey and Son.

One final time, Dickens echoes the refrain of the first half of the chapter: "[Miss Tox] . . . passes the greater part of her time in the ruined house that the rats have fled from: . . . only desiring to be true to the fallen object of her admiration, unknown to him, unknown to all the world but one poor simple woman."[74] As the echoes of that refrain die, Dickens reawakens the work's most dramatic liturgical pronouncement: "Let him remember it in that room, years to come." Bridging the two refrains is a short, but most telling paragraph. Dickens allows Bagstock one final comment on the "fidelity" of Miss Tox: "Damme, Sir, the woman's a born idiot!"[75] In that Florence is about to play the fool, in both Dickens's eyes and in the eyes of many readers, we might suggest that Miss Tox has been elevated by Dickens to fore*shadow* his heroine's final triumph, no small reward for the woman with the "quietest voice" in the novel.

To be sure, the word *fool* does not seem to mean to Dickens what it means to Bagstock—or to many modern readers. Indeed, the sense with which Dickens informs a word like *idiot* in the mouths of the Bagstocks of the world is very dramatically suggested by another soft feminine voice, at the end of chapter 58, just before Dickens launches into the chapter under discussion. Here it is Harriet—another splendid image of the ethical as giving care, being a caregiver, with all the richness Levinas has infused into that concept in his writings, philosophical and theological—who is his vehicle. Sitting at the bedside of the dying Alice, she reads to her from "the eternal book for all the weary, and the heavy-laden; for all the wretched, fallen, and neglected of this earth—read the blessed history, in which the blind, lame, palsied beggar, the criminal, the woman stained with shame, the shunned of all our dainty clay, has each a portion, that no human pride, indifference, or sophistry . . . can take away."[76] Dickens here calls on that aspect of the Christian message that, significantly enough, Milton also invokes as *Paradise Lost* draws to its inevitable conclusion: "Merciful over all his works, with good / Still overcoming evil, and by small / Accomplishing great things, by things deemed weak / Subverting worldly strong, and worldly wise / By simply meek."[77] To believe that the meek will inherit the earth is to elevate the shadow over the substance, art over reality; it is to posit, as a theologian, a philosopher, a novelist, that God exists.[78]

It is no accident that Levinas's contemplations in "Reality and Its Shadow" also end with the essential question of essentialism: "Perhaps the doubts that, since the renaissance, the alleged death of God has put in souls have compromised for the artist the reality of the henceforth inconsistent models, have imposed on him the onus of finding his models anew in the heart of his production itself, and made him believe he had a mission to be creator and revealor. The task of criticism remains essential, even if God were not dead, but only exiled."[79] Just before this, however, Levinas had adduced what might be his final comment on the division between artist and critic: "The most forewarned, the most lucid writer nonetheless plays the fool. The interpretation of criticism speaks in full self-possession, frankly, through concepts, which are like the muscles of the mind."[80] This reverts to Plato, I suspect, but it is an image of the critic that Levinas himself does not accept, except perhaps in theory, for it would render criticism essentially unethical, the conversion of infinity into totality. Without doubt, all language must speak in the manner Levinas describes, but lucid critics could—and should—play the fool just as much as lucid artists. Art evolves into propaganda when artists become critics; criticism evolves into art when critics do what has become almost unthinkable to the postmodernist practice of criticism: listen to the rhythms of the text.[81] Nietzsche, the great admirer of Sterne, did just that: "What is to be praised in [Sterne] is . . . the 'endless melody': an artistic style in which the fixed form is constantly being broken up, displaced, transposed back into *indefiniteness.*"[82]

How then might the "critic as fool" read the return of Florence, certainly one of Dickens's most *foolish* moments?

> Yes. His daughter! Look at her! Look here! Down upon the ground, clinging to him, calling to him, folding her hands, praying to him.
> "Papa! Dearest papa! Pardon me, forgive me! I have come back to ask forgiveness on my knees. I never can be happy more, without it!"
> Unchanged still. Of all the world, unchanged. Raising the same face to his, as on that miserable night. Asking *his* forgiveness![83]

Above all, we might want to pursue Dickens's insistence that we use our eyes and ears, our sensibilities, prior to any urge to redefine the moment in conformity to our own thoughts. To see the image, to listen to the words: this rapt attentiveness to the mixture of sorrow and glory in the human imagination's capacity to envision sacrifice—the hostage, in Levinas's vocabulary—seems to me the primary role of the critical mind as it confronts the inexplicable in the work of art. Everything about the scene would seem utterly impossible, irrational, *idiotic,* to the critical mind, and indeed we share Dombey's incredulity, marked by Dickens's italics: "Asking *his* forgiveness." Surely, he should, logically and in any viable economic exchange, be asking for hers; surely, of all the characters in English literature, Florence is one of those few already with the angels as she walks the earth.[84]

Precisely the need to separate ourselves from Dombey's own incredulity at this moment—as he will shortly himself be separated from it and from the suicidal death of the spirit that he has all along represented—should move us toward that place where disbelief is suspended, scorn rejected, and mockery swallows itself, the proverbial lump in the throat.[85] Does Dickens believe in the reality of the scene? Perhaps the word *unchanged* indicates that he does not, at least not at that level of belief that accounts for reality's insistence on its own duration. Levinas speaks to this issue again and again, but perhaps never quite so perceptively as in *Totality and Infinity,* in the section entitled "The Ethical Relation and Time"; the entire section is philosophically relevant to understanding Florence on her knees, for, far from being a simplistic image of a simpleminded author, the moment is filled with enormous complexity. Here is just part of Levinas's analysis:

> [History] excludes the apology, which undoes the totality in inserting into it, at each instant, the unsurpassable, unencompassable present of its very subjectivity. The judgment at which the subjectivity is to remain apologetically present has to be made against the evidence of history (and against philosophy, if philosophy coincides with the evidence of history). The invisible [which I would suggest is the "image" of "Reality and Its Image"] must manifest itself if history is to lose its right to the last word, necessarily unjust for the subjectivity, inevitably cruel. [The invisible] is produced in the goodness reserved to subjectivity, which thus is subject not simply to the truth of judgment, but to the source of this truth.[86]

Criticism seems to me to poise itself on a cusp between "history" and "subjectivity," thus delineated by Levinas, much as does philosophy, perhaps exactly as does philosophy, which is merely a subspecies of the critical act, and hence of the creative act. The event, the work of art, is dead before us; the cold marble in the unopened museum, the unread book in the library stacks, the unheard sonata, the unrehearsed philosophy— these represent images of death perhaps more forebodingly than any human corpse—so much effort to so little effect. The observer, the reader, the listener—in short, the human being as critic—is required to bring to life the dead work, approaching this inert, unmeaning, and vulnerable object with the judgment of history, or, if I might, the history of judgment. The "judgment of history," predominant today in all modes of critical theory, under the aegis of its guiding truism, "everything is politics," brings the work of art to life by installing it within history, significantly not its own

124 · Textual and Critical Intersections

history, difficult if not impossible to recapture, but within the "history" of the present critic. As Levinas notes:

> The virile judgment of history, the virile judgment of "pure reason," is cruel. The universal norms of this judgment silence the unicity in which the apology is contained and from which it draws its arguments. Inasmuch as the invisible is ordered into a totality it offends the subjectivity, since, by essence, the judgment of history consists in translating every apology into visible arguments, and in drying up the inexhaustible source of the singularity from which they proceed and against which no argument can prevail. For there can be no place for singularity in a totality.[87]

The cruelty Levinas finds in history is, ultimately, its justification for murder; to return to my opening discussion of the illustrations of John Baldessari, our commentary on art, whether by fellow artists, critics, or philosophers, can well awaken the work of art from its moribund state only to kill it again—sometimes unintentionally, but more and more, given the rage and scorn we turn on "bad thinking" (that is, thinking unlike our own), we intentionally attempt to rebury the work of art within the absolute obscurity from which we momentarily have resurrected it.

This would lead us to the "history of judgment," whereby we might learn that the criticism that brings a work to enduring life is that criticism which awakens the work with its apology for disturbing it, as it inevitably must do, with eyes that do not see well, ears that fail to hear all they should, attentiveness that waxes and wanes, and, most importantly, a language that again and again will lapse, as its original sin, into the judgments of history. Is it even possible for us to approach a work of art with the recognition that our judgment of it belongs to a history of judgments, each participating in the life of the work, but doing so only because enlivening criticism offers itself to the work of art in the position of a suppliant, a propitiator? Better, perhaps, that art sleep in its marble death to all eternity than to be awakened only to be tormented by the judgments of history. Surely almost all that has been created by the human mind is better off in this sleep of death from which, blissfully, there is no return. Those few masterworks, however, that disturb history, that force themselves on our attention century after century, asking us to weigh the invisible that is the essence of art against the visible and to find the latter light in the scales, those masterworks demand that we approach them on our knees, humbled because we have come after them, are dependent on them, and have been unable, despite all, to find our way into their heart. For such works, we must take on an infinite responsibility because the dead work of art is, finally, indifferent, irresponsible, and immoral, cold to all that matters in the world, and Levinas is right after all—good criticism, finally, is not an exchange, not an economy, but, as Levinas defines art, "a dimension where commerce with reality is a rhythm."[88]

Put in terms of *Dombey and Son,* all art may be imaged in the figure of Dombey, so often compared to a statue, but ultimately, perhaps, best thought of as the unread book. Florence tries again and again to read him (is any chapter more painful to read in terms of the visible in history than chapter 24, "The Study of a Loving Heart"?), to bring him to life, but to no avail—until this moment of approach, not with her history of the wrongs committed against her, not with her grievances on her sleeve or lips, and not even with a condescending forgiveness of the sinner (only God forgives), but rather, on her knees, in apology, taking his sins on herself as did one of those shadows after which Dickens so clearly modeled his heroine.[89]

One speaks in images and shadows in order to approach something that might resemble truth. There is perhaps no finer approach to truth in literature than Florence on her knees begging forgiveness from Dombey, unless it be Milton, describing the careworn face of Satan: "Dark'n'd so, yet shone / Above them all th' Arch-Angel: but his face / Deep scars of Thunder had intrencht, and care / Sat on his faded cheek."[90] Matthew Arnold surely recognized this when he singled out these few lines as offering a "touchstone" for poetic understanding, for he could not have been ignorant of the fact that Milton's great *care* in his epic poem, pace Blake, was to image Satan as everywhere a darkened shadow of the Divine, even in the "cares" that weigh on both God and Satan as a result of fallenness.[91] Might I suggest that chapter 59 of *Dombey and Son* can serve as a touchstone for the *realistic* novel? If we do not understand how this could be, we perhaps should remain silent for a moment and try again to "listen to what the waves are saying." Eventually we will hear, long before we understand, the truth I think Dickens has found in our shared—and fallen—world.

Originally published in *Philological Quarterly* 84, no. 1 (2005).

Notes

1 For a discussion of this Arion edition, see Melvyn New, "William Hogarth and John Baldessari: Ornamenting Sterne's *Tristram Shandy*," *Word & Image* 11, no. 2 (1995): 182–95. Baldessari made his comments in "John Baldessari: Recalling Ideas," interview by Jeanne Siegel, *Arts Magazine* 62 (1988): 89.

2 Charles Dickens, *Dombey and Son*, ed. Alan Horsman (Oxford: Oxford University Press, 1974), 77.

3 See W. G. Day, "Charles Robert Leslie's 'My Uncle Toby and the Widow Wadman': The Nineteenth-Century Icon of Sterne's Work," *Shandean* 9 (1997): 83–108. In addition to prints, the painting appeared on plates and potlids almost simultaneously with its appearance in Hablot Browne's illustration in chapter 26 of *Dombey and Son*, part 9, issued in June 1847; see Day's discussion, 100–101. For Hogarth's illustrations, see New, "William Hogarth," passim.

4 Dickens, *Dombey and Son*, 316. The presence of the Leslie painting in Browne's illustration was first noted by T. W. Hill (Kentley Bromhill) in "Phiz's Illustrations to *Dombey and Son*," *Dickensian* 39 (1943): 51.

5 Siegel, "John Baldessari," 89.

6 New, "William Hogarth," 193.

7 New, 193–94.

8 Emmanuel Levinas, *Totality and Infinity*, trans. Alphonso Lingis (Pittsburgh, PA: Duquesne University Press, 1969), 262.

9 George Orwell, *1984* (New York: Harcourt Brace, 1949), 271.

10 Michael Steig, *Dickens and Phiz* (Bloomington: Indiana University Press, 1978), 96. Steig had made much the same point in "Iconography of Sexual Conflict in *Dombey and Son*," *Dickens Studies Annual* 1 (1970): 161–67.

11 Steig, *Dickens and Phiz*, 3.

12 Steig, 21.

13 Dickens, *Dombey and Son*, 320.

14 Dickens, 320, 316.

15 Emmanuel Levinas, "Meaning and Sense," in *Basic Philosophical Writings*, ed. Adriaan T. Peperzak, Simon Critchley, and Robert Bernasconi (Bloomington: Indiana University Press, 1996), 41. Levinas continues his thought: "Culture and artistic creation are part of the ontological order itself. They are ontological par excellence, they make the understanding of being possible." As the rest of the essay elaborates, Levinas is directing his argument against the "antiplatonism of the contemporary philosophy of meaning": "the intelligible is not conceivable outside of the becoming which suggests it. There exists no meaning in itself" (42).

16 Levinas, "Reality and Its Shadow," in *Collected Philosophical Papers*, trans. Alphonso Lingis (Pittsburgh, PA: Duquesne University Press, 1998), 12.

17 Levinas, 12.

18 Levinas, 9.

19 Levinas, 9.

20 Levinas, "Reality and Its Shadow," 3.

21 Paul Celan, *Poems*, trans. Michael Hamburger (New York: Persea Books, 1988), 98–99.

22 Levinas, 3.

23 Levinas, 3–4.

24 Levinas, 3. One of the most sympathetic readings of *Dombey and Son* is that by Harry Stone, *Dickens and the Invisible World: Fairy Tales, Fantasy, and Novel-Making* (Bloomington: Indiana University Press, 1979), 146–92. As the title indicates, Stone is highly alert to the "magic" in Dickens, as, e.g., in this comment on Paul: "The introduction of a child's consciousness into *Dombey* is one of the great innovations of the novel, a stunning advance in realistic verisimilitude and psychological portraiture. . . . Yet this realistic advance is the source of wildest fantasy. Paul is encompassed by divination and magic, and this supernatural influence marks him within and without" (160).

25 Levinas, "Reality and Its Shadow," 4–5.

26 Levinas, 10.

27 Levinas, 10–11.

28 Cf. A. E. Dyson, "The Case for Dombey Senior," *Novel* 2 (1969): 123: "Only at the very end of chapter sixteen does Dickens intervene, and at the last moment spoil his effect." Many a critic has had the same reaction to Sterne's passage. Few fictional works of the twentieth century better capture Levinas's concept of "seeing inwardness from the outside" than Virginia Woolf's *The Waves* (1931), the very title of which may reflect the present discussion; certainly, this sentence does: "To be myself . . . I need the illumination of other people's eyes." Woolf, *The Waves* (New York: Harcourt Brace Jovanovich, 1959), 116.

29 Dickens, *Dombey and Son*, 191.

30 Dickens, 191.

31 Levinas, "Reality and Its Shadow," 7.

32 Dickens, *Dombey and Son*, 191.

33 Levinas, "Reality and Its Shadow," 9–10.

34 Levinas, 13.

35 Levinas, 3.

36 Levinas, 1.

37 Critics who *write* about artworks, artists who *illustrate* writings, have, I believe, a slight advantage in this regard, in that the differing media offer a fore-

128 · Textual and Critical Intersections

taste of the sacrament of incarnation (transubstantiation), itself an image of an "ethical aesthetics," by which I would attempt to remystify—and pacify—the process of critical thinking. When the *words* of the text are confronted by the *words* of the critic, the tendency—and in the last thirty years, the imperative—is to argue for victory; or, even worse, to silence the other voice completely:

> Such is the rhetoric that applies, not to speech that seeks to win a case or a position, but rhetoric that eats away the very substance of speech, precisely insofar as it "functions in the absence of all truth." Is this not already the possibility of signification that is reducible to a game of signs detached from meanings? From now on, we face an ideology more desolate than all ideology. . . . This threatening ideology hides in the core of the Logos itself. Plato is confident that he can escape it by means of good rhetoric, but he soon hears within discourse the simian imitation of discourse.

See Emmanuel Levinas, "Ideology and Idealism," in *The Levinas Reader*, ed. Seán Hand (Oxford: Blackwell, 1989), 241. One cannot read very far in Dickens criticism without hearing "simian imitations" of Marx and Freud, Foucault and Habermas, but probably Levinas had Derrida uppermost in mind.

38 Jonathan Swift, *Tale of a Tub* (1704), in *Major Works*, ed. Angus Ross and David Woolley (Oxford: Oxford University Press, 2003), 141.

39 Emmanuel Levinas, "Meaning and Sense" in *Collected Philosophical Papers*, 91.

40 Levinas, 91.

41 If Levinas's philosophic shadow, when placed in juxtaposition with *Dombey and Son*, can help us rethink Dickens's novel, so too can fiction serve as a shadow to help us rethink Levinas's "Reality and Its Shadow." This passage from Hermann Broch's *The Guiltless* ("The Ballad of the Beekeeper") strikes me as a profound commentary:

> Only the blind sing songs they have learned. Those who see (even if in the end they are blinded by too much seeing) may—then more than ever—sing their vision, the perpetually renewed vision of life. . . . It is never an imitation of sounds, but the seen swarming of the bees, the seen flight of the lark, and still more: it is the unseen within the seen, transposed into sound.
>
> For a man's ultimate seeing attains to the invisible: there it is given him to intuit the living in the lifeless, in supposedly dead matter. . . . O eye of man, essence of life. . . . In the eye, the creature is farthest removed from the lifeless but life-receiving dust, out of which he was created. . . . The eye is holy, yet with a mere echoed holiness. For a human act of creation is an echo, communicates only an image of man's vision of life, and man,

knowing himself in his eyes, seeing with his eyes that he himself and what
he has done are good, arrogates to himself an immediate knowledge he
does not possess; his eye makes him vain and he returns to the realm of
dead things, he loses the gift of intuiting life, and his action becomes
a mere wallowing in dead matter, false imitation, empty evil. The false
imitation of God . . . that is the danger facing the artist.

See Broch, *The Guiltless*, trans. Ralph Manheim (San Francisco, CA: North
Point Press, 1987), 82–83.

42 Henri Talon, "*Dombey and Son*: A Closer Look at the Text," *Dickens Studies Annual* 1 (1970): 147.

43 Talon, 148. Talon is citing George Santayana from "Dickens," in *The Dickens Critics*, ed. George H. Ford and Lauriat Lane Jr. (Ithaca, NY: Cornell University Press, 1961), 137; and Étienne Gilson, from *L'Etre et l'essence* (Paris: J. Vrin, 1962), 235. It is telling that while Talon's essay has been ignored, Dyson's "The Case for Dombey Senior," and Julian Moynahan's "Dealings with the Firm of Dombey and Son: Firmness *versus* Wetness," in *Dickens and the Twentieth Century*, ed. John Gross and Gabriel Pearson (Toronto: University of Toronto Press, 1962), 121–31, are two readings from the same period still continually cited. Both agree in their iconoclastic urge: Florence in particular, sentimentalism in general, must be desanctified. Despite the witticisms of Moynahan and the coherence of Dyson, both essays are, to my mind, examples of "Baldessarianism." Moynahan, in particular, exhibits wonderful blindness amid his insights; what are we to think of this outburst, for example: "*Dombey and Son* is a very disturbing book, and its mysteries of characterization and narrative treatment are a part of what makes it disturbing. These mysteries must be faced, if not finally reduced to plain sense through analysis" (122). Dyson is the better reader, but the "uneasiness" he feels is his own shadow cast large on Dickens's text: "Florence's role is closely akin to that of a Christ-figure, despised and rejected, but in the end redemptive through love." Why then, he asks, "should a reader feel uneasy about the ending," and he answers his own question: "The presentation of Florence is to my mind a serious weakness at the very core of the book. Dickens seems determined to wear blinkers when creating her" (129).

44 Levinas, *Totality and Infinity*, 158. Talon, "*Dombey and Son*," 150, cites the French text: "L'absence empirique de l'être humain de sexe feminin dans une demeure ne change rien à la dimension de fémininité qui y reste ouverte, comme l'accueil même de la demeure." Emmanuel Levinas, *Totalité et infini* (The Hague: M. Nijhoff, 1961), 131. Needless to say, because of Levinas's often repeated argument along these lines, he continues to draw fire from those who

find sexism in his concept of the feminine; the most entertaining critique is Luce Irigaray's "Questions to Emmanuel Levinas: On the Divinity of Love," in *Re-Reading Levinas*, ed. Robert Bernasconi and Simon Critchley (Bloomington: Indiana University Press, 1991), 109–18. Patricia Marks, "Paul Dombey and the Milk of Human Kindness," *Dickens Quarterly* 11, no. 1 (1994): 14–25, very ably draws attention to the genderless character of "mothering" in Dickens's novel, responding in large part to Nina Auerbach's influential reading of Dickensian gendering in *Romantic Imprisonment: Women and Other Glorified Outcasts* (New York: Columbia University Press, 1986), 109. Auerbach is convinced that the entire novel is based on "male and female principles [*sic*] who can neither evade nor understand each other, whose tragedy and whose force come from their mutual exclusiveness." Auerbach's thesis is predicated on patriarchal values, whereby power and growth are still more significant human achievements than the vitalization of loss through forgiveness and modesty (118); Levinas's examination of those patriarchal values helps us to see her ethical problem.

45 Talon, "*Dombey and Son*," 150.

46 Talon, 151.

47 Levinas, *Totality and Infinity*, 201. Cf. Moynahan, "Dealings with the Firm of Dombey and Son," 128–29, who labels Sol Gills's back parlor a "quasi-religious community" and is totally dismissive of its "narrow and exclusive standard of values. Its values are simple good nature and simple-mindedness. It leaves out of account intelligence, forceful masculine energy—its males are old men, a simpleton, and Walter." That Dombey must experience a "change of heart that reads like a second childhood" in order to enter this community and "drink of its wine" strikes Moynahan as a surrender of "all those qualities of hardness, self-control, and pride that have made him both human and actual, and inhuman as well." Clearly Moynahan believes his own reading restores the "forceful masculine energy" and "hardness" that Dickens lacks.

48 Talon, "*Dombey and Son*," 153.

49 Dickens, *Dombey and Son*, 569.

50 Dickens, 570.

51 Dickens, 571.

52 Talon, "*Dombey and Son*," 158.

53 Dickens, *Dombey and Son*, 160.

54 Swift, *Tale of a Tub*, 141.

55 Dickens, *Dombey and Son*, 696–97, 700–701.

56 Dickens, 700.

57 Emmanuel Levinas, "Substitution" in Hand, *The Levinas Reader*, 101. See the entire discussion, and especially pages 104–7; and this key summary, which is

given Dickensian manifestation in this chapter: "The for itself signifies self-consciousness; the for all, responsibility for the others, support of the universe. Responsibility for the other, this way of answering without a prior commitment, is human fraternity itself, and it is prior to freedom" (106) Cf. Arlene Jackson, "Reward, Punishment, and the Conclusion of *Dombey and Son*," *Dickens Studies Annual* 7 (1978): 114: "Passivity is an important component in Florence's personality, but Dickens' technique actually increases the sense of passivity in Florence." Jackson tries to redeem the heroine by demonstrating her less than passive nature, her guiltiness, so that in an ethical economy, it is "right" that she ask for forgiveness. Levinas's alternative notion of passivity as "a persecuting obsession" suggests that Dickens's great achievement in the portrayal is precisely that he found a way to image Levinas's infinite responsibility without exchange, the sacrificial gesture that alone is fully redemptive.

58 Emmanuel Levinas, "Humanism and An-archy," in *Collected Philosophical Papers*, 138.

59 Dickens, *Dombey and Son*, 699.

60 Dickens, 699.

61 Moynahan, "Dealings with the Firm of Dombey and Son," 129–30, is merely the wittiest of those who have attacked Dickens from this perspective, and hence the most quotable:

> *Dombey and Son* is also a vision of the transformation of society by love, and as such is something less than adequate. One difficulty is that the vision is neither genuinely religious . . . nor genuinely secular. . . . The book seems to me to exhibit Protestant piety divorced from its doctrinal foundations. . . . Religion has become a set of loose analogies and tropes employed to conceal faulty argument by analogy: people who act like saints will be rewarded like saints in the end. The meek shall inherit the Industrial Revolution.

> He has been well answered by Lynda Zwinger, "The Fear of the Father: Dombey and Daughter," *Nineteenth-Century Fiction* 39, no. 4 (1985): 420–44, e.g., "This dismissive attitude, which duplicates in an unsettling way Dombey's attitude toward his daughter, is itself based on a set of rather loose critical tropes and analogies. The basic critical attitude found in such readings is one of self-congratulation that we are no longer so unsophisticated as to fall for *that*" (434–35). I would add only that neither I nor Moynahan can know what is "genuinely religious."

62 Levinas, *Totality and Infinity*, 155.

63 Dickens, *Dombey and Son*, 5–6, 11.

64 Dickens, 5.

132 · Textual and Critical Intersections

65 Dickens, 5–6.

66 Dickens, 5–6.

67 Emmanuel Levinas, "No Identity," in *Collected Philosophical Papers*, 147. See also Levinas's note to this passage, on that same page: "Subjectivity *signifies* by a passivity more passive than all passivity, more passive than matter, by its vulnerability, its sensibility, by its nudity more nude than nudity, the sincere denuding of this very nudity that becomes a saying, the saying of responsibility, by the substitution in which responsibility is said to the very end, by the accusative of the oneself without a nominative form, by exposedness to the traumatism of gratuitous accusation, by expiation for the other." In this way, our discussion of Miss Tox will lead directly to Florence's act of "responsibility" toward Dombey.

68 Dickens, *Dombey and Son*, 205.

69 Dickens, 315.

70 Dickens, 207.

71 Dickens, 700.

72 Jeremiah 23:28.

73 Dickens, *Dombey and Son*, 701. Dyson's comment, in "The Case for Dombey Senior," 126, seems to me sadly mistaken: "his [Dombey's] sister's dim—and dimly perceived—friend—poor Miss Tox."

74 Dickens, *Dombey and Son*, 701.

75 Dickens, 701.

76 Dickens, 692.

77 John Milton, *Paradise Lost*, 12.565–69, cited from *John Milton: Complete Poems and Major Prose*, ed. Merritt Y. Hughes (New York: Odyssey Press, 1957), 467.

78 Cf. Nancy Klenk Hill, "*Dombey and Son*: Parable for the Age," *Dickens Quarterly* 8, no. 4 (1991): 169–77, and especially 175: "Dickens, in his acknowledgment of suffering and the loss of pride as pre-requisite to entrance into the community of Christian love and caring, expresses a deeply traditional, indeed Anglican theology." Precisely this sort of reading annoys Dyson: "Dickens pushes most of his leading characters too close to allegory," a literary form he finds "flawed, falsifying, and simplified," a "writing in chains." Dyson, "The Case for Dombey Senior," 133–34. He would, presumably, also fault Dante and Dostoevsky—but Theodore Dreiser would emerge unscathed.

79 Levinas, "Reality and Its Shadow," 13.

80 Levinas, 13.

81 One of the finest essays in recent years on *Dombey and Son* is Roger B. Henkle's "The Crisis of Representation in *Dombey and Son*," in *Critical Reconstructions*, ed. Robert M. Polhemus and Roger B. Henkle (Stanford, CA: Stanford

Taking Care: A Slightly Levinasian Reading of *Dombey and Son* · 133

University Press, 1994), 90–110. He finds in the novel two opposing mentalities, two discourses: Paul's "maternal," nondifferentiating way of thinking and Dombey's ethos of the competitive male (92), and he listens to Paul's rhythm:

> As lyrical as such musings are, their otherworldliness detaches them from the richly detailed and grounded social text that is one of the salient qualities of a Dickens novel. Dickens's force lies in his full realization of his world, and Paul's vision seems to draw the imagination away from that world. Our eyes, as readers, are lifted above the scene spread before us; like Paul we seem to be lost in a reverie. . . . In moments such as this, we seem to see *through* Paul, as if he were not there, or as if he were (as so many of Dickens's "spiritual" characters are) a focusing lens for us. (95)

82 Friedrich Nietzsche, *Human, All Too Human: A Book for Free Spirits*, trans. R. J. Hollingdale (Cambridge: Cambridge University Press, 1986), 238.

83 Dickens, *Dombey and Son*, 705.

84 David W. Toise, "'As Good as Nowhere': Dickens's *Dombey and Son*, the Contingency of Value, and Theories of Domesticity," *Criticism* 41 (1999): 323–48, attempts, rather effectively, to return Florence to an economic framework without damaging her essence by suggesting that she sets up "an alternative economy from that in which her father participates: Dombey's economy is based on the exchange of goods, while Florence's is an economy based on the exchange of feeling" (338). But when he expands the argument to suggest that since "Florence seems to love everyone despite what they do or say to her, her love seems both pure and contentless, just as cash (in a system of advanced commodity exchange) is pure value and represents no commodity in particular" (342), he perhaps indicates a flaw in his formulation, since economy (justice) is precisely and always a finite mode of exchange, while Florence's guiltiness before her father has no exchange value whatsoever. It is an acknowledgment of infinite responsibility never fulfilled. Significantly enough, Toise points to one of Dickens's most telling descriptions of Florence, an early impression that forms in Walter's mind: "he could do no better than preserve her image in his mind as something precious, unattainable, unchangeable, and indefinite." Dickens, *Dombey and Son*, 183. One might suggest that Walter has here defined the uneconomic, the nonpolitical—or, more positively, that he has identified the sacramental in the face of Florence. Cf. Jonathan Loesberg, "Deconstruction, Historicism, and Overdetermination: Dislocation of the Marriage Plots in *Robert Elsmere* and *Dombey and Son*," *Victorian Studies* 33, no. 3 (1990): 441–64; Loesberg ties Florence to the Kantian sublime, her ability to love being a "faculty of the mind that surpasses every standard of economics" (458).

85 To be sure, many critics in addition to Moynahan and Dyson have tried to tough it out; hence Mary Armstrong finds Florence the "perfect Victorian female: beautiful to the point of otherworldliness, selfless to the point of invisibility," and then informs us that perfectness is "boring." Armstrong, "Pursuing Perfection: *Dombey and Son*, Female Homoerotic Desire and the Sentimental Heroine," *Studies in the Novel* 28, no. 3 (1996): 282–83. And Nancy Cervetti quotes Sandra Gilbert and Susan Gubar on selflessness: "To be selfless is not only to be noble, it is to be dead." Of this forgiveness scene in particular, she waxes quite indignant: "Where is her sense of personal dignity? Must even a hearth angel be so servile? The humility seems excessive. . . . In order to achieve . . . social connection . . . Florence pays a dear price, forfeiting her dignity, agency, and sexuality. Such sacrifice seems perverse, and we must question the probability and the consequences of such fictional idealization. Florence's abstract character is not constructed with the stuff humans are made of." Cervetti, "Dickens and Eliot in Dialogue: Empty Space, Angels and Maggie Tulliver," *Victorian Newsletter* 80 (1991): 22. See also Jackson, "Reward, Punishment"; and Lisa Surridge, "Domestic Violence, Female Self-Mutilation, and the Healing of the Male in *Dombey and Son*," *Victorian Institute Journal* 25 (1997): 77–103. Even when arguing specific points against him, all these voices ultimately echo Moynahan: "On a harder view, Florence is not a conduit of Grace. The miracles she performs are all arranged for her by the intrusive author. Remove her pall of quasi-religious mystery and Dombey's daughter is at best a sentimentalist lacking decent self-respect, at worst a masochist. She is an image of human feeling devoid of energy, segregated from intelligence and the life of the senses." In fact, he seems to suggest, if her "unlimited sentiment" dominated the world, trains would not run on time; always, the boot stamping on a human face—forever. Moynahan, "Dealings with the Firm of Dombey and Son," 130.

86 Levinas, *Totality and Infinity*, 243.

87 Levinas, 243–44.

88 Levinas, "Reality and Its Shadow," 12–13, 5 (qtd).

89 Cf. Frank McCombie, "Sexual Repression in *Dombey and Son*," *Dickensian* 88, no. 1 (1992): 35: "There is, then, something truly Christ-like, or angelic, about Florence after all (as the novel draws towards its conclusion, she is repeatedly proposed as some kind of 'angel'), and this is not just a recrudescence of mid-century melodrama." Unfortunately, her actions in this forgiveness scene are taken to be a "very clever fictive illustration of Freudian theory"; the Christ complex, one assumes.

90 Milton, *Paradise Lost*, 1.599–602.

91 Matthew Arnold, "Essays in Criticism, Second Series"; see John Shepard Eells Jr., *The Touchstones of Matthew Arnold* (New York: Bookman Associates, 1955), 161–71, and especially his view that "the single line of the passage" to which Arnold was "peculiarly responsive" was indeed "and care / Sat on his faded cheek" (162).

6

Johnson, T. S. Eliot, and the City

> Now Johnson was, in his day, very much a modern; he was concerned with
> how poetry should be written in his own time.
>
> T. S. Eliot, "Annual Lecture on a Master Mind: Milton"

A literary scholar spending years in the company of Laurence Sterne will, if
only as a defense mechanism against the many assertions of Sterne's anticipation of postmodernism, find himself arguing for his far more interesting,
if less obvious, relationship to modernism. Hence, in a series of essays over
the years, I have brought Sterne's writings into proximity with the novels
of Marcel Proust, Italo Svevo, Bruno Schulz, and Virginia Woolf; with the
philosophy of Friedrich Nietzsche; and with the autobiographical *Sentimental Journey* of Viktor Shklovsky—an erratic but sufficiently representative sampling of the modernist movement.[1] What I learned from these
excursions, however, was not only that Sterne anticipated modernism, or
that the predilection among modernists for Sterne's writings (several were
enthusiastic admirers) was of particular importance to their own endeavors but that great authors of any era and any "ism," when placed in proximity by attentive readers, will be overheard engaging in conversations well
worth chronicling.

For example, when reading *Tristram Shandy* alongside *Mrs. Dalloway*,
I believe I heard a conversation between the two works about the modern
worship of proportion, order, and unstoppable progress through science
and technology. Herself a reader of Sterne, moreover, Woolf had a different conversation with him, one sufficient to induce her to write an introduction to an edition of *A Sentimental Journey* that is still a very valuable
commentary on that work.[2] On the other hand, the Polish writer Bruno

Schulz might never have encountered Sterne, but a reader putting his work in proximity with Sterne's may well hear the two authors speaking to one another across languages, countries, and generations. This conversation among the best authors is, I believe, what too many teachers of literature have tended to ignore in a postmodernist era dominated by socially and politically determined reading lists alongside a desire to eschew all that is past in order to emphasize their own agenda of freedom and nonjudgmental evaluation.[3] Modernism, I would argue, instinctively and pervasively sensed and addressed the hazards of leaning too far forward without also looking back.

If Sterne then proves to be an eighteenth-century author in conversation with modernists, is Samuel Johnson another? And, if so, would it be wise to listen first to any conversation that might be heard between Sterne and Johnson, before moving on to Johnson and modernism? We know that he offered several of his patented jibes at Sterne's expense, including one that has proved a wonderful failure of prescience: "Nothing odd will do long. 'Tristram Shandy' did not last."[4] It is a fact, however, that within the single annus mirabilis of 1759, Voltaire's *Candide* was followed closely behind by Johnson's *Rasselas,* and by the first two volumes of Sterne's *Tristram Shandy.* It is certainly possible to align all three authors on numerous topics; I have recently suggested, for example, that their works share a core interest in exposing the flaws of Enlightenment thought.[5] Indeed, the most important conversations modernism has had with the eighteenth century seem always to be reducible to this concern with Enlightenment's implications for both the inherited past and the promised future.

Twenty-five years ago, in a short essay on teaching *Rasselas,* I aligned Johnson's apologue with two modernist texts, Joseph Conrad's *Lord Jim* and André Gide's *The Counterfeiters,* three chronicles of a young man's attempt to find meaning in a world in which, as Gide's Bernard is told, "you can only learn how you ought to live by living" and where Stein's advice for Jim is "to the destructive element submit yourself, and with the exertions of your hands and feet in the water make the deep, deep sea keep you up. So, if you ask me—how to be?"[6] The advice is vague enough to include the characters of Candide and Tristram as well within a modernism that seems to accept the existential autonomy of the individual, but in each instance the author has raised sufficient obstacles to any interpretation that accepts human autonomy as absolute. Rather, these authors across two centuries seem committed to holding fast to an essentialist vision of "how to be" within the jointly perceived "destructive element." Their shared solution entails not only one's own efforts but assistance from higher powers as well, defined as an inherited religion or inherited culture, or perhaps as both. That is to say, we are inheritors as well as innovators, imitators as well as originators. Perhaps the most pertinent distinction to be observed between modernism and academic postmodernism is precisely this, that despite its many quarrels with, deviations from, and innovations to its nineteenth-century inheritance, modernism recognized its inescapable position as heir to Enlightenment and Romanticism. One suspects that the present professorial commitment to starting anew (ab ovo) is already a fading blip, but perhaps that is only a hope. Certainly, for many in the eighteenth and twentieth centuries, whether as writers or as citizens of the world, their grave suspicions concerning Enlightenment have already been realized; it seems quite likely that our present century will come to the same conclusion, given its dire first two decades.

Christianity was one inheritance received by both Johnson and Sterne, an inheritance rich enough to encompass two figures who have come down to us as very different Christians indeed. For the present discussion, the nature and depth of their faith is not as important as its service to both authors, an impediment to the century's emerging and alternative belief system, a newly constructed faith in constant and ameliorating progress, the result of an awakening in the eighteenth century to scientific method, to social improvement, and to political utopianism. Moreover, both authors, while undeniably innovative in thought, form, and style (had anyone before—or after—Johnson written a similar prose sentence?), looked to the past, classical and Christian, early and late Renaissance, for much of their inspiration. It is this mindset, I would argue, that most surely binds Johnson and Sterne together, as two centuries later it would bind Eliot and Woolf.

In a fine essay on "Johnson and Modern Poetry" (1985), David Perkins noted, as have others, the appearance of Johnson in *Little Gidding,* and the strong influence that *The Vanity of Human Wishes* played throughout T. S. Eliot's career. However, it is another observation, concerning Pope's suppressed presence in *The Waste Land,* that suggested to me a path worth pursuing in quest of Johnson's "modernist" links to Eliot, namely Perkins's explanation as to why Eliot thought of including in the archetype of modernist poetry a seventy-line passage imitative of *The Rape of the Lock:*

> [The poem] was about contemporary life in Pope's London (thus extending Eliot's panorama of the city back in time), and, like virtually every other allusion in *The Waste Land,* showed the same life persisting through time: the life of men and women in a bored, materialistic society, aimless and frivolous, in which the cross Pope's Belinda wears about her neck is merely an ornament.[7]

Perkins adds the further astute comment that, as the Romantics rebelled against the Augustans, it was only natural for the modernists, in rebellion against the Romantics, to turn back to writers such as Dryden, Pope, Goldsmith, and Johnson, and he quotes Eliot's 1930 introduction to Johnson's *London: A Poem and The Vanity of Human Wishes:* "Those who demand of poetry a day dream, or a metamorphosis of their own feeble desires and lusts, or what they believe to be 'intensity' of passion, will not find much in Johnson."[8]

While *Vanity* has been combed for its interactions with Eliot's poetry, *London* has remained relatively unexamined, although clearly it pursues, through the genre of "imitation," the city "back in time," importantly so since Juvenal's Rome is certainly among the first to be characterized as "aimless and frivolous." Indeed, in his introduction to the two poems, Eliot returns again to urbanization:

> The verse after Pope, Swift, Prior, and Gay seems an age of retired country clergymen and schoolmasters. It is cursed with a Pastoral convention . . . and a ruminative mind. . . . In this rural, pastoral, meditative age Johnson is the most alien figure. . . . Johnson remains a townsman . . . with no tolerance of swains and milkmaids. He has more in common in spirit with Crabbe than with any of his contemporaries; at the same time he is the last Augustan.[9]

Eliot does judge *Vanity* to be the "finer poem," but then adds that "both of them seem to me to be among the greatest verse Satires of the English or any other language. . . . They are *purer* satire than anything of Dryden or Pope, nearer in spirit to the Latin."[10]

In the Christopher Ricks and Jim McCue edition of Eliot's poems there are several allusions noted to Johnson's writings, but none to *London,* and, indeed, this essay will not attempt to establish verbal influence.[11] Rather, I will be discussing "modernism" as a reaction to urban life, but a reaction significantly different from that of a pastoral-leaning Horatian comparison between city and country life, or a Wordsworthian return to Tintern Abbey, where the country restores the innocence and energy sapped by the city. I will also limit my discussion to Eliot's *Love Song of J. Alfred Prufrock,* although one might suggest the themes to be discussed are more overtly evidenced in *The Waste Land.* But *London* and *Prufrock* have an important biographical connection, being the first successful poems by two young men encountering the city as the place of their chosen residence for the remainder of their lives.[12] Johnson and Eliot (and perhaps Juvenal before them) seem to share the view that the promise of progress, ameliorative change, and, in brief, enlightened modernity that seems always to accompany urban dwelling is indeed a hollow promise. Yet Eliot remained in London throughout his life and never returned (except for occasional visits) to his native country; it would not be far afield to suggest for him a seemingly paradoxical agreement with Johnson's famous paean that "No, Sir, when a man is tired of London, he is tired of life; for there is in London all that life can afford," delivered some forty years after writing *London.* Nor would Eliot disagree with Johnson's many pronouncements marking London as the center of science and learning: "no man, at all intellectual . . . is willing to leave."[13] By placing *London* alongside *Prufrock,* Johnson in proximity to Eliot, I believe we may uncover a foreshadowing of the one aspect of modernism that seems out of place for both authors: their Christian faith. As the careers of both writers developed, this faith became quite overt, but few have wanted to suggest that at this early stage in their careers it was already shaping their vision. I shall argue that this is indeed the case. They portray urbanism as the only environment left to writers and thinkers, but the city confines, corrupts, and finally exhausts everyone; it leaves the writer with no exit, trapped in a violent and corrupt landscape. The choices presented to modern man seem to be limited to adapting to the "destructive element" or withering away; if this is so, modernism, I would suggest, can be defined as a persistent state of psychic depression inherent to this urban experience.

A minor poet, Amy Levy, on the cusp of English modernism in 1889, captured the essence of this urban depression in what is perhaps her best poem, "A London Plane-Tree":

> Green is the plane-tree in the square,
>   The other trees are brown;
> They droop and pine for country air;
>   The plane-tree loves the town.
>
> Here from my garret-pane, I mark
>   The plane-tree bud and blow,
> Shed her recuperative bark,
>   And spread her shade below.
>
> Among her branches, in and out,
>   The city breezes play;
> The dun fog wraps her round about;
>   Above, the smoke curls grey.
>
> Others the country take for choice,
>   And hold the town in scorn;
> But she has listened to the voice
>   On city breezes borne.[14]

Needless to say, any London poet is bound to comment on its fog, although Eliot insisted he had never experienced a London fog before he wrote lines 15–16 of *Prufrock*,[15] but what interests me here is the poet's strained attempt to thrive in London, to ignore the city's destructive environment for all but the one species able to survive amid the fog and smoke and whatever else is borne on "city breezes." It is perhaps unfair to note that Levy committed suicide the year this poem was published, at the age of twenty-seven, but, despite the poem's struggle to be positive, it seems pregnant with a despair generated by entrapment. It is therefore important to point out that in Juvenal's poem (and in Johnson's imitation) the poet is seeing his friend out of the corrupt city but is himself remaining behind. The first thing we might discover by putting *London* into proximity with *Prufrock,* then, is the value of treating the latter as partaking of elements of classical "verse satire"—most particularly here a separation of the speaker

142 · Textual and Critical Intersections

from the observing poet. In *Prufrock,* I would suggest, the young poet accompanies an older man on his city tour, listens to his lament, and ends, as in Juvenal's original poem, on the beach, looking for an exit.

To be sure, that would suggest that the four poets I have invoked, Juvenal, Johnson, Levy, and Eliot, are all *modernists,* an absurdity on the surface but a possibility I nevertheless want to pursue. What the modernist label most suggests to me is a point of view trapped between a worldly dream of a return to an imagined halcyon past (whether a Golden Age or an Eden) and the counterdream of an equally worldly golden or Edenic future. Christian theology and literature are built on an alternative vision, a lost Eden, by which time, sin, and death entered the world, and a possible timeless future in the company of an eternal God, but only through faith in the sacrifice of Jesus Christ. That both Johnson and Eliot famously held tight to this alternative view, is manifest in their biographies and their writings, although both were also quite cognizant of its failure any longer to organize the society around them. Rather, hope for the future had now passed to the promise of a rational political and social amelioration through science and human intellect, the pillars of the urban structure, ancient or modern. Johnson and Eliot envision for us the despair generated by our permanent estrangement from this mythic (as it is to rationalist eyes) story and our equally permanent compensatory commitment to utopian fantasies of progress. Many possibilities have been offered as to the nature of Prufrock's "overwhelming question," but the best answer, I think, is one provided in the Ricks-McCue edition, from Pascal's *Pensées:* "every man who thinks and lives by thought must have his own scepticism, that which stops at the question, that which ends in denial, or that which leads to faith."[16] What most establishes Johnson and Eliot as "modernists" is, I believe, their simultaneous and contradictory embrace, here at the beginning of their careers, of the fraught role of being displaced (or unplaced) *urban Christians,* fully aware of the oxymoronic character of the term. Their response was to undergird their portrait of the city with faint but still audible echoes of Scripture, echoes of doctrine, and echoes of *Paradise Lost.*[17]

Twenty years after *Prufrock* was published, Eliot presented a lecture, "The Christian in the Modern World," to the Church Union Literature Association, that remained unpublished until appearing in the *Times Literary Supplement* in 2017.[18] To my mind, it offers the best commentary on *Prufrock* and urbanism that I have found, beginning with the observation that "so long as people were able to believe—most of them—that the world was making continuous progress in civilization, it was possible for most people to make easy terms with contemporary society.... The social and economic order was far from perfect, but it was on the way towards perfection." For Eliot this progress had one exception, namely that everything was improving "except belief in Christ," and possibly this accounts for his making space for exceptions in his phrasing: "most of them," "most people."[19]

The period 1920–35 (the aftermath of World War I, the ensuing economic collapse, and the preparations for World War II) broke these illusions of progress according to Eliot, but surely the poets of *London* and *Prufrock* were never fully vested in them. As Eliot explores the inevitable failure of the League of Nations, fascism, and communism, he notes that all of them absorbed elements of Christianity: "Various publicists will tell you, that either Marxism, with a few important modifications, is the real Christian attitude; or that Fascism, again with a few important modifications, is the Christian attitude." His own view is crucial: before accepting any political or social system, "consider those Christian elements which are omitted, as well as those that are included." Those elements can be narrowed to two essentials, less familiar in modern times than they were to Johnson, for whom they were the profound bedrocks of the Anglican faith he professed: first, in Eliot's words, "one of the dangerous delusions that the Christian must avoid is that of the perfect human society situated somewhere in the future"; and second, that the "eventual perfection of human nature [can be] brought about exclusively from outside."[20] Johnson would perhaps have been more scriptural: the breach between God (perfection) and humankind, caused by the first Adam's fall into sin and death in the Garden of Eden, can only be healed by absolute faith in, and the assistance of, the second Adam, his sacrifice for—and restoration of—grace to humanity.[21]

In a very useful chapter on *London,* David Venturo notes the poem's contrast between the "georgic existence in lines 210–23 and the 'Dangers' (line 236) of an urban night in lines 224–41," and suggests that because Eliot failed to recognize these "specifically ideological foundations," he questioned the "'sincerity' of Johnson's praise of the country": "That Johnson should ever have contemplated leaving London for the remote promontory of St. David's is so inconsistent with his character, and his confessed sentiments in later life, that we cannot believe he ever meant it."[22] Venturo goes on to express surprise that Eliot would so confound the poet and the poem's "rhetorical spokesman"—that is, his persona (Thales)—and makes the point that "Eliot, of all authors, who could write *The Waste Land* and yet delight in living and working in London, should have been more careful."[23] The observation is important because, as Howard D. Weinbrot long ago demonstrated, there is almost certainly no irony in Juvenal's "georgic existence"—nor would Johnson have believed there was.[24]

It is of course possible that Eliot was simply careless here, but I would suggest another explanation, namely that when Thales speaks of "Some pleasing Bank where verdant Osiers play, / Some peaceful Vale with Nature's Paintings gay," or later when the poet instructs Thales to "There prune thy Walks, support thy drooping Flow'rs, / Direct thy Rivulets, and twine thy Bow'rs," Eliot correctly recognized the diction of satiric parodies of the pastoral tradition, while failing to acknowledge that the same language was Edenic as well.[25] Thus, when Samuel Richardson wants to ridicule the pastoral, he has Sir Charles Grandison talk of a "mossy bank of a purling stream, gliding thro' an enamelled mead . . . the feathered songsters from an adjacent grove, contributing to harmonize and fan the lambent flame"; and when Milton wants to describe life in Eden, his language is similar: "what we by day / Lop overgrown, or prune, or prop, or bind, / One night or two with wanton growth derides / Tending to wild."[26] Johnson may well have built this ambiguity into his poem because while the georgic seems to offer a valid alternative to the city, it ultimately fails—as does the city—to answer the question "how to live?" The eternal oneness with God, represented by Eden or by the pastoral is now possible, only through the mediation of Christ and only after death; it is no accident that Johnson places signs of Christianity not in the country but in the past, the "consecrated Earth" of Elizabeth's time, or "her Cross triumphant on the Main."[27] The tendency to believe the world after the expulsion from Eden to be in a steady and continuing retreat from perfection is precisely the opposite of Enlightenment thought, and hence the story of the Fall becomes the fundamental notion that puts Christian city dwellers in conflict with themselves.[28]

The attempt to find an Edenic existence in the countryside, a mythic return to innocence and harmony, is, within a Christian view, as hopeless a dream as a social and political creation of perfection within the secular state. Given our fallen natures, however, it is highly likely that, even while writing his imitation, Johnson recognized his own "delight" in urban life, the same delight that Venturo notes in Eliot. For both, the city gathers all the conflicts and contradictions of leading a secular life in a God-created world—of being an urban Christian—but there is no other place in which they are willing to live. The past is unrecoverable, at least on earth, but not irredeemable; the future is utterly tainted, both by the impossible dreams postulated but even more so by the tactics those in power will resort to in the belief that they can do what divine power will not do. In Eliot's lecture he opportunely turns to Jacques Maritain:

> In this way (the separation of the secular from the spiritual) the action of States as well as the conduct of wars and conspiracies, revolutions, acts of violence and the rest came to be the work of a tiny group of men who sacrificed their virtue on the altar of public welfare in much the same way that prostitutes sacrifice their honour to maintain the peace of families.[29]

As Johnson's poem suggests, he and those he allied himself to had already identified Robert Walpole and his cohorts as one such "tiny group."[30]

Even as we accept Weinbrot's argument that Juvenal was indeed sincere about a return to country life, and Venturo's assertion that the "pastoral/georgic tradition gives [Johnson] the ideal vehicle for linking rural husbandry and private virtue with the public realm of political virtue,"[31] I suspect that Johnson would have had some reservations, not because he scorned the countryside but because he realized it was no longer a viable alternative, from either a religious or secular viewpoint; his empiricism and his faith would both inform against the pastoral. In this regard, Eliot's reading of the georgic in *London* is valid. He found in Johnson's poem the same inescapable environment into which he imprisoned his own urban dweller. Unlike Thales, however, Prufrock, although equally without "Youth, and Health, and Fortune" cannot (or will not?) escape the city; and, unlike the satirist, he no longer has the "angry Numbers" of Johnson's heroic couplets,[32] backed by Juvenal's majestic severity, but only the fragments of experiences he fears to confront. While both Johnson and Eliot are equally adept, in their different voices, at pointing to the truly destructive and confining environment of urban life, both recognize it as the only

146 · Textual and Critical Intersections

life now available for them. The pastoral alternative, not so much a place as a concept, is no longer possible, and we can perhaps capture their shared dilemma by pointing to the word itself, *pastoral,* denoting as it does both a rural and a religious setting.[33]

Put another way, if one can believe in Lazarus, one can find an alternative to urban life, but Prufrock is not "Lazarus, come from the dead. / Come back to tell you all."[34] The promise of eternal life, figured as the pastoral in literary tradition, as prophecy ("I am no prophet") in the Old Testament, and as John the Baptist in the New Testament ("my head [grown slightly bald] brought in upon a platter"),[35] is now lost to urban dwellers, and its evocation is a hollow promise from the past, no longer functional in the brave new world emerging from that "mythic" spiritual hope into the new secular expectations of modernity.

These overt scriptural allusions are reinforced by less obvious ones. For example, the section begins with the simple "Shall I say," which Ricks and McCue tie to Isaiah 38:15 ("What shall I say") and John 12:27 ("Now is my soul troubled; and what shall I say").[36] The speaker in Isaiah is Hezekiah, who is punished by God for displaying all his wealth, an Orgilio of biblical times, a Great Gatsby of the modern era.[37] In John, the speaker is Jesus, contemplating his own coming death, which will reestablish the connection between God and humanity; significantly, the scriptural chapter opens with an allusion to Lazarus, "which had been dead, whom he raised from the dead."[38] It is appropriate, therefore, that after invoking the prophets, John the Baptist, and Lazarus, Prufrock should confront his fear of death, "from whose bourn / No traveller returns," thus leading us to the Hamlet allusion that has seemed abrupt to some readers.[39]

Unhappily, the lost promise of salvation, a return to the wholeness with God that existed before the Fall, is combined for both poets with a cityscape that makes the new promise of progress equally empty. The result is well described by Andrew Varney, in one of the better essays written on *London:* "Johnson fuses with his public satire a deeply impassioned presentation of the mind in distress that is almost wholly absent from Juvenal and from his other translators and imitators. . . . The strains of querulousness, alarm, unease, fear, and testiness that complicate and enrich the poetic texture of *London* may be missed" if readers concentrate only on the physical and political aspects of the poem.[40] Varney centers attention, instead, on the impact of the city on its inhabitants, bringing Johnson's poem much closer to *Prufrock*, although Eliot is not invoked: "Human minds in this society are fractured, hypocritical, deluded, deceived, or otherwise divorced from their own better interests." For Varney, the poet chronicles the fact that the "social and mental fabric of the city is falling apart," leaving us "nowhere to turn for an assurance of stability,"[41] surely a useful reading, although it does cause him to downplay two additional insights that reading *London* as a modernist poem has perhaps helped bring into focus.

Varney uses a quasi-theological diatribe by Dr. Sacheverell on the moral degeneracy of the times to serve as a contrast to Johnson's more subdued and anguished utterance.[42] The comparison is unfair, reducing the spiritual dimensions of the poem to the caricature of Sacheverell's excessive (and political) certainties; surely, however, when one speaks of the "social and mental fabric" of London, at least in the eighteenth century, one must consider the "spiritual fabric" as well, since most in the century thought of self and state as still fully informed by their religion. Johnson, for example, with poetic subtlety rather than sermonic bombast, several times addresses the presence of religious belief within the landscape of a city without faith. From the "female Atheist" who talks "you dead" to the "Crimes" that "inflame the Wrath of Heav'n," from the often discussed line on the artful French sycophant who will go to hell on your behalf to the invocation of "Heaven's just Bolts" to confound "*Orgilio's* Wealth" with "angry Heav'n's . . . fire,"[43] one finds glimpses of Johnson's Christianity, heavily marked, even at this early date, by three of the four last things that would become the preoccupations of his mind: Death, Judgment, and Hell. Heaven, the end that imparts meaning to a virtuous life, is absent, and in the most famous paragraph in the poem Johnson makes its absence the center of his indictment of London:

> Has Heaven reserv'd, in Pity to the Poor,
> No pathless Waste, or undiscover'd Shore?
> No secret Island in the boundless Main?
> No peaceful Desart yet unclaim'd by SPAIN?
> . . . .
> This mournful Truth is ev'ry where confest,
> SLOW RISES WORTH, BY POVERTY DEPREST.[44]

Obviously, there are economic, social, and political dimensions to this passage, but framing it, I believe, is the now forsaken promise, "Blessed are

148 · Textual and Critical Intersections

the poor in spirit: for theirs is the kingdom of heaven."[45] Matthew Henry's traditional commentary on the passage provides a context for *London* that seems particularly pertinent, as, for example, when he argues that the entire Sermon on the Mount "is designed to rectifie the ruining Mistakes of a blind and carnal World . . . [in which] most *mistake* the End and form a wrong notion of Happiness . . . [they] spend their Days in Mirth, and their Years in Pleasure, . . . eat the Fat and drink the Sweet, and carry all before them with a high Hand."[46] This may strike one as more pertinent to *The Vanity of Human Wishes,* where a more confident Johnson will break away from Juvenal for his own overtly Christian conclusion, but I believe that already in *London* Johnson manifests his world as within and not distinct from his Christian inheritance. It is a perspective that we have difficulty recapturing and crediting after two hundred years of enlightened urbanization, so that if we hear it repeated by a modernist like Eliot, our hackles are raised, and "reactionary" may be the kindest of epithets sent in his direction. Nonetheless, I will here suggest that both *London* and *Prufock* are guided by a similar scriptural response to the modernist question: how are we to live in the destructive element when it is the *only* element in which we can keep afloat? Henry's *Exposition,* in explaining Matthew's difficult phrase "poor in spirit," may provide the answer: "a gracious Disposition of Soul, by which we are *emptied of self,* in order to our being filled with *Jesus Christ.*"[47]

The second aspect of *London* downplayed in Varney's reading is what many critics have noted as Johnson's fondness for city life, a view that the poem projects in various ways, both overt and covert. John Wain perhaps expressed this view most strongly: "the poem welcomes London. In tone, in strategy, in the nature of its art, it is metropolitan. It signals an acceptance of the values of eighteenth-century civilization at their most urbane and sophisticated."[48] If observing this predilection serves only to further a political reading of the poem, the critic's incipient leaning toward Whiggism, it seems misapplied. If, instead, it accounts for the fact that neither Johnson nor Juvenal nor Eliot leaves the city they deplore, it reminds us that the city is now the poets' place, the "intellectual and artistic centre" where they now must live, caught between the fading promise of Heaven and the dubious dream of utopia that have become the defining boundaries of civilization.[49] Within those boundaries, moving from the city's streets to one's own home, the private "city" within the public space, one closes the door in the "*hope* . . . [of] the balmy Blessings of Repose," the "*sacred* Hour of silent Rest," that is, escape from despair into hopefulness, or at least unconsciousness. At this point, we are told that the "faithless Bar" is burst and a violent death ensues.[50] Johnson, always careful in his choice of words, makes the door complicit in the murder, a *faithless* abandonment of duty in a world emptied of hope, whether in the promise of Scripture or enlightened amelioration.

For comparison, we can turn to a scriptural verse that may well have been on Johnson's mind when he reconstructed the passage in Juvenal: "But the day of the Lord will come as a thief in the night; in the which the heavens shall pass away with a great noise, and the elements shall melt with fervent heat, the earth also and the works that are therein shall be burned up."[51] Here the ancient promise is fulfilled, the true end time which is not the building of a perfected city in the future but the final undoing of human self-assertiveness and self-aggrandizement. This particular chapter of Peter's second epistle was, we note, burned into the historical consciousness of every Londoner because the great London fire of 1666 was at first taken as the fulfillment of its prophecy, and afterward as one final warning to that fallen city: "For this they willingly are ignorant of, that by the word of God the heavens were of old, and the earth standing out of the water and in the water: Whereby the world that then was, being overflowed with water, perished: But the heavens and earth, which are now, by the same word are kept in store, reserved unto fire against the day of judgment and perdition of ungodly men."[52]

As Juvenal demonstrates, one does not need Christianity to condemn city life or the corruptions of human beings. My point here is that in eighteenth-century England it would have been impossible, especially given the recent historical past of both plague and fire, to think about London without scriptural reference—and most especially, perhaps, when identifying oneself with a political opposition ready to suggest, even if hyperbolically, that the corruptions and crimes of the Walpole administration were returning the country to all the vices that had justified disaster by plague and fire two generations earlier. Being steeped in Scripture is natural enough for eighteenth-century writers, and almost as natural is an appeal to the authority of the ancients that is always implied by the genre of imitation. Paradoxically, it is this looking back that links Johnson most tellingly to modernism, for, like the modernist, his life and thought clearly committed him to urbanism and its Enlightenment ideals, including scientific progress, better education, and social amelioration. However, this commitment was impregnated with a skepticism, inherent in Christian belief, concerning futuristic schemes. In our own day, modernists, whether in reaction to nineteenth-century naivete or twentieth-century reality, have exhibited a similarly directed skepticism in their writings. Many of these modern writers have also cast an equally skeptical backward look on Christianity,[53] but what binds Johnson and Eliot together is their effort, despite their skeptical empiricism, to retain the single most fundamental truth of their Christian heritage—namely, that we are fallen, mortal and immoral, and all our efforts to replace a virtuous and eternal life by means of the promise of God through Christ with the promise of self-made progress toward secular ideals are almost certainly futile—the city being built is only another Tower of Babel.[54]

The crux of the matter is in such qualifiers in my previous sentence as "efforts" and "almost certainly futile," because it indeed takes strenuous efforts within the cityscape to keep religious faith alive; and because the city dweller can never be certain that human reason will not ultimately reveal the sufficient knowledge and wisdom heretofore thought to be God's alone. We return thus to Varney's "mind in distress," the condition he finds in *London,* but which, I would suggest, is indicative of the more general aesthetic vision we know as modernism. Significantly enough, one sees this distress in a conflict that surrounded the rebuilding of London after the fire, well outlined by Nicholas Hudson. Caught between architects who saw the opportunity for a new rationalized cityscape and what today politicians would call "facts on the ground," "grand projects of urban redesign seemed out of step with the largely undirected and eclectic growth of England's booming metropolis" by the second half of the century.[55] Johnson's first encounter with London reveals, Hudson argues, "the distress and alienation of a small town teacher in the face of the bewildering modernism" of 1738; the fire of 1666 "seems still to be burning," a "particularly bleak and bewildered portrait of a city that other poets were celebrating for its commercial vigor and political liberty"—that is, its resistance to rational organization.[56] Hudson then traces a change in attitude, whereby the city's "twisting alleys and obscure neighborhoods" came to symbolize "the irregular and detailed shapes of human truth, the fabric of 'nature' that he [Johnson] constantly celebrates as the substance of both true art and virtue."[57]

While this argument is quite valid, it may not sufficiently account for Johnson's moral and religious separation from the "commercial ideals" that generated an unplanned city of cosmopolitan complexity and confusion (think of Smollett's portrayals of London), not to mention the problems of crime, poverty, and filth that did not disappear after 1738. For Johnson the city certainly meant intellectual fulfillment, but precisely for that reason, I would argue, it was a residence of livelong conflict and tension, the modernist dilemma of dwelling in despair because there is no other place to dwell.[58] Johnson could never fully become a man of the city, if by that we mean, as we probably must, those occupying their lives only with getting and spending. Thus, although, as Hudson argues, he "rejected schemes informed by neoclassicism, rationalism, and an autocratic vision of government," preferring instead to embrace a city "essentially realist in its artistic outlook, empiricist in its epistemology, and democratic in its political orientation," the fact remains, and Hudson acknowledges this, that he was far from "wholehearted" in embracing the "commercial ideals" that generated this vision of the ad hoc city, showing "little conscious sympathy with those who spent their lives making money."[59]

Putting *London* in proximity with *Prufrock* helps divert attention from the physical, political, and economic aspects of urban life and steers us back to Matthew's "poor in spirit," and the expositor's "*emptied of self.*" Certainly, one dominant theme that Johnson imitates from Juvenal is the triumph of guise and pretense within the city, whether practiced by native inhabitants or invaders from foreign parts. These are the people who empty themselves of self in order to become what others want them to be, all the while ignoring the other half of Matthew Henry's exposition, "in order to our being filled with *Jesus Christ.*" Rather, they are literally "poor in spirit," willing to vote "a Patriot black, a Courtier white," where words also are emptied of substance, and a lie is given "the confidence of Truth."[60] It is particularly telling in this regard that the French invaders are pictured by Johnson (as were the Greeks by Juvenal) as especially skilled in emptying themselves in order to play whatever part is necessary, an actor's talent no longer confined to the stage but now played out in the drawing rooms of the wealthy and powerful: these are the true villains of Johnson's Lon-

152 · Textual and Critical Intersections

don, those who "lye without a Blush, without a Smile; / Exalt each Trifle, ev'ry Vice adore, / Your Taste in Snuff, your Judgment in a Whore."[61] The last line is one of Johnson's more Juvenalian moments, although without actual precedent in his satire, and it leads to what I would suggest is the culmination of Johnson's underlying Christian structure: "For Arts like these preferr'd, admir'd, carest, / They first invade your Table, then your Breast; / Explore your Secrets with insidious Art, / Watch the weak Hour, and ransack all the Heart."[62] Venturo also centers attention on this passage, arguing the seriousness of the portrayal of the French: they are "more dangerous than contemptible. Their silly, protean exterior masks deadly and determined intent. . . . This passage turns on a conceit based on the etymology of the word *insidious,* which is derived from the Latin verb, *insidere,* 'to ambush.'" For Venturo this is primarily of political importance, the Frenchman's design to "invade," "explore," and "ransack" the "inner sancta of his patron's life and thought, but so subtly that the patron fails to notice"; it is, he concludes, "an 'insidious' invasion which results in tacit French rule."[63]

This very apt description of the import of the passage might also lead the reader to the Garden of Eden, indeed, to the already cited (for its pastoral description) book 9, where the temptation and fall of Adam and Eve take place. One might recall first the mask Satan assumes: "The Serpent, subtlest Beast of all the Field. . . . / Fit Vessel, fittest Imp of fraud, in whom / To enter, and his dark suggestions hide / From sharpest sight."[64] In this guise, Satan will approach the "much deceiv'd, much failing, hapless *Eve,*" who will "never from that hour in Paradise" find "either sweet repast, or sound repose," and with *insidious intent* bring sin and death into the world: "Such *ambush* hid among sweet Flow'rs and Shades / Waited with hellish rancor imminent / To intercept thy way, or send thee back / Despoil'd of Innocence, of Faith, of Bliss."[65] If one accepts that Johnson indeed has this passage in mind when he recounts the several "ambushes" awaiting the walker in the streets of London, then surely those subsequent lines, in which the murderer, "Cruel with Guilt, and daring with Despair," disturbs one's hope for the "balmy Blessings of Repose" and "Invades the sacred Hour of silent Rest" can also be seen as a replay of the first loss of innocence that underlies all Christian thought.[66] Without doubt, Johnson's *London* addresses the social, economic, and political corruptions of London in 1738, but the poem is framed, I would argue, by a vision of a world in which the emptying of self is filled not with Christ but with Satan.[67] That being so, the Enlightenment ideals that shape the city must be measured against Eliot's warning: "our duty to change our environment, the environment of our fellow human beings, for the better, must be balanced by our duty to change ourselves."[68]

Neither Milton nor Johnson used the phrase "insidious intent" as I did in the paragraph above, but it was easily recognized, I hope, as a borrowing from *Prufrock:* "Streets that follow like a tedious argument / Of insidious intent / To lead you to an overwhelming question." That question, I have suggested, may be Pascal's choice between denial or faith, but it is a question that Prufrock does not have the courage to ask, having become himself one of those who prepares every day "a face to meet the faces that you meet."[69] Ultimately, those who empty themselves of self but only to be filled with the dreams of infinite knowledge and boundless self-sufficiency (the "sins" of Enlightenment) are not strengthened but weakened. Satan himself is merely a ludicrous pawn in God's divine plan, his existence made possible only through "the will / And high permission of all-ruling Heaven," in order that he can "Heap on himself damnation."[70] Prufrock's enervated state is what has become the archetype of the urban dweller, caught by temptation and indecision, by depression and despair, all "Youth, and Health, and Fortune spent,"[71] but too exhausted to do more than listen to the mermaids of his imagination. Indeed, Prufrock becomes the archetype of modernism, living now in a world east of Eden because Adam and Eve partook of the fruit offered by an insidious flatterer, but himself now not daring to "eat a peach."[72]

It is widely acknowledged that neither Johnson nor Eliot was particularly fond of Milton, as either a "politician" or a "theologian," and only begrudgingly as a poet. It is therefore counterintuitive, perhaps, to suggest that their first poetic successes revolve in some way or another around *Paradise Lost.* In justification, I would argue that we need not posit a concrete influence of Milton on either poet, but rather embrace a more abstract notion: literary genius is always in dialogue with literary genius and no English-language poet whose world has been shaped by Christian thought can avoid entering into a conversation with that one English poet who retold so brilliantly the most essential story of Christianity, from the Fall in the Garden to the redemption through Christ. Johnson quarreled with Milton's politics and Eliot with his poetics, but when Johnson set himself

154 · Textual and Critical Intersections

the task of summarizing *Paradise Lost,* he did so in a manner that suggests a shared heritage of faith with Milton. Eliot, too, shared that faith, and, as well, shared with Johnson a modernism that looked backward in despair over an ever-receding sea of religious faith, and ahead in equal despair over the Enlightenment secular faith that was replacing it. Clinging to both faiths would not be an easy task:

> We all, indeed, feel the effects of Adam's disobedience; we all sin like Adam, and like him must all bewail our offences; we have restless and insidious enemies in the fallen angels, and in the blessed spirits we have guardians and friends; in the redemption of mankind we hope to be included; and in the description of heaven and hell we are surely interested, as we are all to reside hereafter either in the regions of horror or of bliss.[73]

Not coincidentally, I hope, that word *insidious* occurs again. Ironically enough, the shared modernism of Samuel Johnson and T. S. Eliot takes rise in the fact that, despite Enlightenment, they both persisted in having faith in the inherited story that *Paradise Lost* told so well; perhaps that was Milton's own *insidious intent.*

Originally published in *Samuel Johnson among the Modernists* (2019).

Notes

1 See my essays "Proust's Influence on Sterne: A Remembrance of Things to Come," *MLN* 103 (1988): 1031–55; *Tristram Shandy: A Book for Free Spirits* (New York: Twayne-Macmillan, 1994); "Three Sentimental Journeys: Sterne, Shklovsky, Svevo," *Shandean* 11 (1999): 126–34; "Reading Sterne through Proust and Levinas," reprinted as chapter 7 in this volume; "Sterne and the Modernist Moment," reprinted as chapter 8 in this volume.

2 Laurence Sterne, *A Sentimental Journey*, intro. Virginia Woolf (London: Oxford University Press, 1928).

3 In postmodernism's philosophical and aesthetic devaluation of the author as creator and its consequent embrace of pastiche, leveling, and discontinuity, one might find some scattered seeds of the academic postmodernist's present ideologies. Thoughtful postmodernism, however, remains in constant dialogue with the past, and especially with modernism, while its classroom "interpreters" have too often been in communication only with their own cultural moment and no other time. The most characteristic tell defining this crude

reading of postmodern theory is its instinctive flinching when the concept of literary genius or even "very best" authors is introduced into a discussion: "nonjudgmental evaluation" is the oxymoron with which these postmodernist academics wage their war with logic.

4 James Boswell, *Life of Johnson*, ed. R. W. Chapman and Pat Rogers (Oxford: Oxford University Press, 1998), 696 (entry for March 21, 1776). Johnson's belief that literary worth has to do with endurance over time is worth noting.

5 Melvyn New, "Ethics," in *A Cultural History of Comedy: In the Age of Enlightenment*, ed. Elizabeth Kraft (London: Bloomsbury, 2020), 197–219.

6 Melvyn New, "*Rasselas* in an Eighteenth-Century Novels Course," in *Approaches to Teaching the Works of Samuel Johnson*, ed. David R. Anderson and Gwin J. Kolb (New York: MLA, 1993), 122; both Gide and Conrad are cited from this text.

7 David Perkins, "Johnson and Modern Poetry," *Harvard Library Bulletin* 33 (Summer 1985): 307.

8 Perkins, 308, quoting from T. S. Eliot, introduction to *London: A Poem and The Vanity of Human Wishes*, by Samuel Johnson (London: Frederick Etchells and Hugh Macdonald, 1930), 16.

9 Eliot, introduction to Johnson, *London and Vanity*, 15.

10 Eliot, 15.

11 T. S. Eliot, *The Poems of T. S. Eliot*, vol. 1, ed. Christopher Ricks and Jim McCue (Baltimore, MD: Johns Hopkins University Press, 2015). If Ricks's exquisite ear failed to hear any verbal echoes, I doubt any will be found.

12 Johnson had moved to London the year before his poem was published in 1738, when he was twenty-eight years old. Eliot would not move to London until four years after he had in hand a fairly complete draft of the poem in 1911, but he had had some experience of city life in St. Louis, Boston, Paris, Oxford, and London; the poem, he said, was written primarily in Munich. *Prufrock* was first published in 1915, when Eliot was twenty-six. See Eliot, *Poems*, 363.

13 Boswell, *Life of Johnson*, 859. Boswell records many such expressions of Johnson's love of London life; under the main heading for "London: General Advantages," there are six separate passages indicated for "——loves it"; perhaps the entry for September 30, 1769, best summarizes his attitude: "The happiness of London is not to be conceived but by those who have been in it. I will venture to say, there is more learning and science within the circumference of ten miles from where we now sit, than in all the rest of the kingdom" (406).

14 Amy Levy, *The Complete Novels and Selected Writings of Amy Levy, 1861–1889*, ed. Melvyn New (Gainesville: University Press of Florida, 1993), 385. Levy's poem has been enshrined in the Queen's Walk, South Bank, London, along with the work of other "London" poets, including Johnson and Eliot.

156 · Textual and Critical Intersections

15 Eliot, *Poems*, 380, n. to line 15.

16 Eliot, 379, n. to line 10.

17 Eliot of course turned to Dante's *Divine Comedy* for his epigraph (*Inferno*, canto 27, lines 61–62), and elsewhere in the poem. One measure of the historical distance between Johnson and Eliot, but not, I think, the spiritual distance, is Johnson's single mention of Dante recorded in Boswell's *Life*, in a comparison praising *The Pilgrim's Progress*: "It is remarkable, that it begins very much like the poem of Dante; yet there was no translation of Dante when Bunyan wrote" (529).

18 T. S. Eliot, "The Christian in the Modern World," *Times Literary Supplement* (*TLS*), July 7, 2017, 16–18. I quote from *TLS*, but the essay has since been reprinted in *The Complete Prose of T. S. Eliot: The Critical Edition*, vol. 5, *Tradition and Orthodoxy, 1934–1939*, ed. Iman Javadi, Ronald Schuchard, and Jayme Stayer (Baltimore, MD: Johns Hopkins University Press, 2017), 185–95.

19 Eliot, "The Christian in the Modern World," 17.

20 Eliot, 17. Significantly, in view of Johnson's political orientation in *London*, Eliot's lecture moves on specifically to the politics accompanying the secular faith in future perfection that he has been condemning, summarizing a condemnation of realpolitik with "a sentence attributed to Disraeli": "in order to get power and keep it a man must be prepared to do things which neither a punctilious country gentleman nor an honest trader could do in his private capacity without losing his self-respect." Although these words are perhaps characteristic of Disraeli's thought, I have been unable to find evidence of his having spoken or written them. It is noteworthy that the few mentions of Jews in this lecture (that Marx was a Jew, that one of the "limitations of Judaism" was that it believed in a secular perfection) point in a direction particularly pertinent to the present discussion; like Juvenal's Greek invaders and Johnson's French ones, the Jew could be rendered in caricature as embodying urban existence—the ultimate *cosmopolitan*. Amy Levy's short life gives a lie to the stereotype.

21 Anthony W. Lee has provided me several of Johnson's most pertinent statements on the concept of perfectibility. E.g., "the word *perfection* . . . in its philosophical and exact sense . . . can be of little use among human beings," in *The Plan of a Dictionary of the English Language* (1747); or again, from *Adventurer* 85 (1753): "It is, however, reasonable to have perfection in our eye; that we may always advance towards it, though we know it never can be reached." See, respectively, Samuel Johnson, *Johnson on the English Language*, ed. Gwin J. Kolb and Robert DeMaria (New Haven, CT: Yale University Press, 2005), 49; Johnson, *"The Idler" and "The Adventurer,"* ed. John M. Bullitt, W. J. Bate, and L. F. Powell (New Haven, CT: Yale University Press, 1963), 416–17. For

Johnson's possible sympathy with the Arminian position on perfectibility, as preached by William Law and John Wesley, see Richard E. Brantley, "Johnson's Wesleyan Connection," *Eighteenth-Century Studies* 10, no. 2 (1976–77): 143–68.

22 David F. Venturo, *Johnson the Poet: The Poetic Career of Samuel Johnson* (Newark: University of Delaware Press, 1999), 75–76. Venturo is quoting Eliot's "Johnson as Critic and Poet," in *On Poetry and Poets* (New York: Farrar, Straus and Cudahy, 1957), 205.

23 Venturo, *Johnson the Poet*, 76.

24 Howard D. Weinbrot, "Johnson's *London* and Juvenal's Third Satire: The Country as 'Ironic' Norm," *Modern Philology* 73, no. 4, pt. 2 (1976): S56–S65. Weinbrot concludes that "we are to see Thales' departure as intelligent and thoughtful" (S64).

25 Eliot, *Prufrock*, lines 45–46 and 216–17.

26 Samuel Richardson, *Sir Charles Grandison* (1753–54), ed. E. Derek Taylor, Melvyn New, and Elizabeth Kraft (Cambridge: Cambridge University Press, 2022), 591; John Milton, *Paradise Lost*, in *Complete Poems and Major Prose*, ed. Merritt Y. Hughes (New York: Odyssey Press, 1957), book 9, 209–12. This passage begins the debate between Adam and Eve over whether they should separate and divide their labor, which is the immediate opportunity leading to their fall; separation and division of labor are, one might suggest, the essence of urban experience. Johnson, *Dictionary* (1755), cites the Miltonic passage to illustrate "prune." See Milton's extensive description of Eden in *Paradise Lost*, book 4, 205ff.

27 Johnson, *London*, lines 24 and 27.

28 Cf. Robert DeMaria's astute comments on the choice of "Thales" as Johnson's voice in the poem: "Thales is said to be the first philosopher to acknowledge the eternal God and his Providence in governing the world. As a character he is curiously like Demetrius in *Irene*, who goes off with Aspasia to instruct the West. . . . Pious philosophers, combining fundamental Christian beliefs with ancient wisdom and natural science, Thales and Demetrius are embodiments of the Johnsonian hero." DeMaria, *The Life of Samuel Johnson: A Critical Biography* (Oxford: Blackwell, 1993), 49–50. For another connection between *London* and *Irene*, see n. 54, below. DeMaria reinforces the insights of Edward and Lillian Bloom, "The Rhetoric of 'London,'" in *Eighteenth-Century Studies in Honor of Donald F. Hyde*, ed. W. H. Bond (New York: Grolier Club, 1970), 116–17, e.g.: "Thales, that is, acquires a religiosity lacking in Umbricius. . . . Thales is . . . fashioned after many early Christians; they, eager to flee the depravity of the large cities, set forth as lonely wanderers (eremites) through the countryside." I find this identification more convincing than Walter Jackson

158 · Textual and Critical Intersections

Bate's view that Thales is not the Greek philosopher, but the lyric poet mentioned by Plutarch. Bate, *Samuel Johnson* (New York: Harcourt Brace Jovanovich, 1979), 172.

29 Eliot, "The Christian in the Modern World," 17.

30 Venturo, *Johnson the Poet*, 74, argues persuasively that Walpole is figured as Orgilio, and notes that "any reference in 1738 to an arrogant builder of palaces who traded in parliamentary seats and bishoprics (line 204) had to be directed at the prime minister."

31 Venturo, 76.

32 Johnson, *London*, lines 256 and 259.

33 See Johnson, *Dictionary*, s.v. "pastoral": 1. Rural; rustic; 2. Relating to the care of souls.

34 Eliot, *Prufrock*, lines 94–95.

35 Eliot, lines 83 and 82; cf. Amos 7:14 and Matthew 14:6–11, respectively.

36 Eliot, *Prufrock*, line 70; for the biblical citations, see Eliot, *Poems*, 389, n. to line 70. All biblical quotations in the chapter are from the King James Version.

37 See Laurence Sterne's sermon "The case of Hezekiah and the messengers," preached at the resplendent new ambassador's chapel in 1764, a possible rebuke of the earl of Hertford's pride in his possessions (*Sermons* 157–66).

38 John 12:1.

39 Eliot, *Prufrock*, line 111; *Hamlet*, 3.1.78–79; we might recall Hamlet's remark that "Denmark is a prison," his own sense of urban imprisonment. Ricks and McCue find additional scriptural echoes in this section of the poem—most interesting, perhaps, 2 Samuel 12:22, where David recounts his prayer for the unborn child of his adulterous union with the wife of Uriah: "And he said, While the child was yet alive, I fasted and wept: for I said, Who can tell whether God will be gracious to me, that the child may live." It is a prayer that is not answered.

40 Andrew Varney, "Johnson's Juvenalian Satire on London: A Different Emphasis," *Review of English Studies* 40 (1989): 204.

41 Varney, 204, 212.

42 Varney, 213; he quotes a passage from Henry Sacheverell's "inflammatory sermon" "The Perils of False Brethren, Both in Church and State," delivered November 5, 1709, and thus for a service that produced exceptionally rabid sermons recalling the Gunpowder Plot from Anglican pulpits throughout the century; the date itself should thus have warned Varney that it was hardly a representative statement of quotidian eighteenth-century Anglican belief.

43 Johnson, *London*, lines 18, 66, 116, 194, and 209.

44 Johnson, lines 170–73 and 176–77.

45 Matthew 5:3; cf. Luke 6:20.

46 Matthew Henry, *An Exposition of All the Books of the Old and New Testament* [. . .], 3rd ed. (1721–25), vol. 5, 24.

47 Henry, vol. 5, 24. Luke 6:20 reads "blessed are the poor," without the addition of "in spirit," a curtailment that allows the passage to be read more simply in social or economic terms; Matthew's complication moves toward the reading I am suggesting, that Enlightenment faith in the capacity of human intellect and activity to envision and then bring into being a future perfection is in itself a heretical mindset: "'Tis to come off from all Confidence in our own Righteousness and Strength, that we may depend only upon the Merit of Christ for our Justification. . . . The Philosophers did not reckon Humility among their moral Virtues, but Christ puts it first" (Henry, vol. 5, 24). It is important to recognize the increasing significance in the century of Matthew 5:48 ("Be ye there perfect, even as your Father"), partly due to Methodism's influence, but primarily, it might be argued, because the verse embodies a theology seemingly in tune with undeniable economic and social progress. One might reconcile the several texts by placing individual perfection solely in the realm of the eternal, our existence in time rendering claims to perfection a false "Confidence" in one's own "Righteousness and Strength." This would not negate, then, the virtue of striving to perfect both oneself and one's society but would keep in mind that earthly economic and social perfection is not the ethical perfection Matthew 5:48 has in view.

48 John Wain, *Samuel Johnson* (New York: Viking Press, 1974), 86. That the issue of Johnson's attitude toward London remains indeterminate is indicated by Aaron Santesso: "Critics have tended to divide into those who see Johnson's attitude towards London as wholly admiring and those who perceive only stubborn disdain. Each position has its textual evidence." Santesso, "Johnson as Londoner," in *Comparative Excellence: New Essays on Shakespeare and Johnson*, ed. Eric Rasmussen and Aaron Santesso (New York: AMS Press, 2007), 161. Rather than resolving this debate, I hope putting Johnson into proximity with modernism helps explain why a "divided mind" is precisely what the urban Christian must live with. Augustine recognized the dichotomy in his own day, of course, famously positioning the City of God against the City of Man; not the concept, but its continuing relevance is what *London* and *Prufrock* struggle to represent.

49 Obviously, Juvenal worships different gods, but my point is that Johnson cannot help but read his portrait of Rome within his own ethical framework, wherein the conflict between city vice and country virtue becomes the religious/secular struggle I am suggesting. Interestingly, one of Dryden's added lines in his translation of Satire 3 reads "Nor place, nor persons now are sacred held"; and in describing the physical destruction caused by a falling building,

160 · Textual and Critical Intersections

he speaks of "One vast destruction: not the soul alone / But bodies, like the soul, invisible are flown." John Dryden, *The Poems*, ed. Paul Hammond and David Hopkins (London: Longman, 2000), vol. 4, 21, 38 (lines 27, 415–16); the latter translates "quis membra, quis ossa invenit? obtritum vulgi perit omne cadaver more animae" (Who can identify the limbs, who the bones? The poor man's crushed corpse wholly disappears, just like his soul); see *Juvenal and Persius*, trans. G. G. Ramsay (Cambridge, MA: Loeb Classical Library, 1979), 50–53.

50 Johnson, *London*, lines 236–41 (emphasis added).

51 See 2 Peter 3:10.

52 See 2 Peter 3:5–7. When in 1666 a special service was annexed to the *Book of Common Prayer* (*BCP*) in response to the London fire, 2 Peter 3 was included in the Order for Evening Prayer. Obviously, many passages in Scripture tell of divine wrath because of the corruption of the people; e.g., Isaiah 1:7: "Your country is desolate, your cites are burned with fire: your land, strangers devour it in your presence, and it is desolate, overthrown by strangers." This passage, along with passages from Lamentations and Psalms, was part of the special service for September 2, which continued to be observed at St. Paul's until 1859. Most interesting, perhaps, in relation to Matthew's "poverty of spirit," are these passages from the commination for the service: "abandon us not to our selves; but reduce us . . . by any the severest course [and] . . . subdue us unto thy self, and make us see the things belonging to our peace" (*BCP*, 1681). See Jack Gilpin, "God's Terrible Voice: Liturgical Response to the Great Fire of London," *Anglican and Episcopal History* 82 (2013): 318–34.

53 The most obvious example in modernism is *Ulysses*, one foot anchored in Homer, the other in a seeming rejection of Christianity. A question we have yet to resolve concerning modernism is whether any thoughtful and literate mind has yet freed itself from the Christian inheritance, whether even the harshest attacks on the religious heritage are indications of the difficulty of separating from it. Especially for artists, inheriting a tradition steeped in Christian thought, this difficulty seems apparent. Whether whatever postmodernism turns out to be will have success in finally rejecting this inheritance remains to be seen, but for now I suspect those women "talking of Michelangelo" (Eliot, *Prufrock*, line 36), who might provoke disgust in any educated reader because they reduce the portrayer of *The Creation of Adam* and the *Pietà* to cocktail-hour chitchat (not to mention Eliot's comical rhyme), are also possibly reflecting the poem's framework. In my deriving two of the artist's most famous works from Eliot's evocation, I anticipate what I hope to demonstrate in my conclusion: the centrality of Eden and crucifixion to the poem.

54 Johnson seems to have had Babel in mind when he wrote these lines in his play *Irene*, perhaps even as he was also writing *London*:

> How Heav'n in Scorn of human Arrogance,
> Commits to trivial Chance the Fate of Nations!
> While with incessant Thought laborious Man
> Extends his mighty Schemes of Wealth and Pow'r,
> And tow'rs amid triumphs in ideal Greatness;
> Some accidental Gust of Opposition
> Blasts all the Beauties of his new Creation.
> O'erturns the Fabrick of presumptuous Reason,
> And whelms the swelling Architect beneath it. (2.3.1–9)

I quote from the 1749 edition; Johnson is thought to have finished most of the play before he arrived in London in 1737.

55 Nicholas Hudson, "Samuel Johnson, Urban Culture, and the Geography of Postfire London," *Studies in English Literature* 42 (2002): 582.

56 Hudson, 584–85.

57 Hudson, 589.

58 Hudson sees the situation differently: "Here is where Johnson's urban reflections belong to a distinctly bygone era. . . . Since the Romantics, there has been a strong tendency in Western culture to view . . . 'urban man' [as] an alienated and troubled individual, shaped by an environment that overwhelms the senses, confuses traditional beliefs, and destroys communities. . . . But the older Johnson . . . clearly surmounted this alienation" (596). I would suggest, to the contrary, that this alienation was, in Johnson's happier moments, suppressed, but in a lifetime when "much is to be endured and little to be enjoyed" I think his response to the city quite precisely foreshadowed that of the post-Romantic "urban man"; we might claim for him, then, the title of first urban modernist, except that it might better be awarded to Juvenal in Rome.

59 Hudson, 590, 592.

60 Johnson, *London*, lines 152 and 156.

61 Johnson, lines 147–49.

62 Johnson, lines 152–55.

63 Venturo, *Johnson the Poet*, 72.

64 Milton, *Paradise Lost*, book 9, lines 86 and 89–91.

65 Milton, book 9, lines 404 and 406–11 (emphasis added).

66 Johnson, *London*, lines 237 and 240.

67 David Venturo has reminded me, most aptly, that Milton compares the serpent's first sighting of Eve with a simile indicating that Satan is now a city dweller: "As one who long in populous City pent, / Where Houses thick

and Sewers annoy the Air, / Forth issuing on a Summer's Morn to breathe / Among the pleasant Villages and Farms." Milton, *Paradise Lost*, book 9, lines 445–48.

68 Eliot, "The Christian in the Modern World," 17.

69 Eliot, *Prufrock*, lines 8–10 and 27.

70 Milton, *Paradise Lost*, book 1, lines 211–15.

71 Johnson, *London*, line 256.

72 Cf. Eliot, *The Poems*, 398, where Ricks and McCue write, "Like Eve's apple, the peach (*pêche*) tempts to sin (*péché*)."

73 Samuel Johnson, "Life of Milton," *The Lives of the Poets*, ed. John H. Middendorf (New Haven, CT: Yale University Press, 2010), 194.

Sterne

Critical Conversations

7

Reading Sterne through Proust and Levinas

In the whole moral and sensual world the thing whereon my whole life long
I have most dwelt with horror and desire is seduction—inflicted or borne,
active or passive, sweet and terrible, like a command laid on us by a god. . . .
Hence the creative awe as I think of the poem dreamed and planned since
early days . . . put off, the poem of the Brahman's wife, the Pariah-goddess.
There in all the accents of horror I mean to proclaim and celebrate seduction.

Thomas Mann, *Lotte in Weimar,* translated by H. T. Lowe-Porter

A decade ago, in an effort to understand *A Sentimental Journey,* I took a
detour through Marcel Proust and wrote an essay I titled "Proust's Influence on Sterne: Remembrance of Things to Come."[1] As I explained in a
postscript, because we come to Sterne having read—or being in the process
of reading—the best writings of our own era, a writer like Proust unavoid-
ably influences our reading of Sterne. To be sure, one of the referees for the
journal voiced a concern: I had not made enough of the modernist tendencies my reading had made apparent, indeed, had *retreated* from conclusions
necessitated by my own argument. Without altering my text, I responded
in a "Post Postscript" that one aim of the essay all along had been "to disap-
point the desire for a contemporary ideological closure" of Sterne, despite
putting him in proximity with modernism. "What other path is possible,"
I asked, "when we start with Proust, as we all must do in the twentieth century? The text lies passive, almost asleep before our indomitable, aggres-
sive drive to penetrate it, to possess it. It ends, like Albertine, imprisoned
within the cave of our own creating fiction—and also like her, free to deceive us at every turn, while we stand, the Procrustean Guard, at the doors
and windows protecting our possession of a necessary conclusion."[2] I recall
that I was tempted to offer my "Post Postscript" in French.

166 · Textual and Critical Intersections

What strikes me ten years later is how heavily my reading of both *The Captive* (from which I drew my comparisons to Sterne) and *A Sentimental Journey*—and the concluding comments just quoted—was influenced by my reading of Levinas's *Totality and Infinity* (and Derrida's 1964 essay "Violence and Metaphysics"),[3] my only familiarity with Emmanuel Levinas in the mid-1980s. Since then, I have read a good deal more, including Levinas's own encounter with Proust (and, specifically, with *The Captive*), "The Other in Proust," and it is with this particular essay in mind that I would like to revisit the subject. Previously, I had been drawn to what I perceived to be uncanny parallel presentations, through Marcel and Yorick, of sexual desire, seduction, and language; here, by means of a text Sterne was writing simultaneously with *A Sentimental Journey,* his *Continuation of the Bramine's Journal,* unpublished until the late nineteenth century, I would like to suggest a reading of both as Sterne's exploration, in the last year of his life, of an ethical dilemma well exemplified by the last bawdy joke Sterne ever told: the final chapter of *A Sentimental Journey* ends with perhaps the most famous aposiopesis in English literature (*SJ* 165), wherein Yorick stretches his hand across the space separating him from the Piedmontese woman and catches

> hold of the Fille de Chambre's
> END OF VOL. II.[4]

We are nowadays wearisomely familiar with the notion of Sterne's incompleteness, fragmentariness, his celebration of the interruption or aposiopesis, as in the suspended conclusion just quoted. From the perspective of 1768, however, 1767 was Sterne's *final* year, and one must wonder whether he could feel in his terribly worn body, if not in his mind, the impending *closure*—incompleteness may reflect nothing more, nothing less, than our own completion of the life cycle, never experienced but always to be anticipated, especially in a faith as teleologically driven as was Sterne's. With all his dalliance with unendingness, his own end, he knew, was assured—and conveniently summarized by the creed he preached for twenty-five years as the four last things: Death, Judgment, Heaven, Hell. For the martyr or saint, Death and Judgment were most welcome; for the rest of the human race, they were dreaded. Without doubt, one was instructed to have a "sure and certain hope of the Resurrection to eternal life,"[5] if—and it was a momentous *if* for fallen humankind—one were to be "found acceptable" in the sight of God—that is, in Judgment. We need to keep in mind that when, late in *A Sentimental Journey,* Sterne asserts, despite "all the books with which materialists have pester'd the world," that he is positive he has a soul (*SJ* 151), he is asserting not merely a feeling heart, but the belief that he is constituted of substance immaterial as well as material. The importance of the distinction in eighteenth-century thought—and I simplify its many complex discussions of the subject—is that what is immaterial is not subject to death, is eternal, and hence must spend eternity somewhere.[6]

Sterne is said to have called *A Sentimental Journey* his "work of redemption,"[7] and we have taken that to mean, most often, that he heeded the call of his critics to mine his sentimental vein, and thus atone for the bawdiness of *Tristram Shandy.* He was, that is, redeeming his literary reputation; if, as an offshoot of doing so, he also satisfied the Final Judgment, that would be a bonus. But if Sterne thought of *A Sentimental Journey* in that way, he must have assumed a God whose love of the sentimental included depositing crowns into green purses recumbent on the laps of pretty young women. More broadly, he must have thought of a God who would redeem as well the ramblings of *Bramine's Journal,* in which Sterne stretches across an ocean, not merely his hand, but his mind and his morals as well, in order to grasp, in the name of love, an ultimately imaginary woman for whom he felt an absolutely desperate desire.

The few critics who have written about *Bramine's Journal* have spent considerable energy on the question of whether the relationship between Sterne and Mrs. Draper was sexual.[8] One is tempted to quote a Sternean reincarnation in our own age, "It depends on your definition of sex," but in truth the question seems irrelevant. If Mrs. Draper allowed sexual activity of any kind, Sterne would not have been loath; if she did not, he would have remained seductive and ever hopeful. That is to say, I find it quite probable that Sterne's own declining physical condition in 1767, joined to his long practice of seeking (and finding) comfort in sexual activity, would have exacerbated his desires rather than cooled them. The desperate tone of *Bramine's Journal* reflects these desires, but also his awareness that he has, by and large, created Eliza out of them. To the commonplace tale of disappointed love that Sterne might have thus composed from these two elements, he added a third—namely, that our hope for love outlasts all disappointment, all rejection, all shame, all judgment. In *A Sentimental Journey,* if not already in *Bramine's Journal,* this hope turns, I would suggest, into Levinas's ethical question: what is the foundation of our inescapable relationship with the Other?

Sterne's Christian God was infinitely merciful and hence able to redeem whatever lapses he discovered in his balance sheet, but surely Sterne knew better than to abuse that mercy. Why, in the last year of his life, did he not truly mend his ways? The facile answer is, of course, that Sterne did not believe he would die—like all sinners, he had a full intention to reform: tomorrow. Equally facile, I believe, is the suggestion that he could not stop—that the habits of a lifetime were so predominant that despite his best intentions Sterne could not abandon his appetites, whether for bawdiness, for women, or for both together.

I label these facile rather than false solutions because they are both certainly true to some extent. Despite his severe illness, despite his preaching for twenty-five years on the need to prepare for death, Sterne was not exempt from the very human hope of postponement; and perhaps precisely because of his illness, along with his separation from his wife, he could not muster the moral will to turn in another direction. What suggests to me that neither solution plumbs the depths of Sterne at this moment in his life, however, is that so much of both *Bramine's Journal* and *A Sentimental Journey* confront the issue of Judgment and of Heaven.[9] Sterne's mind, in other words, was on redemption during the last year of his life, and his writings suggest not so much a self-justification (though some of that is present) as a desire to find the proper equation between human and divine love. One might thus suggest that *A Sentimental Journey* continues the pilgrimage taken by Chaucer, and that Sterne's Eliza belongs to a tradition that includes Dante's Beatrice, Petrarch's Laura, perhaps, as well, Swift's Stella.[10] It is obvious, of course, that Swann and Odette, Marcel and Albertine, partake of the tradition as well.

Levinas published "The Other in Proust" in 1947.[11] It begins, as Seán Hand points out in the headnote to his translation, with Levinas's most central aesthetic theory, one that links him to Plato in their shared suspiciousness toward art—despite their love *and* practice of it.[12] The theory of the philosopher, both would maintain, deals unequivocally with the object; the theory of the poet, on the other hand, "harbours an ambiguity, for it is concerned not to express but to create the object. Like images or symbols, reasoning is called on to produce a certain rhythm in which the reality that is sought will appear by magic."[13] On the one hand, Levinas would seem to be privileging philosophy in this description, especially when we are told in the next sentence that the "truths" thus produced by art have no value in themselves but are merely "spells and incantations." Yet the word *ambiguity* alerts us to a different valuation, and we are hardly surprised when, in the next paragraph, ambiguity becomes—in a description that surely is applicable to whatever we mean by the work of art—that which renders "absolutely indeterminate" the "contours of events, persons and things," despite "the precision of line and the depth of character type."[14] One might well think of the magnificently *ambiguous* chapter in *A Sentimental Journey*, "The Conquest," when Levinas continues: "We never know right until the end what exactly has happened in this world which is none the less the same as our own and historically and geographically precise. It is a world that is never definitive and where one course of action does not preclude other possibilities."[15]

There is, as I suggested, a strong likelihood that Levinas is not describing the specialness of Proust in these remarks, nor am I claiming Sterne's own specialness in applying them to his writing; rather, the notion of "indeterminateness" may simply serve as another term for the "infinite interest" that masterworks generate, their capacity to respond to—be responsive to—endless commentary. Levinas signals perhaps a major shift in our thinking about aesthetic orderings but chronicles no shift in the production of art itself, in either a modernist or postmodernist phase. The geography of Dante, the theocracy of Milton, the couplets of Pope are no more determinate than *Crime and Punishment*, I would argue, despite Bakhtin's celebration of the polyvalence of the novel form.

We have, however, grown increasingly aware, in some measure because of Levinas and his influence on Derrida, of the value we might place on the indeterminate, although significantly we seem unable to embody that new value in our own critical writings. Postmodern readings continue to provide determinate readings of indeterminate texts, and the boundary between text and commentary continues to assert itself in the very process of examining parameters. In Sterne's case, these parameters take on particular significance not simply in the many ambiguities, primarily sexual innuendos, that we associate with *A Sentimental Journey*, but because he was writing his work of "fiction" alongside a work of "fact," a daily journal kept between April 13 and August 4, 1767, to Eliza Draper, the young married woman from India with whom he had a relationship in London in the spring of 1767, before she departed England to return to her husband.[16] Which objects are, to use Levinas's term, more *magically* produced: Yorick and the women of *A Sentimental Journey* or the Yorick and Eliza of *Bramine's Journal?* Objects of "fiction" or objects of "fact"?

Because for Levinas the ethical is always the starting point, one senses in his comments some disapproval of Proust's infinite play between the indeterminate and (amoral) freedom: "It is curious to note the extent to which Proust's amorality fills his world with the wildest freedom, and confers on definite objects and beings a scintillating sense of possibility undulled by definition. One would have thought that moral laws rid the world of such glittering extravaganzas more rigorously than natural laws and that magic begins . . . where ethics leave off."[17] Sterne's own "wild freedom" is perhaps nowhere more evident than in *Bramine's Journal,* in which a dying fifty-four-year-old married cleric encourages a twenty-three-year-old married woman to think about, among other things, the deaths of their spouses and the union between them that will thus be made possible.[18] If in Proust, homosexuality produces "relations . . . between terms that seemed not to produce them" and thus invokes, for Levinas, Sodom and Gomorrah, Sterne's heterosexuality produces a very similar exceeding of reality itself; everything, as Levinas notes, "is giddily possible."[19]

Let us set aside the question of whether Sterne was born "giddy" or, after an adulthood as a country clergyman, he emerged in his forty-sixth year (1760) as the giddy literary lion whose *Tristram Shandy* had taken London by storm. Rather, I want to concentrate on what is his final giddiness, Sterne's affair with Eliza, an affair that begins with a magical amulet, Eliza in miniature, that he hangs around his neck in order to image himself as riven, bifurcated; he looks at himself looking at the portrait, which, in reality, he has already absorbed into an ego other than the observing self.[20]

"True emotion in Proust is always the emotion of emotions," Levinas suggests,[21] and how easily we might substitute that insight for the many, many books written on the "Age of Sensibility," an era that Sterne is often said to have initiated (and certainly did promote) as a European phenomenon at the end of the eighteenth century. Proustian sensibility,[22] as Levinas defines it, seems a most appropriate parallel phenomenon:

> Proustian reflection, which is governed by a sort of refraction, a gap existing between the ego and its state, puts its own stress on the inner

life. Everything takes place as if the self were constantly doubled by another self, with a friendship that cannot be matched, but equally with a cold strangeness that life struggles to overcome. The mystery in Proust is the mystery of the Other.[23]

Sterne's own sense of a doubling of the self—in the search for sincerity—is apparent throughout his fictions, beginning with the split into Tristram and Yorick in *Tristram Shandy* and the wonderful moment in volume 7 when he responds to the question of his identity:

> ——My good friend, quoth I——as sure as I am I—and you are you——
> ——And who are you? said he.——Don't puzzle me; said I. (*TS* 7.33.633)

But it is in *A Sentimental Journey* that the question is most clearly established, where Yorick divides himself between his ancestor and his present self:

> There is not a more perplexing affair in life to me, than to set about telling any one who I am—for there is scarce any body I cannot give a better account of than of myself; and I have often wish'd I could do it in a single word—and have an end of it. It was the only time and occasion in my life, I could accomplish this to any purpose—for Shakespear lying upon the table. . . . I took up Hamlet, and turning immediately to the grave-diggers scene in the fifth act, I lay'd my finger upon YORICK, and advancing the book to the Count, with my finger all the way over the name—*Me, Voici!* said I. (*SJ* 112)

The uncanny evocation of one of Levinas's favorite scriptural phrases, *me voici* (here I am),[24] perhaps may be taken to suggest that for Sterne, as for Levinas, the readiness of the self to present itself (to make a *present* of oneself) is deeply connected to the self's justification, which is, in turn, connected to the sincerity of the heart that one is prepared to offer versus the temptations to disguise, the first occasion of which was, of course, Adam's *failure* to respond *me voici* in the Garden: "And the Lord God called unto Adam, and said unto him, Where art thou? And he said, I heard thy voice in the garden and I was afraid, because I was naked; and I hid myself."[25] Hence, when Yorick responds to the Count's bawdy insinuation that he

172 · Textual and Critical Intersections

is in France to "spy the nakedness of the land," or of the women, with the assertion that he has come only to "spy the *nakedness* of their hearts, and through the different disguises of customs, climates, and religion, find out what is good in them, to fashion my own [heart] by—and therefore am I come" (*SJ* 111), one may well hear echoes of a Levinasian ethic of unending responsiveness without the categories by which we define (in order to protect) a less sincere self.

This division of the self informs the structure of *Bramine's Journal* as well, except that the estrangement of the self from the self, which Levinas sees as a "spur to the soul" and to which we will shortly return, becomes a collapse of the self into another, who is a double, the same as the self observed. Every aspect of *Bramine's Journal* speaks to this sameness, beginning with the fact that its ground rules indicate Sterne's expectation of and reliance on Eliza's writing a reciprocal journal: "wrote the last farewel to Eliza by Mr Watts *(he saild 23)* who sails this day for Bombay——inclosed her likewise the Journal kept from the day we parted, to this——so from hence continue it till the time we meet again—Eliza does the same, so we shall have mutual testimonies to deliver hereafter to each other" (*BJ* 171).

The motif of mutuality is depressingly obsessional as the journal continues; for example:

April 16: I shall read the same affecting Acc^t of many a sad Dinner wch Eliza has had no power to taste of, from the same feelings & recollections. (*BJ* 172–73)

May 13: Surely 'tis not impossible, but I may be made as happy as my Eliza, by some transcript from her. . . . If not I shall hope—& hope, every week, and every hour of it, for Tidings of Comfort. (*BJ* 189)

June 2: By this time, I trust You have doubled the Cape of good hope—sat down to y^r writing Drawer, & look'd in Yoricks face, as you took out y^r Journal; to tell him so. (*BJ* 194)

June 15: Mark!—you will dream of me this night—& if it is not recorded in your Journal—Ill say, you could not recollect it the day following. (*BJ* 202)

June 21: I long to see [your journal]—I shall read it a thousand times over If I get it before y^r Arrival—What w^d I now give for it—tho' I know there are *circumstances* in it, That will make my heart bleed. (*BJ* 205)

And finally,

July 7: I can see & hear nothing but my Eliza. remember this, when You think my Journal too short, & compare it not with thine, wch tho' it will exceed it in length, can do no more than equal it in Love. (*BJ* 216)

We have here a monologue with an imaginary correspondent, wished into being by the author's own desire. A far more accurate perception of the actual relationship is perhaps supplied by Sterne's depressing assessment of June 30:

I have wrote [a mutual friend] a whole Sheet of paper ab^t us—it ought to have been copied into this Journal—but the uncertainty of y^r ever reading it, makes me omit that . . . which when we meet, shall beguile us of many a long winters night.—*those precious Nights!*—my Eliza!—You rate them as high as I do. . . . They are all that remains to us—except the *Expectation* of their return—the Space between is a dismal Void—full of doubts, & suspence. (*BJ* 210)[26]

The desire for *correspondence* is double edged in *Bramine's Journal.* On the one hand, Sterne wants to bridge the empty space between himself and Eliza, between male and female, with a language that nourishes and heals. Sterne's entries are replete with inquiries into the health of Eliza, echoed by accounts of his own decrepitude at this time—he is inexorably dying, as he himself must surely have realized.[27] On the other hand, the *correspondence* he seeks has at least as much to do with reflecting himself as with reaching another—or, indeed, being reached by another. As he writes his journal, he must *see* Eliza at her desk writing hers.

Indeed, the many references to sensibility and sentiment, sympathy and pathos in *Bramine's Journal* all appear to come from this single urge to find in another human being one's own self, for only then would it be indubitably trustworthy or sincere:

I want You to be on the other side of my little table, to hear how sweetly y^r Voice will be in Unison to all this—I want to hear what You have to say to Y^r Yorick upon this Text.—what heavenly Consolation w^d drop from y^r Lips & how pathetically you w^d enforce y^r Truth & Love upon my heart to free it from every Aching doubt— Doubt! did I say—but I have none—and as soon w^d I doubt the Scripture I have preach'd on. (*BJ* 212, July 3)

The burden of *correspondence,* then, is enormous: "for if thou art false, my Bramine—the whole world—and Nature itself are lyars" (*BJ* 212). Driven by sickness, by a painful estrangement from his wife and daughter, by what he almost certainly feared, his impending death and Judgment, Sterne created in his *Bramine's Journal* a fabric of fictions designed to keep reality at a bearable distance. And the cornerstone of the edifice is the lie of possession, of knowing—the core of Sterne's sad failure, in which he considers his expressions of "doubt" to be "part of the picture of a heart that *again* Languishes for Possession—and is disturbed at every Idea of its Uncertainty" (*BJ* 213). Behind the sentimentalism of *Bramine's Journal,* behind its language of feeling and sympathy and suffering, behind even its empowering of Eliza as both his God ("all powerful Eliza" [*BJ* 216]) and his alter ego ("I resemble no Being in the world so nearly as I do You" [*BJ* 198]), is a desperate push for power, the need to triumph over, to gain control of, his own death and Judgment.

This desperation to find doubleness, sameness, certainty draws a distinct boundary between *Bramine's Journal* and *A Sentimental Journey,* perhaps between fact as fiction and fiction as fact. For in *Sentimental Journey,* as if to comment on the increasingly evident failure of *Bramine's Journal* to create the world as Sterne wanted it to be (a failure, indeed, to create— godlike—the object of his desire as an entity standing before him), he rethinks the male-female relationship as a recomposition of the self in which the woman, in infinite desirability, is imagined as neither mirrored nor doubled,[28] but as other, always happily either just out of reach, unpossessed, or attainable only through a surrender of the self to uncertainty and the transient caress (few writers have had a richer sense of the "magic" of touch—proximity—than Sterne), rather than the assertion of self as knowledge and the permanent grasp.[29]

One familiar with Levinas as a theorist of the Other will have heard the many purposeful echoes of his thought in the account I have just given of the failure of *Bramine's Journal,* and of *A Sentimental Journey* as a corrective; for our present purposes, however, what I most want to emphasize is the appearance of these themes in his "aesthetic" commentary on Proust. Marcel's relationship with Albertine serves Levinas as a paradigm for what does and does not matter if correspondence, proximity, love, are to rise to ethical validation. In the place of *Bramine's Journal's* insistence on reciprocity, for example, we have Levinas's familiar—and profound—insistence on strangeness: "To know what Albertine does, what Albertine sees, who sees Albertine, is of no interest in itself as a form of knowledge but is infinitely exciting because of its fundamental strangeness in Albertine, this strangeness which mocks knowledge."[30] Similarly, Albertine's is the story of a "captive" who disappears, much as Eliza "disappears" over the horizon, returning to India even as Sterne struggles to keep her "presence" before his eyes, captured in a mirror image. It is a gesture commonplace enough in Western romantic literature, marked as it has been by the celebration of unity (a voice in "Unison to all this") or oneness, but it becomes that which one must overcome or escape in Levinas's thought: "The reality of Albertine is her evanescence within her very captivity, a reality made of nothingness. She is a prisoner although she has already vanished despite being a prisoner, since despite the strictest surveillance she possesses the ability to withdraw into herself."[31]

Sterne abruptly ended *Bramine's Journal* within days of receiving a packet of letters from Eliza. One suspects from the parallel composition of *A Sentimental Journey* that he was already disillusioned by his efforts to keep her alive as an entity occupying his divided self, but clearly her response, lacking, one may assume, any hint of the reciprocity he ached to receive, was the direct cause of cessation; she had, in withdrawing from England, withdrawn "into herself." As Levinas astutely perceives, Albertine's death "is the death of the Other, contrary to the view of contemporary philosophy which remains attached to the self's solitary death. Only the death of the Other lies at the crossroads of the journey to rediscover the past."[32] I would suggest, similarly, that Eliza's "death," the death of the Same, the end of the affair, so to speak, opens to Sterne a discovery of the future, of how finally to confront the "self's solitary death," after which Judgment was to follow.

His efforts to defend himself from death through the Eros of possession had led to a death as definitive as a corpse. I find few documents in the

176 · Textual and Critical Intersections

eighteenth century more painful than Sterne's *Bramine's Journal* precisely because few are able to image forth the presence of death so vividly, not Eliza's "death," but the death of the author, the journal keeper whose days close with frightening abruptness, without sufficient warning and without the usual reparative consolation of Heaven; this is aposiopesis as a trope of irretrievable interruption and loss, a trope of death itself. On July 31, having received her letters the day before, which was then spent reading and weeping over them "till I was blind," he returns to the amulet: "I sit contemplating over thy passive picture; sweet Shadow! of what is to come! for tis all I can now grasp . . . remember me, as I remember thee" (*BJ* 222–23). Four days later he stopped the journal completely.

"They order, said I, this matter better in France" (*SJ* 3). Thus Sterne had begun his *Sentimental Journey* soon after starting *Bramine's Journal,* already possessed, I would suggest, of an artist's (or philosopher's?) intuition that the journal would not suffice; perhaps, as well, he had a dying sinner's awareness that Eliza would not be able to justify him in the tribunal before which Toby's oath was famously justified with a tear (*TS* 6.10.511). Yorick continues to wear Eliza's picture around his neck, but only as the "sweet Shadow" of what is *past;* his quest begins anew, and, as Levinas observes of a similar turning in Proust, it seems now to center on two fundamental observations: first, that love justifies itself only by refusing the comfortableness of possession and certainty; and, second, that this love seeks a language different from the language of knowledge, oneness and wholeness, loyalty and faithfulness, with which Sterne had, following a long tradition, tried to create Eliza. Sterne now offers, by way of his own spiritual redemption, an erotic love purged of concupiscence, wherein the word's root in *cupidity,* an urgent desire to possess, is essential to the meaning of what is rejected.

For Sterne, as for a long line of Christian (and non-Christian) male thinkers and writers for whom the celibate Pauline pathway seemed too sterile, too lonely, too difficult, the path to purification, to paradise, began and ended with human love. Put in specifically gendered and sectarian terms, Christian men have for a very long time indulged the Dantesque notion that "Das Ewig-Weibliche / Zieht uns hinan" (The Eternal Feminine / Lures to Perfection)—to deliberately mix my centuries and cultures.[33] Sterne seems to me to be a part of this tradition, significantly caught between Dante and Goethe, whose own sentimental traveler, Werther, comes to grief precisely because he cannot love without seeking a mirror in Lotte, without possession and self-interest; he dies as the Sterne of *Bramine's Journal* dies, contemplating a shadow.

In *A Sentimental Journey,* however, Sterne tries to define a different human connection, as I suspect Goethe understood when he labeled him the most "beautiful spirit that ever lived; who reads him feels free and beautiful; his humor is inimitable."[34] Even more to the point is Goethe's suggestion that Sterne had initiated something he calls "gentle love"[35]—the model, perhaps, of what Goethe would later develop as "elective affinity."

However, Sterne and Goethe would seem to separate themselves from Levinas to the extent that Levinas's version of erotic love, which he reads into Proust, is a love that is free from sexual appetite. Thus, in the death of Albertine as the death of the Other, he finds a death that "nurtures" a love he defines as "ontologically pure": "this Eros is not a relation built on a third term, such as tastes, common interests, or the conaturality of souls, but has a direct relation to something that both gives and refuses to give itself, namely to the Other as Other, the mystery."[36] Insofar as this is a disavowal of possession, one can agree that Proust (and Sterne) had learned much concerning the eroticism of the unpossessed, and, more importantly, the ennui that accompanies possession. But Levinas's impeccable phenomenological credentials have always clashed, it has seemed to me—and to others[37]—with the voice of sexual prohibition he seems to hear from Sinai—the eschewal of "fusion," as a psychological or ethical value, does not seem to me to warrant the evocation of the voluptuous as always a *not yet.*[38] Against that word *pure,* which seems to me quite foreign to Levinas's thought, one might posit Yorick's observation—borrowed, significantly enough, from Montaigne by way of Pierre Charron—after observing a pair of sparrows copulating with great abandon on his window ledge: "But there is nothing unmixt in this world; and some of the gravest of our divines have carried it so far as to affirm, that enjoyment itself was attended even with a sigh—and that the greatest *they knew of,* terminated *in a general way,* in little better than a convulsion" (*SJ* 116).[39]

Still, Levinas and Sterne would seem to begin this journey together; hence Levinas draws away from Proust to generalize on the twentieth century:

178 · Textual and Critical Intersections

The theme of solitude and the breakdown in human communication are viewed by modern literature and thought as the fundamental obstacle to universal brotherhood. The pathos of socialism breaks against the eternal Bastille in which each person remains his own prisoner, locked up within himself. . . . The despair felt at the impossibility of communication . . . marks the limits of all pity, generosity and love.[40]

Yorick, who will shortly have his own encounter with the Bastille, begins his "Preface"—written inside the most unsocial of all vehicles, the *desobligéante*[41] (it would have been better written, he admits at the end of the chapter, "in a *Vis a Vis*" [*SJ* 17])—with a very similar sense of communicative failure:

'Tis so ordered, that from the want of languages, connections, and dependencies, and from the difference in education, customs and habits, we lie under so many impediments in communicating our sensations out of our own sphere, as often amount to a total impossibility. (*SJ* 13)

If in the twentieth century the path most often taken to escape the Bastille of self-enclosure has been that of political liberation movements ("an ideal, a collective representation, a common enemy will reunite individuals who cannot touch or endure one another"), a concomitant path for Yorick is the sentimental journey itself,[42] in which he hopes to "connect" with others—the French, the Italians, women, monks, old soldiers, dwarfs, peasants, philosophes, esprits. But from the very beginning, Yorick shares with Levinas (and Proust) a dubiousness about foreign travel (Italy, in *The Captive*), particularly about the modes of knowledge into which travel had been re-turned by previous travelers and travel writers; all Western travel writing, Levinas might suggest, is nothing more than a footnote to the *Odyssey*, a saga of return. Hence, he continues his analysis of "communication" with the assertion that it has failed precisely "because it is sought as a fusion. One begins with the idea that duality must be transformed into unity, and that social relations must culminate in communion. This is the last vestige of a conception that identifies being with knowledge."[43] And Yorick—whose skepticism in many ways derives from some of Levinas's own sources, particularly Montaigne, Descartes, and Malebranche—echoes the notion:

> Even so it fares with the poor Traveller, sailing and posting through the politer kingdoms of the globe in pursuit of knowledge and improvements.
>
> Knowledge and improvements are to be got by sailing and posting for that purpose; but whether useful knowledge and real improvements, is all a lottery—and even where the adventurer is successful, the acquired stock must be used with caution and sobriety to turn to any profit. (*SJ* 16)[44]

It is a wonderfully Levinasian moment when Yorick exits the *desobligéante* only to be greeted by English travelers ready to engage him in conversation; but "As an English man does not travel to see English men" (*SJ* 17), he retreats to his room; one does not travel to return to one's own mirrored image. On the other hand, one's own room, defined by doors and windows to be opened or closed, is for Sterne—as for Proust—a pervasive image throughout *A Sentimental Journey* of isolation and self-absorption; all of life is in the street below.

Yorick's isolation is broken by contact with a woman, a delicate sexual conversation that takes place while they hold hands in front of the locked door of the inn's coach house. His need to define the situation, to reduce it to knowledge, seems to him a necessity—"a silence of a single moment . . . had been fatal to the situation . . . so I begun the conversation immediately":

> This certainly . . . must be one of Fortune's whimsical doings: to take two utter strangers by their hands—of different sexes, and perhaps from different corners of the globe, and in one moment place them together in such a cordial situation. . . .
>
> —And your reflection upon it, shews how much, Monsieur, she has embarrassed you by the adventure.—
>
> When the situation is, what we would wish, nothing is so ill-timed as to hint at the circumstances which make it so: you thank Fortune, continued she—you had reason—the heart knew it, and was satisfied; and who but an English philosopher would have sent notices of it to the brain to reverse the judgment?

180 · Textual and Critical Intersections

> In saying this, she disengaged her hand with a look which I thought
> a sufficient commentary upon the text. (*SJ* 24)

It is, in many ways, the mistake Sterne had made with Eliza, that Swann so monumentally makes with Odette, and that Marcel repeats with Albertine, the urge to possess through knowledge and definition, and it is no accident that the English empirical (Lockean) tradition of philosophy is invoked—and spurned.

Sterne's relationship with Locke has been debated without resolution this entire century, but surely in this single instance we can agree that Locke has intruded himself into a situation where he has no role: "one does not see," says Levinas, "that the success of knowledge would precisely abolish the proximity of the Other."[45] But Sterne, I would suggest, in this opening encounter of *A Sentimental Journey,* already "knows" what remains always to be again discovered: that it is precisely in the "pulsations of the arteries" he feels along his own "fingers pressing across hers" (*SJ* 25), precisely in this "proximity of the Other," that the end of his search is already present, if only he can resist the temptation to know what those pulsations "mean." Here he perhaps separates himself from Levinas—specifically, from the temptation to distinguish a sexual presence from a nonsexual one. Despite every effort not to "know," Levinas believes he can nonetheless distinguish in Proust what is and is not an ontologically "pure" Eros. I can think of no author of our century more than Proust, however, in whose writings there is less reward for such an attempt; after four thousand pages, everything is indeed possible—except the effort to define a "pure" Eros. And it is in this reassertion of the unknowingness of sexuality—and hence its primal innocence—that I find Sterne's closest link to Proust.[46]

In both authors, however—and here certainly Levinas is a particularly acute reader of Proust—there is absolutely no credence given to the most common "solution" to human sexuality: the "fusion" that comes from knowing in this instance is the clarity with which we have learned to separate love from lust, need from desire; or, as Sterne had put it in *Tristram Shandy,* the certainty with which moralists are able to trace the precise boundary between "the *extreams* of DELICACY, and the *beginnings* of CONCUPISCENCE" (*TS* 5.1.415). Although this fusion into a whole picture of a "known" dichotomy may at times seem to be what Levinas himself attempts in "Phenomenology of Eros," in his encounter with Proust he recognizes such an attempt as the "last vestige of idealism," and certainly Sterne's interest in an anti-Lockean Neoplatonist like John Norris is a sign that he too found himself at the outpost of philosophy in his own bewilderment as to whether he stood justified or not.[47]

Significantly, however, when Sterne invokes Norris in *A Sentimental Journey,* it is to borrow a second time a passage he had first borrowed for a sermon he wrote as early as 1750, now central to his own self-interest in 1767. The sermon is "Our conversation in Heaven," which, for several pages, follows Norris's argument that one must use this life to prepare for the next, for, argues this "very able divine," were "the happiest mansion in heaven . . . allotted to a gross and polluted spirit, it would be so far from being happy in it, that it would do penance there to all eternity" (*Sermons* 280).[48] Readers of Sterne who have never read the sermons will nevertheless find the passage familiar, because Sterne repeats it in *A Sentimental Journey* when discussing Smelfungus and Mundungus, pilgrims so out of sorts with this world that, Yorick opines, they could not possibly find enjoyment in the next:

> Every gentle spirit would come flying upon the wings of Love to hail their arrival—Nothing would the souls of Smelfungus and Mundungus hear . . . they have brought up no faculties for this work; and was the happiest mansion in heaven to be allotted to Smelfungus and Mundungus, they would be so far from being happy, that [their] souls . . . would do penance there to all eternity. (*SJ* 38)

Despite identifying the source, Gardner Stout's annotation makes nothing of the passage, which he reads as typical of latitudinarian hedonism (which never existed): Smelfungus's failure to enjoy the world is contrasted to Yorick's delight in it, the man of ill will versus the man of feeling.[49] However, given the echo of Norris (and the horizon afforded by Levinas), we might read the passage quite differently.

Smelfungus's problem is not that he does not enjoy life, but rather that he is so steeped in life, in the senses, in the disappointments that flesh is heir to precisely because it is flesh (in the *conatus essendi,* Levinas might say),[50] that he is indeed a sinner, an uninstructed bodily presence returning always to earth, excluded from the conversation in Heaven. Sterne is

182 · Textual and Critical Intersections

not, that is, arguing for a heightened physical sensibility toward the world, but the opposite; our journey through life must be a purgation of the senses, a Platonic "purification" and withdrawal from the body "*in order to think well,*" as he says in *Tristram Shandy,* again quoting John Norris (*TS* 7.13.593).[51] To be sure, Tristram disagrees with this notion, but Sterne I think is less certain. That such "purifying" is difficult for the human being is demonstrated on every page of Sterne's works, but neither the Hellenistic nor Christian Platonist, nor the Jewish phenomenologist, for that matter, spells out a path of ease or least resistance for the ethical life. Everything about Platonism seems to go against the human grain, and Yorick's sentimental journey is no exception; somewhere between the sensate rootedness of Smelfungus and Mundungus on the one hand, and the ethereal conviction that our conversation is indeed in Heaven, the man of feeling struggles to "purify" himself in order to be judged worthy at the final assize.[52]

But Sterne does not repeat the error of the idealist in reducing the world to unity, neither the worldly unity of Smelfungus, in which the world is all that matters, nor the "intellectual" unity of Malebranche and Norris, in which the world is all that does not matter. Sterne's desire for a redemptive "love" is to some degree free from "lust" (in part due, I suspect, to physical debility), but to define such love as necessarily without bodily appetite is to return to "knowing" the difference between the two, and Sterne is in the process of rejecting the knowledge that "comes from me," the "definitive quality of our identical existence,"[53] that Marcel had tried to impose on Albertine, and Sterne on Eliza; indeed, that knowledge by which we impose ourselves on the world. Norris, we note, in his celebration of the Pythagoreans, rejects *both* the physical *and* the intellectual appetites, insofar as both are equally sources of inadequate "knowing."

The notion that we can divide the world into fusible dichotomies turns into the image of a fabric in which the "threads of love and desire are [so] entangled" (*SJ* 124) they can never be unraveled. To insist on the category of lust has an aura of gravity (a sinking to the center) about it, an indulgence in the flesh, that, as manifested in both Walter Shandy and Smelfungus, is marked by fears and loathings.[54] Sterne seeks instead a purgation of the body marked by a freedom from *concupiscence,* the urgent need to possess, or the equally urgent need to eschew possession. Sterne's

Reading Sterne through Proust and Levinas · 183

new sexuality is, rather, of a kind that seems to want to weigh the body equally with the mind or soul—but equally here means precisely that: he distances himself from the body by refusing to allow it more importance than the other components of his humanity, refusing to accept the trap of condemning the body so vociferously that the body becomes the site of all ethical conflict—and of all sexual interest as well.

It is a sign of the bad "clarity" with which we "understand" love that Yorick's encounter with the Marquesina F***, the one instance in *A Sentimental Journey* in which a sexual union is openly stated (at least as openly as Sterne ever reveals what he seems to feel is never fully to be expressed in language), has tended to focus critical discussion on the "real" identity of this wonderful Italian woman: who could the F*** possibly stand for?[55] The passage is an image of the most fundamental ethical dilemma: we are standing on a place that belongs to another; as Levinas famously expresses it, our place in the sun is at the expense of the Other.[56] Sterne re-creates a scene that is a moment of felt reality every reader can share: exiting the opera, the Marquesina attempts to sidestep Yorick, who is entering along the same aisleway. It is a beautifully comic version of one of Levinas's most profound insights, what he calls the passivity beyond all passivity that underlies the ethical relationship:

> she was almost upon me before I saw her; so I gave a spring to one side to let her pass—She had done the same, and on the same side too; so we ran our heads together: she instantly got to the other side to get out: I was just as unfortunate as she had been; for I had sprung to that side, and opposed her passage again—We both flew together to the other side, and then back—and so on—it was ridiculous; . . . so I did at last the thing I should have done at first—I stood stock still, and the Marquesina had no more difficulty. (*SJ* 77)

The passage seems to me frankly sexual, and Sterne confirms this suspicion as he concludes the episode:

> Upon my word, Madame . . . I made six different efforts to let you go out—And I made six efforts, replied she, to let you enter—I wish to heaven you would make a seventh, said I—With all my heart, said she, making room. . . .

184 · Textual and Critical Intersections

> I will only add, that the connection which arose out of that translation [of her gesture], gave me more pleasure than any one I had the honour to make in Italy. (*SJ* 78)

This "connection" is a moment of fulfillment, quite alone in *A Sentimental Journey* in its implicit unfettered actualization. It is noteworthy, therefore, that it takes place in the portion of Yorick's journey that remained unwritten—namely, the journey to Italy (of which it is a momentary presage in the midst of his Paris stay). Ten years ago, when I wrote on the passage, I offered two alternatives for his having thus distinguished it: "Perhaps Sterne intended a projection of the fulfillment to be achieved at journey's end, after all has been learned and experienced; or perhaps, more subtly, he intimates that 'connection' must always be that portion of our journey that remains unverbalized, unwritten."[57] I should have known better—the surer reading of Sterne is almost always the more subtle one—and I would now add to the notion of remaining unverbalized and unwritten the even more essential notion of remaining "unknown": it is a "proximity" that, in Levinas's words, "far from meaning less than identification, precisely opens up the horizons of social existence, making the whole surplus of our experience of friendship and love burst forth, and introducing the definitive quality of our identical existence to all the non-definitive possibilities."[58]

The moralist's questions—"Did Sterne have *sex* with Eliza?" and "Was it love or lust?"—are significantly overwhelmed by the Marquesina F***, who points us in a direction of unknowingness: even if we know what F*** "means," we still know nothing about what happens between the self and the Other. As Levinas notes about Marcel, "Marcel did not love Albertine, if love is a fusion with the Other. . . . Tomorrow he will break with the young woman who bores him. He will make that journey he has been planning for so long. . . . But this non-love is precisely love, the struggle with what cannot be grasped (possession, that absence of Albertine), her presence."[59] Sterne had lost Eliza in the very process of binding her so closely to himself, imprisoning her in the miniature around his neck, and in the mirror across from his writing desk, eating table, bed, a mirror in which his own desires were reflected in her necessary reciprocations. Now Yorick knows better; the Marquesina F***, the Other whose presence (present) is fleeting and momentary, is for him the moment in which his journey fulfills itself. She and he both move on; after all, what they are doing ultimately is clearing space precisely so that the other can move on, and Yorick will struggle again and again to find relationship without possession, nondefinitive possibility ("an inexhaustible source of hope," Levinas says of Marcel's theme of solitude that "turns back into communication") without restraint.[60]

Finally, both Yorick and Marcel, in ways that reflect deeply on concepts of communal or political freedom, the great moral desideratum of the last three hundred years, play out their quests within images of repression and restraint. It is not the least strange coincidence between Proust and Sterne that the volume translated as *The Captive* (*La Prisonnière*) is echoed by a chapter with the same title in *A Sentimental Journey,* or that a caged bird is used as an emblem on the title page of volume 3 of the Random House edition. Sterne encounters a caged starling at that moment in his journey in which the possibility of his own imprisonment in the Bastille begins to loom large; he has entered France, still at war with England, without a passport, and the authorities have called for him. The Sterne family used the starling on its coat of arms (identifying its dialectical rendition *starn* with Sterne), and now Sterne identifies himself in prison with the bird, the song of which he "translates," significantly echoing the episode with the Marquesina, as "I can't get out" (*SJ* 93ff.).[61]

The bird cannot "get out," but more to the point, I think, is Yorick's subsequent effort to create a solidarity with "the millions of my fellow creatures born to no inheritance but slavery," and then, when imagination fails, with "a single captive" (*SJ* 97–98). Although in our present age of suspicious and supercilious reading, Yorick's efforts to portray fellow feeling with the oppressed has been faulted, along with the entire sentimental movement, as a mask for bourgeois exploitation,[62] I have little trouble myself with Yorick's sentimentalism; fellow feeling is, after all, still a valuable response to the suffering of others. But as with Marcel, who is imprisoned within the very prison he prepares for Albertine, while she, deceiving him everywhere and with everyone, is quite free, Yorick's attempt to justify himself in the tears he sheds for a bird or for an imagined human being (and the *imagining* is important here) or for a million human beings, proves never to be enough, proves indeed to turn on the self with its own inadequacy, the guilt that knows it has never given enough, done enough, sacrificed enough, to the needs of the Other. Yorick discovers in the star-

186 · Textual and Critical Intersections

ling who is Sterne that at the final tribunal a feeling heart will also be an insufficient passport.

Not only Yorick and his "Bastille," but equally the neo-Marxists who find him an easy target, are caught by, to repeat Levinas's phrase, "the pathos of socialism," which, to be sure, hovers everywhere in Proust's world— and in much critical commentary on that world. Significantly, Levinas will again and again celebrate the instinct for such feelings as the hope of the world;[63] but he will do so only after first opening for us the prison house of language, the self-incarceration of the ethical in a cell, the dimensions of which are defined by the self-preservation and self-survival of the Hobbesian citizen of the world. And Sterne too weighs these moments of social community and communion with that single moment he can never surrender, when, in proximity with the Other—the gendered other, it is important to note—he feels the pulse, no longer wanting to read it in order to understand, and by understanding, to possess the heart that feeds it, but rather, simply because, in the Judgment to come, he is now convinced that "there are worse occupations in this world *than feeling a woman's pulse*" (*SJ* 71). He would seem to be certain of nothing else, but in that pulse, in the mystery of human desire, sexual *and* infinite, he has found "an inexhaustible source of hope," and for someone about to face Judgment, there is probably no greater gift.

Originally published in *Age of Johnson* 12 (2001).

Notes

1 Melvyn New, "Proust's Influence on Sterne: Remembrance of Things to Come," *MLN* 103, no. 5 (1988): 1031–55, reprinted in New, *Telling New Lies* (Gainesville: University Press of Florida, 1992), 137–62.

2 New, "Proust's Influence on Sterne," 1054.

3 See Emmanuel Levinas, *Totality and Infinity*, trans. Alphonso Lingis (Pittsburgh, PA: Duquesne University Press, 1969); Jacques Derrida, "Violence and Metaphysics" (1964), in *Writing and Difference*, trans. A. Bass (Chicago: University of Chicago Press, 1978), 79–153.

4 On Sterne's interest in aposiopesis, see *TS*, Notes 146–47; and Calvin Thomas, "*Tristram Shandy's* Consent to Incompleteness: Discourse, Disavowal, Disruption," *Literature and Psychology* 36 (1990): 44–62.

5 *Book of Common Prayer* (*BCP*, 1745), "Order for the Burial of the Dead."

6 The idea appears, as one would expect, throughout Sterne's forty-five sermons;

a particularly clear statement occurs in sermon 39 ("Eternal advantages of religion," *Sermons* 372):

> The vanity and emptiness of worldly goods and enjoyments,—the shortness and uncertainty of life,—the unalterable event hanging over our heads,—*that in a few days, we must all of us go to that place from whence we shall not return;*—the certainty of this,—the uncertainty of the time when,—the immortality of the soul,—the doubtful and momentous issues of eternity,—the terrors of damnation, and the glorious things which are spoken of the city of God.

The entire passage and much of the sermon are borrowed from John Norris, *Practical Discourses upon Several Divine Subjects* (1691), 9; see *Sermons*, Notes 400. Norris was the last of the Cambridge Platonists and the primary English proponent of Malebranche (and opponent of Locke) at the end of the seventeenth century and into the eighteenth. Sterne's interest in him has not yet been fully explored; see Melvyn New, "The Odd Couple: Laurence Sterne and John Norris of Bemerton," reprinted as chapter 2 in this volume; and J. T. Parnell, "A Story Painted to the Heart? *Tristram Shandy* and Sentimentalism Reconsidered," *Shandean* 9 (1997): 122–35. Certainly Levinas's interest in Descartes and Malebranche would be a good place to begin to understand Sterne's interest in this proponent of Christian Platonism. See, e.g., Emmanuel Levinas, "God and Philosophy," in *The Levinas Reader*, ed. Seán Hand (Oxford: Blackwell, 1989), 166–89.

7 The comment is reported by one of Sterne's acquaintances and imitators, Richard Griffith: "He has communicated a Manuscript to us, that he means soon to publish. It is stiled a *Sentimental Journey*.... [He] calls it his *Work of Redemption*." Griffith, *A Series of Genuine Letters, between Henry and Frances* (1770), vol. 5, 83, quoted from *Letters*, 627n3. Martin C. Battestin, "Sterne among the *Philosophes*: Body and Soul in *A Sentimental Journey*," *Eighteenth Century Fiction* 7 (1994): 17–36, considers the work a "redemption" by way of a refutation of French materialism.

8 See, esp., Arthur H. Cash's "Appendix on the *Journal to Eliza*," in Cash, *Sterne's Comedy of Moral Sentiments: The Ethical Dimension of the "Journey"* (Pittsburgh, PA: Duquesne University Press, 1965), 133–39; and *Laurence Sterne: The Later Years* (London: Methuen, 1986), 270–304. See also Eva C. van Leewen, *Sterne's "Journal to Eliza": A Semiological and Linguistic Approach to the Text* (Tübingen: Gunter Narr Verlag, 1981). One of the best commentaries on the relationship remains that by W. B. C. Watkins in *Perilous Balance* (Princeton, NJ: Princeton University Press, 1939); Watkins recognizes that Sterne's intense need for Eliza is closely connected with his physical collapse in 1767.

188 · Textual and Critical Intersections

I have used Sterne's own title for the work, *Continuation of the Bramine's Journal* (shortened to *Bramine's Journal*); the title "Journal to Eliza" was almost certainly applied by early editors in analogy to Swift's "Journal to Stella," suggesting a relationship between the two journals that is quite unjustified.

9 The gist of this concern is summarized early in *Bramine's Journal*, in the entry for April 27: "I would not part with the Imagination, of how happy I am to be with thee, for all the Offers of present Interest or Happiness the whole world could tempt me with; . . . what are they worth without Eliza? Jesus! grant me but this, I will deserve it—I will make My Bramine, as Happy, as thy goodness wills her . . . & if ever I am false, unkind or ungentle to her; so let me be dealt with by thy Justice" (*BJ* 181–83).

10 See *Letters* 565 (to Eliza, March 1767): "Not Swift so loved his Stella, Scarron his Maintenon, or Waller his Sacharissa, as I will love, and sing thee, my wife elect." In this regard, we would do well to weigh one of Levinas's many confrontations with the problem of gendering in his philosophical writings:

> Let it be understood that if, in order to uphold the thesis of the exceptional position of the feminine in the economy of being, I willingly refer to the great themes of Goethe or Dante, to Beatrice and the *ewig Weibliches*, to the cult of the *Woman* in chivalry and in modern society . . . I do not want to ignore the legitimate claims of the feminism that presupposes all the acquired attainments of civilization. I simply want to say that this mystery must not be understood in the ethereal sense of a certain literature; that in the most brutal materiality, in the most shameless or the most prosaic appearance of the feminine, neither her mystery nor her modesty are abolished. Profanation is not a negation of mystery, but one of the possible relationships with it.

See Emmanuel Levinas, *Time and the Other*, trans. Richard A. Cohen (Pittsburgh, PA: Duquesne University Press, 1987), 86.

11 Emmanuel Levinas, "L'autre dans Proust" (The Other in Proust, 1947), was reprinted in *Noms propres* (Montpellier: Fata Morgana, 1976), 149–56, and recently translated by Michael B. Smith, in *Proper Names* (Stanford, CA: Stanford University Press, 1996), 99–105. I cite, however, the earlier translation by Seán Hand, in *The Levinas Reader*, 160–65.

12 Levinas's attitude appears fairly early in his writings, most specifically in "Reality and Its Shadow," in Hand, *The Levinas Reader*, 129–43; for a much more perceptive account than I am able to offer, see Jill Robbins, *Altered Reading: Levinas and Literature* (Chicago: University of Chicago Press, 1999).

13 Levinas, "The Other in Proust," 161.

14 Levinas, 162.

15 Levinas, 162.

16 The origin and publication history of *Bramine's Journal*, the existence of which was first made public in 1878, and the full text of which did not appear until 1904, in *Complete Works and Life of Laurence Sterne*, ed. Wilbur L. Cross (New York: J. F. Taylor, 1904), are fully outlined in *SJ* xxi–xxx, xxxix–xliii.

17 Levinas, "The Other in Proust," 162.

18 *Letters* 565 (to Eliza, March 1767): "Talking of widows—pray, Eliza, if ever you are such, do not think of giving yourself to some wealthy nabob, because I design to marry you myself—My wife cannot live long"; cf. the journal entry for June 17, wherein Sterne fantasizes: "Mr Draper dying in the Year *****— This Lady return'd to England & Yorick the year after becoming a Widower— They were married" (*BJ* 203).

19 Levinas, "The Other in Proust," 162.

20 In addition to numerous moments in *Bramine's Journal* where he contemplates the portrait as an "act of love," Sterne introduces it into the opening chapter of *A Sentimental Journey*, associating it with the *droit d'aubaine*, the law seizing the property of travelers who die in France: "even the little picture which I have so long worn, and so often have told thee, Eliza, I would carry with me into my grave, would have been torn from my neck.—Ungenerous!— to seize upon the wreck of an unwary passenger" (*SJ* 3). Cf. *BJ* 202 (June 17, 1767): "I have brought y^r name *Eliza!* and Picture into my work—where they will remain—when You & I are at rest for ever." That both passages link the portrait to death is not, to my mind, accidental. One might also note, in drawing some distinctions between fact and imagination, that the miniature did indeed exist (*SJ* 232–34, n. to 3.18–19), and that *Bramine's Journal* would seem to account for *A Sentimental Journey* in real time. On the other hand, since Yorick is traveling to France in 1763, he had not even met Eliza at the time; the miniature has become a fiction.

21 Levinas, "The Other in Proust," 163.

22 Cf. Proust's own interest in the subject in *The Captive*: "[my mother was] always ready to explain to me that one ought not to confuse genuine sensibility [la veritable sensibilité] with sentimentality [la sensiblerie], what the Germans . . . called *Empfindung* and *Empfinderlei*." Marcel Proust, *The Captive*, in *Remembrance of Things Past*, trans. C. K. Scott Moncrieff and Terence Kilmartin (New York: Random House, 1981), vol. 3, 102–3.

23 Levinas, "The Other in Proust," 163. Levinas is echoing *Time and the Other*, significantly published in the same year as his essay on Proust: "The relationship with the other is not an idyllic and harmonious relationship of communion, or a *sympathy* through which we put ourselves in the other's place; we recognize the other as *resembling* us, but exterior to us; the relationship with

190 · Textual and Critical Intersections

the other is a relationship with a Mystery." Levinas, *Time and the Other*, 75 (emphasis added). As Colin Davis notes in *Levinas: An Introduction* (South Bend, IN: University of Notre Dame Press, 1996), 31, Levinas's *sympathie* translates Husserl's *Einfühlung*. One suspects Marcel's mother (and Proust?) would link it to *Empfinderlei*, rather than to *Empfindung*.

24 This is actually Yorick's second use of the phrase; earlier he had suggested that Paris streets were so crowded with other people that it was impossible to get among them with a "'*Me voici! mes enfans*'—here I am" (*SJ* 65). Levinas returns to the phrase again and again in his writings, but see, esp., "Sincerity and the Glory of the Infinite," in *Otherwise Than Being or Beyond Essence*, trans. Alphonso Lingis (The Hague: Martinus Nijhoff, 1981), 144–45, where the intertwined themes of sincerity, Adam, nakedness, and *me voici* are beautifully set forth.

25 Genesis 3:9–10 (KJV).

26 I have discussed this aspect of *Bramine's Journal* previously in "Job's Wife and Sterne's Other Women," in *Out of Bounds: Male Writers and Gender(ed) Criticism*, ed. Laura Claridge and Elizabeth Langland (Amherst: University of Massachusetts Press, 1991), 62–64, in which I concluded, "as the 'space' between them widens, in time and in distance, the idea of possession becomes more and more obsessional: 'and in proportion as I am thus torn from y^r embraces—*I cling the closer to the Idea of you*,' he writes on July 7 [*BJ* 216]. It is, I would suggest, Sterne's lowest point" (64).

27 Cf. Cash, *Later Years*, 288: "Talk about sickness takes up almost as much space in the *Journal* as talk about love"; and Watkins, *Perilous Balance*, 107–19.

28 Mark S. Madoff, "'They Caught Fire at Each Other': Laurence Sterne's Journal of the Pulse of Sensibility," in *Sensibility in Transformation: Essays in Honor of Jean H. Hagstrum*, ed. Syndy McMillen Conger (Rutherford, NJ: Fairleigh Dickinson University Press, 1990), 59n8, calls attention to Georges Gusdorf's notion that "the invention of metal-backed mirrors was a breakthrough in establishing conditions for autobiography," and adds: "Sterne presents Yorick as fixated on Eliza's painted miniature image; because his interest in Eliza is largely narcissistic, a mirror would have been equally appropriate for his·contemplation. In the *Journal*, Eliza as 'other' at best has an uncertain status." Cf. Georges Gusdorf, "Conditions and Limits of Autobiography," in *Autobiography: Essays Theoretical and Critical*, ed. James Olney (Princeton, NJ: Princeton University Press, 1980), 32–33.

29 Cf. Levinas, *Totality and Infinity*, 256–66, and esp. 257:

> The movement of the lover before this frailty of femininity, neither pure compassion nor impassiveness, indulges in compassion, is absorbed in the complacence of the caress.

The caress, like contact, is sensibility. But the caress transcends the sensible.... The caress consists in seizing upon nothing, in soliciting what ceaselessly escapes its form toward a future never future enough.

Sterne's version is, of course, the feeling of the grisset's pulse.

30 Levinas, "The Other in Proust," 163.

31 Levinas, 163.

32 Levinas, 164.

33 See n. 10, above.

34 Johann Wolfgang von Goethe, "From Makarie's Archives," in *Wilhelm Meister's Journeyman Years*, trans. Krishna Winston (Princeton, NJ: Princeton University Press, 1989), 431. I cite this edition for the convenience of those who want to pursue Goethe's comments on Sterne, 434–35, but have used the translation of Alan B. Howes, *Sterne: The Critical Heritage* (London: Routledge, 1974), 433, as more faithful to the original: "Der schönste Geist, der je gewirkt hat; wer ihn liest, fühlt sich sogleich frei und schön; sein Humor ist unnachahmlich." Goethe, *Wilhelm Meisters Wanderjahre* (Frankfurt am Main: Insel, 1982), 485.

35 Johann Wolfgang von Goethe, *Essays on Art and Literature*, trans. Ellen von Nardroff and Ernest H. von Nardroff (Princeton, NJ: Princeton University Press, 1986), 175: "I would like to call attention to a man [i.e., Sterne] who helped initiate, and became the spokesman for, an era . . . which produced more profound understanding of human nature, noble tolerance and gentle love."

36 Levinas, "The Other in Proust," 164.

37 See Luce Irigaray, "Questions to Emmanuel Levinas: On the Divinity of Love," in *Re-Reading Levinas*, ed. Robert Bernasconi and Simon Critchley (Bloomington: Indiana University Press, 1991), 109–18; Irigaray asks a difficult question: "Why, and how long ago did God withdraw from the act of carnal love?" (116). It is a query far more essential, I believe, than her assault on Levinas's supposed gendering of the Other.

38 Levinas, "Phenomenology of Eros," in *Totality and Infinity*, 264. This essay should be read in its entirety (256–66) because Levinas is certainly not as overt about these matters as I (or Irigaray) suggest. The problem, I think, is that in attempting to contemplate the age-old (ethical) distinction between love and lust, Levinas, despite every effort at more subtlety, cannot ultimately resist a sexuality that is disembodied, "pure," "virginal"—or, as Sterne might have written "un——." Had Sterne been chaste, his need to justify appetite might have been less strongly felt.

192 · Textual and Critical Intersections

39 See Melvyn New, "Some Sterne Borrowings from Four Renaissance Authors," *Philological Quarterly* 71 (1992): 302; cf. Pierre Charron, *Of Wisdome*, trans. Samson Lennard (1630), 130–31; and Michel de Montaigne, *Essays*, trans. Charles Cotton (1686), vol. 2, 547. Montaigne's essay is entitled, significantly enough, "Nous ne goustons rien de pur" (That we taste nothing pure). ·

40 Levinas, "The Other in Proust," 164.

41 Sterne defines the vehicle in a footnote: "A chaise, so called in France, from its holding but one person" (*SJ* 12).

42 Levinas, "The Other in Proust," 164. There is some irony, certainly, in Viktor Shklovsky's usurping Sterne's title for his biographical account of the Russian Revolution, but I would suggest that Shklovsky grasped a link between Sterne's travels and his own revolutionary experience, centering precisely on issues of communion and community; see Shklovsky, *A Sentimental Journey: Memoirs, 1917–1922*, trans. Richard Sheldon (Ithaca, NY: Cornell University Press, 1970).

43 Levinas, "The Other in Proust," 164.

44 Yorick prefaces this observation with an anecdote of transplanting a grape stock from one environment to another, and the possibility that the planter, if he grows a grape sufficiently potent, may, "by discovering his nakedness, become a laughing stock to his people," alluding to Noah, Genesis 9:20–22; cf. the discussion of nakedness and shame, important elements in Levinas's discussion of the erotic, in *Totality and Infinity* (esp. 263–64); and see above my discussion of *me voici* and Adam.

45 Levinas, "The Other in Proust," 164.

46 There is a moment in "Phenomenology of Eros" where I think Levinas comes very close to unraveling one clue to Sterne's and Proust's discourses of eroticism, a discussion of laughter, in which "equivocation constitutes the epiphany of the feminine." Levinas, *Totality and Infinity*, 263–64. Sterne, in his own inimitable way, says the same thing when he has Walter Shandy advise Toby to take a much different path than humor in his affair with the Widow Wadman:

> Avoid all kinds of pleasantry and facetiousness in thy discourse with her, and . . . keep from her all books and writings which tend thereto: there are some devotional tracts, which if thou canst entice her to read over—it will be well: but suffer her not to look into Rabelais, or Scarron, or Don Quixote——
> ——They are all books which excite laughter; and thou knowest, dear Toby, that there is no passion so serious as lust. (*TS* 8.34.727)

Sterne and Proust both use their humor to help mystify what "grave folks" believe they know all too well: the ethics of sexuality.

47 See n. 6, above. Two of Norris's most important works are *The Theory and Regulation of Love* (1688) and (with Mary Astell) *Letters Concerning the Love of God* (1695), both of which draw absolute boundaries between sexual love and spiritual love. Interestingly, however, since for Norris, following Malebranche's brilliant formulation, everything is seen "in God," he exhibits great curiosity about a sensual love that is not antisocial.

48 Sterne is quoting John Norris, *Practical Discourses upon the Beatitudes*, 4th ed. (1699), 137; see *Sermons*, Notes 318–19.

49 Laurence Sterne, *A Sentimental Journey*, ed. Gardner D. Stout Jr. (Berkeley: University of California Press, 1967), 338–42.

50 Of Levinas's many discussions of this principle, the one perhaps most relevant to the present discussion is "The Old and the New," in *Time and the Other*, 121–38, esp. 121–22: "Exposed to aging, to an outrage more offensive perhaps than death, . . . in which the human coagulates into an identity, sinking into itself, the Desire for the new in us is a Desire for *the other*; it distinguishes our being from *existing*, which is self sufficient, and which, *conatus essendi*, perseveres in existing, holding, above all, to this very existing. In the natural throbbing of the being of beings, the *human* would thus be the rupture of this ontological rhythm." The last sentence reflects nicely Yorick's interest in pulses, and the fact that the rest of the essay relies heavily on Bergson suggests its applicability to Proust.

51 See also New, "The Odd Couple," in this volume, pp. 38–39. Sterne is borrowing from John Norris, *Practical Discourses upon Several Divine Subjects* (1691), vol. 1, 41–42: "The *Pythagoreans* went higher, and taught their Disciples . . . that they must separate and unwind themselves, even from their very Bodies, if they would be good Philosophers. This in a Qualified and Corrected Sense is true, for the Body is the great Impediment and Disadvantage of the Soul, and therefore all Bodily Passions and Inclinations, as well as Intellectual Habits and Appetites must be put to *Silence*, in the still and Attentive Search and Inquiry after Truth." One might note in the last sentence Norris's allusion to Malebranche's "attention of the soul," a phrase of great interest to Levinas; see, e.g., his discussion of the poetry of Paul Celan in *Proper Names*, trans. Smith: "'Attention, like a pure prayer of the soul,' of which Malebranche speaks: . . . extreme receptivity, but extreme donation; attention—a mode of consciousness without distraction, i.e. without the power of escape through dark underground passages; full illumination, projected not in order to see ideas, but in order to prohibit evasion; the first meaning of that insomnia that is conscience" (43).

52 I have called attention to the various forms of *pure* in this paragraph to highlight the Platonic urge I think lurks in Levinas's "ontologically pure Eros." For

Norris and for Sterne, however, insofar as Platonism has been Christianized, "pure Eros" is Christ alone, and purification an unceasing, crucifying process of departure and ascension.

53 Levinas, "The Other in Proust," 164.

54 Still one of the best essays on Sterne is Sigurd Burckhardt, "*Tristram Shandy's* Law of Gravity," *ELH* 28 (1961): 70–88.

55 From this general naivete, I must exempt Madeleine Descargues, "*A Sentimental Journey*, or 'The Case of (In)delicacy,'" in *Critical Essays on Laurence Sterne*, ed. Melvyn New (New York: G. K. Hall, 1998), 243–53, originally published as "*A Sentimental Journey*, ou 'le cas d'indélicatesse,'" *Études Anglaises* 46 (1993): 407–19. Her conclusion about *A Sentimental Journey* may or may not be the same as my own; we have not, fortunately, been able to decide: "Its putting forward the platonic intent of Yorick's quest is another way of considering the pursuit of fidelity to oneself and to others, when infidelity and fickleness stand at the very core of self-consciousness." Descargues, "*A Sentimental Journey*," 251–52.

56 Levinas uses the phrase for one of his epigraphs for *Otherwise Than Being*, borrowed from Pascal, *Pensées*: "'That is my place in the sun.' That is how the usurpation of the whole world began." A second epigraph, also from *Pensées*, is equally applicable to this discussion: "They have used concupiscence as best they could for the general good; but it is nothing but a pretense and a false image of charity; for at bottom it is simply a form of hatred."

57 New, "Proust's Influence," 1039.

58 Levinas, "The Other in Proust," 164.

59 Levinas, 164–65.

60 Levinas, 165.

61 On the starling, see *SJ* 324–25, n. to 95.10–11. For a fuller analysis of the "caged bird" image shared by Proust and Sterne, see New, "Proust's Influence," 1040–42, including Marcel's final words on Albertine: "Set free once more, released from the cage in which, here at home, I used to leave her for days on end without letting her come to my room, Albertine had regained all her attraction in my eyes; she had become once more the girl whom everyone pursued, the marvellous bird of the earliest days." Proust, *The Captive*, 481.

62 The best of these readings is Robert Markley, "Sentimentality as Performance: Shaftesbury, Sterne, and the Theatrics of Virtue," in *The New Eighteenth Century: Theory and Interpretation*, ed. Felicity Nussbaum and Laura Brown (London: Methuen, 1987), 210–30; still, see my comments in "Something New under the Sun," *Eighteenth Century: Theory and Interpretation* 40 (1999): 187–94 (an issue devoted to "Levinas and the Eighteenth Century"). Two particularly supercilious readings along these lines are Judith Frank,

"'A Man Who Laughs Is Never Dangerous': Character and Class in Sterne's *A Sentimental Journey*," *ELH* 56 (1989): 97–124; and George E. Haggerty, "Amelia's Nose; or Sensibility and Its Symptoms," *Eighteenth Century: Theory and Interpretation* 36 (1995): 139–56. A fine antidote to both essays is Donald R. Wehrs, "Levinas and Sterne: From the Ethics of the Face to the Aesthetics of Unrepresentability," in New, *Critical Essays on Laurence Sterne*, 311–29.

63 See, esp., Emmanuel Levinas, "Ideology and Idealism," in *Of God Who Comes to Mind*, trans. Bettina Bergo (Stanford, CA: Stanford University Press, 1998), 9: "Like the requirements of scientific rigor, like anti-ideology, the revolt against a society without justice expresses the spirit of our age."

8

Sterne and the Modernist Moment

"To define——is to distrust," as Tristram triumphantly informs Euge-nius, although he immediately realizes he has a victory without laurels: "I triumph'd over him as I always do, like a fool" (*TS* 3.31.258). Similarly, I have foolishly managed over the past fifteen years to write about Sterne and modernist authors without ever defining modernism or postmod-ernism. I have, for example, written about Sterne and Proust, Sterne and Nietzsche, Sterne and Svevo,[1] but have continued to believe all along that Sterne is neither proto-modernist nor proto-postmodernist, neither an anticipation of Joycean stream of consciousness nor a foretaste of a Der-ridean breakdown between signified and signifier (which, assuredly, first happened in Eden, not in Paris). Rather, Sterne, like all great artists, was a writer of his own time and place; all that we can really mean when we assign a prophetic aura to his work is that authors of a later period have read Sterne in ways that we must now take seriously, their powerful lenses proving to be filters we are unable to avoid. As I expressed it in explain-ing Proust's influence on Sterne: "twentieth-century readers, reading the best that has been produced in their own century, come to earlier literature through that experience and cannot free their reading from it."[2]

With this in mind, let me define *modernism* in the narrowest possible sense, keeping in mind that by *modernism* I mean *modernism,* and "noth-ing more, or less," as Sterne says about defining the word *nose* (*TS* 3.31.258). It was a condition of Western thought that started with Nietzsche, but perhaps earlier with Kierkegaard, and perhaps before that with Hume and Kant—a condition that some believe ended with the anointing of post-modernism and Derrida at Johns Hopkins University in 1968, although here, again, precursors might be discovered, every messiah having had his

John the Baptist. Still others would argue that postmodernism was merely a contrarian moment, fueled by politics, in a modernist age, and that, this moment having passed, we continue to be modernists into the twenty-first century, like Jews holding fast to Torah and Talmud, unswayed by false messiahs and new testaments. In short, by *modernism,* I mean the question that should stand uppermost in our consideration of what it means to be human in our own time: how is it possible in this most hair-raising of eras still to stand erect? "What a life of it has an author, at this pass!" (*TS* 3.33.262).

Put alternatively, we might suggest that the singular aim of postmodernism was to demonstrate the flaws of modernist thought by means of a philosophical-linguistic-sociological (and, thinking of *Tristram Shandy* [*TS* 1.21.72], all other categories of thought "ending . . . in *ical*") assault on its aesthetic and metaphysical (counter-materialist) tendencies. To reassert, then, the meaning of *modernism,* we should allow the aesthetic and metaphysical to speak for themselves. More narrowly formal definitions have their uses, and to think of modernist narration in terms of its characteristic disruptions of temporal sequence, narrative framing, and the realist illusion is at least to approach the affinity with Sterne acknowledged by writers such as Joyce, and subsequently overdetermined by critics.[3] Yet modernism begins by placing the very concept of definition itself under question, and its manifestations—in works of literature, music, art—are everywhere a warning against the definitional process, the defining of matter by form. For this reason, I will eschew generalizations and instead examine very closely two representative excerpts from two modernist fictions; what is most worth observing about Sterne in proximity to the artists of the modern era will, it is hoped, emerge from this examination.

The first passage, pertinently enough since I have invoked an image of the modernist as persistent Jew, is to be found in *Street of Crocodiles* (1934) by Bruno Schulz (1894–1942), a Polish Jew shot to death in his hometown, Drogobych, by the gestapo.[4] The second passage is from Virginia Woolf's *Mrs Dalloway,* published some nine years before *Street of Crocodiles.* Needless to say, Woolf was not a Jew (though married to one), but the persistence with which she cleaves to the notion that her formal innovations in the face of modern dilemmas had to be steeped in familiarity with her aesthetic past will here suffice for what I will suggest is one of modernism's most paradoxical characteristics: a persistent metaphysical engagement with the past, whatever the present or the future might hold. Woolf greatly admired Sterne, and indeed wrote an introduction to a new edition of *A Sentimental Journey* three years after writing *Mrs Dalloway*.[5] Schulz, on the other hand, gives no explicit indication that he had read Sterne, but he did read and translate Kafka, who certainly read Nietzsche, who called Sterne "the most liberated spirit who ever wrote"—only three degrees of separation.[6]

Bruno Schulz was an art teacher at a local high school for all of his adult life. *Street of Crocodiles*, a collection of loosely connected short stories, was published when he was forty, followed by a second collection, *Sanatorium under the Sign of the Hourglass*, in 1937; he was supposedly working on a novel, *The Messiah*, when he was murdered in 1942. Like Tristram, the narrator of the stories in *Street of Crocodiles* has a theory-driven father, Jacob, "that incorrigible improviser, that fencing-master of imagination . . . that metaphysical conjurer."[7] His primary theory is nothing less than a new thesis of creation, unfolded in two linked stories, "Tailors' Dummies" and "A Tractate on Tailors' Dummies, or The Second Book of Genesis."[8] Jacob formulates not only a commentary on Schulz's own disorienting and magnificently innovative fictions, but also a useful window through which to view whatever we eventually come to define as modernism.

The "Dummies" are connected to Jacob's dry-goods shop and serve for the fitting and cutting of garments; for Jacob, however, it is not the garments but the remnants that become the foundation of his theory, the "heap of cuttings, of motley rags and pieces . . . the thousand scraps, the frivolous and fickle trimmings."[9] If this notion moves us closer to the world of *Tristram Shandy* (where the planet itself is said to be made of the "shreds and clippings of the rest" [*TS* 1.5.8], where a marbled page serves as a "motly emblem" of the work [*TS* 3.36.268], and where Uncle Toby's virtue is finally reduced to "nothing but *empty bottles, tripes, trunk-hose, and pantofles*" [*TS* 9.22.777]), so does Jacob's concomitant interest in the seamstresses (*grissets*) drop us into the very middle of *A Sentimental Journey*, Yorick, and the beautiful grisset in Paris. Responding to the "magnetism of his strange personality," the young women allow Jacob to "study the structure of their thin and ordinary little bodies," to feel their pulses, so to speak. On one particular occasion, the theory is formulated: "pull-

Sterne and the Modernist Moment · 199

ing Pauline's stocking down from her knee and studying with enraptured eyes the precise and noble structure of the joint," Jacob revises Genesis: "If . . . I were to attempt a criticism of creation, I would say 'Less matter, more form!' Ah, what relief it would be for the world to lose some of its contents. More modesty in aspirations, more sobriety in claims."[10] Sterne makes the same point in using a sentence from Epictetus as his title-page motto for volumes 1 and 2 of *Tristram Shandy:* "We are tormented with the opinions we have of things, and not by things themselves."

Like Walter Shandy, Jacob lives in an intellectualized universe where matter matters most. Both are driven by a persistent urge to find the proper forms (their theories) for all that matters (and for all matter), and, most significantly, to reduce or dismiss whatever matter they cannot contain within their forms as matter that does not matter, the refuse of their lives. For both Walter and Jacob, the overflow of matter is a cause of constant alarm, and while they both might sensibly wish for relief from the agitations of theorizing, both remain insensibly mounted and agallop on the hobby-horses of their *form*ulations. Sterne and Schulz, however, remain skeptical concerning this world of thought and *form*ation, and acutely aware that "Pauline's white calf," released "from the prison of her stocking," has the capacity to *de*form and *re*form the world.[11] In that single insight, I would locate one of the hinges on which Sterne opened his own door to modernism.

Jacob struggles to elucidate his theory in his "Tractate," reminiscent of "Slawkenbergius's Tale" on the one hand, the *Tristrapædia* on the other: "Matter grows under our hands.—Let no man say,—'Come—I'll write a *duodecimo*'" (*TS* 5.16.446). The monism of "thinking matter," one of the heresies of rationalism in Sterne's century, is for Schulz the "Great Heresy," and for Jacob, "Our Heresiarch," who mesmerizes his small audience with his "dangerous charm," his insistence that "matter has been given infinite fertility, inexhaustible vitality, and, at the same time, a seductive power of temptation which invites us to create as well. . . . The whole of matter pulsates with infinite possibilities."[12] Even without informing spirit, in other words, matter is already alive and fecund in itself. Schulz's portrayal of this matter as feminine is mirrored by Sterne's association of masculinity with Walter, the *philosophus gloriosus* (formalism), with Toby, the *miles gloriosus* (militarism, triumphalism), and, significantly enough in both instances,

200 · Textual and Critical Intersections

with impotence, which, in James A. Work's succinct formulation, "hovers like a dubious halo over the head of every Shandy male, including the bull."[13]

As Jacob spins his theory, its dangers become more and more apparent. Matter is

> pliable like a woman, submissive to every impulse, it is a territory outside any law, open to all kinds of charlatans and dilettanti, a domain of abuses and of dubious demiurgical manipulations. Matter is the most passive and most defenseless essence in [the] cosmos. Anyone can mold it and shape it; it obeys everybody. All attempts at organizing matter are transient and temporary, easy to reverse and to dissolve.[14]

The further one carries the theory, the more appalling it becomes, the passivity of matter suggesting that each new formalism can be freely imposed on it, that between Hegel and Heidegger (to invoke the philosophical bookends of modernism), the reduction of all matter to a new formalism, ever and always in the name of history and the reality of things (what "really *matters*"), was not only acceptable but demanded: "Homicide is not a sin. It is sometimes a necessary violence on resistant and ossified forms of existence which have ceased to be amusing."[15] Or, as Jacob concludes, with the blindness of Uncle Toby pursuing the "great ends of [his] creation" as he delivers his apologetical oration in defense of warfare (*TS* 6.32.557), "here is the starting point of a new apologia for sadism."[16]

Modernism, I suggest, is an aesthetic (and metaphysical) attempt to confront the *sadism* inherent in the mind's encounter with matter. Put in Sterne's language, with a nod toward Keats, could we ride our hobbyhorses "peaceably and quietly along the King's high-way," and not compel others to "get up behind [us]" (*TS* 1.7.12), could we celebrate the infinitude of matter without any "irritable reaching after fact and reason," we could indeed celebrate a world of rich fecundity without guilt or shame or tartuffery.[17] And indeed, "They order . . . this *matter* better in France," a land of *grissets* and *filles de chambre* (*SJ* 3, emphasis added). That is not, however, the world in which we find ourselves, and the forms by which we attempt to control matter's infiniteness, even when they begin "in jest," always end "in downright earnest" (*TS* 1.19.61). This entire passage from *Tristram Shandy* is worth contemplating as an indication of the incipient "sadism" of Walter's theorizing: "he was serious;—he was all uniformity;—he was systematical, and, like all systematick reasoners, he would move both heaven and earth, and twist and torture every thing in nature to support his hypothesis" (*TS* 1.19.61). As the twentieth century bears witness, formalisms always begin with a rhetorical demonstration (Walter) and always—at least in our cultural memory—end in warfare (Toby).

Clearly, however, this cannot be the only view of formalism entertained by Sterne, or by modernists, both being so often brilliant formalists themselves. Art is, after all, a complicating rather than a simplifying discourse, the antithesis of the political. Modernist aesthetics is intensely aware of its own implication in the containment of matter. Here is a description of Jacob, a fragment broken loose from a story written by a Polish Jew in 1934:

> As my father proceeded from these general principles of cosmogony to the more restricted sphere of his private interests, his voice sank to an impressive whisper, the lecture became more and more complicated . . . and the conclusions which he reached became more dubious and dangerous. . . . He half-closed one eye, put two fingers to his forehead while a look of extraordinary slyness came over his face. He transfixed his listeners with these looks.[18]

Is there anyone who has read *Tristram Shandy* who will not here recognize Walter Shandy, a fragment within a novel written by an Anglican cleric between 1759 and 1767? The mind creates the formal linkage, binds the two figures and two fragments together, and then prepares to publish its insight to the world: "What could be wanting in my father but to have wrote a book to publish this notion of his to the world? Little boots it to the subtle speculatist to stand single in his opinions, - - - - unless he gives them proper vent" (*TS* 1.19.63). We do not, as yet, destroy those who disagree with us about such literary links (the *matters* of literature do not seem to *matter* very much), but as the nation of Israel (Jacob) discovered, transfixing listeners (the act of conversion) is the beginning of the justification of conviction, control, sadism, and war.

Modernism—in its complicated aesthetic engagement with formalism, in its ironies and self-conscious skepticism that turns most evidently on its own doubts, its own heresies, its own relationship with its heritage—is a desire to *deconvict* the world. Sterne may be considered one of those authors who first suggested that such an irenic or pacific vision might pos-

202 · Textual and Critical Intersections

sibly be more Christian than the doctrinalism that his world inherited; he called such doctrinalism "polemical divinity," but significantly enough, when asked to define it, Yorick pulls out a copy of Rabelais and reads a page (*TS* 5.28–29): there has perhaps never been an era in which the "modernist" urge to *deconvict* has not been accompanied by the counter-urge to re*form* the world to the shape of one's own *convictions*. Precisely for this reason, such skeptical foresight—or insight—into the habitual tenacity of human beings with "important" ideas ought not be labeled "modernism," which only celebrates yet another formalism, that of precursiveness. It is more useful, perhaps, to suggest that, in the infinitude of matter's potential, Schulz is the lens through which we can locate the modernist moment in Sterne, just as Sterne is the lens through which the modernist moment in Rabelais comes to light—and to fruition. Hence, the modernist, as opposed to the postmodernist, has no predominant instinct to destroy the forebears (the art of politics), but rather, as with Sterne, a paradoxical embrace of the past alongside both innovation and a highly individualized, not to say idiosyncratic, vision: the unexpected always depends on the expected.

One more point may help to complicate further this shared moment between Sterne and Schulz. As noted, Jacob's entire theory begins with a woman's body, and, indeed, it also collapses in the same encounter. The women of his audience discover how easy it is to break his spell, and in a gesture rich with scriptural significance, one of the girls moves "her chair forward and, without getting up from it, lifted her dress to reveal her foot tightly covered in black silk, and then stretched it out stiffly like a serpent's head."[19] In case we miss his point, Schulz repeats the image: "Adela's outstretched slipper trembled slightly and shone like a serpent's tongue. My father rose slowly, still looking down, took a step forward like an automaton, and fell to his knees. The lamp hissed in the silence of the room . . . whispers of venomous tongues floated in the air, zigzags of thought."[20] As with Sterne, human sexuality—the crevice in the fireplace, Slawkenbergius's nose, the cursed slit in the petticoat, the making of sausages, and countless other images, male and female—calls formalism back to matter, the infinite fertility of matter, and the inadequacy of human efforts to subdue it. We can return to the Garden for our explanation, or we can accept, with Rabelais and Sterne, Freud and Proust, Nietzsche and Schulz (that is, with modernists of every era), that the human mind, that fortress of conviction and certainty, is always and everywhere vulnerable to the zig-zaggery of sexuality's—the body's—approaches.

Hence, it should not surprise us that when Tristram encounters the fact that "matter and motion are infinite," it is embedded within Trim's funeral oration *and* a discussion of his persuasive genius. Death, along with impotence, hovers over both Shandy Hall and Toby's bowling green, but it is important to Sterne's ultimately Christian vision that love and sexual desire hover there as well. Where Sterne differs from his era, perhaps, is in his willingness to entertain the possibility that this overlapping, here on earth and in the constant interplay of human interaction, is preparatory to salvation.[21] That Trim's oration is pieced together from the *Book of Common Prayer* is telling; but it is equally noteworthy that Trim, alongside his mourning, offers us a lesson in persuasiveness—and seduction. The dropping of his hat as an emblem of death works precisely because we are "not stocks and stones . . . but men cloathed with bodies, and governed by our imaginations" (*TS* 5.7.431–32). For Sterne, this vulnerability marks the pathway of persuasiveness, and he opens to the reader, much as Schulz would do almost two centuries later, the dangerous landscape of modernity:

> Ye who govern this mighty world and its mighty concerns with the *engines* of eloquence,—who heat it, and cool it, and melt it, and mollify it,——and then harden it again to *your purpose*—
>
> Ye who wind and turn the passions with this great windlass,— and, having done it, lead the owners of them, whither ye think meet—
>
> Ye, lastly, who drive——and why not, Ye also who are driven, like turkeys to market, with a stick and a red clout—meditate—meditate, I beseech you, upon *Trim's* hat. (*TS* 5.7.433)

The world of twentieth-century political positiveness, whether from the Right or from the Left, and the instruments of its persuasiveness, from oratory, rhetoric, and propaganda to torture and warfare, are here foreshadowed with a deftness of touch that almost seems, again, a justification for sadism; in the space between "eloquence" and "a stick and a red clout," one can locate perhaps every historical event of a most anguished century.

Sterne refuses, however, to let this vision dominate his text. The courting of Susannah turns vulnerability into a relationship that Sterne will not allow us to ignore, much less to condemn: the persuasion or seduction to human sexuality. As he talks about death and corruption, Trim directs his speaking toward Susannah: "What is the finest face that ever man looked at!—I could hear *Trim* talk so for ever, cried *Susannah*,—what is it! (*Susannah* laid her hand upon *Trim's* shoulder)—but corruption? ——*Susannah* took it off" (*TS* 5.9.435). Our most profound theories and thoughts—even those offered as an alternative Genesis, or as reparation for the sin and death entailed by the Fall therein—are tinged with what it means to be human, to have "this delicious mixture" (*TS* 5.9.435) within us.[22] These "threads of love and desire . . . entangled with the piece" (*SJ* 124) must always be acknowledged, not as matter to be overcome, not as sin, or disease, or madness, but as the site of love and caring, that single gesture of openness toward a fellow creature that might deconvict the world of its certainties, that might disarm its violence, and that might, just possibly, have saved us from the twentieth century. *Modernism* is that single gesture defined aesthetically, and while both Sterne and Schulz acutely (and humorously) chronicle the opposing human embrace of closure (close-mindedness), they continue to dream, each in his own way, of the harmonies that could change the world. It is certainly no accident that both authors image themselves, finally, as a human being stretching across an abyss in search of the bodily matter of the human being on the other side (figure 7).[23]

Virginia Woolf was a close and appreciative reader of Sterne, but for our present purpose, I want to concentrate on one particular passage in *Mrs Dalloway* that is, to my mind, Woolf's most poignant illustration of what I take modernism to be—and of the demons it was designed to confront. If Jacob and Walter Shandy can be reduced to one formal construct, so might an even more unlikely pairing—the highly successful Harley Street physician Sir William Bradshaw and the Yorkshire sesquipedalian Dr. Slop—be reduced to another, at least insofar as both represent the ultimate weapon in the reduction of matter to form, the advent of science and technology. Perhaps no image in literature is more pregnant with the dangers of the finite mind (and its yearnings for conviction) than Dr. Slop's forceps, designed to engage matter with precisely the right force, but sufficiently flawed, despite its set screws and other mechanical precautions, that one's nose is in constant danger. Needless to say, his other "instruments of deliv-

Figure 7. *Sleeping Adela and Edzio,* by Bruno Schulz, circa 1934.

ery" are instruments of death, instruments, significantly enough, that impale and carve the infant skull for its easier removal from the womb.

I have, on occasion, considered Sterne a satirist in the tradition of Swift, Pope, and the Scriblerians, but nothing he ever wrote is equal to the savage indignation informing Woolf's portrait of Sir William. She begins with a slight undercurrent of irony at his expense: "a heavy look, a weary look (the stream of patients being so incessant, the responsibilities and privileges of his profession so onerous), which weariness, together with his grey hairs, increased the extraordinary distinction of his presence and gave him the reputation . . . not merely of lightning skill and almost infallible accuracy in diagnosis, but of sympathy; tact; understanding of the human soul."[24] His diagnosis of Septimus Warren Smith marks the conviction of true science: "He could see the first moment they came into the room (the Warren Smiths they were called); he was certain directly he saw the man; it was a case of extreme gravity. It was a case of complete breakdown—complete physical and nervous breakdown . . . he ascertained in two or three minutes (writing answers to questions, murmured discreetly, on a pink card)."[25] The repressed anger in this description is obvious enough, but at its core is Woolf's own engagement with history, as we recall how and why Septimus has become a challenge to the medical profession (even if only a three-minute challenge), a victim of that warfare Uncle Toby practices so benignly (in the eyes of many a Tobyphile, at any rate) on his bowling green; in fact, is Woolf not recalling Sterne aurally when she defines Septimus's war as "the European War—that little *shindy* of schoolboys with gunpowder"?[26]

Against the "heroism" of warfare, the human attempt to subdue matter to its own dimensions, as Swift would have it,[27] Septimus has an alternative vision, that he has "committed an appalling crime and been condemned to death by human nature."[28] We might well ask, what is the *matter* with Septimus, the primary medical (and psychiatric) question, but Septimus already knows that, as a defender of what *mattered* to some people, he has destroyed—and seen destroyed—what *mattered* to others. The aborting of the infinite fecundity of matter, the inability after the fact to keep straight the difference between what matters (what we preserve) and what did not seem to matter (what we discard, destroy), that is his disease—the matter of (and with) his mind. Sir William's diagnosis is, it would seem, wonderfully correct: "he was not mad, was he? Sir William said he never spoke of 'madness'; he called it not having a sense of proportion."[29]

Is it possible that modernism, as both form and matter, can be defined simply by its lack of Sir William's "sense of proportion"? Similarly, is Sterne's purchase on modernism the fact that his eponymous hero is not born until the third volume, and is only five years of age when the ninth volume concludes—epical signifiers of disproportion? Obviously so, but with one vital qualification if we are to distinguish between modernism and postmodernism, each of which might claim "lack of proportion" as its raison d'être, each of which lays claim to Sterne (if not to Woolf) as its prescient ancestor. Woolf can, perhaps, help us locate the distinction.

Sir William is, I would suggest, Woolf's own prescient ancestor of postmodernism, for his worship of proportion—"Proportion, divine proportion, Sir William's goddess"[30]—is ultimately science's response to the world's formlessness, to the lamentable fecundity of matter that calls forth the mind's unceasing efforts—by means of forms, formulas, formulations— to exercise sufficient control. If Sir William attempts to "cure" the world of its "prophetic Christs and Christesses, who prophesied the end of the world, or the advent of God," by prescribing a glass of milk and better sleeping habits, so too has postmodernism attempted, at long last, to relieve the world of "Christ (a common delusion),"[31] insofar as Christ, in John's Gospel formulation, is the Word, the Logos, the guarantee that there is, after all, some relationship between our words and the world—or, as Sterne's Yorick would have it, between a mother and her son, despite the best reasonings of canon law and visitation diners (*TS* 4.30.393–94). If Sir William finds madness in the "advent of God," so the postmodernist finds it there as well, although *God* is not as useful a theoretical word as *truth, determinacy, certainty* (that is, *untruth, indeterminacy, uncertainty*) or any of the other evasions of late twentieth-century dogmatism. What unites the doctor and the theorist, in other words, is their absolute embrace of positive knowledge, not as an alternative possibility within matter's fecundity, but as the signifier of matter's impotence in the hands of science and the theoretical, the power of the human mind.

In both instances, however, it is not the content of the theory that matters (after all, as Woolf astutely notes, "we know nothing about—the nervous system, the human brain"),[32] but the reductive systemization that makes possible the Harley Street professionalism of the physician, the academic institutionalization of the theorist: the certainties of the politician. For "Proportion has a sister," Woolf writes,

> less smiling, more formidable, a Goddess even now engaged—in the heat and sands of India, the mud and swamp of Africa, the purlieus of London, wherever, in short, the climate or the devil tempts men to fall from the true belief which is her own. . . . Conversion is her name and she feasts on the wills of the weakly, loving to impress, to impose, adoring her own features stamped on the face of the populace. At Hyde Park Corner on a tub she stands preaching. . . . How he would work—how toil to raise funds, propagate reforms, initiate institutions! But Conversion, fastidious Goddess, loves blood better than brick, and feasts most subtly on the human will.[33]

It is modernism's acutely nervous foreshadowing of the "Goddess of Conversion"—a foreshadowing arising, perhaps, from the events ticking all across Europe and Asia from the mid-nineteenth century to the doppelgänger explosions of communism and fascism—that separates modernism from postmodernism. As modernism wanes, "conversion" reenters the marketplace of ideas as a new mode of orthodoxy and respectability, the nonaesthetics of a world in which everything is political; it is a world Sterne, Schulz, and Woolf deplored. Indeed, Sterne's own nervous foreshadowing of the decline of Christian thought—"I hesitate not one moment to affirm, that in half a century, at this rate, we shall have no souls at all; which being the period beyond which I doubt likewise of the existence of the Christian faith, 'twill be one advantage that both of 'em will be exactly worn out together" (*TS* 7.14.595)—ties him far more closely to the modernist than to the postmodernist. We see this not only in his creation of Walter Shandy, that great converter through logic and argumentation, but even more so in his figure of Uncle Toby, whose bowling-green activities bespeak a world at war, much in the same way that Sir William in Harley Street and the preacher on his tub at Hyde Park Corner (Sterne's great progenitor Swift is surely summoned by that image) reinscribe for Woolf (and Septimus) the horrors of war. To suggest that Septimus's guilt is madness, as Sir William does, is perhaps the mirror image of the suggestion that Uncle Toby is innocent; in both instances, we fail to recognize the impetus that drives both Sterne and the modernist artist: a dread of the orthodox, the straight line, the insistence of form over matter, the reformation of matter by way of conforming it to the dimensions of one's own science, one's own theories, one's own militant occupation of the seemingly empty spaces of the world, otherwise known as what "matters" to other people.

It is to Sterne's credit that he never confuses the straight line of orthodoxy with that mode of Christianity that lovingly embraces all that cannot be known or contained. Schulz, with his strong acquaintance with kabbalistic Judaism, shares that same sense of religion, not as definitive truth but as infinite possibility. It is not, finally, Christianity that modernism seeks to recover (as a careful reading of the greatest of modernist poets, T. S. Eliot, would show), but art and metaphysics, both of which were most overtly manifested in Western thought in the wake of ineffable monotheism.

Bruno Schulz, Virginia Woolf, and Laurence Sterne would not necessarily agree with this *form*ulation of their work, or the notion of modernism it entails. In responding to the exercise of finding the modernist connection in Sterne, I have already accepted the postulate that some "sense of proportion" exists between the two, that it would require only a proper ordering of observations and insights to "solve" the equation, repair our previous lack of knowledge, cure our ignorance. I suspect, however, they would—in their own unique voices—ask me to dismount my hobby-horse. Or perhaps—if I have been able to capture the modernist spirit in any way—they might see in my zigzag approach to the question not Uncle Toby's tactical march to the very center of the place (which, we note, may prove a place of impotence after all), but the paths of a maze (another Shandean image) from which neither I nor my reader can emerge with any positive sense of the ground traversed, much less a sense of proportion or convertible knowledge. Life and art converted into knowledge: the devastating path of conversion on which Hegel set us in the interval between Sterne, who foresaw his visionary scheme (our systems of knowledge, Tristram declares [*TS* 1.21.72], have "gradually been creeping upwards towards that Ακμή of their perfections, from which . . . we cannot possibly be far off"), and Schulz and Woolf, who had to live with its consequences. All three authors worked to invert that seeming inevitability of matter subdued to knowledge, all three in their own ways (and it is, I would maintain, a modernist credo—if modernists had credos) worked to convert knowledge back into art and thus into life. In that celebration of art (and life), Sterne joined with Schulz and Woolf to shape a modernist possibility: ☞ "But this is not matter of SYSTEM; . . . nor is it matter of BREVIARY——for I make no man's creed but my own——nor matter of FACT——at least that I know of; but 'tis matter copulative and introductory to what follows" (*TS* 8.8.665). That this is the eighth and last paragraph in the eighth chapter of the eighth volume of *Tristram Shandy* is probably—but not assuredly—an accident: the modernist mind can leave it at that.

Originally published in *The Cambridge Companion to Laurence Sterne* (2009).

Notes

1 See my essays "Proust's Influence on Sterne: A Remembrance of Things to Come," *Modern Language Notes* 103, no. 5 (1988): 1031–55; *Tristram Shandy: A Book for Free Spirits* (New York: Twayne, 1994); "Three Sentimental Journeys: Sterne, Shklovsky, Svevo," *Shandean* 11 (1999): 126–34; and "Reading Sterne through Proust and Levinas," reprinted as chapter 7 in this volume.

2 New, "Proust's Influence on Sterne," 1053.

3 For the broad spectrum of twentieth-century authors interested in Sterne, see the essays collected in David Pierce and Peter de Voogd, eds., *Laurence Sterne in Modernism and Postmodernism* (Amsterdam: Rodopi, 1996); see also its list

of works cited. Pierce's introduction to this volume cites Joyce's famous invocation of Sterne to explain his attempt "to build many planes of narrative with a single esthetic purpose" in *Finnegans Wake* (10).

4 *Street of Crocodiles* is quoted from *The Complete Fiction of Bruno Schulz*, trans. Celina Wieniewska (New York: Walker, 1989). For Schulz's life, see Jerzy Ficowski, *Regions of the Great Heresy: Bruno Schulz, a Biographical Portrait*, trans. Theodosia Robertson (New York: Norton, 2003).

5 See Miriam L. Wallace, "Thinking Back through Our Others: Rereading Sterne and Resisting Joyce in *The Waves*," *Woolf Studies Annual* 9 (2003): 193–220; while the essay itself is an example of postmodernism run amok, the quotations garnered from Woolf's essays and manuscripts concerning Sterne are well worth recovering.

6 On Nietzsche and Sterne, see Duncan Large, "'The Freest Writer': Nietzsche on Sterne," *Shandean* 11 (1999): 9–29. The phrase "freest writer" is from *Human, All Too Human* (1886), quoted by Large (11): "How, in a book for free spirits, could there be no mention of Laurence Sterne, whom Goethe honoured as the freest spirit of his century! Let him accept the honour here of being called the freest writer of all time, in comparison with whom all others seem stiff, square, intolerant, and boorishly direct." I discuss this passage at length in *A Book for Free Spirits*, 15–17, 113–18.

7 Schulz, *Street of Crocodiles*, 24.

8 The translation reads "Treatise," but as others have noted, "Tractate," with its allusion to Talmudic commentary, is perhaps a more telling rendition.

9 Schulz, *Street of Crocodiles*, 27.

10 Schulz, 29.

11 Schulz, 29.

12 Schulz, 30.

13 See James A. Work, ed., *Tristram Shandy* (New York: Odyssey Press, 1940), lx.

14 Schulz, *Street of Crocodiles*, 30.

15 Schulz, 30.

16 Schulz, 31.

17 *Letters of John Keats*, ed. H. E. Rollins (Cambridge, MA: Harvard University Press, 1958), vol. 1, 192 (December 21, 1817). For Sterne's understanding of tartuffery, a mode of domineering hypocrisy that pervades his satire, see New, *A Book for Free Spirits*, 113–34.

18 Schulz, *Street of Crocodiles*, 31.

19 Schulz, 33.

20 Schulz, 34.

21 See, in particular, sermon 29, "Our conversation in Heaven," and the discussion of it as a commentary on *A Sentimental Journey* (*SJ* 273–75, n. to 38.4–13).

Sterne and the Modernist Moment · 211

22 Cf. *SJ* 116: "But there is nothing unmixt in this world; and some of the gravest of our divines have carried it so far as to affirm, that enjoyment itself was attended even with a sigh—and that the greatest *they knew of,* terminated *in a general way,* in little better than a convulsion." For a discussion of this passage and its roots in Montaigne (another modernist), see *SJ* 346–47, n. to 116.7; see also *SJ* 124 ("The Conquest").

23 See the concluding aposiopesis of *A Sentimental Journey*: "so that when I stretch'd out my hand, I caught hold of the Fille de Chambre's / END OF VOL. II" (*SJ* 165); see also Jerzy Ficowski, ed., *The Drawings of Bruno Schulz* (Evanston, IL: Northwestern University Press, 1990), esp. "The Book of Idolatry," 52–107.

24 Virginia Woolf, *Mrs Dalloway*, ed. David Bradshaw (Oxford: Oxford World's Classics, 2000), 81.

25 Woolf, 81.

26 Woolf, 81 (emphasis added). Cf. Toby's "apologetical oration": "If, when I was a school-boy, I could not hear a drum beat, but my heart beat with it—was it my fault?" (*TS* 6.32.555).

27 "For what man in the natural state or course of thinking, did ever conceive it in his power to reduce the notions of all mankind exactly to the same length, and breadth, and height of his own? Yet this is the first humble and civil design of all innovators in the empire of reason." Jonathan Swift, *A Tale of a Tub and Other Works*, ed. Angus Ross and David Woolley (Oxford: Oxford University Press, 1986), 80.

28 Woolf, *Mrs Dalloway*, 82.

29 Woolf, 82.

30 Woolf, 84.

31 Woolf, 84–85.

32 Woolf, 84.

33 Woolf, 85; cf. *TS* 2.5.106: "When a man gives himself up to the government of a ruling passion,——or, in other words, when his HOBBY-HORSE grows headstrong,——farewell cool reason and fair discretion." Once again, we find Swift's *Tale of a Tub* underlying the notion: "But when a man's fancy gets *astride* on his reason, when imagination is at cuffs with the senses, and common understanding as well as common sense, is kicked out of doors; the first proselyte he makes is himself, and when that is once compassed, the difficulty is not so great in bringing over others" (82). Swift's proselyte and Woolf's converter meet, I would maintain, not only in Walter's study, but on Toby's bowling green as well: warfare is, after all, persuasion by other means.

9

Richardson's *Sir Charles Grandison* and Sterne

A Study in Influence

In an essay revisiting, yet again, Sterne's purported relationship to the novel tradition of Fielding, Smollett, and Richardson, Tim Parnell offers as one small piece of evidence Alan Dugald McKillop's 1956 suggestion that Richardson's close attention to gesture in *Sir Charles Grandison* may have influenced Sterne. It is one of the more convincing suggestions among the many that have been reiterated by Tom Keymer and others to place Sterne in the "novel" tradition of midcentury, even if as a parodist, but it leads Parnell to preface his response to McKillop's suggestion with what must surely have occurred to most readers: "Hard as it is to imagine Sterne ploughing his way through *Grandison.*" He then goes on to suggest, quite rightly I believe, that if Sterne did indeed derive his interest in gesture from Richardson, it was by no means as a target for parody.[1]

Having "ploughed" my own way as a scholarly editor through all of Sterne's works and, most recently, *Sir Charles Grandison,*[2] I was quite surprised to find many points of congruity between them, enough, in fact, to lead me to wonder why this should be the case. As an editor of both *Tristram Shandy* and *A Sentimental Journey* I found no verbal echoes but instead a strong argument against considering Sterne's fictions within the novel "tradition"; indeed, I found quite a few arguments to the contrary and in support of my suspicion that Sterne as a novelist was merely the rather haphazard construct of later literary historians, those unwilling to account for other modes of prose fiction and instead using "novel" as a convenient catchall label for any imaginative work in prose. Now, looking through our annotations to *Grandison,* wherein Sterne is far more often cited than Defoe, Behn, Manley, Haywood, or Smollett,[3] it seemed imperative to reopen the case for *Grandison* as an influence on Sterne.[4]

Literary influence between authors is usually posited, logically enough, when we can find a later author borrowing directly from an earlier; this claim is greatly facilitated by textual evidence, the clear echo of a sentence or passage, or by biographical evidence, that is, when authors have specifically named their influences, their favorite authors and favorite works; or, in the case of parody and satire, authors particularly scorned. Hence, when Richardson specifically quotes "the words of a great poet" that "*The godlike man ... has nothing to conceal*" we can find the exact text in Edward Young, and find also a second reference to Young a few pages further on, as "my favourite author." And we can also point to the fact that Richardson printed or reprinted works by Young no fewer than twenty-six times.[5] Similarly for Sterne, when we are told that Yorick carries an account of a battle between "*Gymnast* and captain *Tripet*" we can be certain that the book is *Gargantua and Pantagruel*, and can easily annotate the quoted material (*TS* 5.28–29.463–64) as from that work, indeed, quoted verbatim from the Urquhart-Motteux translation; we can also, for further proof, point to his probable first attempt at what became *Tristram Shandy*, his "Rabelaisian Fragment" (see *TS*, Notes 376–77).[6]

Less convincing as evidence of influence, but still having much credence, is the belief that earlier authors permeated the literary world in which later authors find themselves; can anyone writing poetry, drama, or fiction in England in 1760 not have been "influenced" by Shakespeare, Cervantes, and Milton—not to mention Scripture? We might also suggest authors of the preceding half century—some still read in our author's time, some not—who would have left their imprint: Pope and Swift, Thomson and Young, certainly; Eusden and Blackmore, Philips and Tate, less likely.[7] In annotating *Grandison*, for example, it is impossible to avoid Richardson's borrowings from Restoration stage figures, most particularly Charlotte's numerous invocations of Congreve's Millamant;[8] or, less directly, the influence of late Restoration "she-tragedies" (but stretching back to *Hamlet*'s Ophelia) on Clementina's mad scenes.

With still less certainty we might posit not an authorial or performance aura but rather an influence of form or style on the one hand, zeitgeist on the other. This may be what Keymer seems to be uncovering as influences;

214 · Textual and Critical Intersections

Sterne may or may not have read Fielding and Richardson, but by 1760 their efforts had created an environment in which any long fiction, particularly a "biographical" narrative, must have been influenced by them. Similarly, an epistemological urge for a more "realistic" fiction must have had its effect on all those writing after Locke's *Essay concerning Human Understanding* (1689) changed the direction of philosophical discourse.[9] Similarly, those who continue to accept the nineteenth-century notion of a dormant eighteenth-century church and a concomitant century-long "ascent" toward secularism will find that worldview reflected in the literature of the period. One discovers, in short, that at this level of influence studies one is able to paint with a far broader brush than that supplied by verbatim borrowings, but with far less precision. At its furthest reaches, we have fully entered the realm of interpretation.

And yet this stage does not yet exhaust the scale of credibility regarding influence, because beyond what I have just been describing is an emerging industry fostered by both internet resources, and by social and political concerns. If we accept that all authors of long fictions published in the 1760s had to be influenced by Fielding and Richardson, does it follow that they would also have to be influenced by Defoe, Behn, Smollett, and Haywood, or by William Goodall, Francis Coventry, William Toldervy, and Edward Kimber? The last four names are gathered quite unfairly from the footnotes to Parnell's essay simply to emphasize their distinction from the first four. One could, of course, spiral even further down the oiled slide into obscurity, but Goodall and company (not to mention the writers skewered in the *Dunciad*) can serve to represent a new level of influence discourse, one I find particularly disturbing. Setting aside Smollett's nonfiction, *Travels through France and Italy,* we have no evidence that Sterne was aware of or influenced by the first four writers, whatever might be our own waning and waxing interest in them; the second four represent authors who wrote in a tradition that Wayne C. Booth labeled self-conscious narrative fiction, and into which he tried to place Sterne.[10]

We might want to believe that an earlier such forgotten work, *Life and Memoirs of Mr. Ephraim Tristram Bates, Commonly Called Corporal Bates* (1756) did indeed influence Sterne, but the sole reason for that supposition is the obvious one;[11] for other such titles, we have Parnell's puzzlement that despite Booth, "Keymer's is the solitary sustained attempt to read Sterne in relation to the fiction written by his contemporaries." He promises "far more attention" to such works in the future, which is, I fear, an accurate prediction. With the internet, we can now search for any few words in Sterne's writings, find them in an earlier work, and posit an influence.[12] More and more we are able to dredge from well-deserved obscurity the literary detritus of a society, whether for social and political reasons or simply because we are enabled by search engines to do so—or because, to offer Johnson's always pertinent observation, "Truth, Sir, is a cow which will yield such people no more milk, and so they are gone to milk the bull."[13] At some point in the scale of influence, however, these dwellers in the depths simply do not matter (excepting, obviously, a verifiable quotation higher on the credibility scale); it is perhaps for that reason alone that no one until Keymer picked up on Booth's efforts, although he does so with a quite different purpose: to reinsert Sterne into the novel tradition rather than distinguish him from it. For the same reason, a century after Hughes's recovery, *Tristram Bates* remains as only three minimal footnotes in the Florida Edition (*TS*, Notes 76, 93–94, 144–45); critics have found nothing to say about the relationship between the two works because, in fact, Sterne and the anonymous author never entered into conversation with one another. I will return to this point more than once in this essay, but suffice it here to keep in mind that authors can borrow verbatim or otherwise from authors with whom they are not in conversation and, conversely, not borrow in any obvious way from those with whom they are richly and necessarily engaged.

There is another, less traveled road to approach this question of influence and its varying degrees of credibility, one that bypasses both the influencer and influenced. There is always a third party present, the reader who posits the influence, particularly that very specialized reader, the scholarly editor or critic for whom finding relationships is stock-in-trade. The perception of an influence is always lodged in the beholder's eye, which accounts for the fact that hundreds of years after publication a source can be found where no one had ever before thought to look. Particularly pertinent to this discussion, then, is an observation about the work of scholar-critics that is rarely if ever discussed, the proximity of texts in their own reading history. That is to say, our reading (like life itself) is always sequential, so that when we begin to analyze one work (E) we will always be bringing along with us the works (A, B, C, D) we have most recently read. This is rather obvious for scholars who are also active instructors (as most are) because they are accustomed to reading books in the sequential confines of a designed course; for example, surrounding *Tristram* in the all too usual eighteenth-century "novel" course will be Fielding and Richardson on one end, Burney and Austen on the other. Moreover, instructors will almost certainly link one book to the next, asking students at each step to comment on the development they perceive as the course progresses. Even the perception of differences is locked into the overall structure of a sequence that necessarily seems compelled to move from "beginning" to "conclusion."[14] It is often said to annotators, as a rule of thumb, that the nearest source is the most telling, but nothing, to resituate that advice somewhat, is nearer to the mind of annotators than their just previous readings, nothing more vital to literary critics than the works they are reading immediately prior to or alongside the work under discussion.

Perhaps because it is so obvious, this proximity is rarely mentioned as an element of source studies, much less of criticism in general. Surely, however, to offer a Levinasian reading of Sterne or to point out John Norris's influence on him (to implicate myself) is the result of having read Levinas or Norris with Sterne something of a fixture (not to say hobby-horse) of my mind.[15] I can find little fault with this procedure except our frequent blindness to it; as scholars we read continuously, and each reading influences the next thing we read; and if one text is in our mind more than any other, then readings of multiple works may be said to circle around that one work; we are consciously or unconsciously looking for signs of influence, possibilities of application, similarities and differences that will tie any two titles together.

Thus it is that I came away from more than a decade's immersion in *Sir Charles Grandison* with the dubious conviction not only that Sterne "ploughed" through it, but that it may well be the key to understanding two seemingly irreconcilable aspects of Sterne's works, the bawdry and the Christian sentimentalism. By qualifying "sentimentalism" with "Christian" I hope to distinguish Sterne's (and Richardson's) sentimentalism from its secular version, the gemütlichkeit that begins and ends with the warmth of a self-approving heart. Rather, the original Man of Feeling for both writers, I would suggest, is Jesus, and sentimentalism is always explored against the human effort, as Tristram describes it, to get *"out of the body, in order to think well"* (*TS* 7.7.593). He attributes the saying to the Pythagoreans and offers the sentence in Greek as well as in English. The Florida editors admitted to being unable to find the passage among the Pythagoreans, a good indication that even when authors tell us their sources they need to be verified by the reader. In this instance, subsequent reading found the entire passage in an author we have lately come to realize was very important to both Sterne and Richardson, namely John Norris of Bemerton (1657–1711), in this instance, his *Practical Discourses upon Several Divine Subjects* (1691).[16]

For Richardson, sentimentalism is a very similar struggle against self-ishness and self-centeredness, or as Harriet says at one point, "Self, my dear Lucy, is a very wicked thing; a sanctifier, if one would give way to its partialities, of actions, which, in others, we should have no doubt to condemn." Sir Charles, too, speaks of the need to "divest" himself "of Self."[17] That is to say, for both writers, sentimentalism suggests a struggle of human beings to be more than human; paradoxically, when they are found to be humane (e.g., "head over heels in love"), it is not because their true natures have been revealed, but just the opposite—sentimentalism is an act of strength (through faith) by which we overcome our fallen state, the condition of man that is the starting point for both Richardson and Sterne.

This fallen state, both authors also seem to agree, must account for three entities: the body, the mind, and the soul. This is, without doubt, reductive, but a useful entry to an eighteenth-century construct still reliant on a theology that was also, and perhaps not accidentally, based on the triune nature of the divine. We can substitute other equally simplistic (because unexamined) terms (e.g., *sense, will, spirit;* or, *feeling, reason, heart*), but will always return to the existence of an entity we understand as our sensate body, a second we label our thinking mind, and a third entity that we do not understand because it is other than body or mind—like the word *God, soul* is the name the century (following a long tradition) gave to an unknowable, ineffable, unnamable essence, the existence of which seemed necessary to almost everyone. Moreover, as part of being human, authors will spend their century and their intellects (again, following a long tradition) trying to know precisely what they label unknowable. We may trace, in fact, from their beginnings in Scripture to the present day the efforts of both philosophy and theology to define what the eighteenth century, with the confidence of its Christian inheritance, continued to call soul, without coming to a conclusion more telling, perhaps, than that all this intellectual energy is just one further manifestation of human vanity, Self's appetitive

218 · Textual and Critical Intersections

need to assert its own significance. The belief that human thought is driven by human appetites is no more than to reclaim for the center of Christianity, the Fall in Eden; perhaps not fortuitously, even the author of *An Essay concerning Human Understanding* acknowledges this centrality in the very first sentence of his *Reasonableness of Christianity* (1695): "'Tis obvious to anyone who reads the New Testament, that the Doctrine of Redemption, and consequently of the Gospel, is founded upon the Supposition of *Adam*'s Fall. To understand therefore what we are restored to by Jesus Christ, we must consider what the Scripture shews we lost by *Adam*."[18]

Sterne highlighted the body's assertive nature by means of his infamous bawdry and innuendo; and Richardson, by means of his equally infamous puritanical refusal to acknowledge its existence. Yet one immediately recognizes, I hope, the carelessness of *infamous* opinions: as was early recognized by at least some of Sterne's more astute contemporaries, his bawdry produces no bodily appetites, no lustful thoughts; we have to strain our moral urges to wax indignant (as many, no doubt, did) over a furred cap that is worth stroking in just the right way.[19] On the other hand, few authors in the eighteenth century entered more readily into the sexual appetites of both their characters and readers than did Richardson. Fielding spotted this immediately, and one might well believe that Richardson's hostile response had something to do with being caught out. The pursuit of innocence is obviously not always erotic and titillating, but in Richardson's hands it most certainly is.[20] We do not need to strain our morality to condemn the male pursuit, if only because Richardson so clearly points our way, but we do have to pretend not to be aroused (male and female reader alike) by Richardson's elaborate and detailed descriptions of beauty and innocence threatened with violation. The long history of literature, up to the present day, indicates that the pleasures of literature do not always coincide with our ethics.

The opening volume of Richardson's final novel deals almost exclusively with the same situation, beauty and innocence threatened by violence, the kidnapping of Harriet by the villainous (if inept) imitation of Lovelace, Sir Hargrave. When that situation resolves itself, however, it does not end the novel's erotic appeal but opens a new opportunity for the reader, the contemplation of a polygamous relationship, as the eponymous hero is set to decide between—and the physical description is vital—the *loveliest* woman in England and the *loveliest* woman in Italy;[21] "sister excellencies" he calls them, and Richardson's correspondence while writing *Grandison* indicates his willingness to tease his female circle with the option of Grandison having both women. Mr. B.'s and Lovelace's fantasies become in *Grandison* the underlying plot.[22] It is almost impossible to read the correspondence without realizing that both author and recipient were aroused by the notion; on riskier grounds, but still quite possible, one might see in the correspondence (especially with Lady Bradshaigh) Richardson's own displaced desire for multiple wives, often, as with his hero, labeling the women he wrote to as "sisters" or "daughters." This too is less innocent than it might seem, since incest also hovers over the novel, in Charlotte's all-too-obvious attraction to her brother and in his young ward's sexual awakening to him as well. Moreover, these are not concealed desires: Grandison's sisters are fully aware of mutual attraction between Harriet and Sir Charles (they never are "brother" and "sister" despite his oft-repeated "third sister"), all three women are aware of Emily's idolatry, and Sir Charles is also not blind to the situation. The world of *Grandison* is aquiver with physical desire.[23]

Still if we encounter a passage in *Grandison* like the following, we almost certainly would pass it over without comment, as seems to have been true up to now. The situation is one in which Sir Charles tries to discover whether Charlotte is open to a marriage with Lord G. She, in turn, is interested in playing the coquette as long as possible; as Richardson often does in the novel, he creates a dialogic scene, striving perhaps for the sharp repartee, as already noted, of the Restoration stage:

> [*Sir Ch.*] But perhaps, madam [Harriet], to me, you will be so good, as, in one word, to say, No, or Yes, for Charlotte.
>
> *Miss Gr.* What, Sir, to be *given up* without a preface!—I beg your pardon. *Less* than *ten words* shall not do, I assure you, tho' from my sister Harriet.
>
> *Sir Ch.* Who given up, Charlotte? *yourself?* If so, I have my answer.
>
> *Miss Gr.* Or Lord G.—I have not said which. Would you have my poor Lord rejected by a slighting monosyllable only?
>
> *Lady L.* Mad girl!
>
> *Miss Gr.* Why, Lady L., don't you see that Sir Charles wants to take me by *implication?* But my Lord G. is neither so soon lost, nor Charlotte so easily won.[24]

220 · Textual and Critical Intersections

Sterne never, to my knowledge, plays with *monosyllable* but many others did, including Fielding in *Shamela*.[25] More surprising, Richardson also uses it in *Pamela II,* where Pamela recounts an evening spent with Mr. B.'s rakish friends, their discussion concluding with affirming the way Sir Jacob was tricked into acknowledging Pamela: "Ye——as, by my Soul, (drawling out the affirmative Monosyllable) I was used most scurvily; faith I was . . . for I have hardly been able to hold up my Head like a Man ever since."[26] Rivero does not annotate the passage, and perhaps it is only because I come to Richardson from Sterne that I find bawdiness in it; were *monosyllable* the only suspect word I might have been more cautious, but put together with "hold up my Head like a Man" surely one may grow suspicious. And when in *Grandison monosyllable* recurs, and warrants from the speaker's sister, "Mad girl!," one may be justified in finding Richardson not only writing a bawdy exchange, but allowing the joke to be stated and knowingly reacted to by female characters. Still, for generations of readers who believe Richardson's writings indicate a mind diametrically opposed to whatever was Sterne's way of thinking, the annotator might be the culprit. Guiltily then, keeping Sterne in mind as is inevitable given my previous annotating of his text, the very next sentence is unfortunately also susceptible to bawdy interpretation: *implication* (Latin *implico* = enfold, embrace, join) is used in *Tristram Shandy* (*TS* 3.7.198) with obvious sexual application, to describe a knot made "by the duplication and return of the two ends of the strings through the annulus or noose made by the second *implication* of them—to get them slipp'd and undone by——I hope you apprehend me" (the Shandean wink at the end of the passage ensures that the unwary reader returns to get Sterne's, well, *implication*).

It is almost certain that few scholars, even those willing to acknowledge Richardson's bodily oriented novels, would want to follow me down this path, so obvious will it seem to them that only someone who has a Shandean-filled head could come up with the possibility that Samuel Richardson (and his readers!) enjoyed a bawdy joke. It is this Shandean bent, however, that I wish to emphasize in this discussion of sources, analogues, and influences, because we all approach the target text with some other readings uppermost in our mind; were it not Sterne's works but, say, Aubin's novels, we would almost certainly read the passage in a more straightforward and literal manner: Charlotte's "slighting monosyllable" refers only to the yes or no required by Sir Charles; and her thought of Sir

Charles taking her by *implication* (and the italics are Richardson's, always a careful user of emphasis), means only that her silence will be interpreted as a no.[27]

On the other hand, the possible validity of a Shandean reading of this passage may be in our minds when we turn back to an earlier moment in the same volume. Here the assembled company are discussing "Love and Courtship," a topic on which Sir Charles proves to be as expert as on every other subject under consideration in this voluminous novel. His conclusion is to hold in abeyance any declaration of love to avoid driving "a Lady into reserves; since that would be to rob myself of those innocent freedoms . . . to which an honourable Lover might think himself intitled; and which might help him [Don't be affrighted, Ladies!] to develope the plaits and folds of the female heart."[28] The women are indeed a bit shocked, and cousin Everard (the rakish bad seed of the family) sums up the feeling with a proverbial observation: "Sir Charles may with more safety *steal a horse,* than I *look over the hedge.*"[29] As Richardson indicated many times in his correspondence, and as Harriet and Charlotte attest on more than one occasion, his virtuous hero had to be given "rakish" qualities if he were not to turn into a Mr. Hickman, virtuous but dull. How exactly is Sir Charles's observation rakish?

In her annotation to the passage, Jocelyn Harris reads *plaits* as meaning "hidden recesses, implying artifice and deceit," which gives the word a rather chastising tone. However, the connection with *folds* may suggest a more playful usage (plaits = pleats), a metaphor of robing and disrobing. Johnson's *Dictionary* gives credence to this reading with his definition of *develop* as "to disengage from something that enfolds and conceals; to disentangle"; his illustration is from Pope's *Dunciad,* book 4, lines 268–70: "We bring to one dead level ev'ry mind. / Then take him to devellop, if you can, / And hew the Block off, and get out the Man." Johnson's illustration for *plait,* from Addison's *Remarks on Several Parts of Italy* (1705), is also apropos: "'tis very difficult to trace out the Figure of a Vest thro' all the Plaits and Foldings of the Drapery."[30] At this point, one is tempted to suggest, again, that Sterne hovers in Richardson's pages (or vice versa): "there was a plainness and simplicity of thinking [in Uncle Toby], with such an unmistrusting ignorance of the plies and foldings of the heart of women" (*TS* 6.29.550). Yorick seems to understand Sir Charles at this point better than most, and thus he protests to the Count that he has come to France

222 · Textual and Critical Intersections

to spy not on the nakedness of its women, but on "the *nakedness* of their hearts" (*SJ* 111).[31]

If modern readers have missed the "implications" of these similarities, Richardson's first editor (of his letters) did not. Anna Laetitia Barbauld very acutely uses the same language to comment on the author's understanding of the female character: "Richardson had been accused of giving a coldness to his female characters in the article of love . . . but he has made ample amends for the imputed omission in his Grandison, where he has entered into the passion with all the minuteness, and delicacy, and warmth, that could be desired, and shewn the female heart to be open to him in all its folds and recesses."[32] Barbauld was no fan of Sterne, but that she singles out this image of the folds and recesses as both delicate and warm seems to suggest that she was familiar with its potential sexual connotations. Had she recalled Lovelace's usage, she would have had no doubt—indeed, perhaps she had remembered: "the seal [of Clarissa's and Anna's letters in his hand] would have yielded to the touch of my warm finger . . . and the folds, as other plications have done, opened of themselves to oblige my curiosity."[33] And lest we assume that only a despicable rake could speak in that manner, we may summarize what has been suggested with one final passage from *Grandison,* where Sir Charles "innocently" plays the rake with Lady Beauchamp: "Surely, Lady Beauchamp, a man of common *penetration* may see to the *bottom* of a woman's heart. A *cunning* woman cannot hide *it*. A *good* woman will not."[34]

If reading Sterne before reading Richardson can produce bawdry in *Sir Charles Grandison,* can Sterne reciprocate by deepening our understanding of Richardson's Christian sentimentalism? The critical consensus would indicate otherwise: Richardson was a printer and novelist who aspired to the role of a parson; Sterne, a parson, who seemed to want to be anything but one. Nonetheless, having read *A Sentimental Journey* before *Grandison,* one will certainly hear an echo of one of its most frank passages in the following sentence and its several repetitions in the final volumes of Richardson's novel:

Adieu, my dear Dr. Bartlett [Sir Charles writes]. "In the highest of our pleasures, the sighing heart will remind us of imperfection." It is fit it should be so.[35]

Yet may there not be a fulness in joy [Harriet writes], that will mingle dissatisfaction with it? If there may, shall I be excused for my solemnity, if I deduce from thence an argument, that the human Soul is not to be fully satisfied by worldly enjoyments; and that therefore the completion of its happiness must be in another, a more perfect state?[36]

. . . this odd situation added *uneasiness* to my indisposition: A dissatisfaction, that I find will mingle with our highest enjoyments . . . [again Harriet's report].[37]

"The sighing heart," [Harriet remembers Sir Charles saying] "will remind us of imperfection, in the highest of our enjoyments."[38]

And one more illustration, again from Harriet, although it is not the last such occurrence in the work: "How often do I revolve that reflexion of your brother, that, in our happiest prospects, the sighing heart will confess imperfection!"[39] Within the context of *Sir Charles Grandison,* the sentiment voiced here may well be the Christian cement that binds the novel together. While writing a "comedy" companion piece to the "tragedy" that is *Clarissa,* Richardson's meaning is compounded in both instances by a Christian crosscurrent: Clarissa assuredly ascends to Heaven in what is, after all, a Divine Comedy; in *Grandison,* however, Heaven awaits another day, the characters all locked into an ongoing earthly life that remains a Pilgrim's Progress. Hence, although Sir Charles and Harriet are married and expecting a child, Clementina remains the deliberately unresolved third party, casting the pall of the mundane world over the bliss of the couple.[40] To a lesser extent, so also does the equally unresolved fate of "poor Emily" (the immediate reason for the last expression [with the "sighing heart"] of the sentiment quoted above).

Richardson could have heard the notion that the world is able to deliver only incomplete enjoyment countless times from the pulpit had he attended church; since he did not, in later life,[41] he could have found it in hundreds of sermons, so commonplace is the observation. Two occurrences (note, I do not say "sources"), however, are of particular pertinence to the discussion here. The observation is made, for example, in William Sherlock's *A Practical Discourse concerning Death* (1689), which reached

224 · Textual and Critical Intersections

a twenty-sixth edition in 1754, a book Harriet's grandmother is reading when Sir Charles surprises her with his visit and proposal to pursue Harriet, a dramatic moment in the novel[42]—and a visit recorded within the same letter in which Harriet, for the first time, voices the sentiment of life's incomplete joys. Sherlock's version is worth quoting:

> For setting aside the Miseries and Calamities, the Troubles and Inconveniences of this Life, which the happiest men are expos'd to (for our Experience tells us that there is no compleat and unmixt Happiness here;) setting aside, that this World is little else than a Scene of Misery to a great part of Mankind . . . yet if we were as happy as this World could make us, we should have no reason to complain that we must exchange it for a much greater Happiness.[43]

Richardson admired Sherlock and perhaps considered his contributions to Christian theology entirely, even increasingly, relevant. That is the conclusion I draw, with some hesitation, from a letter to Thomas Edwards in which he celebrates the timely republication of the "noble Discourses of Sherlock" as an apt foil to the deistic heresies espoused by Lord Bolingbroke in his just published posthumous *Works* (5 vols., 1754).[44] Sherlock is echoing, obviously, a long line of Christian sermonists in preaching a doctrine that would be invoked to argue for the existence of an afterlife as a balance for the sorrows in this world of virtuous believers, and for a soul characterized by its yearning for a happiness that no earthly delights can quench. The inadequacy or incompleteness of everything that the world calls pleasure is the ethical lesson repeated Sunday after Sunday during the entire century. Of course, in addition to sermons, Richardson would have found the sentiment in Pope's famous couplets: "Hope springs eternal in the human breast: / Man never Is, but always To be blest: / The soul, uneasy and confin'd from home, / Rests and expatiates in a life to come";[45] or in various passages from his favorite poet, Edward Young, his *Night Thoughts.*[46] Indeed, from the preacher in Ecclesiastes to Johnson's *Vanity of Human Wishes,* the sentiment's constant repetition can be matched only by the equally constant inability of human beings to accept its logic. It is this failure, perhaps, that energizes the efforts of authors like Richardson and Sterne to attempt another path, what we might label "ethical realism," for reconciling time-bound humanity to an eternal God.

A sermon published in 1760, and hence not possibly influencing *Grandison,* contains yet another restatement of the idea: "Lastly, When we reflect that this span of life, short as it is, is chequered with so many troubles, that there is nothing in this world springs up, or can be enjoyed without a mixture of sorrow, how insensibly does it incline us to turn our eyes and affections from so gloomy a prospect, and fix them upon that happier country, where afflictions cannot follow us, and where God will wipe away all tears from off our faces for ever and ever? Amen" (*Sermons* 102). The sermon is titled "Job's account of the shortness and troubles of life, considered" and appears in the second volume of *Sermons of Mr. Yorick,* published the same year *Tristram Shandy* awakened a London audience to the satire, comedy, and bawdry of the unknown Reverend Mr. Sterne from Sutton-on-the-Forest, Yorkshire. Sterne may have borrowed the sentiment from William Sherlock (he borrows elsewhere from him), although much of this particular sermon echoes William Wollaston's *Religion of Nature Delineated* (1722), a popular work of Christian ethics, in its eighth edition by 1759.[47]

Sterne's earlier version of this Christian truism, and its possible sources, is not, however, as important for my purposes as is his final statement of it in *A Sentimental Journey:* "But there is nothing unmixt in this world; and some of the gravest of our divines have carried it so far as to affirm, that enjoyment itself was attended even with a sigh—and that the greatest *they knew of,* terminated *in a general way,* in little better than a convulsion" (*SJ* 116). In case the bawdy intent of this restatement is missed, the rest of the brief chapter has Yorick's recall of the "grave and learned Bevoriskius" observing copulating sparrows on his sill and seeing them as a sign of God's blessings to "his creatures," followed by an intrusive exclamation from the narrative voice: "Ill fated Yorick! that the gravest of thy brethren should be able to write that to the world, which stains thy face with crimson, to copy in even thy study" (*SJ* 116–17). We are certainly not too far from another version of "incomplete enjoyment," Rochester's "The Imperfect Enjoyment," the sources for which stretch back to classical parallels in Ovid, Lucretius, and Petronius, up to French sources in the seventeenth century—but rarely to Christian ones.[48]

As the Florida annotation indicates, Sterne's immediate source for this passage is Pierre Charron's *Of Wisdome:* "Good things, delights and pleasures cannot be enioyed without some misture of euil and discommodity; *... Euen from amidst the fountains of delights do arise alwayes some bitternesse, which euen in the height of pleasure doe annoy.* The highest pleasure that is, hath a sign and a complaint to accompany it; and being come to perfection is but debility, a deiection of the minde, languishment."[49] Charron is here paraphrasing his mentor, Montaigne, the essay "That We Taste Nothing Pure." Without doubt, Montaigne himself opened the door to Charron's and Sterne's innuendo: "Of the Pleasures and Goods that we enjoy, there is not one exempt from some mixture of ill and inconvenience. . . . Our extreamest Pleasure has some Air of groaning and complaining in't. Would you not say that it is dying of Pain?"[50] The passage I elided in both Montaigne and Charron is a Latin tag from Lucretius, *Of the Nature of Things* (book 4, lines 1133–34), translated by Montaigne as "Something that's bitter will arise / Even amidst our jollities." It seems clear from Lucretius's context that the sexual suggestiveness originated with him, passed through Montaigne and Charron, and reached its culmination in Sterne.[51] The classical source is important because it again teaches what we all know but find difficult to accept: it would be impossible, perhaps, to find an observer of life, classical or Christian, early or late, priestly or promiscuous (or both), who would not subscribe to the truism endorsed by Sir Charles and Harriet: "In the highest of our pleasures, the sighing heart will remind us of imperfection."[52] It is significant that Richardson puts the sentence in quotation marks; and equally significant that as annotators we were not able to locate a specific source.

Or is the source the annotator himself? We can be certain that Richardson did not borrow his bawdry or his Christian vision from Sterne, but at this point can we share with Parnell the view that it is doubtful Sterne slogged his way through *Grandison?* We might instead surmise that *A Sentimental Journey* is a conscious rewriting of Richardson's "sentimental journey," remembering that much of *Grandison* takes place on the Continent. And that *Tristram Shandy* is a parody of Richardson's novel—after all, parodying his writings was almost a cottage industry by the 1760s. Sir Charles is perhaps the most organized, most potent, and most rational hero ever to be brought to life, often within his own detailed narrative account, in the pages of serious fiction; Tristram is the least organized, garters in hand, irrational and inept character ever to try to tell his own story. One might have thought of *Tristram Shandy* as primarily in the Scriblerian tradition, a satiric view of human nature, its excesses and deprivations, but perhaps instead it is a novelistic undoing of Samuel Richardson's ideal good man. Surely that would suit the narrative being written by those aspiring to fit Sterne into the purported dominant genre of the middle of the century, the novel, a sophisticated return to an earlier version of *Tristram* as an "anti-novel."[53]

This path would certainly assist readers in confronting the dilemma created by the reverberations linking the two authors, bawdy echoes, on the one hand, the notion, theological or otherwise, of incomplete enjoyments on the other. Once again, the third party in influence claims must acknowledge a role. Keymer's monograph on Sterne came ten years after his significant study of Richardson, in which Sterne plays a minor but telling part in a discussion of the indeterminacy of the ending of *Grandison*.[54] Unfortunately, finding "much higher moral and political stakes" in *Clarissa*, Keymer pursued indeterminacy in that novel, while more or less dismissing it in *Grandison* as a playful abdication of authorial responsibility.[55] In the same year as this study of *Clarissa* appeared, I too was drawn to the question of Sterne's "indeterminacy," in an essay suggesting the term was ill applied to *Tristram Shandy*.[56] With *Grandison* now more thoroughly in my head, I believe Keymer's linking of Sterne with Richardson's final novel was quite perceptive, although for reasons having less to do with the form of fiction—whether novel, biography, autobiography, or satire—and far more with their shared theology, or, again, with what I have labeled Christian sentimentalism.

We might begin with the observation that with all his other virtues, Sir Charles is the most feeling of men. For 750,000 words, he enacts the role of the physical and mental hero, the perfections of body and mind in the human trinity mentioned earlier. Even more perfect (the solecism is deliberate), he is the embodiment of sentimentalism, whether we locate sentiment in his soul—or, where Sterne most often locates sentiment, in his heart. He is in love, he is in agony; he is the good brother lamenting the follies of his sister, the good son, weeping for his mother, again the good son, following his religiously trained heart rather than his head in obeying his quite evil father. Above all, he is the man of sentiment agonizing to the point of ill health over a "divided heart," a "divided love," for almost the entirety of the novel. Tristram, we might note, after diminishing his father's head (reason) as inadequate to the world in the first half of

228 · Textual and Critical Intersections

Tristram Shandy, spends the remainder of the work (excepting volume 7) exploring the heart of Uncle Toby, before finding it equally inadequate— in both instances, the emphasis on one facet of the human trinity fails to account for the other two. It is in volume 7, however, where Tristram momentarily abandons both Walter and Toby for his flight to France, that he seems most to invoke Sir Charles; both seek happiness in a foreign setting.

Sterne reportedly called *A Sentimental Journey* his "work of *redemption,*"[57] and most critics have read that as indicating a turn away from satire and bawdry toward a kinder and "cleaner" writing, signaled by its title. However, since the work almost certainly continues his interest in the body's sexual urges (the work ends, of course, with Yorick reaching across the space between two beds, coming in touch with the fille de chambre's "END OF VOL. II") (*SJ* 165), is it not at least possible that Sterne's particular "redemptive" act in his last fiction was again to journey abroad in order to redeem Tristram's attitude toward what awaited travelers abroad, namely, foreigners and Roman Catholicism? It has rarely drawn forth comment that for this second journey he chose Yorick for his traveler, his clerical persona, long since dead within his fictional chronology, rather than Tristram, his "other" self, still alive and well at the end of nine volumes, and already a traveler to France.

With the guns of the Seven Years' War barely silenced, Tristram rushes through France, scorning other travel writers by denigrating the towns he passes through, ridiculing French roads and post chaises, belittling French dining, and throughout the volume seeming to prefer Janatone's dimensions to those of any famous cathedral or fortification. His encounters with the Roman Church are equally negative. Thus he reacts to disturbances when he is trying to sleep in his coach during a baiting: "Monsieur le Cure offers you a pinch of snuff——or a poor soldier shews you his leg— —or a shaveling his box" (*TS* 7.16.597). Yorick will enter Calais with the same attitude but rather quickly (and for several motives, sexual appetite certainly not the least of them) will enter into a snuff-box exchange with a Franciscan monk, a scene that became an icon of sentimentalism for the next fifty years (*SJ* 26–27; see the annotations to this exchange, *SJ* 258–59).

Tristram passes through St. Dennis without looking at the abbey: "Richness of their treasury! stuff and nonsense"—thus dismissing the collection of relics (e.g., *"Judas's lantern"*) that marks one essential difference between Catholic and Protestant practice (*TS* 7.16.598). Paris's streets are "nasty," its walls "are besh—t," its illumination inadequate, and the horses are all "puny." Indeed, on leaving Paris he has decided that "spleen" is the "best principle in the world to travel speedily upon" (*TS* 7.17.599–604). One might almost accuse him of reacting to France as did Smollett, the infamous Smelfungus of the *Journey.*

Ridicule of the abbess of Andoüillets and her novice Margarita, who together manage a masterpiece of casuistry to avoid forbidden words while enveloping themselves in a plethora of bawdy possibilities, takes up chapters 21–25. And when the reader chides the story as a "strange" one, Tristram responds with ridicule of the monastic life by suggesting that readerly tastes would have been better satisfied had his story been "upon some melancholy lecture of the cross—the peace of meekness, or the contentment of resignation . . . or upon the purer abstractions of the soul, and that food of wisdom, and holiness, and contemplation, upon which the spirit of man (when separated from the body) is to subsist for ever" (*TS* 7.26.615). In short, Tristram travels through Catholic France embracing Walter Shandy's view from decades earlier: "he hated a monk and the very smell of a monk worse than all the devils in hell" (*TS* 7.27.619). So splenetic has Tristram been throughout his mad dash through France that when, in the final episode of his journey, Nannette dances up to him with amity and amiableness in her eyes, he "dances off" (*TS* 7.43.649–50). Possibly this invitation is a challenge to his dubious virility noted by Jenny just a few chapters earlier (*TS* 7.29.624), but it is of a piece with his French journey: he travels through a country in which he has little if any relationship with the "foreigners" who live there—not even the inviting women, whose dimensions (body) he might take, but nothing else.

As a traveler, Sir Charles Grandison is diametrically the opposite. He is at home in every country, in France, in the courts of Germany, in Turkey, wherever he sets his welcome feet. Where Tristram is deathly sick crossing the channel (*TS* 7.2.578), Grandison considers sea voyages, back and forth to Italy, summer or winter, as just another lame impediment to the good he is intent on doing: "Seas are nothing to him. . . . he considers all nations as joined on the same continent; . . . if he had a call, he would undertake a journey to Constantinople or Pekin, with as little difficulty as some others would . . . to the Land's-end."[58] Above all, of course, he has entered into a sufficiently close relationship with a Catholic Italian family so that a marriage is at stake. Although he offers various qualifications—and after meeting Harriet has the alternative of a Protestant English woman—he remains willing to consummate this foreign marriage because his honor is engaged. Indeed, Richardson is given insufficient credit for his quite radical approach to toleration, national and religious both, lodging in his good man, his Christian hero, a belief that nations and religious "sects" are less important than the hopes and the inadequacies that bind all to all. It is a lesson Richardson derives from Scripture in a manner that many do not, and it forms the core of his Christian sentimentalism. More to my point, it is a vision of the righteous soul firmly tied to what I have suggested is the defining core of the novel, the repeated adage that "in the highest of our pleasures, the sighing heart will remind us of imperfection."

Sterne's erotic use of the same Christian truism in *A Sentimental Journey* perhaps opens this interpretative door wider than scholarly caution dictates, but that is the point of my argument. Putting a close textual knowledge of Sterne into proximity with an equally close reading of *Grandison* is to discover these small and scattered similarities and then face the challenge of explaining them. The easier path toward explanation would be to embrace the rather dubious thesis, suggested above, that Sterne, our best biographical instincts to the contrary, did indeed plow through the multiple volumes of *Sir Charles Grandison*.[59] Then in 1759, after writing a local satire on the York clerical establishment (*A Political Romance*) and two chapters, in the mode of Pope's *Peri Bathous,* of an aborted "Rabelaisian Fragment," he decided to shape his next creative efforts as responses to Richardson, first, a parody of his good man (*Tristram Shandy*), then an embrace of his Christian sentimentalism (*A Sentimental Journey*). We might also suggest, as part of this explanation, either that Sterne's bawdry was a critique of what he considered Richardson's reticence to discuss the body as part of the human condition (overlooking those passages that his own texts have helped us recover); or, if we prefer to think of Sterne as a more careful reader, that his bawdry was intended to make overt what he realized was the underlying, necessary, and too often overlooked physical (sexual) prowess of Richardson's "good man."

Richardson's highly appetitive Mr. B. and Lovelace have attracted a great deal of modern attention, but when even the author's modern biographers opine that *Grandison* "is not a good novel," and its twentieth-century editor, that it "was the book that Richardson had no desire to write," modern readers may be excused for not giving it careful attention.[60] Instead, they have tended to accept quite literally Sir Charles's often repeated insistence that mind and soul are all that matter to him, and certainly not a woman's beauty, much less her sexuality; love transcends the body, and in every possible way his hero was created to eschew the physicality of, say, the human, all too human character of Tom Jones. Reading *Grandison* in juxtaposition with Sterne may, however, help us to a better understanding of a badly underrated novel and its hero.[61]

Just as Yorick's journey is, among other possibilities, a quest for a satisfying union with a foreign other, well-illustrated as mentioned earlier by Yorick's final act of stretching forth his hand to the Piedmontese "lady ... with a glow of health in her cheeks" only to reach the Lyonoise maid's "END" instead (*SJ* 162–65), so in *Grandison,* Sir Charles stretches his hand from England to Italy in order to grasp Clementina, only to have Harriet stumble into the gap between the two. In both instances the possible ménage à trois defines inadequacy more than possibility. Sterne never does contemplate, teasingly or otherwise, the divided heart, but his bawdry throughout both fictions covets the same shock value as does Richardson's play with polygamy: here is our ideal world, in which Madam Reader harbors no such thoughts, and here is our reality, in which an author's language is never quite free from appetitive implication. Richardson's final novel takes polygamy as its theme for precisely the same reason, partly in jest (as when shocking his correspondents), but partly also in sober consideration of what it represents, the faith of innocence in eternal and unchanging love coming to terms with the realities of a transitory and mutable life. Significantly enough, Richardson concludes his work without resolving the triangle, at least insofar as Clementina remains uncommitted to anyone but Sir Charles as the novel ends.[62]

Indeed, a carefully constructed image of the three lovers together strongly suggests he had no intention (despite the urgings of his readers) to resolve the novel in a more traditional way (as with *Pamela* and *Clarissa,* where the "afterlives" of characters are sketched to almost everyone's satisfaction). Here we have, instead, Clementina's surprise flight to London and a (temporary) union of the three lovers. While it is never a sexual consummation, their interlocked togetherness does suggest Richardson's attempt to find in his threesome what might be the closest approach human beings can make to completeness in the incomplete and imperfect mundane world in which we work out salvation. Thus, in this very long novel's penultimate chapter, the three stroll into a garden, Grandison holding each woman by the hand, the Protestant and the Catholic, English and Italian, wife and virgin. Within the garden, they stand with "the Orangery on the right-hand; that distant clump of Oaklings on the left," while Clementina asks them a second time to promise to visit her in Italy (the first promise was given, significantly enough, with the dual vow: "We do!—We do!"): "Be *This* the spot to be recollected as witness to the promise. . . . We both repeated the promise; and Sir Charles said . . . that a little Temple should be erected on that very spot, to be consecrated to our triple friendship."[63] Richardson has come as close as possible to reconciling the conflicts of his novel within a world where such resolutions come dangerously close to the distinctly heretical act of creating a Heaven on earth; thus the notion of polygamy hovers over the scene.[64] And thus also the setting returns us to the unresolved political conflict that many readers have found infiltrating every part of the work (beginning with the Grandison family names—Charles, Charlotte, Carolyn), given that the "Orange" was a longstanding image for William of Orange, the "Oak" for the Jacobite cause.[65] Divided loves and divided loyalties seem to be set aside, momentarily at least, political settlements being, perhaps, in Richardson's eyes, merely political versions of polygamy.[66]

Toleration, the acceptance of otherness, even to the attempted reconciliation of persistent, seemingly unending oppositions, is Richardson's suggestion for the best we can do within a world in which the soul can never be satisfied. It is a path that Sterne seems also to trace, not only in his fictions but throughout his sermons, hewing as they do to the standard latitudinarian orthodoxy outlined at the beginning of the century by Tillotson, Sherlock, Norris, and a host of other "practical" theologians.[67] In *Tristram Shandy,* the exploration of life's inadequacies permeates the work, beginning with the damaged homunculus wending its way home and ending with Walter Shandy's diatribe (via Charron's *Of Wisdome*) against the various humiliations he finds in the act of making love (*TS* 9.33.806; and see *TS,* Notes 549–51).[68] In *Sentimental Journey,* his "work of *redemption,*" Sterne finds the same inadequacies, but moves toward Richardson's acts of reconciliation, beginning, of course, with the begging monk, then es-

Richardson's *Sir Charles Grandison* and Sterne: A Study in Influence · 233

tablishing Yorick by means of a passport, as a legitimate traveler through France, and finally by Yorick's participation in the dance with the French peasants, an ultimate image of reconciliation labeled, significantly enough, "The Grace"—the love feast of ancient Christian tradition.[69] One might even point to the fact that while Yorick is still in France, his most satisfying encounter is with the *Italian* countess F***, an encounter that begins with that most basic of human efforts to live in harmony with another. Meeting face-to-face in an attempt to proceed in opposite directions, each tries to make way for the other but steps to the same side, thus again blocking one another (*SJ* 77–78). As with so many episodes in Sterne, it is an experience everyone has had but few have been able to imbue with as much meaning as in *Sentimental Journey*: "I will only add, that the connection which arose out of that translation, gave me more pleasure than any one I had the honour to make in Italy" (*SJ* 78).

Even this intrusion of an Italian countess, however, cannot convince me that Sterne had read *Grandison*, much less based his fictions on Richardson's writings. Rather, I believe it is the critic who has read both in near juxtaposition who will create a relationship between the two, because that is what readers do. At times that same critic, as an annotator, may find a verbatim borrowing that seems to confirm a source relationship between one author and another. At other times, historical and biographical evidence can provide substantial proof of influence. But at the level of veracity I am suggesting, it is as possible to write achronologically about Sterne's influence on Richardson as about the chronologically possible Richardson's influence on Sterne.

Reading Richardson in proximity to Sterne helps us to suggest something about Richardson's bodily and Sterne's spiritual concerns, but critics have certainly pointed in both directions without putting the two authors in touch with one another.[70] What proximity does seem to reveal about the two authors, who might be joined together or separated in terms of the formal aspects of their writings or their life experiences, is that both share a Christian sentimentalism that is essentially the playing out of Christian doctrines in Christian practicalities. The range of theological and naturalistic meanings inhering in the single phrase "incomplete enjoyment" is at the center of their shared religion and their art, so much so that one might want to believe the two are in an ongoing conversation with one another,

234 · Textual and Critical Intersections

a conversation that never took place in actuality yet can be overheard by readers willing to acknowledge that great authors, put in proximity, will always talk to one another.[71]

We often fail to hear that conversation because of our own louder conversations about our reading. At times we drown it out with theoretical constructs, at times with textual minutiae, and at still other times overwhelm it with the flotsam and jetsam of every literate society, the multitude of texts produced in any age and the accumulated accompanying "received wisdom" regarding them. Thus, Richardson is prudish, Sterne is promiscuous—what could they possibly have to do with one another, especially when the "received wisdom" also tells us that eighteenth-century Anglicanism was moribund or that Sterne and Richardson are sexists. What I would like to suggest, however, is that these two authors are sharing in a conversation that we must be quiet and *attentive* in order to hear, a conversation in which great works of literature are constantly engaged, as long as there are readers for them. Moreover, it is that conversation that draws us to these works more than to others, the works that ultimately shape what we today scorn as the canon. Without doubt, both authors were extensive readers, and one can recover many odds and ends of that reading afloat in their own writings. Ultimately, however, it is not Sterne's absorption of Johann van Beverwyck (Bevoriskius) or Richardson's of Penelope Aubin that matters, but rather the conversation with the canon that enabled them to use their reading, large and small, to effect. We can readily accept that Richardson was in conversation with Milton; I would hope that overhearing the Richardson-Sterne conversation now suggests to us that Sterne was also in conversation with Milton, writing two works steeped in the incomplete enjoyments, mental, physical, and spiritual, that resulted from the Fall. But both authors are also in conversation with Proust, as I have previously suggested about Sterne; can anyone doubt that Proust's *La prisonnière* (*The Captive*) is also talking to—and is talked to by—*Clarissa?*

I believe we diminish authors when we fail to read them within the canon they received and passed on. Certainly the canon changes over time, authors leaving and entering as succeeding generations evolve in their literary tastes. There is a historian's (and editor's) interest in reading Sterne alongside *Tristram Bates* but quite another mode of interest when reading him alongside Richardson or Proust. We know that Austen was very favorably inclined toward *Sir Charles Grandison,* but it may only be when we put her work in proximity with Pope or Dickens, that we can better understand the conversation Austen had with Richardson; and, conversely, coming to Richardson through Austen has certainly shaped our view of his accomplishments. To extend this argument a bit further, while literary scholars should pay attention to conversations most immediate to their primary text (that is, eighteenth-century writers talking to one another), we should also remain open to putting other masterworks in proximity with eighteenth-century texts. Happening, for example, to be reading Robert Musil's *Der Mann ohne Eigenschaften* (*The Man without Qualities*) while working on the edition of *Grandison,* I believe I overheard Musil's antihero Ulrich and Sir Charles speaking to each other across centuries, most particularly when Ulrich's contemplated incest (in part 2) seems to be playing the same role as polygamy in Richardson's world. Unless we are willing to listen to such conversations, we do not perform our only true function as professors of literature: to preserve and pass on the very best literature of all ages by listening to, and reporting on, the conversations these great authors continue to have with one another.

Interestingly, when Richardson and Sterne wanted to embody their notion of ethical being, both invoked not the omniscience of God or providential intervention, stalwarts of an immanent theology, but instead incomplete enjoyment, an experience that entails the changes and chances of earthly time, and thus an opening into an eternal and unchangeable future. Incomplete enjoyment also leads inevitably to our past, the origin or cause of the separation between our ability to conceive perfection and our inability ever to achieve it. Literature (including Scripture, if one is inclined to include it) returns again and again to human incompleteness, the immeasurable distance between the finite world it seeks to describe and the infinite world beyond conception; the literary tradition is, indeed, a writer's best evidence of incompleteness ("of making many books there is no end; and much study is a weariness of the flesh"),[72] humanity's ceaseless effort to comprehend its lack of comprehension. In the literature that matters, we find both the past and the future, but the present disappears from sight; the modern shibboleth for pleasure, living for and in the present, is anathema to the religious mind and also, I suggest, to those authors engaged in the conversation I have been describing. Again and again, the great authors of our literary past reaffirm the spiritual reality of literature, an aesthetic and ethical notion that is as mystical as anything the Judeo-Christian tradition has created, whether the unknowable, ineffable God or the monotheistic mystery of the Trinity. When we consider Richardson and Sterne from this perspective, in proximity, they do indeed speak to one another.

Originally published in *Modern Philology* 115, no. 2 (2017).

Notes

1 Tim Parnell, "Sterne's Fiction and the Mid-Century Novel," in *The Oxford Handbook of the Eighteenth-Century Novel*, ed. J. A. Downie (Oxford: Oxford University Press, 2016), 271. Thomas Keymer's argument is made in *Sterne, the Moderns, and the Novel* (Oxford: Oxford University Press, 2002), 41–43, 128–30. One assertion is particularly puzzling: "Sterne cannot, of course, have known the sophistication of Richardson's thinking about reader response as set out in letters that were then unpublished, and he does indeed seem to have read *Clarissa* and *Grandison* as unavailing exercises in hyperrealistic narration and interpretative ultimatum" (Keymer, 42). Surely this begs the question of whether or not Sterne read either work.

2 Samuel Richardson, *Sir Charles Grandison*, ed. E. Derek Taylor, Melvyn New, and Elizabeth Kraft (Cambridge: Cambridge University Press, 2022). Hereafter cited as *Grandison*.

3 Fielding is, as to be expected, cited more often than Sterne, but primarily in comparing and contrasting *Amelia*, written the year before *Grandison*; we know that Richardson read at least the first volume and deplored it. See, e.g., his letter to Anne Donnellan, February 22, 1752: "You guess that I have not read Amelia. Indeed I have read but the first volume. I had intended to go through with it; but I found the characters and situations so wretchedly low and dirty, that I imagined I could not be interested for any one of them." *The Correspondence of Samuel Richardson*, ed. Anna Laetitia Barbauld (1804), vol. 4, 60. And, again, to Lady Bradshaigh, February 23, 1752: "I have not been able to read any more than the first volume of Amelia. Poor Fielding! I could not help telling his sister, that I was equally surprised at and concerned for his continued lowness." Samuel Richardson, *Correspondence with Lady Bradshaigh and Lady Echlin*, ed. Peter Sabor (Cambridge: Cambridge University Press, 2016), vol. 1, 204. Other citations of Fielding are almost always negative.

4 See *Grandison*, 1928n53, on the close attention both authors pay to descriptive details. We (the editors of this volume) offer a different passage from the one quoted by McKillop and Keymer, and alluded to by Parnell (see *Grandison*,

Richardson's *Sir Charles Grandison* and Sterne: A Study in Influence · 237

314), there being many possible examples; we suggest the drama rather than the novel as an influence. The speechifying attitudes of the good Sir Rowland are an earlier example of a shared interest in describing gestures—but also may suggest, as does the McKillop passage, a context other than the "rise of the novel": "And that, let me tell you, Ladies, for the following reasons—standing up, and putting the fore-finger of his right-hand, extended with a flourish, upon the thumb of his left" (*Grandison*, 42). Cf. *TS* 4.7.333: "he holds the fore-finger of his left-hand between the fore-finger and the thumb of his right." Our *Grandison* annotation also points to the fact that within this speech, Sir Rowland's "Know you, Ladies, that *wit* and *wisdom* are too [*sic?*] different things, and are very rarely seen together?" voices an opinion central to Tristram's "Author's Preface" (*TS* 3.20.227–28). What might be beyond the annotator's purview, however, is a further observation that both authors here may not, in fact, be seeking some "hyperrealistic narration" but rather reflecting commonplace manuals of rhetoric (pulpit and otherwise), stretching back at least to the seventeenth century. See, e.g., John Bulwer, *Chirologia, or The Natural Language of the Hand; and Chironomia, or The Art of Manual Rhetoric* (1644); see also the very useful study by Paul Goring, *The Rhetoric of Sensibility in Eighteenth-Century Culture* (Cambridge: Cambridge University Press, 2005). To focus minute attention on gesture as necessarily a novelistic concern is to overlook the "art of oratory," pervasively taught in the schools for the practical use of both clerics and politicians and ripe for the parodic treatment of speechifying old men.

5 *Grandison*, 308, 319. The line is from Edward Young, *The Complaint, or Night-Thoughts* (1742–45), night 8. For Richardson's printings of Young, see Keith Maslen, *Samuel Richardson of London, Printer* (Otago, New Zealand: University of Otago, 2001), items 929–54.

6 That Sterne here mingles his most definitive statement of valuing practical over scholastic theology with the words of a writer best known for ludicrous bawdry is worth keeping in mind as this discussion progresses. For the "Rabelaisian Fragment," see *MW* 152–75.

7 I perhaps beg the question by endorsing Pope's taste: "And Eusden eke out Blackmore's endless line; / She saw slow Philips creep like Tate's poor page." Alexander Pope, *The Dunciad* (1742), book 1, 104–5, in *The Poems of Alexander Pope*, ed. John Butt (New Haven, CT: Yale University Press, 1963), 725.

8 See, e.g., in *Grandison*: "when the Lover becomes the husband, the over-lively mistress will be sunk in the obliging wife" (827); or, "But, high-ho!—There's a sigh, Harriet" (833); and one more example, "But marriage itself, Sir, shall not give you a privilege to break into my retirements" (840). In William Congreve, *The Way of the World*, see, respectively, 4.5.70–72, 2.4.44, and 4.5.65–

238 · Textual and Critical Intersections

69, in *Works of William Congreve*, ed. D. F. McKenzie (Oxford: Oxford University Press, 2011), vol. 2, 184, 145, 184.

9 The influence of Locke on Sterne has been central to much criticism on *Tristram Shandy*, at least since John Traugott's *Tristram Shandy's World* (Berkeley: University of California Press, 1954), and has been tracked to the beginning of the century in an important essay by Darrell Jones, "Locke and Sterne," *Shandean* 27 (2016): 83–111. Perhaps his most useful point is that too often literary scholars working at this level of influence study fail to read the philosophical work under question with sufficient expertise. We might add to this caveat another, namely, that Locke wrote other important works too often ignored by literary critics.

10 See Wayne C. Booth, "The Self-Conscious Narrator in Comic Fiction before *Tristram Shandy*," *PMLA* 67 (1952): 163–85. The essay formed part of Booth's brilliant effort, in *The Rhetoric of Fiction* (Chicago: University of Chicago Press, 1961), to explore modes of fiction more precisely than is possible when critics reduce all long nonfictions to simply one sort of novel or another.

11 See Helen Sard Hughes, "A Precursor of *Tristram Shandy*," *Journal of English and Germanic Philology* 17 (1918): 227–51.

12 Parnell, "Sterne's Fiction," 265. I have discussed this problem briefly in "Sterne's Bawdry: A Cautionary Tale," *Review of English Studies* 62 (2011): 80–89.

13 James Boswell, *Life of Johnson*, ed. R. W. Chapman and Pat Rogers (Oxford: Oxford World Classics, 1980), 314.

14 One may, of course, try to define a course that defies a sequential experience, just as one may read a dozen books simultaneously, but such efforts simply reinforce my point that both literature and its readers are time bound. Years ago, I experimented with "extreme" nonsequential reading by offering courses wherein we read eight or nine modern "classics," selected only because their authors' surnames began with the same letter. My primary question: Would students be able to hear any conversation between these major literary figures across centuries and cultures? Would they be able to draw maps of influence, patterns of similarities and differences between Pasternak, Perec, Pirandello, Platonov, Poe, Proust, Pushkin, and Pynchon? Note that even the order of reading is arbitrary—at first I arranged the authors chronologically, but that obviously influenced the outcome; now, alphabetically, *Swann's Way* and *Eugene Onegin* emerge in sequence. Surely "obsession" will suggest itself to alert readers, cemented by the next work, Thomas Pynchon's *V.* We might want to conclude, therefore, that these three authors have conversed with one another, hence influenced one another; we might also conclude that the list reflects the instructor's taste for literature tilted toward authors obsessing about obses-

sion. With either conclusion, the point is that in all studies of literary influence, readers and their reading remain a crucial element of the equation.

15 See my essays "The Odd Couple: Laurence Sterne and John Norris of Bemerton" and "Reading Sterne through Proust and Levinas," reprinted as chapters 2 and 7 in this volume, respectively. This second essay in turn was an offshoot of my earlier "Proust's Influence on Sterne: A Remembrance of Things to Come," *Modern Language Notes* 103 (1988): 1031–55, the title and substance of which are also, perhaps, the seeds of this present essay.

16 John Norris, *Practical Discourses upon Several Divine Subjects* (1691), 41–42. See Melvyn New, "'Scholia' to the Florida Edition," *Scriblerian* 27 (1994): 94–95. For Norris's importance to Sterne, see New, "Odd Couple"; Tim Parnell, "A Story Painted to the Heart? *Tristram Shandy* and Sentimentalism Reconsidered," *Shandean* 9 (1997): 122–35; Geoff Newton, "The Sermons of Laurence Sterne, Neoplatonism, and Two Short Works," in *Divine Rhetoric: Essays on the Sermons of Laurence Sterne*, ed. W. B. Gerard (Newark: University of Delaware Press, 2010), 149–63; and Geoff Newton, "Divine and Human Love: Letters between John Norris and Mary Astell, Laurence Sterne and Eliza Draper," in *Theology and Literature in the Age of Johnson: Resisting Secularism*, ed. Melvyn New and Gerard Reedy, SJ (Newark: University of Delaware Press, 2012), 183–201. For Norris's importance to Richardson, see E. Derek Taylor, *Reason and Religion in "Clarissa": Samuel Richardson and "The Famous Mr. Norris, of Bemerton"* (Burlington, VT: Ashgate, 2009).

17 *Grandison*, 495, 1115, 1122; and see 879, 1476, 1482, all passages where the "divesting of Self" is iterated. And compare Clarissa's lament: "But still upon *Self*, this vile, this hated *Self!*" Samuel Richardson, *Clarissa* (1747–48), vol. 6, 10 (letter 2).

18 John Locke, *Writings on Religion*, ed. Victor Nuovo (Oxford: Clarendon Press, 2002), 91. That Norris was the first English philosopher to write in opposition to Locke, and that his *Essay towards the Theory of the Ideal or Intelligible World* (1701–4) can be read as an attempt to reconcile Lockean epistemology with Christianity, is important when weighing Norris's influence on both Richardson and Sterne. For the century-long continuation of this effort at reconciliation, see especially the very thorough and persuasive study by Richard E. Brantley, *Locke, Wesley, and the Method of English Romanticism* (Gainesville: University Press of Florida, 1984).

19 See *TS* 8.11.670: "By all that is hirsute and gashly! I cry, taking off my furr'd cap, and twisting it round my finger . . . 'tis an excellent cap too (putting it upon my head and pressing it close to my ears)—and warm—and soft; especially if you stroke it in the right way." See also *Gentleman's Magazine* 37 (February 1767):

75–76: "It has been charged with gross indecency . . . but indecency does no mischief, at least such indecency as is found in *Tristram Shandy*; . . . It tends as little to inflame the passions as *Culpepper's Family Physician*." Or again, from Richard Griffith's *Posthumous Works of a Late Celebrated Genius* (*The Koran*) (1770), vol. 1, v: "The very worst part of his writings, might be only, that they were as indecent, but as innocent, at the same time, as the sprawling of an infant on the floor." Both of these latter passages are reprinted in *Laurence Sterne: The Critical Heritage*, ed. Alan B. Howes (London: Routledge, 1974), 180, 212. Richardson condemned the little he had read of *Tristram Shandy* (the first two volumes) as "execrable," but also opined: "One extenuating circumstance attends his works, that they are too gross to be inflaming." Richardson to Bishop Mark Hildesley, Winter 1761, in Barbauld, *Correspondence*, vol. 5, 146. This bawdry in the penultimate volume of *Tristram* (*TS* 8.11.670) does suggest that far from abandoning his wit for sentiment, as some critics urged him to do, Sterne seems quite deliberately not to have done so; no passage in *Tristram* calls attention to the body more frankly than this one.

20 The critical literature attesting to Richardson's sensuality is legion, so perhaps I will be forgiven for citing just one particularly astute (and entertaining) discussion, Juliet McMaster, "*Sir Charles Grandison*: Richardson on Body and Character," *Eighteenth-Century Fiction* 1, no. 2 (1989): 82–102.

21 Harriet is called the "loveliest woman in England" a dozen times, Clementina almost as many, changing only the country; many other indications are given of the physical perfections of both women—and of Sir Charles, "handsomest of men." Setting aside Richardson's love of superlatives, the important point is that in all his novels, bodily beauty matters, despite all the nods to "mind" and "soul"; Clarissa, we recall, first demonstrates her rich physicality by her abhorrence of Solmes's "ugliness."

22 As early as April 22, 1752, citing scriptural precedent, Richardson twitted Lady Bradshaigh about the possibilities of polygamy, but it had long been on his mind as a particularly alarming "solution" for his rakish male characters: both Mr. B. and Lovelace fantasize about it. The subject was bandied back and forth with Bradshaigh for almost a year before Richardson suggested they end the discussion (February 24, 1753), but even then it returns in late December as Richardson teases Bradshaigh with his undisclosed ending for *Grandison*. See Sabor, *Correspondence*, vol. 5, 209, 216, 221, 229, 232, 315. For a thorough analysis of Richardson's (and his period's) interest in polygamy, see David Macey, "'Business for Lovers of Business': *Sir Charles Grandison*, Hardwick's Marriage Act and the Specter of Bigamy," *Philological Quarterly* 84 (2005): 333–55. Macey (336) notes that polygamy "was very much on the minds of English readers during the period" and, quoting from Lawrence Stone, *Broken Lives:*

Separation and Divorce in England, 1660–1887 (Oxford: Oxford University Press, 1993), 22, notes that there were "thousands, perhaps tens of thousands" of bigamous unions in the century. See also the broad discussion by Howard Weinbrot, "Johnson's *Irene* and *Rasselas*, Richardson's *Pamela Exalted*: Contexts, Polygamy, and the Seraglio," *Age of Johnson* 23 (2015): 89–140; oddly, Weinbrot fails to explore the extended "bigamous" plot of *Grandison*. See also Carol Houlihan Flynn, *Samuel Richardson: A Man of Letters* (Princeton, NJ: Princeton University Press, 1982), 234. Finally, it might be noted that Richardson printed the first and second editions of Patrick Delany's *Reflections upon Polygamy, and the Encouragement given to that Practice in the Scriptures of the Old Testament* (1737, 1739); Dean Delany was, of course, one of the Richardson "circle," along with Mary Delany.

23 Perhaps the most blatant instance is the attempt of Sir Thomas Grandison's steward, aptly named Mr. Filmer, to push him into marriage with a "fine young creature, not more than sixteen," even while Sir Thomas is on his deathbed; one must assume at least "keeping," had death not intervened. *Grandison*, 377–78.

24 *Grandison*, 606–7.

25 "Mrs. *Jewkes* took a Glass and drank the dear *Monosyllable*; I don't understand that Word but I believe it is baudy." Henry Fielding, *Joseph Andrews and Shamela*, ed. Douglas Brooks-Davis (Oxford: Oxford World's Classics, 1999), 328.

26 Samuel Richardson, *Pamela in Her Exalted Condition*, ed. Albert J. Rivero (Cambridge: Cambridge University Press, 2012), 257–58.

27 See Richardson's preface to Penelope Aubin, *Collection of Entertaining Histories and Novels* (1739). The first rule Richardson derives from her fiction is telling: "First, *A* Purity of Style and Manners, *that nothing may be contained in them that has the least Tendency to pollute or corrupt the unexperienced Minds, for whose Diversion they are intended.*" Samuel Richardson, *Early Works*, ed. Alexander Pettit (Cambridge: Cambridge University Press, 2012), 94. Whether Richardson, when he picked up his own novelistic pen, would think of his audience as limited to "*unexperienced Minds*" is a question worth exploring.

28 *Grandison*, 457 (Richardson's brackets).

29 *Grandison*, 457.

30 Samuel Johnson, *Dictionary* (1755), s.vv. "develop," "plait"; Pope, *Dunciad*, book 4, 268–70, in Butt, *Poems*, 780; Joseph Addison, *Remarks on Several Parts of Italy*, 5th ed. (1745), 192.

31 The Florida Edition annotators of *Tristram* and *Journey* failed to suggest the "influence" of Richardson on either passage.

32 Barbauld, *Correspondence*, vol. 1, cxviii–cxix.

242 · Textual and Critical Intersections

33 Richardson, *Clarissa*, vol. 6, 190 (letter 48).

34 *Grandison*, 790 (emphasis added).

35 *Grandison*, 1061.

36 *Grandison*, 1223–24.

37 *Grandison*, 1251.

38 *Grandison*, 1258.

39 *Grandison*, 1387.

40 Some very fine recent work on *Grandison* has justified the inconclusive conclusion, including Lois A. Chaber, "*Sir Charles Grandison* and the Human Prospect," in *New Essays on Samuel Richardson*, ed. Albert J. Rivero (New York: St. Martin's Press, 1996), 193–208; and Emily Friedman, "The End(s) of Richardson's *Sir Charles Grandison*," *Studies in English Literature, 1500–1900* 52 (2012): 651–67. In the general introduction to the Cambridge *Grandison*, E. Derek Taylor offers a persuasive argument for Richardson's Christian purpose in leaving several key relationships in the novel unresolved.

41 Richardson to Lady Bradshaigh, late November 1749: "I am pleased with your principal motives of going to church, example and public prayer; a duty, the one, I have long (shall I say) neglected; a benefit, the other, I have as long been deprived of by my nervous malady, which will not let me appear in a crowd of people." See Sabor, *Correspondence*, vol. 5, 83.

42 *Grandison*, 1220.

43 William Sherlock, *A Practical Discourse concerning Death*, 13th ed. (1705), 29.

44 Samuel Richardson, *Correspondence with George Cheyne and Thomas Edwards*, ed. David E. Shuttleton and John A. Dussinger (Cambridge: Cambridge University Press, 2013), 353. Richardson goes on to condemn Bolingbroke for being willing to "frame a Religion to his Practices. Poor Man! He is not a Doubter now!" I believe he had Sherlock's *Practical Discourse concerning Death* in mind, but some hesitation is appropriate, given Dussinger's identifying "Sherlock" as Thomas Sherlock, author of *Use and Intent of Prophecy* (1725), which he identifies as a strong and popular argument against deism, and in press at the time. As noted, however, a twenty-sixth edition of *Practical Discourse* was published in 1754 ("so seasonably publish'd," Richardson wrote in his January 15, 1755, letter to Edwards); the fifth edition of *Prophecy* was published in 1749, and the sixth was advertised in January 1755. In either case, both Sherlocks would have recognized that imperfect enjoyment and the afterlife are intimately and thoroughly entwined in their theology. Richardson's gloating triumph over Bolingbroke is yet one more indication that he strongly believed in an afterlife in which judgment would be passed and all imperfect pleasures would be perfected for the righteous.

Richardson's *Sir Charles Grandison* and Sterne: A Study in Influence · 243

45 Pope, *An Essay on Man*, epistle 1, lines 95–98, in Butt, *Poems*, 508; even Bolingbroke would be pressed to discover a deistic reading of these lines, whatever
his influence on Pope's thought.

46 For example:

> Can we conceive a disregard in Heaven,
> What the worst perpetrate, or best endure?
> *This* cannot be. To *love*, and *know*, in man
> Is boundless appetite, and boundless power;
> And these demonstrate boundless objects too.
> Objects, pow'rs, appetites, Heav'n suits in all.

Or again:

> Why by *reflection* marr'd the joys of *sense*?
> Why *past*, and *future*, preying on our hearts,
> And putting all our *present* joys to death?

And one last example:

> Why life, a moment; infinite, desire?
> Our wish, eternity? our home, the grave?
> . . . .
> Why happiness pursu'd, tho' never found?
> Man's thirst of happiness declares *it is*
> . . . .
> That thirst unquencht declares *it is not here.*

See Edward Young, "The Infidel Reclaimed" (night 7), in *The Complaint,
or Night-Thoughts on Life, Death, and Immortality*, 7th ed. (1747), 177, 189.
I follow Robert G. Walker, *Eighteenth-Century Arguments for Immortality
and Johnson's "Rasselas"* (Victoria, BC: University of Victoria, 1977), in citing particular passages among the many in Young's poetry that are apropos.
Walker's study remains one of the most useful and thorough discussions of the
century's efforts to continue its belief in immortality and judgment.

47 See *Sermons*, Notes 150–51, where possible sources for Sterne's version of the
idea are suggested. Despite its title, Wollaston's work is by no means "naturalistic," arguing throughout for an afterlife.

48 See, however, Nicholas Fisher, "'Damn'd in the Cup': Faith, Poetry, and the
Earl of Rochester," *English: Journal of the English Association* 62 (2013): 166–
92. That Sterne would expose Tristram to a similar "imperfect enjoyment" (*TS*
7.29.624), when he stands before Jenny, "garters in my hand, reflecting upon

what had *not* pass'd," ought not be forgotten in the present discussion; nor the fact that, as with Tristram and Uncle Toby, the maiming of the groin hovers over *Grandison* as well. Both Jeronymo and Mr. Merceda suffer wounds at the hands of those aggrieved by their sexual transgressions and trying to ensure they would never be able to thus sin again.

49 Pierre Charron, *De la sagesse* (Bourdeaux, 1601), trans. Samson Lennard, 1612; the quotation is from the 1630 ed., 130–31. Charron's book was an important source for Sterne; see *TS*, Notes 39–40, 549–50, that is, annotations to passages at the outset and conclusion of the work, where the topic is the act of human procreation. Sterne's debt to this valuable source was first noted by Françoise Pellan, "Laurence Sterne's Indebtedness to Charron," *Modern Language Review* 67 (1972): 752–55; that Sterne quotes Charron in the opening chapters of *Tristram* and returns to him seven years later for the conclusion seems to have been overlooked by those determined to posit the work's postmodern disorganization.

50 Michel de Montaigne, *Essays*, trans. Charles Cotton (1685–86), vol. 2, 547; Sterne used this translation.

51 In lines just before the passage cited, Lucretius discusses the power of love, recommending that one dissipate the appetite by spreading it among many; such a lover, he maintains, "tastes more certain and more unmixed Delight," than those who depend on one partner: "The Lover hopes, perhaps, that his Flame may be extinguished by the same Object that first blew the Fire, but Experience shews the contrary of This; for This is the only Thing which, the more we enjoy of it, our Soul still burns with the eager Desire of more." Lucretius, *Of the Nature of Things* (1743), vol. 2, 91.

52 *Grandison*, 1061.

53 See Keymer, *Sterne, the Moderns, and the Novel.* For recent examples of the effort to explain Sterne within the contexts of his own time and the genre of the novel, see Scott Enderle, "The Vulnerable Page: Patronage, Copyright and the Material Text in *Tristram Shandy*," *Shandean* 23 (2012): 57–76; Moyra Haslett, "Eccentricity, Originality, and the Novel: *Tristram Shandy*, Volumes 1 and 2," in *Reading 1759: Literary Culture in Mid-Eighteenth-Century Britain and France*, ed. Shaun Regan (Lewisburg, PA: Bucknell University Press, 2013), 169–85; and Amit Yahav, "Sonorous Duration: *Tristram Shandy* and the Temporality of Novels," *PMLA* 128 (2013): 872–87.

54 Thomas Keymer, *Richardson's "Clarissa" and the Eighteenth-Century Reader* (Cambridge: Cambridge University Press, 1992), 72–76. Keymer is making a broader case for indeterminacy as part of Richardson's ethical strategy: "There can . . . be little doubt about the centrality of textual indeterminacy

and readerly creativity to his project for the reader's education. His last novel, *Sir Charles Grandison*, gives the method its freest rein" (72).

55 Keymer, *Richardson's "Clarissa" and the Eighteenth-Century Reader*, 75–76.

56 See my essay "Sterne and the Narrative of Determinateness," reprinted as chapter 1 in this volume. It is hardly coincidental that Keymer and I were both writing about "indeterminateness" in the 1990s; readings of past works will always be influenced by the particular critical hobby-horses of present time.

57 The phrase is actually Richard Griffith's, whom Sterne met while beginning his *Journey*; twenty years later, in his *Series of Genuine Letters between Henry and Frances* (1786), Griffith reported seeing the first part of the manuscript: "It has all the Humour and Address of the best Parts of *Tristram*, and is quite free from the Grossness of the worst.... He ... calls it his *Work of Redemption*." Quoted in Howes, *Laurence Sterne*, 185; and see *SJ* lxii–lxiii. Martin C. Battestin makes much of the phrase in his articles "*A Sentimental Journey*, Sterne's 'Work of Redemption,'" *Bulletin de la Société d'Etudes Anglo-Américaines des XVIIe et XVIIIe Siècles* 8 (1994): 189–204; and "Sterne among the *Philosophes*: Body and Soul in *A Sentimental Journey*," *Eighteenth-Century Fiction* 6 (1994): 17–36.

58 *Grandison*, 525–26.

59 The catalog of Sterne's library contains other collections as well; it lists one odd volume of *Grandison*, and nothing else by Richardson. It also includes some seven hundred volumes that Sterne purchased "dog cheap" in 1761, but almost certainly did not spend enough time at Coxwold to read; it thus offers little evidence of Sterne's actual reading. See *Letters* 202, 204n11; Keymer, *Sterne, The Moderns, and the Novel*, 59–60.

60 T. C. Duncan Eaves and Ben D. Kimpel, *Samuel Richardson: A Biography* (Oxford: Clarendon Press, 1971), 387; Jocelyn Harris, ed., *Sir Charles Grandison* (London: Oxford University Press, 1972), vol. 1, viii. Harris's paradoxical influence in both making *Grandison* available to modern readers and yet marginalizing the work by her thesis that it was a disorganized patchwork quilt of a cooperative effort between author and coterie, will be, it is hoped, corrected by the new Cambridge edition, which, briefly, wholeheartedly endorses Barbauld's response to the idea of others helping Richardson's reticent pen: "The works of Richardson bear all the internal marks of having been written by one person. The same sentiments, the same phraseology, the same plan sedulously followed from beginning to end, proclaim the hand of a single author. . . . Where could Richardson have found a pen able to supply his own, except in some detached ornament or trifling appendage." Barbauld, *Correspondence*, vol. 1, cxl–cxli.

246 · Textual and Critical Intersections

61 Obviously, Sterne's presence is not necessary to produce fine readings of *Grandison*, as exemplified by several recent efforts to redeem the work; see, Friedman, "The End(s) of Richardson's *Sir Charles Grandison*"; Alison Conway, "*Sir Charles Grandison* and the Sexual Politics of Toleration," *Lumen* 30 (2011): 1–19; Patrick Mello, "'Piety and Popishness': Tolerance and the Epistolary Reactions to Richardson's *Sir Charles Grandison*," *Eighteenth-Century Fiction* 25 (2013): 511–31; M. J. Koehler, "The Problem of Suspense in Richardson's *Sir Charles Grandison*," *Eighteenth Century: Theory and Interpretation* 54 (2013): 317–38. My reading here is very much indebted to their work, along with that of my *Grandison* coeditors, Elizabeth Kraft and E. Derek Taylor.

62 Some of Richardson's readers immediately asked for a continuation that would resolve the undecided fate of Clementina (and other dangling aspects as well), to which he responded with a privately printed *Copy of a Letter to a Lady, Who Was Solicitous for an Additional Volume to the History of Sir Charles Grandison* (1754), which he distributed to his friends. While the text tries to satisfy them to some extent by rehearsing all the issues he did resolve, his defense of incomplete satisfaction is particularly pertinent: "Permit me further to observe, that the conclusion of a *single story* is indeed generally some great and decisive event; as a *Death*, or a *Marriage*: But in scenes of life carried down nearly to the present time . . . all events cannot be decided . . . ; since persons presumed to be still living, must be supposed liable to the various turns of human affairs." Samuel Richardson, *Correspondence Primarily on "Sir Charles Grandison,"* ed. Betty A. Schellenberg (Cambridge: Cambridge University Press, 2015), 189. That this is not merely the rationalization of an author tired of writing is suggested by a similar reply he made years earlier to Lady Bradshaigh's desire for a happy ending to *Clarissa*:

> Let us attend Clarissa in the Issue of her supposed Nuptials. We will imagine her to have repeatedly escaped the Perils of Child birth. How many Children shall we give her? Five? Six? Seven? How many, Madam? Not less I hope. . . . Well but we have supposed her past these Dangers. And we will suppose that her Children have all of them escaped the manifold Hazards of the Infantile State. . . . Good Parents are not sure they shall have good Children. But suppose all their Children dutiful, prudent, good, and suppose them to continue so, Sons and Daughters, till marriageable Years: How *then* are the Cares of the anxious Parents encreased? If ever so worthy may not the Daughters marry unworthy Men, the Sons unworthy Women?

See Sabor, *Correspondence*, vol. 1, 34 (December 15, 1748). Clearly for Richardson, human existence is an experience characterized by "changes and chances," one that could not be "completed" except by death and the judgment that would follow. Compare Sterne's frequent use of the phrase "changes and chances" in his sermons (*Sermons* 95, 146, 239, 330), which also occurs in the *Book of Common Prayer* (Oxford, 1740), in one of the collects ending the communion service: "among all the changes and chances of this mortal life, thy servants may ever be defended by thy most gracious and ready help."

63 *Grandison*, 1685.

64 It is difficult to find a garden in Richardson's fictions that does not more or less adumbrate Eden. In *Grandison*, the question had earlier been raised as to whether Sir Charles, the "best" of men, would have "been so complaisant to his Eve as *Milton makes Adam*" or "done *his own duty*, were it but for the sake of posterity, and left it to the Almighty, if such had been his pleasure, to have annihilated his first Eve, and given him a second." *Grandison*, 1136–37. The allusion to Milton is to *Paradise Lost*, book 9, lines 905–12, where Adam very quickly decides to fall with Eve:

> for with thee
> Certain my resolution is to Die.
> How can I live without thee, how forgo
> Thy sweet Converse and Love so dearly join'd,
> To live again in these wild Woods forlorn?
> Should God create another *Eve*, and I
> Another Rib afford, yet loss of thee
> Would never from my heart.

See John Milton, *Complete Poems*, ed. Merritt Y. Hughes (New York: Odyssey Press, 1957), 399. As many have pointed out, Harriet is precisely the second Eve, provided for Sir Charles after he resists the first, Clementina, but the more essential point is that any resolution will produce an Adam (Charles) for whom the future is unknown; having made his choice, Charles must accompany the two women out of the garden and into the world of change and chance.

65 See, e.g., Margaret Ann Doody, "Richardson's Politics," *Eighteenth-Century Fiction* 2 (1990): 113–26; and Teri Doerksen, "*Sir Charles Grandison*: The Anglican Family and the Admirable Roman Catholic," *Eighteenth-Century Fiction* 15 (2003): 539–58.

66 As Neil Guthrie suggests, "oaklings" had a specific meaning: "In a withered or 'stricken' form, frequently with the motto *revirescit* ('it revives, it grows green again, it shoots again'), the oak is a symbol of eventual restoration and regeneration with christological significance." Guthrie goes on to note that a "pamphlet of 1716 which expresses support for the Hanoverian succession is titled *A Dialogue between an Oak and an Orange-Tree*, the implication being that

248 · Textual and Critical Intersections

the two species are incompatible within the same grove." Guthrie, *The Material Culture of the Jacobites* (Cambridge: Cambridge University Press, 2014), 44. Richardson here seems to indicate just the opposite, although the return to Eden is again a polygamous vision; "incompatibility" is, perhaps, fallen nature's ecological version of incompleteness and inadequacy.

67 While reading latitudinarian sermons remains the best way to understand the Anglican attempt to move beyond the religious conflicts of the seventeenth century without losing their faith (as many in the nineteenth century believed had happened), a very thorough scholarly account is provided by Patrick Müller, *Latitudinarianism and Didacticism in Eighteenth-Century Literature: Moral Theology in Fielding, Sterne, and Goldsmith* (Frankfurt: Lang, 2007). He notes that "in 1689, the publication of Locke's *Letter Concerning Toleration* marked yet another climax in the reception of Latitudinarian thought" (35). In that work Locke argues that "No Man by nature is bound unto any particular Church ... but every one joins himself voluntarily to that Society in which he believes he has found that Profession and Worship which is truly acceptable to God. The hopes of Salvation, as it was the only cause of his entrance into that Communion, so it can be the only reason of his stay there." Indeed, the opening sentence of *Toleration* loudly proclaims Locke's stance: "I esteem that Toleration to be the chief Characteristical Mark of the True Church." John Locke, *Letter concerning Toleration*, ed. Mark Goldie (Indianapolis, IN: Liberty Fund, 2010), 15, 7. *An Essay concerning Human Understanding* has attracted almost all suggestions of Locke's influence on the literature of the century, but perhaps *Toleration*, along with *Two Treatises on Government* and *The Reasonableness of Christianity*, might prove equally fertile ground.

68 Few passages in Sterne's works are more pertinent in justifying his emphasis, through bawdry, on the ways in which society (and religion) have turned the natural act of procreation into something that "turns all the wisdom, contemplations, and operations of the soul backwards"; an act, also, that "all the parts thereof ... are held as to be conveyed to a cleanly mind by no language, translation, or periphrasis whatever" (*TS* 9.33.806).

69 "It was not till the middle of the second dance ... I fancied I could distinguish an elevation of spirit different from that which is the cause or the effect of simple jollity.—In a word, I thought I beheld *Religion* mixing in the dance" (*SJ* 159). For Sterne's "internationalism," see the excellent essay by Stephanie DeGooyer, "The Poetics of the Passport in *A Sentimental Journey*," in *Sterne, Tristram, Yorick: Tercentenary Essays on Laurence Sterne*, ed. Melvyn New, Peter de Voogd, and Judith Hawley (Newark: University of Delaware Press, 2016), 201–18; and for a particularly profound reading of Sterne's ethical thrust, see,

in the same volume, Donald R. Wehrs, "Anarchic Signification and Motions of Grace in Sterne's Novelistic Satire," 77–99.

70 At least two critics, by very different routes, reach a conclusion about the non-resolution of the plot similar to the one I am suggesting. John Allen Stevenson argues that it is a means of "attack[ing] the [illusory] satisfactions we expect of courtship narratives"; see Stevenson, "'A Geometry of His Own': Richardson and the Marriage-Ending," *Studies in English Literature 1500–1900* 26 (1986): 475. Rebecca Anne Barr finds the nonending a means of "insisting upon the inevitability of mitigated happiness"; see Barr, "Richardson's *Sir Charles Grandison* and the Symptoms of Subjectivity," *Eighteenth Century: Theory and Interpretation* 51 (2010): 407.

71 The word *great* will undoubtedly raise modern hackles, as does *genius*. They are meant to do so: see "'A Genius of That Cast': Celebrating Sterne," reprinted as the coda to this collection.

72 Ecclesiastes 12:12 (KJV).

10

Boswell and Sterne in 1768

On earth the righteous man takes the form of a tedious Grandison, in whose eyes even a Venus of the streets would be sexless.

Honoré de Balzac, *Cousin Pons*

It has often been observed that 1759 was a banner year in literature, producing three masterpieces that seem to have much in common, most pertinently, perhaps, that in the so-called age of the novel not one of them fits comfortably into that genre. I refer, of course, to Voltaire's *Candide,* Johnson's *Rasselas,* and the first two volumes of *Tristram Shandy.* We know there were hundreds if not thousands of literary publications in 1759, but only a very few of equal genius. Adam Smith's *Theory of Moral Sentiments* might thus qualify, but certainly not *Memoirs of the Celebrated Miss Fanny Murray.* Both, however, are quite rightfully assigned chapters in *Reading 1759: Literary Culture in Mid-Eighteenth-Century Britain and France.*[1] In celebrating Sterne's final year, 1768, I prefer to eschew the notion of "culture," literary or otherwise, that makes Fanny's *Memoirs* includable, and concentrate instead on a genius equal to Sterne's, pursuing my belief that some writers influence each other because when we read their work we inevitably put them into an overheard conversation.[2] At times that intercourse can involve authors widely separated by time and space, authors who have never actually talked to each other; at other times, as in the present instance, they may be contemporaries or neighbors, intimate or distant as the case may be. What distinguishes the conversation I am listening to, in other words, is not any actual or conscious dialogue but rather one that emerges from works of genius put in proximity. Obviously, readers are the ones overhearing this conversation, indeed creating it, but I invoke the too-often slighted concept of *literary genius* to validate their reports:

genius finds itself justly reflected in conversations not with mediocrity but only with another genius. That, at any rate, is the premise of the conversation I overhear when I bring James Boswell and Laurence Sterne into proximity for the sole reason that both created works of genius in 1768.[3]

A project of this sort clearly requires a certain amount of blindness or deafness. Sterne was writing his final work while staving off death, in part by clinging to the fantasy-driven hope of "new love." He survived only long enough to finish two of the projected four volumes of *A Sentimental Journey*. Boswell, on the other hand, was still a very young man, reluctantly beginning his career in law, dreaming of an alternative career as a famous writer, falling in and out of love with great (ir)regularity but convinced that marriage was the only cure for his appetite for life—and women. These highly significant differences matter little once we put his *Account of Corsica* into proximity with *A Sentimental Journey*.[4] Our deafness will also extend to the historical events and the social and economic innovations of the 1760s, and, even more pertinently given my literary emphasis, to the many voices clamoring for recognition in 1768. Frances Burney began her journals this year, Edward Gibbon started and abandoned his "History of the Swiss," and Henry Mackenzie began writing *The Man of Feeling* (published in 1771). Oliver Goldsmith, Hugh Kelly, George Coleman, Richard Cumberland, and David Garrick all had new plays staged during the 1767–68 season. Poets we might have listened to would include the undervalued Francis Fawkes, a Yorkshire resident, to whose first collection (1761) Sterne had subscribed; this year he published his fine edition of the *Poems of Theocritus*. That the internet allows us to recover tens of thousands of pages of "literature" written in any given year tempts us to believe we can derive from it the year's "literary culture." I suspect, however, that what we will actually derive from this access to an unmanageable wealth of information is evidence only for our preconceived notions, the thousands of pages being irreducible to meaningful interpretation of the actual content of literature.

For example, if I had the opinion that "Scriblerian" satire did not exist, I could sort through a thousand documents with a title that includes *satire* or *satiric* and point to many of them that pay no attention to Swift or Pope: QED. On the other hand, if I believe that the term "Scriblerian" captures a unifying element of the genius of those canonized authors and helps to define the age, I can put them into relationship with another genius and find their existence documented to my own satisfaction. In the two months preceding Boswell's *London Journal,* from September 14 to November 13, 1762, he recorded a journey from Auchinleck to Edinburgh en route to London, his so-called Harvest Jaunt.[5] For his entertainment on the road, Boswell armed himself with several volumes of the Pope-Swift *Miscellanies* (1727), along with Orrery's biography of Swift (1751). On September 17, he refers to "Memoirs of P. P. Clerk of the Parish" (probably by Pope), and five days later to Swift's "Letter to a Young Lady Newly Married." Then, on September 30, he entertains Lord Kames by reading *The Art of Sinking in Poetry,* "a performance which cannot be too often read, as its inimitable humour must always please."[6] All are in *Miscellanies.* That Boswell in 1762, at the age of twenty-two, found the collection worth taking on his journey suffices in my judgment to indicate the reality—indeed the vitality—of the Scriblerians into midcentury—and, of course, our own present day.

Donald R. Wehrs has beautifully confronted this problem in reviewing a book based on electronic research, Brad Pasanek's *Metaphors of Mind: An Eighteenth-Century Dictionary,* a work celebrating "surfing the web, wandering wither the search engine listeth." The results, Wehrs argues, can be useful for readers and scholars, but may also "encourage confusion of appearances of learning with its substance, and invite mistaking industry for achievement. These dangers are prominently satirized by Sterne, Swift, Cervantes, Rabelais, and Erasmus and associated by those writers with reservations about modernity that one might expect eighteenth-century scholars to be cognizant of when they reflect on digitized modernity." Wehrs goes on to note that "availability is no guarantee of significance," and that being able to locate "long unread, out-of-print texts" by using a search engine and "keyword" (e.g., *1768*) and grant such works posthumous recognition is "the scholarly equivalent of a trophy for participation." Rather, he suggests, "the work of time and judgment in regulating forgetting" should not be undone.[7] With this in mind, I want to listen to the conversation Sterne and Boswell had in their works of 1768, the year of the death of one, and the first literary triumph of the other.

It is important to preface my account by acknowledging the fully valid argument of James J. Caudle that much if not all the legend of a Boswell-Sterne relationship in London in 1760 was a construct of Boswell's imaginative mind, a "cock-and-bull story."[8] Boswell would spend much of the ensuing decade in Europe, while Sterne traveled abroad first between January 1762 and June 1764, then again between November 1765 and June 1766. Some cities they had in common, but at different times: for example, Boswell was in Turin in January 1765, Sterne ten months later; in Naples, they missed one another by eleven months, in Rome by a full year. We have some letters written by Sterne during his travels but nothing that compares to Boswell's records. Still, while Sterne would have had little if any reason to think about the young man he may or may not have encountered in his whirlwind days in London, in Utrecht Boswell characterized his journal keeping by recalling Sterne's masterpiece:

> I can never resist anything laughable that presents itself, whether there is occasion for it or not. In this I follow the example of Rabelais, Tristram Shandy, and all those people of unbridled imagination who write their books as I write my themes—at random, without trying to have any order or method; and for that reason they have acquired great reputation among people of unregulated vivacity who do not wish to give themselves the trouble of thinking even in their amusements.[9]

A second mention of Sterne during the decade also occurred in Utrecht, when Boswell was in the company of Robert Brown (1728–77), a fellow Scot and minister of the English Presbyterian Church at Utrecht, who was "a useful and reasonably sympathetic friend" to him during his year of legal studies.[10] Brown is known to Sterne scholars as the author of perhaps the most perceptive and enthusiastic response to the first two volumes of *Tristram Shandy* that we know of: "Never did I read any thing with more delectation. What a comical Fellow the author must be! & I may add also what a Connoisseur in Mankind!" (July 25, 1760; *Letters* 691).[11] One may at least hope that Brown and Boswell held some discourse about Sterne during their many hours together, but the only other mention is that Brown shared Sterne's correspondence with him on March 13, 1764. Whether it was Sterne's reply on September 9, 1760, to the July letter or to more recent letters we do not know.[12]

This is rather scant documentary evidence on which to construct a relationship between the two authors, and especially if we elaborate on the many and enormous differences already suggested. During the 1760s,

254 · Textual and Critical Intersections

while Sterne was writing seven more volumes of *Tristram Shandy*, Boswell first studied law in Utrecht before proceeding on a prolonged Grand Tour through Germany and Switzerland (1764–65), then to Italy and France (1765–66), all the while—in the telling modern title of the final journal volume of the decade—"in search of a wife." Sterne traveled for his health, in part to pursue his wife, who had decided that life in France was better than life with him, in part to keep distance between them. After a bout of severe depression in Utrecht, Boswell was a hale and hearty twentysomething (except for his many episodes of sexually transmitted diseases—or, as he would have put it, "clapt again!"). Sterne, on the contrary, was a wasted body, fleeing from death across the Continent, as he reveals in a telling autobiographical detail at the opening of volume 7 of *Tristram Shandy;* he was also, it might be mentioned, trying to convince Eliza, if not himself, that he was not being treated for a venereal disorder (*BJ* 176–77).

Boswell fell seriously in love with several women during the decade and engaged in sex with countless others, important experiences that filled him with guilt and an abiding concern with the mysteries of free will, sin, and final judgment. The counterweight to this worrisome state of being was an equally abiding faith that he was destined to atone for his weaknesses with great accomplishments. Sterne's sexual activity in the decade, so far as we know, was more limited, but culminated in a love affair with a married woman half his age; he left behind some letters and a portion of his onesided journal to her, a journal that opens to us one strain of the conversation between Sterne and Boswell: the inclination to chronicle their days in terms of their encounters with women. As has been often observed, it is a structuring frame in *A Sentimental Journey*, which was written alongside the *Bramine's Journal*. Finally (although it would be impossible to exhaust all the differences between them), Sterne was to publish his second masterpiece on February 27, 1768, just three weeks before his death—his "work of redemption" as he is said to have labeled it.[13] Nine days before *A Sentimental Journey* appeared, Boswell had published his first masterpiece (February 18), a work that would make him an instant celebrity ("Corsica Boswell"), and also one we might accurately label—if we accept its probable motives—a "work of redemption."[14]

Prior to Boswell's experiences in Corsica, the highlight of his travels was his meeting with Rousseau and Voltaire, both living in Switzerland at the time. Setting aside his ever-present urge to meet famous men and his concomitant desire to be praised by them, one might posit a third motive, already evident in his seeking Johnson's company at the beginning of the decade. More than most men, Boswell was enormously disturbed by the question of free will for the very obvious reason that his life to this point was one in which he constantly willed himself to have control over his sexual and social practice and, with equal constancy, acted otherwise. He had already quickly entered and exited the Roman Catholic Church, which has its own solutions to the problem—namely, celibacy and confession; the first he found impossible, the second was precisely what led him to Johnson, Rousseau, Voltaire, and a host of friends, male and female, to whom he revealed his weaknesses and from whom he sought both advice and reassurance.

We have Boswell's scattered notes of his meeting with Voltaire on December 29, 1764, during which the conversation took a turn indicative of these concerns, one that offers a most useful intersection with Sterne.[15] Pursuing his desire to be known to everyone as the most open and frank young man ever to seek an audience with fame, Boswell tells Voltaire that he had expected to find him great but "very bad," an expectation which sincerity makes him admit; now, although finding him more virtuous than he thought he would, he nevertheless confronts Voltaire with his entry on *soul* in the *Dictionnaire philosophique*. It had bothered Boswell, and he refuses to accept Voltaire's judgment that it was "a good article." Boswell objects most particularly to the notion that immortality is just a "pleasing imagination," insisting instead on its reality: "It must be so." Boswell was quite proud of himself in this encounter and wrote about it to Voltaire a few weeks later (January 15, 1765): "You may remember that I showed no mean timidity; and while I maintained the immortality of my soul, did I not glow with a fire that had some appearance of being divine? I am exceedingly happy that I have had an important conversation with you. . . . Although I am sincerely sorry at your being prejudiced against the doctrines of consolation and hope."[16] Again, in April, he returned to this discussion in a second letter to Voltaire: "It is curious after all to reflect that the Soul is really the All, the man, the thinking principle, the source of everything noble and elegant. . . . (You must forgive my zeal for immortality. I am a melancholy man, I know not how. In this world my prospect is

256 · Textual and Critical Intersections

clouded. I cheer my hours of gloom with expectations of a brighter scene after death, and I think I have a strong probability that I shall not be deceived)."[17]

Where Boswell had written "It must be so," Pottle has interpolated into the text "Like Cato, we all say. . . ." Most readers of *A Sentimental Journey*—and most literate people of the eighteenth century—would not have needed the prompt. Yorick comes to the same passage from Joseph Addison's *Cato* (1713) late in *A Sentimental Journey,* and for the same reason Boswell has invoked him. A few pages earlier, Yorick's meeting with Maria, and his sympathy for her, had culminated in precisely the assertion of positive belief that Boswell wants for himself and finds lacking in Voltaire:

> I felt such undescribable emotions within me, as I am sure could not be accounted for from any combinations of matter and motion.
>
> I am positive I have a soul; nor can all the books with which materialists have pester'd the world ever convince me of the contrary. (*SJ* 151)

This is soon followed by his apostrophe to "Dear sensibility," the "divinity which stirs within" him, although at times this evidence for the existence of a soul is overwhelmed by "sad and sickening moments," when his soul "*shrinks back upon herself, and startles at destruction*'—mere pomp of words!" (*SJ* 155). The Florida editors provide context for the quoted material (*SJ* 372–73). The lines from *Cato* occur at the opening of the fifth act, when Cato sits with "Plato's Book on the Immortality of the Soul" in his hand and a sword in front of him, contemplating suicide:

> It must be so—Plato, thou reason'st well!—
> Else whence this pleasing hope, this fond desire,
> This longing after immortality?
> Or whence this secret dread, and inward horror,
> Of falling into nought? Why shrinks the soul
> Back on herself, and startles at destruction?
> 'Tis the divinity that stirs within us;
> 'Tis heaven itself, that points out an hereafter,
> And intimates eternity to man.
> Eternity! Thou pleasing, dreadful thought![18]

Equally telling are these lines from Nicolas Rowe's *The Fair Penitent* (1703), also, it would seem, on Sterne's mind when constructing the passage: "Hast thou e'er dared to meditate on death? . . . Say, has thou coolly thought? / 'Tis not the stoic's lessons got by rote, / The pomp of words, and pedant dissertations / That can sustain thee in the hour of terror."[19]

Thomas Keymer finds both "sentiment and satire" in *A Sentimental Journey*'s encounter with Maria and in Yorick's assertion of a soul, a combination of "casual sympathy and smug self-approval."[20] I would suggest instead that Yorick and Sterne—and even Boswell—might have considered the "failure of feeling" as the universal failure of Christians when they measure themselves against what they believe is expected of them, both by God and by the soul (conscience) they believe He planted within them. In this process of self-examination, with eternity at stake, the mixture of righteous and condemned behavior in almost every encounter with reality would seem to preclude smugness (or "callous egotism," as Keymer amplifies his disapproval of Sterne), an attitude directly opposed to those who seek salvation with fear and trembling. Of course, this entails reading their writings as if they believed in the soul, in eternity, and in judgment, which is the argument of this essay.

For both Boswell and Sterne, I suggest, the existence of a soul and an afterlife is consistently and frighteningly connected to the possibility of free will. Simply put, both men—one entering his prime, the other sharply aware of impending death—knew that despite every effort, their bodies had triumphed over their better intentions with too-frequent regularity. If they indeed had a soul looking toward immortality, it was in dire straits. Boswell's well-chronicled bouts of dark despair were manifestations not of religious doubt but rather of his worthiness or, more to the point, his unworthiness for religion's promise of immortality. This overt distress helps us toward an understanding of the dying Sterne, who left behind far less by way of personal confessions but in their place a work that transforms Boswell's journalized anxieties into a fictionalized confession of faith, a final statement on the end of a Christian's life. Immersed in both loneliness and illness, when juxtaposed to Boswell, Sterne is an old man confessing to the world what Boswell, as a young man, confessed to Johnson, to Voltaire, to Rousseau, indeed to anyone who would listen: his life was too often a contradiction to his beliefs—and hence to his hopes for immortality.

258 · Textual and Critical Intersections

The suggestion that Boswell, and especially Sterne, would agonize over theological issues is somewhat less suspect than it was a few decades ago, although perhaps we still tend to evaluate their religious faith through secular eyes. Putting the two authors in proximity may encourage us to improve our perspective on what can be so difficult for the modern mind to grasp, that belief in Christian dogma is neither a sign of imbecility nor hypocrisy, neither the privilege of immaturity nor the desperation of the deathbed. With rare exceptions, those who were born in that time and place considered themselves bound by Christianity's truths. Whatever the French Enlightenment produced (and both Sterne and Boswell touched its headsprings, the one with visiting Diderot and d'Holbach, the other with Voltaire and Rousseau), it did not free the vast majority of the British population, and among them the most profound geniuses of the day, into the slumber of secularism[21] that has all too often characterized literary and historical studies of the eighteenth century.[22]

Without doubt, every age adds something to the crucible of Christianity, and the eighteenth century was no exception; but its contribution was something far more important than the rational or empirical knowledge that Enlightenment has come to signify as being essentially hostile to religion. Sterne apostrophizes this new "discovery": "Dear sensibility! source inexhausted of all that's precious in our joys, or costly in our sorrows! thou chainest thy martyr down upon his bed of straw—and 'tis thou who lifts him up to HEAVEN—eternal fountain of our feelings!" (*SJ* 155). Thus opens the paragraph that winds its way to Cato's theorizing of a world without that divine spark of sympathy the soul shares with the "great— great SENSORIUM of the world! Which vibrates, if a hair of our heads but falls upon the ground." The Florida annotators suggest that "Sterne's argument—we awaken to God's presence through our most generous feelings—is well within orthodox boundaries" (*SJ* 373), and indeed it is. I would also suggest, however, that orthodoxy itself subtly shifted from one end of the century to the other, so that now a religion of the heart has, for many, replaced one of the head.[23] Boswell's primary love while in Holland (and for some time thereafter), Belle de Zuylen (Zélide), seems to have anticipated Sterne by some four years: "Blest Sensibility! Zélide will never disown thee, thou sole offset for the misfortune of nice discernment and exacting taste. Thou who causest her to cherish the sweets of Nature, thou who dost bind her to the Arts."[24] That she summons Rousseau's *Émile* at the end of her invocation perhaps separates her from the providential-ism of Sterne's expression,[25] but the distance is a narrow one. Sensibility, from the Cambridge Platonists at the end of the seventeenth century to Rousseau at the end of the eighteenth, was an incorporation of the divine within the human, a turning of Jesus into the original "man of feeling." The reasonableness of self-interest and the urgency of physical desire both had to be overcome by a counterintuitive and disruptive force that embodied belief in an immaterial and immortal essence characterized by its essential distinction from both reason and appetite.[26] Those virtues the self and body could not practice were nonetheless the passport to eternal life, and for Boswell and Sterne the soul became the repository of whatever hopes they retained for an eternity spent in the presence of God.

Boswell wonderfully embodies this most difficult conflict again and again in his travels but perhaps never so starkly as in the following few entries made while he was still in Holland (and trying to practice celibacy). On Sunday, April 15, 1764, he writes in his journal: "Think if GOD really forbids girls," and two days later he writes to his good friend (and another confessor) William Johnson Temple: "Sometimes I think myself good for nothing, and sometimes the finest fellow in the world. . . . I, who am conscious of changes and waverings and weaknesses and horrors, can I look upon myself as a man of dignity?"[27] This attitude pervades much of his Utrecht journal, his periodic "dismal" periods, but we must pay equal attention (and credence) to the path by which he overcomes these moments: "I am now again at rest. I view Deity as I ought to do, and I am convinced that Jesus Christ had a divine commission, that through him the justice of GOD is satisfied; and that he has given us the most exalted morality: 'To love GOD with all our heart, and our neighbour as ourselves'" (to Temple, June 11, 1764).[28] What I would stress here is that for both Boswell and Sterne, confrontation with one's own devices and desires, and one's hope to overcome them and achieve promised salvation, leads to the most mundane and fundamental doctrines of belief: providential care and the Golden Rule—both involved with caring for others more than for oneself.

We have come to think of Sterne as proleptically engaged with theories of the mind, struggling to unravel the novelistic practices by which thought could be displayed on the page. Boswell may help us to see that ideation was not Sterne's preoccupation but that of the age, including those who were never preoccupied with narrative technique: "How strange is the mind of

260 · Textual and Critical Intersections

man! How are our ideas lodged? How are they formed? How little do they depend upon realities!"[29] The problem returns frequently because of Boswell's journalizing; for example, "I find it is impossible to put upon paper an exact journal of the life of man. External circumstances may be marked. But the variations within, the workings of reason and passion, and, what perhaps influence happiness most, the colourings of fancy, are too fleeting to be recorded. In short, so it is that I defy any man to write down anything like a perfect account of what he has been conscious during one day of his life, if in any degree of spirits."[30] Where most Sterne scholars would immediately cite John Locke's *Essay concerning Human Understanding* at this point, Boswell might more pertinently have had Montaigne in mind—or even Augustine's *Confessions,* since the impetus for Boswell's puzzlement is as ethical as it is aesthetic, returning us again and again to his struggle with a will that seems anything but free and most particularly when he deals with desire: "I must observe of myself that from my early years I have never seen an agreeable lady but my warm imagination has fancied as how I might marry her and has suggested a crowd of ideas."[31] We might observe a very similar attitude in Yorick, as with his first encounter with a woman in France: "—Good God! how a man might lead such a creature as this round the world with him!—." In a gesture that he will repeat again and again in *A Sentimental Journey,* the thought then leads him to justify his soul: "In a word, I felt benevolence for her; and resolved some way or other to throw in my mite of courtesy" (*SJ* 22–23), only to allow the body to be reasserted by bawdy innuendo: ". . . if not of service."[32] As Boswell could tell him, he could tell Boswell: the promise of Heaven depends on a will that seems irrepressibly self-destructive, a central mystery of a religion that embraces both omnipotence and free will, divine goodness and the presence of mundane evil. A secular mind may simply dismiss as willful abstraction the desire for immortality and salvation, as Voltaire seems to have done, but as Sterne and Boswell are unable to do.

However, they order things better in France. Boswell, too, was enamored of the idea that a change of place could renew his life: "had I been told that by being drawn some hundreds of miles in a certain machine, seeing another assemblage of houses and some more of those miserable two-legged animals called human . . . I should feel myself a happy man, should view the Creation in an agreeable light . . . I should most certainly have treated him who told me so . . . a very ignorant fellow."[33] But the old

Boswell, filled with regrets and dismal thoughts, never quite disappears, and the usual culprit is temptation: "Bless me, have I now committed adultery? . . . Should I now torment myself with speculations on sin, and on losing in one morning the merit of a year's chastity. No: this is womanish. . . . Let it go. I'll think no more of it. Divine Being! Pardon the errors of a weak mortal. Give me more steadiness. Let me grow more perfect."[34] We might try to resist the secular instinct to dismiss these moments as hypocrisy or as self-deceiving and smug pieties. Instead, if we are willing to rouse ourselves from the dogmatic slumbers of secularism and return to those of Christianity (a fair-enough exchange to make when trying to overhear conversations taking place among believers), we will find in Boswell an honest and painful awareness of his inability to control himself and an often-incapacitating (if increasingly "old-fashioned") dread of final judgment because of it. We might be influenced by different dogmas but still no more able to control our desires than was Boswell. When, therefore, we suspend our secular dismissal of Boswell's anguish and our tut-tutting at Sterne's unclerical conduct, we may then be better prepared to overhear a conversation about being human, still meaningful to the modern reader although it took place 250 years ago.

We left Yorick before the *remise* door, hand in hand with the woman in Calais, contemplating whether he could be of "service" to her. His next words are, "Such were my temptations—and in this disposition to give way to them, was I left alone with the lady with her hand in mine" (*SJ* 23). It is a scene often repeated in *A Sentimental Journey,* tactile encounters where approach and avoidance wrestle with one another.[35] Yorick does not have Boswell's futuristic hope to "mature" and become virtuous. Rather, conflated with Sterne, he is a dying man, painfully aware that his hope is lodged in a Heaven more understanding of weakness than is human judgment. When Yorick first dismisses the fille de chambre, it is with a "kiss of charity, as warm and holy as an apostle" (*SJ* 90), but when he meets her a second time, with thoughts "not in strict unison with the lesson of virtue" (*SJ* 124) of their first meeting, and finally tumbles her on the bed, he rises to the occasion with a dramatic apostrophe: "Yes——and then—Ye whose clay-cold heads and luke-warm hearts can argue down or mask your passions—tell me, what trespass is it that man should have them" (*SJ* 124). Sterne did believe they were a trespass, however, and the rest of the chapter wrestles with the hope that "providence" will take into account the interweaving of body in the same narrow space occupied by head, heart, and soul; his language, typically enough, mirrors exactly this "entangled" web, a plea to God: "Let me feel the movements which rise out of it [the situation], and which belong to me as a man—and if I govern them as a good one—I will trust the issues to thy justice, for thou hast made us—and not we ourselves" (*SJ* 124). The challenge when reading *A Sentimental Journey* is to find in "movements," "as a man," and "issues" not disqualifying bawdry but rather the very essence of the anxieties and fears of Sterne's final illness. We will return to this encounter shortly, but here it suffices to indicate that Sterne's invocation at this point to the "great governor of nature" is really a plea to his God to forgive his lifelong inability to disentangle the conflicting threads of inclination and conscience. For those who believe in possible eternal separation from the Creator, this is a persistent anxiety; and for those who believe they have no such conflict to deal with, I might suggest a rereading of Sterne's "Abuses of conscience" sermon.[36]

For Boswell, almost every encounter with a woman entailed a decision and hence a question of his free will. One such occasion, when Boswell is presented by Louis Dutens[37] to the French Ambassador's wife, will bring Yorick immediately to mind:

> I had the honour to hand her to her coach. About the middle of the stair we were met by a marquise, who of course was to turn back. But the great question was, who should be led first to her coach? *Madame la marquise! Madame l'ambassadrice!* I was simple enough to be tossed from the one to the other, as I did just what I was bid; while the rogue Dutens enjoyed my perplexity and probably studied from it something to insert among his notes on Leibnitz on determining motives. At last her Excellency of France took the *pas*.[38]

The question of protocol here becomes more overtly sexual in Yorick's meeting on the stairs in Milan with another marquise, the Marquesina di F*** (*SJ* 77–78); in both instances one sees an everyday encounter turned into a puzzle that the mind alone seems unable to solve, a mundane puzzle of motivation as Boswell astutely observes in this instance, even while he admits to feeling so helpless a depression over the incident that it spoils the remainder of his evening.

At the end of the seventeenth century the journeys of Boswell and Sterne might well have been written under the sign of John Bunyan's *Pil-*

grim's Progress, wherein each encounter is a temptation to overcome. We tend to slight Bunyan today, but as Samuel Johnson noted in 1773, "it has had the best evidence of its merit, the general and continued approbation of mankind. Few books, I believe, have had a more extensive sale."[39] Not coincidentally, the *Divine Comedy* is part of this same conversation, another literary classic that reflects the pervasiveness of journeying as Christianity's predominant metaphor for each individual existence. When Johnson accepted the task of accompanying Boswell as far as Harwich to begin his travels in 1763, I suspect he saw himself setting the young man forth on a pilgrimage into adulthood. While there they attend church, and, Boswell writes, "Johnson . . . sent me to my knees, saying, 'Now that you are going to leave your native country, recommend yourself to the protection of your CREATOR and REDEEMER.'"[40] That the conversation then turned to Berkeley's immateriality and Johnson's famous kick is significant because if Berkeley was correct, the struggle Boswell felt between his physical and metaphysical parts would have seemed meaningless.[41] Given the challenge of Berkeley, however, and of Locke and Descartes before him, we might suggest that for eighteenth-century Christian travelers, neither Dante nor Bunyan, but Miguel de Cervantes created their model in the knight of La Mancha, Don Quixote. Much has been made of the shifting interpretation of Cervantes's hero during the eighteenth century, whereby the ludicrous madman becomes the idealist creating a better world, but it is worth noting that *Don Quixote* was written some seventy-five years before *Pilgrim's Progress* and in a Roman Catholic country. It is, I suggest, as Christian a work as *Divine Comedy* and *Pilgrim's Progress,* and one that spoke with pertinent significance to mid-eighteenth-century travelers.

Sterne's many allusions to Cervantes have often been commented on, and indeed Gardner Stout sees *Don Quixote* as central to *A Sentimental Journey.*[42] In Yorick's meeting with Maria, during which (as noted) he asserts his assurance that he has a soul, he had begun the episode by picturing himself "like the Knight of the Woeful Countenance, in quest of melancholy adventures" and then had added, "but I know not how it is, but I am never so perfectly conscious of the existence of a soul within me, as when I am entangled in them" (*SJ* 149). Boswell is not as multifold in his allusiveness to Cervantes, but on the day he sat down to begin writing his *Account of Corsica* (March 27, 1767) he reports that his father was reading *Don Quixote* and was "much entertained with him. . . . Joked on my Account;

called it quixotism." Earlier in the same month, he had written to Temple: "You say well that I find mistresses wherever I am. But I am a sad dupe, a perfect Don Quixote."[43] Nine years earlier, at the age of eighteen, Boswell had already recognized something quixotic in his relationship with women, again in his correspondence to Temple, on July 29, 1758: "You used to admonish not to turn an Old Man too soon, dont be thunderstruck, if this same fellow, should all at once, subito furore obreptus, commence Don Quixote for his adorable Dulcinea. But, to talk seriously, I at first fell violently in love with her."[44]

While both Sterne, especially with his letters and journal to Eliza, and Boswell, with almost every woman he meets, partake of Quixote's imaginary romance with Dulcinea, it is in the *Account of Corsica* and *A Sentimental Journey* that we find the most striking influence of Cervantes. Early in Cervantes's opening volume, Quixote recites at length to a company of shepherds the perfections he plans to restore, creating a world in which there is "no fraud, no deceit, no malice intermixed with plain-dealing truth: justice . . . undisturbed and unbiassed by interest and favour, which now impair, confound, and persecute her."[45] The speech precedes the first of several similar inset tales, often masterful versions of the idyllic fictions Cervantes parodies through his woeful knight: in this particular romance, the shepherd Chrysostom dies of love, rejected by the beautiful Marcella. Both Quixote and Chrysostom are willing to die for the cause of a beautiful, harmonious, and peaceful world, whether found in the books read by Quixote, or in the woman loved by the shepherd, but their desire for a return to Edenic purity entails no reciprocal response from those whom they encounter. Indeed, as Quixote all too often discovers, his attempts arouse hostility or comic dismissal from those whom he intends to convert to his own vision of the good.

On the other hand, Cervantes and his readers surely knew these scriptural verses: "Where is the wise? . . . hath not God made foolish the wisdom of this world?"[46] a verse at the heart of Erasmus's *Praise of Folly* and still foundational, if reluctantly so, to the ethics of the Enlightenment. Erasmus states the proposition thus: "The entire Christian religion seems to bear a certain natural affinity to folly, and to relate far less clearly to wisdom. . . . You see that no fools are more distracted than those whose ardent zeal for Christian piety has wholly eaten them up. They discard their belongings, swallow insults, put up with trickery, . . . subsist on fasts, vigils, tears, toils, and humiliations. They shun life, seek death . . . as if their souls existed somewhere else, not in their bodies."[47] The conclusion of *Praise of Folly* is replete with difficult ironies and paradoxes, but importantly it opens a counterintuitive pathway for the appraisal of Quixote as a character quite other than a mere fool; he now becomes, theologically, a "fool for Christ."

As the Enlightenment progresses, the two "fools" will merge into a composite whole, Quixote becoming an admired, indeed beloved, but *secular* idealist, a stubborn reformer who, in the words of his twentieth-century incarnation, will dream "impossible dreams." Where Erasmus's fool attempts to gain salvation by reenacting the simplicity and sacrifice of Christ, Enlightenment's fool wages war on the ills of the world in the belief that humankind will be saved by human effort. No longer a fool, no longer a fool for Christ, the new Quixote will eventually become a force for social and political good (and, sadly enough, for totalitarian states, an embodiment of their own versions of what is good for others). For Boswell and Sterne, however, in the middle of the eighteenth century, the fool melds the two strands of reformer and soul seeker into the figure of sensibility. We can see this in one of Boswell's laments while in Turin, a hotbed of sexual temptations: "I saw that amongst profligate wretches a man of sentiment could only expose himself." Or again, "My sensibility is so delicate that I must fairly own it to be weak and unmanly. It prevents me from having a decent and even conduct in the course of ordinary life."[48] Boswell sees "sensibility" as a cause of both strength and weakness, a duality he confronts most cogently when deriving from Pasquale de Paoli's character a lesson for life:

> I saw from Paoli's example the great art of preserving young men of spirit from the contagion of vice, in which there is often a species of sentiment, ingenuity and enterprise nearly allied to virtuous qualities.
>
> Shew a young man that there is more real spirit in virtue than in vice, and you have a surer hold of him, during his years of impetuosity and passion, than by convincing his judgment of all the rectitude of ethicks.[49]

One has in this character of Paoli the essence of what Boswell wanted to learn on his Grand Tour, his own quixotic search for self-control on the one hand, greatness on the other. The quixotic at midcentury is, I am suggesting, the visionary future in which all evils will be overcome by Enlightenment, including the evils of sickness, sinfulness, separation, even death—and, in contrast, a continuing belief in the truth of a religion that considers sin and death inherent to the human condition and hence a fool's or madman's errand (knight-errantry)[50] to reform oneself or the world. Reformation is embodied for both authors in the failures of their wills, Enlightenment, in their desire to assert their souls.[51]

On the Friday Sterne died (March 18, 1768), Boswell was once again traveling, this time from Edinburgh to York; he made no inquiry after the Yorkshire native, but on Saturday visited York Minster ("Saw the cathedral. It is a prodigiously noble Gothic edifice"), where Sterne preached at times, and on Sunday went to a play at the York Theater and then had an excellent supper.[52] Between these activities he also pursued a very young girl, Mary, "a pretty, lively little girl whom accident had thrown in my way a few days before," whom he has decided to save from profligate men after first testing her "virtue": "I find I am still somewhat of a Don Quixote, for now am I in love with perhaps an abandoned, worthless being."[53] A second encounter then calls forth this exclamation: "How strange is this! The author of the *Account of Corsica* the sport of a frivolous passion. Shall my mind ever be all solid and rational? Yes. A room which is hung with the slightest chintz and gaudiest paper may by and by be hung with substantial velvet or even thick arras hangings with scripture stories wrought upon them. My walls are good, so they will bear any sort of hangings."[54]

The juxtaposition of Mary and Corsica is what at the outset of *Tristram Shandy* Sterne calls the "*cervantick* tone" (*TS* 1.12.34),[55] which might be simplified, for the present purpose, as a voice aware of the conflict between vision and reality, between a desire to improve ourselves and our world and the persistent resistance to that desire. Boswell's brief time in York is part of his journey to London to celebrate the publication of his *Account*. Johnson was in Oxford at the time, but he sent Boswell a most typical letter of deflation: "I wish you would empty your head of Corsica, which I think has filled it rather too long" (March 23, 1768).[56] Boswell's epistolary response soars to quixotic heights:

But how can you bid me "empty my head of Corsica?" . . . Consider fairly what is the case. The Corsicans never received any kindness from the Genoese. . . . They owe them nothing; and when reduced to an abject state of slavery by force, shall they not rise in the great cause of liberty and break the galling yoke?[57] . . . Empty my head of Corsica! Empty it of honour, empty it of humanity, empty it of friendship, empty it of piety. No! while I live, Corsica and the cause of the brave Islanders shall ever employ much of my attention, shall ever interest me in the sincerest manner.[58]

A very useful discussion of the meaning of Corsica to Boswell and his age can be found in the introduction to the Boulton-McLoughlin edition, as well as an awareness of the conflict I am exploring:

One of the compelling reasons for Boswell to visit Corsica was that he wanted to see for himself the native islanders who were fighting for their freedom. Rousseau was perhaps the first to bring him to focus on this singular example in Europe of a people striving for nationhood. . . . There are aspects of Boswell on the Grand Tour that bring him close to Pope's caricature, "The Stews and Palace equally explor'd / Intrigu'd with glory, and with spirit whor'd." But the seriousness of his curiosity about Corsica more than makes up for this.[59]

Despite the "best intentions" of the Corsicans and Boswell, General Paoli was defeated by the French in May 1769, and Corsica became a French territory (and remains so today); six months after that, Boswell married his cousin Margaret Montgomerie (November 1769), was reconciled to his father, entered seriously into the profession of law, and paraded his Corsican outfit at Garrick's Shakespeare festival. In quixotic terms, the world reasserted itself—and the fate of human will in its struggle with the realities of body and mind remained unresolved, if not defeated. And yet, when we position ourselves to listen to a conversation between Boswell and Sterne, are we not saying, as did Addison's Cato, "it must be so"? Are we not, when overhearing any conversation from the past, listening to a "divinity that stirs within us," providing an "intimation of eternity"—or, as Wordsworth would phrase it, "intimations of immortality"? Stripped of the Christian promise, our only access to what Boswell and Sterne thought when they

268 · Textual and Critical Intersections

invoked "this pleasing hope, this fond desire, / This longing after immortality" (their "souls") is our capacity to overhear the sensibilities of one enduring author conversing with another. Indeed, it seems quite possible that just such dialogues have always been what humanity has taken (and mistaken) to be the voice of God.

Boswell would live the second half of his life after 1768, and his major literary achievement was still ahead of him. In the same month that he began writing *Corsica,* Sterne began a journal to Eliza Draper, whom he had met some three months earlier: "you shall see it, for if I live not till your return to England, I will leave it you as a legacy" (*Letters* 550). Whatever flights of fancy Sterne indulged in when writing to Eliza, his dying is the final truth to which all his dreams revert. And he does dream excessively, much induced by illness we can assume, but certainly a portion of his desire for Eliza was to justify his sexual life with a final bodiless encounter with his own Dulcinea; she is, after all, "not handsome," but still appeals to a "man of sense, tenderness, and feeling"; in short, she possesses "that bewitching sort of nameless excellence, that men of *nice sensibility* alone can be touch'd with" (*Letters* 553). This chord is struck again and again in his address to her, entwined with biblical snatches, prayers for her safe passage, and dreams of his wife's demise, with Eliza's husband also fading from the scene and a future idyllic life for the two of them, happily forever after. The quixotic underwrites the entire affair, as Sterne caroms between his own dying body and his desire for justification.

What appears in rather naked and desperate openness in the *Bramine's Journal* and Sterne's letters to Eliza is given aesthetic cover in *A Sentimental Journey,* but it is an often-committed error of interpretation to overlook the biographical fact that its author was a dying man, fearful, even as a good Christian still has to be, of the righteous judgment awaiting him. He had been sanctified to preach this day of judgment to others for more than thirty years, but as with his congregants, he had too often ignored in life what he preached in church. Nowhere is this conflict more evident than in his sermon "The Levite and his concubine," wherein he preaches three different lessons: (1) it is very difficult for a body to live without human companionship; (2) a loving God understands this and forgives weaknesses of the body; and (3) that same God is far more forgiving (and virtuous) than one's gossiping neighbors.

The first truth returns us to the struggle between our will and our reason: thus, when Sterne presents the "concubine," he asks his congregation to consider that "our actions stand surrounded with a thousand circumstances which do not present themselves at first sight; . . . the difficulties and temptations under which they acted,——the force of the passions ——the suitableness of the object, and the many struggles of virtue before she fell,——may be so many appeals from justice to the judgment seat of pity" (*Sermons* 168).[60] When he turns to the Levite, his justification echoes the writings of John Norris of Bemerton, whose presence in both *Tristram Shandy* and *A Sentimental Journey* has come to be recognized as central to Sterne's theology. Thus where Sterne writes, "Yet still, '*it is not good for man to be alone:*' nor can all which the cold-hearted pedant stuns our ears with upon the subject, ever give one answer of satisfaction to the mind; in the midst of the loudest vauntings of philosophy, Nature will have her yearnings for society and friendship" (*Sermons* 169–70), he is copying from Norris's discourse "Of Solitude": "We all . . . stand in need of one anothers help at every turn, both for the *Necessities* and *Refreshments* of Life. And therefore I am very far from commending the undertaking of those *Asetics,* that out of a pretence of keeping themselves *unspotted from the World* . . . abandon all Human Society." Unless one is a God, Norris continues, "*It is not good for man* (tho in *Paradice* it self) *to be alone.*"[61] Sterne was preparing this sermon for the press even while writing *A Sentimental Journey,* as reflected in the words of Yorick's second encounter with the fille de chambre, already quoted: "Yes——and then—Ye whose clay-cold heads and luke-warm hearts [etc.]" (*SJ* 124).[62]

In the sermon's next paragraph, Sterne gives yet another version of the "cold-hearted pedant," the "*Asetics,*" the "clay-cold heads": "Let the torpid Monk seek heaven comfortless and alone——GOD speed him! For my own part, I fear, I should never so find the way: let me be wise and religious—but let me be M A N: wherever thy Providence places me, or whatever be the road I take to get to thee——give me some companion in my journey" (*Sermons* 170). The road and the journey come naturally to the sermonizer as images for life itself and return us to Quixote and Boswell as well as to the man Sterne as opposed to the priest. All three wanted to do more than seems possible for a man to do, all three are again returned to the world and its realities.

Still, Quixote's dream of correcting the injustices of the world becomes part of the Enlightenment dream of progressive amelioration of ourselves and others, and Boswell's own knight-errantry entitles him to a sense of accomplishment and achievement that endures to this day: in Corsica's struggles, he had placed himself and the Corsicans on the right side of history. As for Sterne, his Eliza was perhaps just another Dulcinea, a work of an overheated imagination; and his letters and journal to her, just his own attempt at knight-errantry, replete with language using the clichés from those books Cervantes both satirized and, in his interpolated tales, imitated. Sterne's final exploit, however, is the writing of *A Sentimental Journey,* a work that makes him, perhaps, the most quixotic hero of the three. It is a book written with all the marks of the author's humanity about him, a man still striving toward forgiveness and immortality although staking his claim not on a reformation that eludes him, but rather on an insistence that his God would know him for the divided being He had created. Sterne's *Journey* is the final heroic declaration he left behind for us all, but particularly in conversation with Boswell, assuring him that for the duration of his journey or pilgrimage through life, every moment of Grace (as in the title of its penultimate chapter),[63] every connection in life where we believe we can, with awakened sensibility, perceive "*Religion* mixing in the dance," will be followed by a "Case of Delicacy," his final chapter. Ever and again, the body will be confronted by irresistible temptations in defiance of our reason and our piety, and we will end with our hand stretched across the empty space surrounding us, seeking whatever solace we hope is out there. For Sterne, facing his own death and judgment, *A Sentimental Journey* is a particular act of quixotic heroism, a final assertion that being human, all too human, can also promise immortality, or, "in the tender strokes of nature which the poet has wrought up in that pathetic speech of Perseus: '*O Cupid, prince of God and men &c.*'" (*SJ* 45).

Originally published in *Laurence Sterne's "A Sentimental Journey": A Legacy to the World* (2021).

Notes

1 See, in Shaun Regan, ed., *Reading 1759: Literary Culture in Mid-Eighteenth-Century Britain and France* (Lewisburg, PA: Bucknell University Press, 2013): Nigel Wood, "Adam Smith's *The Theory of Moral Sentiments* in 1759: Specta-

torship, Duty, and Social Improvement," 57–74; and Mary Peace, "'On the soft beds of luxury most kingdoms have expired': 1759 and the Lives of Prostitutes," 75–91.

2 I have pursued this line of inquiry over three decades, beginning with "Proust's Influence on Sterne: A Remembrance of Things to Come," *MLN* 103 (1988): 1031–55; and more recently in "'A Genius of That Cast': Celebrating Sterne" and "Richardson's *Sir Charles Grandison* and Sterne: A Study in Influence," reprinted as the coda and chapter 9 in this volume, respectively.

3 Concomitant with the concept of genius is that of literary canonization, which, as with its religious counterpart, remains for me a telling act of spiritual belief. The capacity to be canonized derives from an achievement that measures itself against those who are already canonized and should (although it rarely does) remain beyond all the social or political considerations that might motivate those who are empowered to add to—or subtract from—the canon. Despite efforts, early and late—e.g., F. R. Leavis, *The Great Tradition* (New York: Doubleday, 1954), 11n2 (where he refers to Sterne's "irresponsible [and nasty] trifling"); or Donald Greene, "The World's Worst Biography," *American Scholar* 62, no. 3 (1993): 365–82—Sterne and Boswell remain canonized literary geniuses, whose conversation we can hear if we quiet contemporary conversations about our own predilections and concerns.

4 For the best edition of *An Account of Corsica*, see James Boswell, *An Account of Corsica, The Journal of a Tour to That Island, and Memoirs of Pascal Paoli*, ed. James T. Boulton and T. O. McLoughlin (Oxford: Oxford University Press, 2006). Citations to these texts refer to this edition.

5 See James Boswell, *Boswell's London Journal*, ed. Frederick A. Pottle (London: William Heinemann, 1951; numbered edition only), 43–111.

6 Boswell, 46, 56, 65.

7 Donald R. Wehrs, review of *Metaphors of Mind: An Eighteenth-Century Dictionary*, by Brad Pasanek, *Scriblerian* 50, no. 1 (2017): 79. The concept of rightful and necessary "forgetting" is Nietzsche's, what Wehrs characterizes as "an evolutionarily valuable skill."

8 James J. Caudle, "'Fact' or 'Invention'? James Boswell and the Legend of a Boswell-Sterne Meeting," *Shandean* 22 (2011): 30–55.

9 James Boswell, *Boswell in Holland, 1763–1764*, ed. Frederick A. Pottle (New York: McGraw Hill, 1952), 68–69 (November 1763) (hereafter, *Holland*). Boswell refers specifically to the daily exercises he wrote in his journal in the languages he was, at that moment, trying to master. It is important to note that throughout this essay I have consulted only the "trade" edition of Boswell's writings; generalizations, therefore, await final validation from the "research" edition.

10 *Holland,* 23n2.

11 That Brown singled out the influence of Montaigne ("he is no stranger to Montaigne; nay . . . he is full as well acquainted with him, as with the book of common prayer"; *Letters* 692) is noteworthy. Perhaps only Boswell among eighteenth-century British authors exhibits an equal engagement with *Les Essais.*

12 *Holland,* 180.

13 The comment was reported by Richard Griffith in *A Series of Genuine Letters between Henry and Frances* (1786), vol. 5, 83: "It has all the Humour and Address of the best Parts of Tristram, and is quite free from the Grossness of the worst. . . . He . . . calls it his *Work of Redemption.*"

14 Boswell wrote to his friend William Johnson Temple on May 3, 1769: "Never did there live such a man as myself. I beseech you write to me without delay: Dublin is address enough for *Corsican Boswell.*" James Boswell, *Boswell in Search of a Wife, 1766–1769,* ed. Frank Brady and Frederick A. Pottle (New York: McGraw-Hill, 1956), 202 (Hereafter, *Search*). Typically enough, Boswell was on his way to Ireland to court the latest of his possible wives, Mary Ann Boyd, traveling with his cousin Margaret Montgomerie, to whom (Margaret) he would propose a few months later, and marry in November 1769. We recall that Sterne too was so popular it was rumored that "A Letter addressed to Tristram Shandy in Europe shou'd reach him" and indeed did, if we believe for once the usually unreliable John Croft in "Anecdotes of Sterne," *Shandean* 19 (2008): 54, originally published in Charles Whitefoord and Caleb Whitefoord, *The Whitefoord Papers,* ed. W. A. S. Hewins (Oxford: Clarendon, 1898). Croft wrote his anecdotes in 1795.

15 James Boswell, *Boswell on the Grand Tour: Germany and Switzerland, 1764,* ed. Frederick A. Pottle (New York: McGraw-Hill, 1953), 303–4 (hereafter, *Germany*).

16 *Germany,* 319.

17 *Germany,* 322.

18 Here quoted from Joseph Addison, *Cato: A Tragedy and Selected Essays,* ed. Christine Dunn Henderson and Mark E. Yellin (Indianapolis, IN: Liberty Fund, 2004), 88 (act 5, scene 1, lines 1–10); the editors point out that Cato is reading Plato's *Phaedo.*

19 Nicholas Rowe, *The Fair Penitent,* ed. Malcolm Goldstein (Lincoln: University of Nebraska Press, 1969), 63 (act 5, scene 1, lines 77, 79–82).

20 Thomas Keymer, "*A Sentimental Journey* and the Failure of Feeling," in *The Cambridge Companion to Laurence Sterne,* ed. Thomas Keymer (Cambridge: Cambridge University Press, 2009), 90–91.

21 I allude to Kant's famous awakening from the "dogmatic slumber" induced

by Hume's dismissal of metaphysics, without engaging with the arguments of either; suffice to say, the dogmatic slumbers of religious faith can too easily be replaced with the dogmatic slumbers of secularism, both equally smug in their certainties. Enough scholarly progress has been made in recent years toward modifying our secularist views so that younger scholars may feel I have exaggerated our past smugness. An exchange between myself and an unnamed scholar fictionalized in my introduction to *Theology and Literature in the Age of Johnson: Resisting Secularism*, ed. Melvyn New and Gerard Reedy, SJ (Newark: University of Delaware Press, 2012), xiv–xvii, will suggest the atmosphere thirty years ago, when the actual exchange took place in the pages of *Eighteenth-Century Life* in 1992–93.

22 Boswell's account of Voltaire's direct encounter with disbelief is telling: "He expressed his veneration—his love—of the Supreme Being, and his entire resignation to the will of Him who is All-wise. He expressed his desire to resemble the Author of Goodness by being good himself. . . . He does not inflame his mind with grand hopes of the immortality of the soul. He says it may be, but he knows nothing of it. And his mind is in perfect tranquility." But then, in asserting his sincerity of belief, Voltaire goes on, "I suffer much. But I suffer with patience and resignation; not as a Christian—but as a man." Perhaps we should take Boswell's account of Voltaire cum grano salis, but the opposition between tranquility and suffering, between being a Christian and a man, is certainly present in both Boswell and Sterne, if not in Voltaire, who, we must remind ourselves, when told by Boswell that Johnson was "orthodox," replied: "He is then a dog. A superstitious dog. No worthy man was ever superstitious." *Germany*, 294, 300.

23 My longtime colleague Richard E. Brantley, over a course of seven full-length studies of nineteenth-century British and American authors, has argued with cogency for an evangelical (Methodist) merger of mind and heart, studies that culminate with a reading of Emily Dickinson: "The poet collapses distinction between mind and heart and creates thereby an uneasy but sympathetic composite of common humanity." Brantley, *Transatlantic Trio: Empiricism, Evangelicalism, Romanticism* (Ames, IA: Culicidae Press, 2017), 34. For Sterne and Boswell such a "collapse" of distinction was not possible, because their minds and hearts rarely merged. Sensibility was the century's fresh attempt to reconcile mind and heart by turning from oneself to others, an attempt codified, e.g., in Adam Smith's *Theory of Moral Sentiments*. It was enthusiastically preached from Anglican as well as dissenting pulpits, with a stress on caring for rather than judging others, emulating God's mercy rather than justice. This shift in emphasis between two teachings both easily derived from Scripture was Christianity's attempt to reconcile religious faith with empirical knowl-

edge (the challenge of Enlightenment), but an "empirical faith" seems remote from both Sterne and Boswell. Sternean ironies and Boswellian fear and trembling reflect far more Kierkegaard's impasse than the age's embrace of sensibility.

24 *Holland*, 188. Cf. in the same volume Boswell's friend George Dempster to Boswell, August 22, 1763: "Adieu, thou mass of sensibility!" (11).

25 Sterne alludes to Matthew 10:29–31, the most fundamental providential assertion in Scripture. See also Luke 12:7 and several Old Testament versions, including 1 Samuel 14:45, 2 Samuel 14:11, and 1 Kings 1:52.

26 One will recognize in this formulation a dependence on the excellent work of Donald R. Wehrs, "Levinas and Sterne: From the Ethics of the Face to the Aesthetics of Unrepresentability," in *Critical Essays on Laurence Sterne*, ed. Melvyn New (New York: G. K. Hall, 1998), 311–29; and Wehrs, "Anarchic Signification and Motions of Grace in Sterne's Novelistic Satire," in *Sterne, Tristram, Yorick: Tercentenary Essays on Laurence Sterne*, ed. Melvyn New, Peter de Voogd, and Judith Hawley (Newark: University of Delaware Press, 2016), 77–99.

27 *Holland*, 222, 223.

28 *Holland*, 282.

29 *Germany*, 16.

30 *Search*, 242.

31 *Germany*, 23.

32 The biblical echo, "And there came a certain poor widow, and she threw in two mites" (Mark 12:42), is played against *service*, a word Sterne well knew could evoke the Shandy bull, kept "for the service of the Parish" (*TS* 9.33.807).

33 *Germany*, 35.

34 *Germany*, 91.

35 Ray McDermott, applying his training as an ethnologist, examines in minute detail the complexity of Yorick's interaction with his partner in this scene; see McDermott, "Yorick's Ethnographic Journey," in New, de Voogd, and Hawley, *Sterne, Tristram, Yorick*, 169–86, esp. 180. See also, Anne Bandry, "Les livres de Sterne: Suites et fins," *XVII–XVIII: Revue de la Société d'études anglo-américaines des XVIIe et XVIIIe siècles* 50 (2000): 132–33, where she notes that in *A Sentimental Journey* Sterne uses the word *hand* more often than *heart* (107 occurrences to 62), or any other common noun except *man*. Sterne's tactile sensitivity, a hyperawareness of human touch, is matched by Boswell's: e.g., "I sat [at the opera] vis-à-vis to her and pressed her legs with mine, which she took very graciously." James Boswell, *Boswell on the Grand Tour: Italy, Corsica, France*, ed. Frank Brady and Frederick A. Pottle (New York: McGraw-Hill, 1955), 28 (January 10, 1765) (hereafter, *Italy*). Or again,

"I sat close behind the Princess, and at the most affecting scenes [of *Othello*], I pressed my hand upon her waist. She was in tears, and rather leaned to me." *Search*, 109 (December 24, 1767). A distinction between touching and groping might not have occurred to either party, although Boswell does seem more culpable than Yorick—we do not know about Sterne. At a time of increased electronic isolation, it is perhaps well to recall one of Boswell's astute comments about his social nature: "in the immense multiplicity of human beings, the more attachments we can form, the better." *Search*, 116.

36 I think it no accident that Sterne published this sermon three times, once in 1751 in a pamphlet, then in volume 2 of *Tristram Shandy* (1759–60), and a third time in volume 4 of the *Sermons of Mr. Yorick* (1766). It is, perhaps, his most complete statement of what he perceived to be the basis of human nature, his own included: in a word, self-deception.

37 This is the same Louis Dutens who met Sterne at a dinner in Paris and was amused by Sterne abusing him to the guests, not realizing he was at the table (*SJ* 278, n. to 40.2); he subscribed to *Sermons* in 1769. As Boswell and Sterne crisscrossed Europe, they often encountered the same people, including many English travelers; Boswell, however, had far more contact with the nobility than did Sterne, wealth and property (and the title baron) having more sway than genius, then and now.

38 *Italy*, 30.

39 James Boswell, *Life of Johnson*, ed. R. W. Chapman and Pat Rogers (Oxford: World Classics, 1980), 529.

40 Boswell, 333.

41 What could Boswell (or Sterne) do with this typical conclusion from Berkeley: "Not to mention that the apprehension of a distant deity, naturally disposes men to a negligence in their *moral* actions, which they would be more cautious of, in case they thought him immediately present, and acting on their minds without the interposition of matter, or unthinking second causes." George Berkeley, *Three Dialogues between Hylas and Philonous*, ed. Robert Merrihew Adams (Indianapolis, IN: Hackett, 1982), 90.

42 Laurence Sterne, *A Sentimental Journey*, ed. Gardner D. Stout (Berkeley: University of California Press, 1967), 44–46 and passim.

43 *Search,* 45, 35.

44 *The Correspondence of James Boswell and William Johnson Temple, 1756–1795*, ed. Thomas Crawford (New Haven, CT: Yale University Press, 1997), vol. 1, 6.

45 Miguel de Cervantes, *The History and Adventures of the Renowned Don Quixote*, trans. Tobias Smollett, ed. Martin C. Battestin and O M Brack (Athens: University of Georgia Press, 2003), 74 (part 1, book 2, chapter 3).

46 See 1 Corinthians 1:20 (KJV).

276 · Textual and Critical Intersections

47 Desiderius Erasmus, *The Praise of Folly and Other Writings*, trans. Robert M. Adams (New York: W. W. Norton, 1989), 82–83.

48 *Italy*, 39, 112.

49 *Account of Corsica*, 180.

50 Cf. Temple to Boswell, January 8, 1768: "Undoubtedly . . . my dear Boswell; the romance of knight-errantry is no more. . . . Does not this shock the sensibility of your enthusiastic soul?" Temple, as he often does, confronts Boswell with his weakness: "The great Baron, the friend of Rousseau and Voltaire, the companion of Paoli, the author of that immortal work, the Account of Corsica, is dwindled into a whining, fawning lover, the slave of a fair hand and a pair of black eyes." *Search*, 120, 119.

51 I deliberately invoke the capitalized terms, Reformation and Enlightenment, to suggest that, as Erasmus perceived, both movements contained within themselves the countermovements, if not self-destructive impulses, that twentieth-century modernism, in art and literature, had to confront.

52 *Search*, 135–36.

53 *Search*, 135. *O tempora! O mores!* Today we are often appalled, as here, by Boswell's (and Sterne's) rather overt objectification and demeaning of women; it is quite impossible to predict what will appall readers 250 years from now about our own age, but, again, Sterne's sermon on conscience and "self-deception" might provide one clue.

54 *Search*, 137. In one of those eerie moments of confluence, Boswell at this time also engages in a coffeehouse discussion about Corsica with Sir George Armytage (MP for York, 1761–68) and receives Armytage's compliments on the *Account of Corsica* ("authentic and very accurate") without revealing his identity as the author. Sir George had subscribed to Sterne's *Sermons* in 1760; one suspects *A Sentimental Journey* never came up in their conversation.

55 The Florida annotation to this passage (*TS*, Notes 75, n. to 34.25) indicates the far greater complexities triggered by Sterne's several allusions to Cervantes and his tone; see also, *TS*, Notes 216, n. to 200.6.

56 *Search*, 164–65.

57 Sterne's own brief encounter with the issue of slavery has received outsize attention in recent years, both favorable and unfavorable, indicative of our proclivity to enlist past authors into our own party—or to exclude them. Here we shall simply note Boswell's own reflection on sighting prison ships in the harbor of Marseilles, imagining how the prisoners might think: "If we could escape, we should certainly do it. A bird shut up in a cage desires freedom, and so much the more should a man desire it." *Italy*, 243. I am inclined to praise their sensibility, but of course we tend to believe our own sensibilities far better honed than those of the past.

58 *Search,* 164–65. Corsican tradition, it is worth noting, considerably helped Boswell to leave his whoring behind: "They told me that in their country I should be treated with the greatest hospitality; but if I attempted to debauch any of their women, I might expect instant death." *Account of Corsica,* 165. Significantly, *An Account of Corsica* had every bit as much success as the first two volumes of *Tristram Shandy* a decade earlier. It was quickly translated into Dutch, French, German, and Italian; and Benjamin Franklin "did not find it difficult to draw political analogies between the Corsicans and the American colonists on the subject of liberty." *Account of Corsica,* li. One might also claim for the *Account* an influence on Byron's fierce interest in Greek independence.

59 *Account of Corsica,* xxxi.

60 As has often been observed, Sterne does not pursue the quite horrid subsequent events of Judges 19.

61 John Norris, *A Collection of Miscellanies,* 2nd ed. (1692), 159, quoted from *Sermons,* Notes 208. Some very good work has been done on Norris and Sterne in recent years, but for the present subject perhaps the most pertinent is Geoff Newton, "Divine and Human Love: Letters between John Norris and Mary Astell, Laurence Sterne and Eliza Draper," in New and Reedy, *Theology and Literature in the Age of Johnson,* 183–201. Significantly, another important borrowing from Norris in *Journey* concerns the unfitness for Heaven of Smelfungus and Mundungus (*SJ* 38; see also 273, n. to 38.4–13). See also Melvyn New, "Job's Wife and Sterne's Other Women," in *Out of Bounds: Male Writers and Gender(ed) Criticism,* ed. Laura Claridge and Elizabeth Langland (Amherst: University of Massachusetts Press, 1990), 55–74.

62 The Florida annotations (*Sermons,* Notes 208) point significantly enough to the opening paragraph of Johnson's sermon on marriage: "That society is necessary to the happiness of human nature, that the gloom of solitude, and the stillness of retirement . . . neither extinguish the passions, nor enlighten the understanding, that discontent will intrude upon privacy, and temptations follow us to the desert, every one may be easily convinced, either by his own experience, or that of others." *The Sermons of Samuel Johnson,* ed. Jean Hagstrum and James Gray (New Haven, CT: Yale University Press, 1978), 3. Surely when Boswell confessed his failures in 1762, Johnson provided just such consolation to him.

63 Cf. *Account of Corsica,* 165, when Boswell is sailing to the island of Corsica: "At sunset all the people in the ship sung the Ave Maria, with great devotion and some melody. It was pleasing to enter into the spirit of their religion, and hear them offering up their evening orisons."

II

Single and Double

Memoirs of Martinus Scriblerus and *Tristram Shandy*

Is it not *Demonstration* to a person of your Sense that, since *you cannot find it,* there is *no such thing?*

The Society of Free-Thinkers to Martinus Scriblerus

In an earlier essay, I brought James Boswell's early triumph, *Account of Corsica,* into juxtaposition with Laurence Sterne's final triumph, *A Sentimental Journey,* both written in 1768, as an example of how literary genius talks to literary genius across disparities in age, in intention, in genre. I began that discussion with Boswell's "Harvest Jaunt" in 1762, but since that essay was focused on the end of Sterne's career (and life) in 1768, I did not amplify on a point made early in the essay concerning Boswell's reading on his journey from Auchinleck to Edinburgh in route to London between September 14 and November 13, 1762.[1] The aspiring author had armed himself with several volumes of the Pope-Swift *Miscellanies* (London: Benjamin Motte, 1727), along with Orrery's *Remarks on the Life and Writings of Dr. Jonathan Swift* (1751). On September 17, his journal refers to "Memoirs of P. P., Clerk of this Parish" (probably by Pope), and five days later to Swift's "A Letter to a Very Young Lady, on her Marriage." Then, on September 30, he entertained Lord Kames by reading *The Art of Sinking in Poetry,* "a performance which cannot be too often read, as its inimitable humour must always please."[2] All are in *Miscellanies.* That Boswell in 1762, at the age of twenty-two, found the collection worth taking on his journey suffices, for some of us, to indicate the reality and vitality of the Scriblerians into midcentury—and, of course, to our own present day. Quite probably a search of Eighteenth Century Collections Online (ECCO) can find a

Single and Double: *Memoirs of Martinus Scriblerus* and *Tristram Shandy* · 279

thousand authors thinking of themselves as satirists without evidencing any sign of having read the *Miscellanies*—much less competence in imitating them—but it seems telling that the young Boswell, heading toward his now famous London meeting with Samuel Johnson (if not Laurence Sterne),[3] thought that Pope and Swift were fit road companions. Like theological concepts, canons form themselves in mysterious ways.

Sterne was not a young man when he turned toward his writing career, but a middle-aged vicar of a country parish in Yorkshire. It was a local church dispute involving the diocese of York that inspired him in 1758 to try his hand at satire, petty ambitions, pride, and hypocrisy always being fit targets for literary chastisement. With this impetus to write something, we might be surprised to learn that Sterne did not turn directly to Locke or Hume, not even to Fielding or Richardson, but rather to the same volumes of *Miscellanies* that four years later would accompany Boswell to London. It is a point made by several readers of Sterne's early works, and one hopes with more thoroughness in the annotations of the Florida Edition, where it is suggested, for example, that *A Political Romance* was influenced particularly by the second volume of *Miscellanies*. "Memoirs of *P. P., Clerk of this Parish*" (Pope), "Stradling *versus* Stiles" (Pope), *A Key to the Lock,* and Arbuthnot's John Bull pamphlets are all cited when annotating specific passages. And, without doubt, Pope's *Peri Bathous,* also published in the *Miscellanies,* was Sterne's model for the Kerukopædia, the planned "art of sermon-writing that forms what little there is of design in the two surviving chapters of what we now call the 'Rabelaisian Fragment'" (*MW* 91–92, 153–54).

Fifty years ago, when the specter of a Scriblerian influence on *Tristram Shandy* was suggested in my *Laurence Sterne as Satirist* (1969), the emphasis was, quite rightly, on the influence of *A Tale of a Tub* and *The Dunciad* on Tristram's "life and opinions."[4] More recently, Marcus Walsh has continued that emphasis, richly aided by insights gained from his work on a new scholarly edition of the *Tale* for the Cambridge Edition of the Works of Swift.[5] Without repeating here any of the arguments concerning *Tristram Shandy*'s genre made over the last half century, perhaps their thrust might today be usefully reframed as a conversation: when Sterne turned toward a literary career in 1758, he entered, self-consciously, into a dialogue with Pope and Swift, *The Dunciad* and *A Tale of a Tub,* an exchange with two particular writers who continued to speak to him with acute cogency despite the intervening years. However, since these authors came to Sterne embedded in what was already part of the received canon of Scriblerian satire, represented by two particular publications, the *Miscellanies* and *Memoirs of the Extraordinary Life, Works, and Discoveries of Martinus Scriblerus* (1741), these are also voices heard in that conversation. While the notes to the Florida Edition paid ample attention to the *Miscellanies*, especially in volume 9, Sterne's own *Miscellaneous Writings*, revisiting Sterne's relationship with *Martinus Scriblerus*, I suggest here, may prove of value, most especially in testing the hypothesis that Sterne differed from the early satirists by embracing humanity, physicality, and diversity, while they eschewed all three.

I will begin with an author who was highly influenced by the Scriblerian project when writing one of the most famous of all eighteenth-century satires, *Gulliver's Travels*. Taking my cue from Charles Kerby-Miller's insightful analysis of *Memoirs'* chapter 16, "*Of the Secession of* Martinus, *and some Hint of his* Travels," I restate what has always been obvious, namely that the "differences between the *Memoirs* and the *Travels* are so great . . . that the reader does not accept the identification easily."[6] But beginning with the valid observation that Swift, as an early Scriblerian, would have had the travels of Martinus in mind as he started work on *Gulliver,* Kerby-Miller addresses the necessary formal changes required when moving from a piecemeal satire like *Memoirs* to an "extended narrative satire, especially of a pseudorealistic variety where the reader's credulity and sympathy may be insensibly aroused, thus destroying most of the effectiveness of the satire,"[7] which, he suggests, is the immediate and striking contrast of sense and senselessness. To compensate, he argues, the satirist may create a positive character in a negative environment, a negative character in a positive one, or a combination of both. This is perhaps overly simplified, both in his telling and in my retelling, but his test cases, *Don Quixote, Hudibras, Candide, Connecticut Yankee,* and *Gargantua and Pantagruel* give verifying substance to his argument. Specifically, the uniformity of Martinus as a satiric target (which, Kerby-Miller admits, is a weakness in the work as it was delivered to us) is contrasted with the complexity of Gulliver:

> Swift's double attitude toward his hero and the peoples he visits produced a uniquely effective satiric pattern. An almost universal failing of long satires is that their rigid pattern tends to blunt the reader's

Single and Double: *Memoirs of Martinus Scriblerus* and *Tristram Shandy* · 281

appetite and keenness of appreciation. . . . By not making a clear-cut division of "right" and "foolish" between Gulliver and his successive hosts Swift avoided this weakness. He was aware of the advantage his flexible satiric pattern gave him. . . . The reader of the *Travels* is seldom allowed to slip into a fixed attitude toward the characters and events and is not permitted to anticipate for any considerable length of time the character of the satire he is to encounter.[8]

And one final thought from Kerby-Miller: "It is necessary to make clear . . . that the literary changes which Swift introduced were not matched by corresponding intellectual ones. *Gulliver's Travels* is thoroughly Scriblerian in its basic intellectual attitudes and even . . . in its specific objects of satire. It therefore fits into the broad Scriblerus scheme without difficulty."[9]

Thirty-two years after *Gulliver's Travels,* when Sterne sat down in 1758 to write his *Political Romance,* then his aborted version of *Peri Hupsous,* the "Rabelaisian Fragment," and finally to embark on *Tristram Shandy,* he faced a similar formal problem. First, narrative fiction had overtaken most other forms of literature in popularity between 1726 and 1759; and, second, in an age of sensibility and sentiment, satire as it had been written during the lifetimes of Pope and Swift had lost an audience. Still, Kerby-Miller's description of the relationship of *Gulliver's Travels* to *Memoirs* seems at least worth considering as a scenario for Sterne as well. This is especially true when one confronts Ashley Marshall's *The Practice of Satire,* the primary intent of which is to put into doubt any notion of a continuing Scriblerian influence on the satire of the century. Her summary of the critical debate concerning the genre of *Tristram Shandy* is fair enough, coming down to the end of the twentieth century as a division between a view of the work as a part of the Scriblerian tradition, as I have argued, or *not* a "Scriblerian throwback," as Thomas Keymer has counterargued.[10] The trouble with my approach, she believes, is that it "exaggerates the degree to which Sterne is Swiftian, representing *Tristram Shandy* as centrally an attack on pride and obscuring the book's amiability and humor."[11] Keymer, on the other hand, is faulted because despite his argument that *Tristram* is a satire on novel writing, he also finds it "heavily conditioned by satirical traditions that culminate with Swift," and a work that "cleverly capitalizes on a potentiality that *A Tale of a Tub* had intimated but been unable to fulfil."[12] For Marshall, there is no "central satiric target" in the work, and my and Keymer's suggestions are dismissed for representing "only a small part of what the novel 'does,' and [Sterne's] satire shares little with Pope or Swift in technique, tone, or principal object. What they denounced in their different ways, Sterne makes playful fun of in the midst of a multifocused and exceptionally jumbled book. He is doing something different."[13]

This is the point Marshall repeats several times within her brief discussion. She emphasizes, for example, Sterne's "amused acceptance as an alternative to despair," his "good cheer, a sense of humor, and manifest warmth toward humankind"; he is having "too much fun to be gloomy" (quoting Howard Weinbrot), and then, quoting Peter Briggs, "*Because* man lives in this world amongst riddles and mysteries, *because* he cannot gain a consistent grasp upon his own experiences and upon the values and perceptions of others, he should be generous, patient, honest, and good-humored."[14] Finally, Marshall succinctly states her own point of view: "But all of this satire comes in one of the liveliest, friendliest books in the language. Unlike Pope and Swift and many other satirists, Sterne is not really passing judgment."[15]

To her credit, Marshall does cite several modifications I have made in my too long career riding the hobby-horse of *Tristram Shandy* as a satire, but she is probably also correct in assuming that my view has not fundamentally altered.[16] To be sure, in 1969, I had belabored the differences between prose satire and the novel, following the excellent direction of critics like Northrop Frye, Wayne C. Booth, and Sheldon Sacks, and their attempt to stem the increasingly lazy inclusion of all prose fiction into the catchall "novel" category—a laziness still in evidence today, as Marshall's use of the term for a "multifocused and exceptionally jumbled book" suggests.[17] Despite Marshall's range covering 112 years of satire, her view of both the genre's depth and breadth remains narrow. Many major works of satire have managed to combine judgment and humor, from Rabelais to Samuel Butler, even warmth toward humankind (Erasmus to Cervantes), and if Pope, Swift, Gay, and Arbuthnot were not enjoying themselves, where is literary enjoyment to be found? In her limiting satire to anger and despair, Marshall assigns the impetus of satire to the author's sentiments and sensibilities rather than to the true origin of satire in the realm of ethical thought. The notion that a Juvenal or a Pope writes satire in the white heat of anger is fundamentally flawed; in this Wordsworth and Coleridge were right: literature comes from emotion recollected in tranquility.

Single and Double: *Memoirs of Martinus Scriblerus* and *Tristram Shandy* · 283

The telling comment that Sterne is "not really passing judgment" is, in fact, a quite judgmental statement itself, a desire to believe that this eighteenth-century author, enlightened by Enlightenment, shares the modern reader's view that discrimination contains a Pandora's box of evils, and that the judgmental, "discriminating" person is not "one of us." The "playful fun" of diversity, inclusiveness, nonjudgmentalism may lead to a jumbled book, but one quite free from the evaluations that make *Peri Bathous* and *The Dunciad* so challenging to critics who no longer want (or know how) to discriminate between good and bad poetic lines. In this respect, Keymer seems to me quite correct in finding an incipient satire of the novelists in *A Tale of a Tub* because, proleptically, it chronicles the century's quiet evolution of the concept of discrimination (judgment) from a good trait to a bad one, an evolution mirrored by, among other changes, the amalgamation of all prose writers into novelists. In the character of Tristram, writing a long narrative satire about his life and opinions, Sterne has lodged this same core of ethical change. Significantly enough, in 1759, when he published the first two volumes of *Tristram Shandy,* two other *satires* appeared, *Rasselas* and *Candide,* both lazily identified as *novels* today. All three works, to my mind, exhibit the very same ethical core: an assertion of the value—indeed the necessity—of a discriminating mind in a world offering multiple and at times destructive alternatives.

In Peter Briggs, Marshall finds reinforcement for her idea that in a world of "riddles and mysteries" satiric judgment or discrimination is indeed the evil thing we now believe it to be: how can we judge others when we do not understand ourselves or our world? Indeed, for much of the second half of the twentieth century, the "riddles and mysteries" passage, quoted twice in *Tristram Shandy,* was considered an anticipation of existential angst and deconstructive indeterminateness, an indication that Sterne was indeed "one of us." In his first usage, Tristram arrives at the phrase when trying to account for the "instantaneous impulse" by which "*Nature . . . dear Goddess*" directs us to particular bodily movements, "we know not why—But mark . . . we live amongst riddles and mysteries—the most obvious things, which come in our way, have dark sides, which the quickest sight cannot penetrate into; and even the clearest and most exalted understandings amongst us find ourselves puzzled and at a loss in almost every cranny of nature's works" (*TS* 4.17.350). The second instance is toward the end of the work (*TS* 9.22.776), the first sentence of a chapter that discusses

"Nature's" ineptitude in "making so simple a thing as a married man": "WE live in a world beset on all sides with mysteries and riddles."

The Florida Edition notes that "riddles and mysteries" is echoed in two of Sterne's sermons (19 and 44): "That in many dark and abstracted questions of mere speculation, we should erro——is not strange: we live amongst mysteries and riddles, and almost every thing which comes in our way, in one light or other, may be said to baffle our understandings" (*Sermons* 182); and, again: "Nay, have not the most obvious things that come in our way dark sides, which the quickest sight cannot penetrate into; and do not the clearest and most exalted understandings find themselves puzzled, and at a loss, in every particle of matter" (*Sermons* 415). The editors also cite an essay that found in the passage the "scepticism of Hume."[18] They cautioned, however, that the echoing of the sermons might suggest that "'mysteries and riddles' is simply a restatement of some very commonplace Christian beliefs" (*TS*, Notes 313).

The validity of that caution was established when the source of the sermons' phrasing was located in John Norris's *Practical Discourses* (1691): "We live among Mysteries and Riddles, and there is not one thing that comes in at our Senses, but what baffles our Understanding" (*Sermons*, Notes 218).[19] Norris then goes on, as does Sterne, to suggest that while the senses rarely deceive us (for example, in distinguishing hot from cold), we are still "so very much out in our Judgments . . . in the conduct of Life, and in the great Ends and Measures of it" (*Sermons*, Notes 238). Sterne's sermonic point is similar, that it would "dishonor" God to suggest he failed to give us sufficient judgment to distinguish extremities, but despite God's "judgment, like his heart" being upright, unfortunately in human beings "there is a secret bias some how or other, hung upon the mind, which turns it aside from reason and truth" (*Sermons* 183).[20] Significantly enough, these passages in Norris and Sterne are based on several passages in Locke's *Essay concerning Human Understanding.*[21] The annotation in *Sermons* also quotes a similar sentiment in John Tillotson (*Sermons*, Notes 219) before remarking on the convergence of Norris, Locke, Tillotson, and Sterne as indicative of a Christian truth rather than a modern one: "When Sterne uses such words as 'mystery' or 'riddle' it is far more valid to hear echoes of 1 Corinthians 13:12, where the Greek *ainigma* (as in [Matthew] Poole's marginalia, 'in a riddle') is the heart of the verse, 'we see through a glass darkly'; and echoes as well of those contemporaries of Locke, such as Tillotson and Norris, who worked to incorporate his insights into their received notions of fallen human reason" (*Sermons,* Notes 219–20; *darkly* is the word Poole is glossing).

For the Enlightenment thinker, "riddles and mysteries" exist as problems to be solved, science and technology increasingly giving human beings the tools necessary to do so. Rather than having to face the darkness associated with not knowing the world, it seemed now possible that the human mind, the processes of ratiocination, could elevate us all into the realms of light and certainty, quite erasing the darkness of error and chance.[22] Much has been made of Locke's concept of identity, the separation of an autonomous self, an independent thinker able to process the world as an open system consistently responsive to informed reason. That interpretation of *Essay* is perhaps superficial, however, because Locke, as exemplified in "The Extent of Humane Knowledge," continued to operate in the same closed world as did Norris and Tillotson, one in which autonomous identity remained inextricably tied to limitation, the emergence of finite mankind from infinite divinity.[23] The secular self that we would like to find in Locke is quite different from the religious self, most obviously in Locke's persistent separation of knowledge of the world from knowledge of God.[24] However, it also receives statement in the same section in which he evoked riddles and mysteries:

> Our Knowledge being so narrow, as I have shew'd, it will, perhaps, give us some Light into the present State of our minds, if we look a little into the dark side, and take a view of *our Ignorance:* which being infinitely larger than our Knowledge, may serve much to the quieting of Disputes. . . . The meanest, and most obvious Things that come in our way, have dark sides, that the quickest Sight cannot penetrate into. The clearest, and most enlarged Understandings of thinking Men find themselves puzzled, and at a loss, in every Particle of Matter.[25]

Locke certainly challenged the theologians of his time (and it is worth pointing out that Norris was the very first to respond questioningly to *Essay*),[26] but primarily because he had, despite his intentions, left the door ajar for the Enlightenment celebration of a thoroughly demystified world,

286 · Textual and Critical Intersections

and for its inhabitants, enlightened seekers of ameliorating truths, to pursue happiness as their attainable goal. No wonder then, that, in Briggs's formulation, "riddles and mysteries," even those not immediately solvable, would now lead humanity to be "generous, patient, honest, and good-humored."

It is tempting at this point to invoke, as one anti-Enlightenment statement, Keats's famous letter advising poets to remain "in uncertainties, Mysteries, doubts, without any irritable reaching after fact & reason";[27] or, as another anti-Enlightenment observation, the depressing history of twentieth-century inhumanity, in which the search for solutions led to "final" ones in both Europe and Asia. However, we can just as appropriately invoke the Scriblerians, because at the very moment when Europe was setting autonomous beings free to solve the mysteries of existence, to enter into an enlightened era peopled by the effusive "man of feeling," and the nonjudgmental "man of good-humor," the satirists were targeting more precisely than ever before those who believed in their own autonomy and capacity to change the world for the better by unriddling or demystifying it. That such satiric targeting faded as a vehicle for great literature in the more hopeful nineteenth century is suggested by the decline, even extinction, of the literary genre of satire. One can, obviously, still find distinct traces of Scriblerian doubts about a nonjudgmental autonomous self in authors ranging from Dostoevsky to Tolstoy, Balzac to Flaubert, Dickens to Trollope, but by embedding those doubts within a prose form committed to the exploration of personal identity as its primary ethical consideration, the great novelists abetted the increasing secularization of literature even as their actual fictions kept alive the continuing Mystery at the core of re-creating worlds through words—the Logos that speaks before being spoken.

By the end of the twentieth century, when historical experience demanded a reexamination of Enlightenment ethics,[28] even from the most ardent believers in reason's possibilities, literary scholars reacted, as might be expected, by altering the vocabulary with which they explained books and the world: riddles and mysteries became deconstructions and indeterminacies. Every literary work, every event in it, up to and including the rape of Clarissa, was found to be unknowable, a fertile if paradoxical arena for the critic, who, while seemingly suspicious of solutions, was still imbued with the joyous activity of providing enlightening and definitive ones.[29] To be "exceptionally jumbled" became a sign of authorial puzzlement that only the sharpest critic could unravel for the untrained reader. And *Tristram Shandy,* the unwanted stepchild of the eighteenth-century "novel" up to mid-twentieth century, became the eighteenth-century scholar's prime example of a work that reveled in disorder and chaos, joyous in its celebration of multiplicity of meanings, sympathetic to, and tolerant of, every idea and every soul (including that of a poor fly), a work that confessed and enjoyed language's inability to express any truth at all. Of course, this "ethical stance" of tolerance and sympathy best suited the values of the modern critic, so they became Sterne's values as well, a solution that enabled *Tristram Shandy* to be reintegrated into the curriculum as a major Enlightenment advancement into modernity.

That modern critics are unable to rest content in riddles and mysteries is merely to observe that they are "human, all too human," that the search for "solutions" did not suddenly arise in a period labeled "Enlightenment" but is part of our genetic makeup—we are puzzle-solving animals. What is different in the present, post-Enlightenment era, however, is how we now react when, in Locke's words, the "clearest, and most enlarged Understandings of thinking Men find themselves puzzled, and at a loss, in every Particle of Matter."[30] Jewish theology, for example, believes God to be ineffable and unknowable but has spent a vast amount of its intellectual energy on explicating God's moods and motives. Christian theology, based on Talmudic practice, also posits an unknowable God, a "Mystery" at the heart of its theology, but spends the next two thousand years both raveling and unraveling the Trinity, a unitary and multiple God, one, two, and three simultaneously. This quest for knowledge, or inability to accept what is unknown, is theologized as the original sin; Swift, it should be observed, eschewed all attempts to "solve" the triune nature of God.[31] This surrender to the unknown, acknowledging the incapacity of the autonomous individual to unravel transcendent mysteries is an overcoming of self (the sinful self, Swift would have said) by communion with others.[32] That is, riddles and mysteries are subjected to communal and community knowledge; accepting a particular received solution to an unsolvable mystery is one's entry fee to that (un)enlightened state of being comfortable with (and comforted by) the infinite unknown.

Pedagogic authority in today's literature classrooms operates to some extent in imitation of theological authority. The instructor explicates an original text and texts generated by it, but also posits mystery (that is, indeterminacy) at the heart of its meaning, a play of language that can only be unraveled by the interpretive key held by the authorities. But while the theologian is able to hold two conflicting ideas at once, that the text must be endlessly explicated until all its mysteries are revealed yet that doing so is to commit the sin of overreaching the human condition (pride), the modern critic, unable to agree (with George Steiner, for one) that the literature we should be reading is always theological, transcendent, and unknowable, will accept no downside to explication, and no upside to communion. There is no "otherwise than interpretation," and so the ethical dilemma exists in which we celebrate our own reading as correct but equally the right of others to their incorrect readings. We continue to share Enlightenment's suspicion of communion and community: ambiguities and indeterminacies are to be viewed by each autonomous reader, professional or layman, as necessarily susceptible to explication, at times responsive to an accepted authority, but the imperative to interpretation can also be claimed at will by the autonomous self as a privilege, indeed a right.

The breakdown of communion in the modern approach to the riddles and mysteries, the transcendence of great literature, has several manifestations, perhaps most telling, the breaking into "schools" of critical approach, smaller and smaller communities identified in most cases by the name of the prophet whose approach is being followed, from Lacan to Latour, Derrida to Deleuze, the present life span of such schools being approximately a decade. Critical study today resembles the Protestant sectarian era, without its violence. Communal breakdown also manifests itself in the abandonment of the canon, replacing texts kept alive by communion and community with texts that rely on nondiscriminatory judgments to replace those previously included by generations of discriminating readers. As troubling, we see this breakdown of a community of interpretation in a diminishing respect and care for the text and the words in it.[33]

For our present purpose, however, a particularly telling illustration of our inability to be silent in the face of unknowingness is the blank page in *Tristram Shandy* (*TS* 6.38). For recent critics, saddled with theories of the inadequacy of words, readerly participation in "making meaning," the substitution of visualization for language, blankness here is an irresistible invitation for the autonomous critic, autonomy's final triumph, all the unknowns of silence and emptiness solved by self-assertion. And

Single and Double: *Memoirs of Martinus Scriblerus* and *Tristram Shandy* · 289

yet, Tristram has very specifically detailed his instructions for how to fill that blank page, and, unless we have a death wish, we had best not exercise our freedom: "Sit down, Sir, paint her [the Widow Wadman] to your own mind——as like your mistress as you can——as unlike your wife as your conscience will let you—'tis all one to me——please but your own fancy in it" (*TS* 5.38.566). That we ignore the text at this point, and for the sole purpose of focusing on our freedom instead, suggests, among other failings, a lack of awareness that for the eighteenth century, consciousness and conscience were linguistically, philosophically, and theologically very closely intertwined; whatever invitation blankness offers to consciousness, as always in Sterne's masterpiece conscience (and the abuse of conscience) will set limitations to self-assertion.

The Scriblerians would not have missed Sterne's humor, nor would Stella or Eliza Haywood, even though it seems to be at their gender's expense.[34] Having read the entire book, they would have known that Sterne was an equal opportunity satirist of both male and female vanities; it is, after all, Mrs. Shandy who mentions her husband's short stature compared to Tristram's height. Put another way, the influence of the Scriblerians on Sterne is to be found not only in the many passages and techniques he borrowed from them, but perhaps far more significantly in their being his comprehending audience. Sterne obviously wrote not for the tut-tutting Victorians, but not to the overwrought readers of our own time either who cannot see themselves in the ethical mirror provided by Sterne's bawdry, the "riddle and mystery" of those masterworks of satire from Petronius and Lucian onward, in which ridicule of the "poor bare forked animal that we are" never defies serious ethical intent but creates it.

As has often been commented, Sterne was a master of the double entendre, and nowhere more so than in sexual allusion. Within an autonomous human world, his ridicule may indeed invoke hostility, labels like sexist and homophobic, because there is no frame of reference able to weigh and measure the divine origin of humanity against its present condition. This duality, body and soul, finite and infinite, material and immaterial, translates itself most often not into mysteries of indeterminate and multiple meanings, but into the *double* entendre, where *two* meanings are indicated: thus, *nose* is not at all a slippery indeterminate term in *Tristram Shandy*, despite numerous critics arguing it is: *nose* means *nose* or it means *penis,* one or the other, and sometimes both; it does not mean *chair* or *window*. In addition to his obvious enjoyment of such doubling, Sterne shares with the Scriblerian tradition its usefulness in calling attention to the pride and hypocrisy that seem to accompany human aspirations to a status above their bodily urges and odors.

Reading Sterne without acknowledging this particular doubleness of human folly and the author's appeal beyond the human in order to judge it makes it difficult if not impossible to comprehend why he included the following passage in the very last chapter of *Tristram Shandy*. The speaker is Walter Shandy, but he is repeating the words of Pierre Charron (1541–1603), who is himself echoing Montaigne: all of them are voicing, we believe, Sterne's most fundamental insight into his own sexual existence and his clerical duty: why, it is asked, should "so exalted and godlike a Being as man" reproduce by means of "a passion . . . which couples and equals wise men with fools . . . more like satyrs and four-footed beasts than men . . . what reason is it, that all the parts thereof . . . the instruments, and whatever serves thereto, are so held as to be conveyed to a cleanly mind by no language, translation, or periphrasis whatever?" (*TS* 9.33.806). The second half of the lament, namely that we are not only ashamed of our body and its sexual actions in bringing new life into the world, but quite unashamed and indeed proud of our weapons by which we destroy life, is also borrowed, almost verbatim, from Charron: "The act of killing and destroying a man . . . is glorious—and the weapons by which we do it are honourable" (*TS* 9.38.806).[35] It is worth pointing out that both Charron and Sterne do not in any way suggest that our language is inadequate for expressing sexuality, but only that we are ashamed that such bodily urges detract from the sense of ourselves as "exalted and godlike" and so we mask them. Montaigne, as a source for Sterne, was quickly recognized by the Reverend Robert Brown, who wrote to Sterne in July 1760 that he guessed he was "no stranger to Montaigne" (*Letters* 692).[36]

Sterne's Scriblerian inheritance is to feel comfortably at home with this duality that makes us both "exalted and godlike a Being" and a four-footed (or two-footed, as Shakespeare would have it) "beast." But this is not the same as Jonathan Lamb's "double principle," for Sterne would have recognized something oxymoronic in a "principle" that could organize "duality."[37] Lamb's "principle," that is to say, exhibits a modernist discomfort

Single and Double: *Memoirs of Martinus Scriblerus* and *Tristram Shandy* · 291

with doubleness (or multiplicity), despite his seeming to relish it, because his effort continues the Enlightenment's aspiration to demystify that particular doubleness whereby the self or one's identity is always accompanied by that which is not oneself—God in the eighteenth century, Otherness in various modern theologies. While Sterne uses "riddles and mysteries" to lead readers away from ludicrous theories and inadequate solutions and toward communal truths beyond the isolated and autonomous self, Lamb praises diversity and multiplicity as modes of indeterminacy and mystery but remains committed to a unitary vision, to a solution that reduces diversity to two sides of the same human coin. To be sure, since diversity is a virtue, lack of diversity a vice, the ethical imperative is as dominant in his work as any ethical position might have been in the eighteenth century, whether in a sermon or a satire. Lamb shows little awareness, however, that the literature he is reading could embody a very different doubleness, one absolutely closed to ratiocination or analytic exposition, the tools of Enlightenment by which all difficult distinctions and differences could be absorbed by discovering a unifying principle.

Every great work of art defies that "human, all too human" urge to reduce its diversity to principle, its doubleness to oneness. While artistic genius does this as a matter of course (the inability to exhaust commentary being the defining hallmark of canonicity), it was the Scriblerians who recognized, simultaneously with the rise of the autonomous self, that the new concept of doubleness was a threat to both art and ethics, being a doubleness whereby all that was unknown could eventually be known, reduced to a principle, a solution, by the enlightened unaccompanied human being. Against this, they posited another mode of doubleness, an ethical truth that confronted the autonomous self and its consciousness with the communally created conscience, thus allowing them to write freely of this world's riddles while always keeping their eye on another source for their measures, and thus avoiding Keats's "irritable reaching after fact & reason." One chapter of *Martinus Scriblerus,* in particular, "The Double Mistress," may prove useful as a measure of Sterne's relationship to whatever we mean by Scriblerian satire, in part because it seems to have been the production primarily of Arbuthnot, corrected by Pope, without the presence of Swift's dominating Scriblerian voice first (and still most brilliantly and influentially) articulated in *A Tale of a Tub, The Battle of the Books,* and

A Discourse concerning the Mechanical Operation of the Spirit. A sentence in the introduction of the chapter may, indeed, establish a verbal link with Sterne:

> The style of this Chapter in the *Original Memoirs* is so singularly different from the rest, that it is hard to conceive by whom it was penn'd. But if we consider the particular Regard which our Philosopher had for it, who expresly directed that *not one Word of this Chapter should be alter'd,* it will be natural to suspect that it was written by himself, at the Time when *Love* (ever delighting in *Romances*) had somewhat tinctur'd his Style.[38]

When Sterne sent his *Political Romance* to his York printer, Caesar Ward, in 1758, he warned him, "That, at your Peril, you do not presume to alter or transpose one Word, nor rectify one false Spelling, nor so much as add or diminish one Comma or Tittle, in or to my *Romance*" (*MW* 117); and a year later, when writing to Dodsley about his intention to publish the first two volumes of *Tristram* in York, he stressed his own correcting of the "Proof, [so that it] shall go perfect into the World" (*Letters* 97). The Florida editors connect these assertions to the story of Toby's amours, described as "so nice and intricate a one, it will scarce bear the transposition of a single tittle" (*TS* 8.7.663–64). Marcus Walsh is certainly right in suggesting another parallel with *A Tale of a Tub,* when Peter warns his brothers "not to add to, or diminish their Coats"; and in noting an allusion to Revelation 22:18–19: "If any man shall add unto these things, God shall add unto him the plagues that are written in this book: And if any man shall take away the words of the book of this prophecy, God shall take away his part out of the book of life."[39] This care concerning the accuracy of transcription, even when parodically expressed, is suggestive: even in their most ludicrous moments, the capacity to distinguish between, yet recognize the dependent relationship of, human language and the ultimate authority of the creating Word partakes of the same devotion to a doubleness that informs both rabbinical and patriarchal commentary: words matter because the Word matters, and Walter Shandy's penknife scratching of his text into conformity with his theories is the fate these authors are both fearing— and predicting—for their texts at the hands of Enlightenment's irritable demystifiers.[40]

Single and Double: *Memoirs of Martinus Scriblerus* and *Tristram Shandy* · 293

While the arrangement of chapters in *Memoirs* often seems merely the haphazardness of its compositional history, the two chapters immediately preceding the "Double Mistress" episode are valuable in establishing its Scriblerian design. Chapter 11 is Pope's account of the curing of the disease of "self-love," hardly an original subject for satire in any age, but given our discussion thus far, a pertinent comment on autonomous selfhood: "There are people who discover from their very youth a most amorous inclination to themselves."[41] In several ways, the chapter anticipates the coming discussion of doubleness by illustrating the self "doubling" back on itself, almost as its principle of organization: thus, "bawds and pimps that go between a man and himself"; "Whom does he generally talk of? Himself." Most telling is the cure: "Let all Looking-glasses, polish'd Toys, and even clean Plates be removed from him, for fear of bringing back the admired object."[42] And in the end, there is mock despair at finding a cure for self-love; if none is found, Martinus "must e'en leave the poor man to his destiny. Let him *marry himself,* and, when he is condemn'd eternally to himself, perhaps he may run to the next pond to get rid of himself, the Fate of most violent Self-lovers."[43] One might almost suspect that the germ of "Double Mistress" was in the phrase "*marry himself,*" a prognosis of impotence, sterility, and death that might also anticipate the opening chapters of *Tristram Shandy,* wherein the marriage bed is a place of singular occupancies.[44]

More complicated but equally reflective of both "Double Mistress" and Scriblerian satire is chapter 12, "*How* Martinus *endeavoured to find out the Seat of the* Soul, *and of his Correspondence with the* Free-Thinkers." As Kerby-Miller's valuable discussion and annotations make clear, the materiality of the soul was as vital to Enlightenment thought as its immateriality was to Christian believers. Sterne revisits the debate through Walter Shandy's theory that natural birth damaged the pineal gland, home of the physical soul according to Descartes. The Florida editors trace Sterne's winding path through Chambers's *Cyclopædia,* as he follows the cross-references to pertinent learned articles to shape Walter's argument;[45] they also point to this chapter in *Memoirs* and to its ultimate relocation of the soul from the pineal gland to "the Organ of Generation." Here again, Locke's vacillation is important, returning us to his chapter "Of the Extent of Humane Knowledge": "I say not this, that I would any way lessen the belief of the Soul's Immateriality: I am not here speaking of Probability, but Knowledge."[46] That one hiccup allowed the materialists all the hesitation they required, the soul becoming for them "that Theological Non-entity" according to the free-thinkers' letter to Martinus.[47] Even serious theologians like Samuel Clarke now felt compelled to demonstrate to enlightened thinkers that the unknowable mysteries of immateriality and immortality could be explicated to their rational satisfaction; he was doomed to failure, as the Scriblerians could have informed him.

One of Descartes's arguments for the pineal gland, as summarized by Kerby-Miller, is particularly pertinent to my argument: "It alone of all parts of the brain is single and thus is the only place from whence thought, which is single, might emanate."[48] While Descartes had self-identity in mind in this sentence, it may also serve as an apt summation of the crippling boundary set by Enlightenment thought to the riddles and mysteries offered by existence: "Is it not *Demonstration* to a person of your [Martinus's] Sense, that, since *you cannot find it,* there is *no such thing?*"[49] The appeal to Martinus's ego in this letter from the free-thinkers, their enthusiastic endorsement of his intellect as the sole measure of existence, is the fertile soil in which Scriblerian satire, whether in the 1720s or 1760s, takes root and flourishes.[50] It is no accident, then, that the soul's materiality leads to the concomitant assertion that the mind is also material, a mere mechanism that the virtuosi among the free-thinkers will try to duplicate as an automaton. To the twenty-first century reader this perhaps sounds all too natural (even desirable) a result of scientific thinking, but the Scriblerian response is worth keeping in mind to measure the three hundred years between their time and ours. As in the previous chapter on human pride, which ended with the idea of death, so too does this chapter: Crambe advises Martinus "by no means to enter into their [the free-thinkers'] Society, unless they would give him sufficient security, to bear him harmless from any thing that might happen after this present life."[51] Like Sterne's black leaf in the opening pages of *Tristram Shandy,* the Scriblerians offer a second chapter-ending memento mori to seal their discussion of autonomous individuals confronting the mysteries of existence without acknowledging all they are unable to fathom, a way, perhaps, of saying to the free-thinkers, "where are your gambols now?"

When the discussion of the material seat of the material soul moves to the material nature of thought, it is obvious that the free-thinkers are quarreling with Locke, who argued for an immaterial *consciousness* against the notion of thinking matter.[52] What is most worthy of note, however, is just how "unenlightened" Locke's argument is, returning at several key points to restore contact with a consciousness that is also conscience.[53] Thus the "Goodness of God" is invoked to assure us that the consciousness of another person cannot be transferred to our consciousness and "by a fatal Error" make us responsible for a deed that "draws Reward or Punishment with it."[54] And again, in language one would not expect from an empiricist: "And thus we may be able without any difficulty to conceive the same Person at the Resurrection, though in a Body not exactly in make or parts the same which he had here, the same consciousness going along with the Soul that inhabits it." And yet again, "But in the great Day, wherein the Secrets of all Hearts shall be laid open, it may be reasonable to think, no one shall be made to answer for what he knows nothing of; but shall receive his Doom, his Conscience accusing or excusing him."[55] This appeal to a just Judge emerges tellingly alongside Locke's notion of selfhood, a "Forensick Term appropriating Actions and their Merit; and so belongs only to intelligent Agents capable of a Law, and Happiness and Misery." Reaching the end of his argument that although human justice can punish us for a crime committed in drunken forgetfulness ("Humane Laws punish . . . with a Justice suitable to their way of Knowledge"), a different law is lodged in the Apostle's promise that "at the Great Day, when every one shall *receive according to his doings, the secrets of all Hearts shall be laid open*" and "the Sentence shall be justified by the consciousness all Persons shall have, that they *themselves* in what Bodies soever they appear, or what Substances soever that consciousness adheres to, are the *same,* that committed those Actions, and deserve that Punishment for them."[56]

In that last sentence Locke is melding two scriptural passages, the first from 1 Corinthians 14:25, the second from 2 Corinthians 5:10. Sterne had quoted the first (unnoticed by the Florida editors), appropriately enough in a passage overtly Scriblerian: "Let no man say from what taggs and jaggs hints may not be cut out for the advancement of human knowlege. Let no man . . . ever rise up and say again . . . [what] may not be struck out, to carry the arts and sciences up to perfection.——Heaven! Thou knowest how I love them [enquirers];——thou knowest the secrets of my heart," at which point Tristram pledges his shirt if he could "satisfy one feverish enquirer" with a clue leading to the desired perfection (*TS* 6.26.546–47).

296 · Textual and Critical Intersections

In the scriptural passage, Paul weighs the multitude of tongues proclaiming truths against the inspired word of those who, in the commentary of Matthew Henry,

> plainly interpret Scripture, or preach, in Language intelligible and proper, the great Truths and Rules of the Gospel, a *Heathen* or unlearned Person, coming in, would probably be convinced, and become a Convert to Christianity, *ver.* 24, 25. His Conscience will be touched; the Secrets of his Heart will be revealed to him, he will be condemned by the Truth he hears, and so will be brought to confess his Guilt, to pay his Homage to God, and own that he is indeed among you, present in the Assembly.[57]

Every aspect of Sterne's passage is illuminated by its scriptural context, from his ministerial endorsement of practical versus polemical divinity, to his Scriblerian distrust of human knowledge as capable of perfection in any area, to his Christian acceptance of guilt and divine judgment, and, finally, to his anti-autonomous endorsement of communion.

Sterne's use of the second scriptural passage is equally telling. It occurs in a sermon, "Vindication of human nature" that is a favorite with those who want to find Sterne a man of kindly sentiments and warm feelings toward humankind, Marshall's and Briggs's Sterne, and certainly not a satirist. Without belaboring the point, as I do in my headnote (*Sermons,* Notes 118–20), the sermon's message is, via John Tillotson, well within orthodoxy, a "vindication of human nature . . . irrevocably embodied in redemption through Jesus Christ and not in unaided human beings" (*Sermons,* Notes 119). When we examine our life, we will find it "so beset and hemm'd in with obligations of one kind or other, as to leave little room to suspect, that *man can live to himself*" (*Sermons* 72). The mutual dependence between human beings is then compared to the individual's relation to God, beginning with the thought that "there is a GOD who made me," and that "I am accountable for my conduct and behavior to this great and wisest of beings, before whose judgment seat I must finally appear and receive the things done in my body,—whether they are good, or whether they are bad" (*Sermons* 72). As with Locke, as with the Scriblerians, dependency rather than autonomy creates a world where consciousness is conscience, because judgment awaits. There is always a judgment necessary to communal living here on earth, although it may or may not be fair (much like satire,

Single and Double: *Memoirs of Martinus Scriblerus* and *Tristram Shandy* · 297

one might suggest). But there is also a judgment to come, an idea not only hostile to the general intent of enlightened thought, but equally uncomfortable to modern minds. Interpretation that fails to take that discomfort into account reduces the most important "doubleness" of the past (human and divine) to the singleness of the knowable world.[58]

In approaching the "Double Mistress" episode by way of its preceding chapters on human pride and material theories of the soul and consciousness, one moves away from absorbing it into recent discussions of monstrous births and gender inequality, and back to the more likely interests of the Scriblerians: human folly arising from pride, intellectual arrogance, and material appetites. In passing, it is worth observing the ease with which the Scriblerians were able to assume diverse voices, without losing sight of their satiric purpose—heroic- and romance-writing worthy of Aphra Behn, farcical comedy recalling Shakespeare's clowns and Dickens's attorneys, scholarly arguments derived from scholasticism, and legal jargon appropriate to Blackstone or William P. Barr. That the episode quickly becomes a legal debate is not unexpected, not only given my prior discussion, but also within the context provided by contemporary reactions to the historical "twins" on which "Double Mistress" is based.

When the original twins were exhibited in 1708, the questions asked often raised theological and legal issues.[59] For example, "*Whether each of the twins . . . hath a distinct soul, or whether one informs both?*"; "*is it lawful for them to marry?*"; "*Whether if any marry one of the two children, when grown up . . . he be guilty of incest?*"; and, significantly enough, in view of Locke's distribution of justice between earthly and divine: if one of the twins should commit a crime entailing the death penalty, "*how should it be punish'd, and justice be satisfy'd, if it cannot be without the death of the innocent?*" The answers are also rather predictable within the eighteenth-century context: "Each hath doubtless a separate soul, since their passions and affections are as different, as if they had entirely separate bodies";[60] if they had been otherwise joined, marriage would be possible but "these are of so peculiar a nature, that the forementioned sin [of incest] is unavoidable. This therefore is an abundant cause and just impediment, why neither of them can be join'd with a man in holy matrimony"; and, particularly pertinent to our discussion, it is argued that if the innocence of one twin can be established, the "equity of our common law will bear her harmless . . . [because] it is preferable that the guilty should go unpunish'd, rather than

298 · Textual and Critical Intersections

the harmless, the innocent, should suffer."[61] And there is a moment when the discussion of the 1708 twins will sound familiar to readers of *Tristram Shandy:* in answering a question about the comparative healthiness of one twin and weakness of the other, it is suggested that the latter, being the second born, "'tis likely that by the compression of the head, the brain receiv'd some damage."[62] (Compare Walter's defense of podalic delivery to prevent "the violent compression and crush which the head was made to undergo, by the nonsensical method of bringing us into the world by that part foremost" [*TS* 3.19.175]).

For the Scriblerians, Martinus's dilemma revisits their previous discussion of the unsolvable mystery of both human and divine doubleness, the body and soul of the one, the Father and Son of the other. That he seeks his answer in the law courts[63] is already to admit defeat, for as Penny-feather points out, Martinus "maintains no less an absurdity than this, that *One is Two.*"[64] Such an "absurdity" is at the core of Christianity, indeed multiplied into an even deeper "absurdity," "*One is Three.*"[65] Were it possible that the free-thinkers' dismissal of that "Theological Non-entity commonly call'd the *Soul*" was erroneous, Martinus might appeal, like a "wise Petitioner" to "the *very Throne* and *Judgment-Seat* of the Monarch,"[66] instead of the secular courts, but within his world that phrase has only a bawdy meaning, what Tristram labels the *Argumentum ad Rem,* one of several "unanswerable arguments" he proudly adds to the arsenal of rhetoric (*TS* 1.21.79). Having thus avoided the mystery of divine doubleness, the legal quarrel limits itself to human doubleness, the conflict between the material body and (im)material soul, a dual nature intensified by both the intellectual pride that denies human physicality and the lust that overwhelms consciousness (conscience).

As just noted, Sterne would seem to have had this chapter of *Memoirs* in mind when he writes: "As for the *Argumentum Tripodium* [argument addressed to the third leg], which is never used but by the woman against the man;—and the *Argumentum ad Rem* [argument addressed to the thing], which, contrarywise, is made use of by the man only against the woman" (*TS* 1.21.79). This chapter is one of the most Scriblerian in all *Tristram Shandy,* promising, first, that knowledge is moving toward the apex of perfection, "from which, if we may form a conjecture from the advances of these last seven years, we cannot possibly be far off," then exploring Uncle Toby's sexual modesty caused by Widow Wadman's inquiry concerning the wound on his groin, and ending in its description of Walter as a "speculative,—systematical" philosopher (*TS* 1.21.72, 74–75, 76).

From the classical period to modern day, satirists have used scatology and sexuality to remind us of this doubleness, a body and a conscience that are often misused and abused. Martinus's search for the seat of the soul culminates in Penny-feather's argument that, if the "*Principle* and *Essence* of *Individuality*" is an identical soul in an identical body, it must be that "the organ of Generation is the true and only *Seat of the Soul.*" Both science and law in the seventeenth century were still swayed by the homuncular theory of generation, whereby, as Penny-feather argues, the "whole man, both Soul and body, is *there* form'd."[67] Not coincidentally, perhaps, Sterne opens *Tristram Shandy* with Walter advocating the same theory; for both Arbuthnot and Sterne, homunculism was already outmoded by advances in microscopy that gave better evidence for ovulist theories, but both found it a convenient means of ridiculing the deep inquirer after truth.[68] Penny-feather runs into immediate difficulty, however, on two fronts. First, his argument fails to account for the woman's "organ of generation," convinced as he is that the male organ carries *ex traduce* the "whole man, both Soul and body." And second, by including the "Soul" as also originating *ex traduce,* he materializes the soul, and thus—despite his assertions to the contrary—commits heresy.[69]

As with all theological topics, *ex traduce* had been argued and reargued for centuries, but for our present purposes, the definition in Johnson's *Dictionary* suffices: "to propagate; to increase by deriving one from another."[70] While the idea was supported by homuncular theories of generation, according to which the physical human being was in the first seed of Adam and passed on thereafter and was useful (indeed necessary) in order to explain the transmission of original sin, the notion that the soul was also thus passed on had been deemed heresy by Aquinas and all other theologians since. Significantly, Johnson offers for his illustration of *ex traduce* a quatrain from Sir John Davies's *Nosce teipsum,* the first part of which was "Of Humane Knowledge" and the second, "Of the Soule of Man, and the Immortalitie thereof" (1599), reprinted well into the eighteenth century, indeed, as late as 1787. Davies speaks so directly to Penny-feather that we might well believe he is being invoked: "None are so grosse as to contend for this, / That soules from bodies may traduced be, / Betweene whose natures no proportion is, / When root and branch in nature still agree." In his next stanza, Davies also denies traduction as the origin of souls: "But many subtill wits have justifi'd, / That *Soules* from *Soules* spiritually may spring; / Which if the nature of the *Soule* be try'd, / Will even in nature prove as grosse a thing."[71]

The authors of *Memoirs* would have fully expected their readers to recognize that Dr. Penny-feather was simply continuing Martinus's argument that the soul is a material object, lodged in the male organ and passed on from generation to generation. They might also have expected the very mention of *ex traduce* to remind many eighteenth-century readers of the doctrine of Original Sin, the eating of the Tree of Knowledge in Eden. Not by accident, then, Adam and Eve become the center of Dr. Leatherhead's counterargument, an attempt to celebrate whatever might be divine within the human being by refusing to acknowledge the body. The echoes of the passages already quoted from Walter's attack on sexuality at the very end of *Tristram Shandy* are palpable: "Neither the individual Essence of mankind, nor the Seat of the Soul, doth reside in the Organ of Generation . . . for unreasonable indeed must it be, to make that the Seat of the Rational Soul, which alone sets us on a level with beasts. . . . In a word, what can be a greater absurdity, than to affirm Bestiality to be the Essence of Humanity, Darkness the Centre of Light, and Filthiness the Seat of Purity."[72] Like Walter Shandy, Leatherhead then summons the "most eminent Philosophers of all ages" to affirm the impudence of degrading "the Rational Soul, to the very lowest and vilest Apartments."[73] His ultimate argument, however, is that in the Garden "our first Parents, in the state of Innocence, did in no wise propagate their species after the present common manner of men and beasts," but rather in some "pure and spiritual manner, suitable to the dignity of their station." The argument becomes more and more fanciful; Adam and Eve had no sexual organs at all until after the Fall, the "immediate Excrescence of Sin . . . to render them fitter companions for those Beasts among which they were driven." Or, another argument, namely that in the Garden "Adam was endow'd with a continual uninterrupted Faculty of Generation" while it is well known "that the present (male) part of Generation is utterly incapable of this continual Faculty."[74] It has often been remarked that "impotence" hovers over the entire Shandy family, includ-

Single and Double: *Memoirs of Martinus Scriblerus* and *Tristram Shandy* · 301

ing Tristram, with garters in hand, apologizing to Jenny for what has not passed (*TS* 7.29.624).

The legal debate ends, then, with a choice between denying the materiality of the body or the immateriality of the soul, human pride and self-love being behind both errors. It is no accident that *Memoirs* returns us to Eden and the Fall, a story, in Milton's grand retelling, that wielded outsize influence throughout the literature of the eighteenth century. To be sure, a prose genre was emerging that would attempt to escape the weighty influence of Christianity, but the Scriblerian satirists connected to the nascent novel primarily with suspicion of any literary endeavor attempting to mirror this world and the doubleness of its creatures without reference to that other doubleness, the Father and Son, who created both. Like Defoe, Fielding, and Richardson, they addressed a readership of believers, but where the budding novelists found their ethical interest in chronicling just how far autonomous characters could rise *and* fall in this new world of possible earthly amelioration, the Scriblerians were impelled by a different ethical impetus, one limited or expanded by their belief in a judgment and afterlife, Crambe's final words to Martinus, to beware of death and judgment. We are, of course, still more inclined toward the novelists today, reading literature as Martinus reads Lindamira, an object to be penetrated by his desire to possess her; her doubleness, the unpossessed twin by her side, will either succumb to his possession or, as Dr. Leatherhead warns, he will have to commit "Bigamy, Rape, or Incest"—a violation of the material doubleness both of the twins and of all literary texts that capture the dual nature of humanity, a body containing a soul, a soul within a body. That is what happens when as readers and scholars we explicate any "double principle."[75]

But from another viewpoint, Marshall is quite right in suggesting that Scriblerian satire was not the dominant mode of eighteenth-century satire. It had many imitators, but few who could capture within their literary work the second doubleness we have been talking about, the presence of the immaterial or spiritual, embodied for Christians in God and the Son, but for any artist found within their ability to capture a transcendence that we are asked to witness in the great art of any era. The audience for Scriblerian satire was primed to see that doubleness as part of a God-ordained story of creation, sin, death, and judgment (Milton's story of the Word made flesh); today's author must find a different transcendence for a different audience, but when that audience can believe they are again in touch with literary greatness, usually but not always tested by endurance over time and translation, we can attest to its presence even when we are unable to define it, perhaps exactly because we cannot define it.

Sterne is a Scriblerian satirist not because he shares with the Scriblerians an overarching dubiety about Enlightenment solutions to the divided nature of humanity, but because his artistry is at their transcendent level, energized by his Christian faith in the immateriality and immortality of the soul. With that belief comes all the informing ideas of *Tristram Shandy,* beginning with a black page as memento mori, an Enlightenment virtuoso, a sermon on the abuses of conscience, a sentimental soldier, and everywhere, a linguistic versatility that rubs our noses in human sexuality. Sterne forces us to confront the forked animal that we know we are with acceptance, amusement rather than disgust (and we would maintain Swift's scatology has the same effect), and the spiritual creature that we hope we can become without any irritable search to uncover the Mystery of that immateriality through which ethical human beings, in Sterne's communion, realized their truth. Writing this essay, seeking "principles," I too have sinned against the texts I have analyzed, but that is an awareness Scriblerian satire leads me to even if it cannot restore my chaste enjoyment of what I am reading—"chastity, but not yet!"

The echoes of *Memoirs* in *Tristram Shandy* are important keys to understanding Sterne, but even more important, I believe, is his absorption with its authors when he began his own creative work, his compatibility with the satiric world of their imagination in which human beings are the creation of God, not autonomous, and where all efforts toward social and political amelioration are met with the still embraced story of a Fall in Eden due to pride and the temptation to forbidden knowledge. Maintaining such a view was not at all incompatible with good humor, kindness, charity, laughter, or tolerance, but it did separate the satirists from those of our own time who want to find Swift a cynical misanthrope and Sterne an existential postmodernist. Sterne was not Swift, and the Swift who wrote *A Tale of a Tub* was not the Swift who wrote *Gulliver's Travels,* just as the Pope who wrote *The Rape of the Lock* was not the Pope who wrote *The Dunciad.* But binding them all together, along with other eighteenth-century Scriblerians, both those who wrote satire of equal genius and those who failed

Single and Double: *Memoirs of Martinus Scriblerus* and *Tristram Shandy* · 303

to achieve their brilliance, is a shared belief (Anglican and Catholic) in a world and its people characterized by irreducible doubleness: "the glory, jest, and riddle of the world!"[76]

Originally published in *Swift Studies* 36 (2021).

Notes

1 See my essay "Bosewll and Sterne in 1768," reprinted as chapter 10 in this volume; see also James Boswell, *Boswell's London Journal*, ed. Frederick A. Pottle (London: William Heinemann, 1951; numbered edition only), 43–111.

2 Boswell, *London Journal*, 46, 56, 65.

3 James J. Caudle has effectively demolished most of the traditional accounts of a Boswell-Sterne meeting; see "'Fact' or 'Invention'? James Boswell and the Legend of a Boswell-Sterne Meeting," *Shandean* 22 (2011): 30–55.

4 Melvyn New, *Laurence Sterne as Satirist: A Reading of "Tristram Shandy"* (Gainesville: University of Florida Press, 1969), 1–3.

5 Marcus Walsh, "Scriblerian Satire, *A Political Romance*, the 'Rabelaisian Fragment,' and the Origins of *Tristram Shandy*," in *The Cambridge Companion to Laurence Sterne*, ed. Thomas Keymer (Cambridge: Cambridge University Press, 2009), 21–33; Jonathan Swift, *A Tale of a Tub and Other Works*, ed. Marcus Walsh (Cambridge: Cambridge University Press, 2010).

6 *The Memoirs of the Extraordinary Life, Works, and Discoveries of Martinus Scriblerus*, ed. Charles Kerby-Miller (1950; New York: Oxford University Press, 1988), 315 (hereafter cited as *Martinus Scriblerus*).

7 *Martinus Scriblerus*, 317.

8 *Martinus Scriblerus*, 318.

9 *Martinus Scriblerus*, 320.

10 Ashley Marshall, *The Practice of Satire in England, 1658–1770* (Baltimore, MD: Johns Hopkins University Press, 2013), 280–81. Marshall is referring to my *Laurence Sterne as Satirist* and to Thomas Keymer, *Sterne, the Moderns, and the Novel* (Oxford: Oxford University Press, 2002).

11 Marshall, 280.

12 Marshall, 281.

13 Marshall, 281.

14 Marshall, 281. Howard Weinbrot is quoted from *Menippean Satire Reconsidered: From Antiquity to the Eighteenth Century* (Baltimore, MD: Johns Hopkins University Press, 2005), 11; Peter Briggs from "Locke's *Essay* and the Tentativeness of *Tristram Shandy*," *Studies in Philology* 82 (1985): 517–18.

15 Marshall, *The Practice of Satire in England*, 282.

304 · Textual and Critical Intersections

16 Of my work, she points in particular to *Tristram Shandy: A Book for Free Spirits* (New York: Twayne, 1994); more pertinent might have been "Swift as Ogre, Richardson as Dolt: Rescuing Sterne from the Eighteenth Century," *Shandean* 3 (1991): 49–60; "Sterne and the Narrative of Determinateness," reprinted as chapter 1 in this volume; and "Swift and Sterne: Two Tales, Several Sermons, and a Relationship Revisited," in *Critical Essays on Jonathan Swift*, ed. Frank Palmeri (New York: G. K. Hall, 1993), 164–86.

17 Northrop Frye, *Anatomy of Criticism: Four Essays* (Princeton, NJ: Princeton University Press, 1957); Wayne C. Booth, *The Rhetoric of Fiction* (Chicago: University of Chicago Press, 1961); and Sheldon Sacks, *Fiction and the Shape of Belief: A Study of Henry Fielding* (Berkeley: University of California Press, 1964). Marshall lists only Frye in her bibliography.

18 Francis Doherty, "Sterne and Hume: A Bicentenary Essay," *Essays and Studies*, n.s., 22 (1969): 71–87.

19 The source is Norris's "A Discourse concerning the Folly of Covetousness," in *Practical Discourses upon Several Divine Subjects* (1691), vol. 2, 238.

20 For an extensive discussion of Sterne's absorption of Norris's theology, see "The Odd Couple: Laurence Sterne and John Norris of Bemerton," reprinted as chapter 2 in this volume. For example, Sterne seems to be echoing the last portion of the passage just quoted in the "Abuses of conscience" sermon, first published in York in 1751, and subsequently included in *Tristram Shandy* (*TS* 2.17.147): "was it certain that self-love could never hang the least bias upon the judgment." That in this part of the sermon he is actually following Swift's "On the Difficulty of Knowing One's Self" should not be ignored; see *The Prose Works of Jonathan Swift*, ed. Herbert Davis et al. (1948; Oxford: Basil Blackwell, 1963), vol. 9, 358, 360. Despite *Tristram Shandy* being an "excessively jumbled" work, there is hardly an episode in it that does not respond to the ethical awareness of the fallacies of human judgment in the conduct of life, as discussed in both Swift's and Sterne's sermons that address self-knowledge and conscience.

21 John Locke, *An Essay concerning Human Understanding*, ed. Peter H. Nidditch (Oxford: Clarendon Press, 1975), IV.3.543, 553, 556 ("The Extent of Humane Knowledge," specifically, paragraphs 6, 22, and 25).

22 The best most recent account of an "enlightened" thinker is Jacopo Agnesina, *The Philosophy of Anthony Collins: Free-Thought and Atheism* (Paris: Honoré Champion, 2018). Agnesina convincingly argues that Collins denied God's divine attributes, intelligence, and design, along with substance duality, affirming instead materialistic monism. See also Sarah Ellenzweig, *The Fringes of Belief: English Literature, Ancient Heresy, and the Politics of Freethinking*,

1660–1760 (Stanford, CA: Stanford University Press, 2008); James A. Herrick, *The Radical Rhetoric of the English Deists: The Discourse of Skepticism, 1680–1750* (Columbia: University of South Carolina Press, 1997); and Roger D. Lund, ed., *The Margins of Orthodoxy: Heterodox Writing and Cultural Response, 1660–1750* (Cambridge: Cambridge University Press, 1995).

23 The vexed history of Locke's influence on Sterne is carefully analyzed by Darrell Jones, "Locke and Sterne: The History of a Critical Hobby-Horse," *Shandean* 27 (2016): 83–111. Long before that essay, however, D. R. Elloway made a particularly pertinent point about Locke, Sterne, and language in demolishing John Traugott's existential reading (*Tristram Shandy's World: Sterne's Philosophical Rhetoric* [Berkeley: University of California Press, 1954]), and many future readings as well, by correctly observing that Locke never suggested that language had to be severely defined and disciplined in order to serve as a means of communication. Rather, Locke was fully aware that communication without discipline takes place every day (it is not words but predilections—hobby-horses—that interfere with the Shandy brothers' understanding of one another), which was precisely his point: scientific language needed far more precision than commonplace human conversation, and Locke's *Essay* was addressed to the advancement of science. Elloway, "Locke's Ideas in *Tristram Shandy*," *Essays in Criticism* 6 (1956): 326–34.

24 Locke, *Essay*, IV.10.619–30.

25 Locke, IV.3.553.

26 John Norris, *Cursory Reflections upon a Book Call'd "An Essay concerning Human Understanding,"* in *Christian Blessedness, or Discourses upon the Beatitudes of Our Lord and Saviour Jesus Christ* (1690). For a useful discussion of Norris's objections and Locke's responses, see W. J. Mander, *The Philosophy of John Norris* (Oxford: Oxford University Press, 2008), 169–98.

27 *The Letters of John Keats*, ed. H. E. Rollins (Cambridge: Cambridge University Press, 1953), vol. 1, 193–94. Keats's capitalization of "Mystery" is worth noting, as is his offering Coleridge as an example of a person who cannot exercise "Negative Capability," because he is "incapable of remaining content with half knowledge." According to Coleridge, "The poet is not only the man made to solve the riddle of the Universe, but he is also the man who feels where it is not solved and which continually awakens his feelings." Samuel Taylor Coleridge, *Lectures on Shakespeare, 1811–1819*, ed. Adam Roberts (Edinburgh: Edinburgh University Press, 2016), 88 (lecture of December 12, 1811).

28 What has already become hackneyed, Theodor Adorno's "no poetry after Auschwitz," might more accurately have been rendered, "no novels after Auschwitz," novels being the genre that rose and fell with the Enlightenment;

modernists like Joyce and Woolf recognized this after World War I, but many only now are realizing that new (or older) forms of prose fiction will be needed to deal with the failure of autonomous human beings to embody, in any truthful (or ethical) way, their rendition of the world into words. László Krasznahorkai is one of the best of these authors, and Colm Tóibin, a better blurb writer than most, gets to the heart of the matter in labeling him "one of the most mysterious artists now at work." Cover blurb for *Seiobo There Below* (2008; New York: New Directions, 2013).

29 William B. Warner's *Reading Clarissa: The Struggles of Interpretation* (New Haven, CT: Yale University Press, 1979) is one example, but my favorite would be Judith Wilt's "'He Could Go No Farther': A Modest Proposal about Lovelace and Clarissa," *PMLA* 92 (1977): 19–32, where the Scriblerian subtitle might suggest that criticism should now devour innocent texts as a solution to the poverty and hunger of trying to live by bread alone.

30 Locke, *Essay*, IV.3.553.

31 Swift, "On the Trinity," in *Prose Works*, vol. 9, 159–68. The sermon remains undated but was probably written some twenty years before publication in 1744. In it, Swift recognizes that we are naturally impelled to follow our reason, but that if we are "directly told in Scripture, that *Three* are *One*, and *One* is *Three*," we "could not conceive or believe it in the natural common Sense of that Expression, but must suppose that something dark or mystical was meant. . . . It is plain, that God commandeth us to believe there is a Union and there is a Distinction; but what [each is] all Mankind are equally ignorant, and must continue so, at least till the Day of Judgment" (161). It seems quite possible that some aspects of the "Double Mistress" episode from *Martinus Scriblerus* were in Swift's mind when composing this sermon.

32 The celebration of the self by enlightened nonbelievers was echoed, significantly enough, by some Dissenters, most particularly in their eschewal of communal ritual. Sterne had addressed the importance of a worshipful community in an untitled sermon little read by Sterne scholars, known as "Efficacy of prayer," wherein he is critical of "the doctrine of those who would resolve all devotion into the inner man" depending on one's "purity and integrity of heart,—unaccompanied either with words or actions" (*Sermons* 402). Saddled with a body ("We are not angels, but men cloathed with bodies" [402], a phrase repeated in *TS* 5.7.431–32), we need all the "external helps" that places of worship afford, necessary to both the worshipper and "civil society" (403). Sterne would have found the same view in Norris, among many other eighteenth-century Anglican clerics, always based on the doubleness of the human being: "Fellowship and Communion" is required because a "Worship purely Mental and Intellectual is too Abstract and Sublime for a Nature allied

to Sense, and depending upon it. . . . God has given you a Soul and a Body in Conjunction." John Norris, "Spiritual Counsel, or The Father's Advice to His Children," in *Treatises upon Several Subjects* (London: S. Manship, 1698), 467–68, quoted from *Sermons*, Notes 433, where Sterne's passage is annotated with several similar statements from the Anglican pulpit stressing human doubleness.

33 Without insisting on Talmudic rigidity, a glance through the reviews of present-day scholarship in the *Scriblerian* turns up more and more lists of miscitations and misquotations, more and more indications of the use of inadequate texts, more and more foolish errors of reading, for example that the black page of *Tristram Shandy* commemorates Tristram's death, or that Jonathan Swift wrote a letter to Laurence Sterne in 1708—both statements to be found in recent scholarly publications. The latter error resulted, pertinently enough, from a careless reading of a Kerby-Miller annotation mentioning Swift's letter to "Stearne" about the actual joined twins who formed the basis of "Double Mistress"; this was Bishop John Stearne, Swift's friend; Laurence would not be born for another five years. See *Martinus Scriblerus*, 143.

34 On the other hand, sadly typical of today's programmatic reader, Carolyn D. Williams finds the entire passage appalling: the author, "Lawrence [*sic*] Sterne . . . is so firmly convinced that all women want sexually active men with generously proportioned genitalia [that he] totally sacrifices Widow Wadman's individuality." This comes toward the end of an essay that seems to formulate the eighteenth century's attitude toward women based on Pennyfeather's arguments in *Martinus Scriblerus*, beginning with a brief skirmish with Locke, who is found almost to "annihilat[e] the soul" by equating it with an evanescent "consciousness"—a rather doubtful reading of Locke's *Essay*, II.27, "Of Identity and Diversity"; see Williams, "'Another Self in the Case': Gender, Marriage and the Individual in Augustan Literature," in *Rewriting the Self: Histories from the Renaissance to the Present*, ed. Roy Porter (London: Routledge, 1997), 113–14. To my knowledge, no one before this has ever accused the Widow Wadman of worrying over the *size* of Toby's penis.

35 The parallels to Charron, *Of Wisdome*, trans. Samson Lennard (1612), 83, 85, 138, are provided in *TS*, Notes 548–49. For a discussion of Sterne's divided attitude toward Toby and his bowling green, see Melvyn New, "Laurence Sterne and William Falconer: Soldiers and Sailors," *Philological Quarterly* 99 (2020): 229–44.

36 Brown goes on to suggest that Sterne knew Montaigne better than the *Book of Common Prayer*, to which he responded, "'As for my conning Montaigne as much as my pray'r book'—there you are right again,—but mark . . . I have not said I admire him as much" (*Letters* 168).

308 · Textual and Critical Intersections

37 Jonathan Lamb, *Sterne's Fiction and the Double Principle* (Cambridge: Cambridge University Press, 1989). One suspects this was the sort of book one had to write in the deconstructive 1980s, but Lamb's earlier essay "Sterne's Use of Montaigne," *Comparative Literature* 32 (1980): 1–41, remains the more convincing effort.

38 *Martinus Scriblerus*, 143 (italics reversed). Kerby-Miller attributes the concluding sentence of the "Introduction: To the Reader" (*"whenever [the reader] begins to think any one Chapter dull, the style will be immediately changed in the next"*) to a desire to give cover to the multiple authorship of *Martinus Scriblerus*, and links it specifically to the "different style employed in the Double Mistress episode" (183n24).

39 Walsh, "Scriblerian Satire," 23, 32n7.

40 A particularly significant scriptural chapter concerning the Word versus the chatter of many words (the "gift of tongues") is 1 Corinthians 14; see Locke's and Sterne's similar use of verse 14:25 below.

41 *Martinus Scriblerus*, 134.

42 *Martinus Scriblerus*, 135–36.

43 *Martinus Scriblerus*, 136.

44 Kerby-Miller points to the presence in this chapter of Robert Burton's *Anatomy of Melancholy*, one of Sterne's favorite sources as well; see especially Walter Shandy's cures for love (*TS* 8.34.725–28; *TS*, Notes 522–27), mostly taken from Burton's section on "Love-Melancholy." One of the best recent discussions of Burton's influence on the Scriblerians and Sterne is Christopher Tilmouth, "Sceptical Perspectives on Melancholy: Burton, Swift, Pope, Sterne," *Review of English Studies* 68, no. 287 (2017): 924–44. Considering the changing attitude toward melancholy in the century, mirroring similar evolutions for ideas such as *enthusiasm* and *quixotism*, Tilmouth argues that Pope and Swift were already enmeshed in this change, and adds: "It makes sense to think of Sterne as continuing the Scriblerian vein of satire" (925n5). Tilmouth ultimately finds that Sterne's "robust scepticism about man's intellectual pretensions" is alleviated by "a good-humoured ironic light," and that Burton oscillated between melancholy and laughter while in Sterne they are *"co-present."* Whether oscillation and co-presence can be differentiated seems to be a problem confronted by the "Double Mistress" episode, not to mention the Mystery of Trinity. By concentrating on a "double perspective" or "mutually incompatible positions" in Burton, the Scriblerians, and Sterne, and their treatment of melancholy, Tilmouth demonstrates the inconsistencies possible within the material body, but leaves untouched the immaterial soul or spirit, which is, as he notes in one key sentence, where Swift's "allegiance is" (929).

45 Sterne has too often been read in the last fifty years as the leading metaphysi-

cian of the eighteenth century, so it is worth reminding ourselves that much of his "philosophical" knowledge is garnered from Chambers's *Cyclopædia* and similar digests; one might suspect of him what Kerby-Miller notes about Swift's role in the arguments of this chapter, namely, that "his lack of interest is, of course, to be traced to his detestation of metaphysical argument and religious speculation." *Martinus Scriblerus*, 284. Sterne's reduction of "polemical divinity" to the antics of Rabelais's Gymnast and Tripet (*TS* 5.29.463–64) may indicate his similar actual indifference to metaphysics and theology, except as fodder for his satiric wit.

46 Locke, *Essay*, IV.3.6.541.

47 *Martinus Scriblerus*, 138.

48 *Martinus Scriblerus*, 287.

49 *Martinus Scriblerus*, 138.

50 The free-thinkers' first argument for the materiality of thought is that since the "*meat roasting* Quality" of a smoak-jack resides in all its several mechanical parts, so too can consciousness reside in the many material parts of a human being rather than immaterially in a unified self. We might recall Uncle Toby's response to his brother's suggestion that the mind operates as a magic lantern (a metaphor borrowed from Locke, *Essay*, II.14.9.184): "mine are more like a smoak-jack" (*TS* 3.18.225). The Florida editors annotate this passage with a sentence from Pope, "Thoughts on Various Subjects," (no. 81): "Some men's Wit is like a dark lanthorn, which serves their own turn and guides their own way: but is never known (according to the Scripture Phrase) either to shine forth before Men, or to glorify their Father in heaven." *The Works of Mr. Alexander Pope, in Prose* (1741), vol. 2, 337. Swift's "Mechanical Operation of the Spirit" is also at play in the passage; see *TS*, Notes 233–34.

51 *Martinus Scriblerus*, 142.

52 Locke, *Essay*, II.27.328–48, "Of Identity and Diversity." The free-thinkers believe the brain is a "*Congeries* of Glands," a gland being a canal, so that when "two of these Canals disembogue themselves into one, they make what we call a Proposition; and when two of these propositional channels empty themselves into a third, they form a Syllogism, or a Ratiocination." *Martinus Scriblerus*, 141. This, in turn, is very much like the process outlined in Crambe's *Treatise of Syllogisms*, where ideas copulate and engender conclusions (*Martinus Scriblerus*, 121); attempts to explain the process of ideation solely in material terms seem at home in sexual metaphors, nowhere more richly than in Sterne's own play throughout *Tristram Shandy* on creation and procreation, and particularly in his several uses of *ejaculation* (a mode of disemboguement, one might note). See Melvyn New, "Sterne," in *Cambridge Companion to English Novelists*, ed. Adrian Poole (Cambridge: Cambridge University Press,

2009), 63–79. And see also *TS* 3.40.280–81: "THE gift of ratiocination . . . is the finding out the agreement or disagreement of two ideas one with another, by the intervention of a third . . . just as a man, as *Locke* well observes, by a yard, finds two mens nine-pin-alleys to be of the same length . . . by *juxta-position*." Tristram alters Locke (*Essay*, IV.17.18.685), just enough to turn his idea into a disemboguement. As with the Scriblerians when writing *Memoirs* and with Swift's *Tale of a Tub*, language proves so richly fecund that its capacity to re-create reality to its own wishes and dimensions (Peter and Jack in the *Tale*, Martinus in *Memoirs*) is never in question. Tristram exhibits the same rich capacity, but in the Scriblerian mode it is the language of an autonomous being, adequate for fully expounding one's life and opinions but unable to assess itself in relation to the transcendent otherness of Christian belief. That inability is the ethical core of Scriblerian satire, the abuse of conscience (or consciousness) that Sterne knowingly placed at the very center of his vision.

53 See, e.g.: "So that this consciousness not reaching to any of the Actions of either of those Men [Nestor or Thersites, in Locke's dismissal of transmigration of souls], he is no more one *self* with either of them, than if the Soul or immaterial Spirit, that now informs him, had been created, and began to exist, when it began to inform his present Body." Locke, *Essay*, II.27.14.339.

54 Locke, II.27.13.338.

55 Locke, II.27.13.340, 344.

56 Locke, II.27.13.346, 343–44. A particularly valuable reading of this section of *An Essay concerning Human Understanding* is provided by R. C. Tennant, "The Anglican Response to Locke's Theory of Personal Identity," *Journal of the History of Ideas* 43 (1982): 73–90. Tennant grants that "Locke perhaps did believe that the soul was immaterial, but as a philosopher he could only regard the doctrine as unintelligible"; and again, "Locke was anti-Christian in the impact his work made on eighteenth-century thought" (77). Tennant believes Locke was "theologically naïve and destructive" of Christianity, which is certainly possible, although in my own reading I suggest that rendering some questions to be "unintelligible," while naive from an Enlightenment point of view, is highly sophisticated within a theological exposition. Tennant seems to acknowledge this when he turns to "opponents" of Locke like Berkeley, Joseph Butler, and William Law, "who each . . . had a wide influence among evangelicals, and who may even be described as mystics: that is, they knew by personal experience the suprarational, non-linguistic character both of direct communion between the soul and God and of the understanding of the redemptive scheme" (78–79). That Locke left room for this experiential faith within his epistemology (and ontology) is splendidly argued by Richard E.

Single and Double: *Memoirs of Martinus Scriblerus* and *Tristram Shandy* · 311

Brantley, *Locke, Wesley, and the Method of English Romanticism* (Gainesville: University of Florida Press, 1984).

57 Matthew Henry, *An Exposition of All the Books of the Old and New Testament*, 3rd ed. (1721), vol. 6, 120.

58 Sterne's "Abuses of conscience" sermon, published on three separate occasions in his lifetime, offers a useful counterbalance to the reading of *Tristram Shandy* as nonjudgmental, and may account for Sterne's having included it, an early warning to those who wanted to find Tristram "one of us." The last paragraph, significantly enough, iterates this same division between human and divine justice: "And . . . remember this plain distinction, a mistake in which has ruined thousands,—that your conscience is not a law:—No, God and reason made the law, and have placed conscience within you to determine;—not like an *Asiatick* Cadi, according to the ebbs and flows of his own passions,—but like a *British* judge in this land of liberty and good sense, who makes no new law, but faithfully declares that law which he knows already written" (*TS* 2.17.164).

59 The questions appeared in the *British Apollo* between June and October 1708. I quote from a collected edition, *The British Apollo*, 3rd ed. (1726): 300–301, 316. Kerby-Miller's suggestion that the questions and answers might have been Arbuthnot's seems based solely on the similarity between them and the issues raised in "Double Mistress." Possibly, instead, they reflect concerns that would have occurred to most observers in 1708 and the decades following.

60 *The British Apollo*, 301.

61 *The British Apollo*, 316. See also Locke, *Essay*, II.27.19.342: "And to punish *Socrates* waking, for what sleeping *Socrates* thought, and waking *Socrates* was never conscious of, would be no more of Right, than to punish one Twin for what his Brother Twin did, whereof he knew nothing, because their outsides were so alike, that they could not be distinguished; for such Twins have been seen."

62 *The British Apollo*, 301.

63 In scholastic terms, the appeal is *in Foro Legis* (the outer forum, that is, in the eyes of the law) rather than *in Foro Conscientiæ* (the inner forum, that is, in the eyes of God, the conscience).

64 *Martinus Scriblerus*, 156.

65 See n. 31, above, the passage from Swift's sermon "On the Trinity"; indeed, the entire sermon is a significant commentary on "Double Mistress."

66 *Martinus Scriblerus*, 159.

67 *Martinus Scriblerus*, 157–58.

68 See *TS* 1.2.2–3 for Tristram's elaboration of the "homunculus" thesis; see also *TS*, Notes 44–47. That the "preformation" theory was held by many scientists

312 · Textual and Critical Intersections

of the day is given further credence by Arbuthnot's using it in a 1710 contribution to the *Philosophical Transactions of the Royal Society of London*, "An Argument for Divine Providence, taken from the Constant Regularity Observed in the Births of Both Sexes," namely that "there seems to be no more probable cause to be assigned in physics for this equality of the births, than that in our first parents seed there were at first formed an equal number of both sexes." See John Arbuthnot, "An Argument [. . .]," *Philosophical Transactions Abridged* 5 (1809): 606–9. Arbuthnot's mathematical probability formulas are, to the nonmathematical, quite dazzling.

69 Frank Palmeri, "*Martinus Scriblerus*, Diderot's *Dream*, and Tiepolo's *Divertimento*: Eighteenth-Century Representations of Aggregate Identity," *Comparative Literature Studies* 38 (2001): 330–54, takes a very different view of this passage, beginning with his belief that the homunculus is housed in the woman (an error caused, it would seem, by the traditional use of the female pronoun to indicate the soul). Most significantly, he suggests that the "ridiculous conundrums" implied by materialist philosophy "[meet] no rational or substantial refutation" (334); I am arguing, to the contrary, that precisely the lack of a "materialist" or rational refutation is the immaterialist's strongest argument in favor of divine ineffability.

70 Johnson, *Dictionary* (1755), s.v., "to traduce."

71 Sir John Davies, "Of the Soul of Man and the Immortalitie thereof," in *The Poems of Sir John Davies*, ed. Robert Krueger (Oxford: Clarendon Press, 1975), 27. Davies's discussion of "knowledge" is of much significance to our argument; that a theological work of 1599 was still being reprinted throughout the eighteenth century is the sort of historical detail too often ignored by literary scholars; Swift, we might note, included it on his Moor Park Reading List, 1697–98; see Dirk F. Passmann and Hermann J. Real, "Annotating J. S.: Swift's Reading at Moor Park in 1697/8," in *Reading Swift: Papers from The Seventh Münster Symposium on Jonathan Swift*, ed. Janika Bischof, Kirsten Juhas, and Hermann J. Real (Paderborn, Germany: Wilhelm Fink, 2019), 101–24. In the second stanza quoted, Davies aligns himself with those who argued that the soul was united with the body by God at birth—how this was done was a mystery. Johnson's second quotation illustrating *traduce* casts less light, but that was its intention: "Some [believe the soul is] made by *God*, some by *Angels*, and some by the *Generant*. Whether it be immediately *created*, or *traduced*, hath been the great ball of contention to the Later Ages." Joseph Granvill, *Scepsis Scientifica, or Confest Ignorance, the Way to Science* (London: E. Cotis for Henry Everston, 1665), 14.

72 *Martinus Scriblerus*, 160.

Single and Double: *Memoirs of Martinus Scriblerus* and *Tristram Shandy* · 313

73 *Martinus Scriblerus*, 161. The observation of human hypocrisy concerning bodily functions is hardly new, stretching back at least to Aristophanes and Petronius; in the twentieth century it is perhaps Yeats who captured it best, in "Crazy Jane Talks with the Bishop": "But Love has pitched his mansion in / The place of excrement; / For nothing can be sole or whole / That has not been rent." W. B. Yeats, *Collected Poems* (New York: Macmillan, 1958), 255. In more recent decades, Arundhati Roy, *The God of Small Things* (1997; New York: Random House, 2017), 218, writes: "He tells stories of the gods, but his yarn is spun from the ungodly human heart."

74 *Martinus Scriblerus*, 161.

75 It is quite possible, in fact, that one can possess both Lindamira and Indamora, a parody of the actual doubleness of human beings, the body and soul of Locke's unitary being; the great novels go very far in allowing us to think that the author has indeed succeeded in fully understanding a Madame Bovary or a Charles Swann. That these great works of art continue to generate readings does suggest the difficulty if not impossibility of full possession; what is always left over, we might suggest, is indicative of transcendence, what always remains of the work beyond interpretation.

76 Alexander Pope, *An Essay on Man*, ed. Maynard Mack (1950; London: Methuen, 1964), 56 (epistle 2, line 18).

12

"The Life of a Wit is a warfare upon earth"

Sterne, Joyce, and Their Portraits of the Artist

> I am sick, I must die.
> Lord have mercy on us.
> Thomas Nashe, "A Litany in Time of Plague"

It would have been impossible for me to write about Sterne during the past half century without encountering James Joyce,[1] most especially because I have had a particular interest in connecting Sterne to twentieth-century modernism, with published essays putting him in proximity to Marcel Proust, Virginia Woolf, Bruno Schulz, and Italo Svevo, among others.[2] Yet, looking back over my engagement with Sterne and Joyce, I find primarily a history of evasion and avoidance: I have occasionally (and validly, I hope) protested any attempt to link stream-of-consciousness with Sterne's Lockean train of ideas—they do not produce the same narrative mode, and it is simply a slipshod reading of both authors that equates them as narratologists. Far more specifically, I assisted a former doctoral student, Stephen Soud, with his published argument that the copy of *Aristotle's Masterpiece* Leopold Bloom finds in a bookstall is a nineteenth-century reproduction of the seventeenth- or eighteenth-century midwifery manual that Tristram consults on several occasions. To be honest, however, my contribution stemmed simply from the luck of a book collector who bought random copies of the *Masterpiece* whenever he found one; the image on the Winter 1995 cover of the *James Joyce Quarterly* is from my copy, now housed in the University of Florida's Special Collections; the essay inside that issue is Soud's solid explanation of its close resemblance to Bloom's copy.[3]

My fullest engagement with Joyce was again rather superficial. In 1994 I organized an extended reading of *Tristram Shandy* (Twayne's Masterwork Studies) by beginning and ending each chapter with a quotation from Nietzsche—and borrowed my title from him as well, *Tristram Shandy: A Book for Free Spirits*. More to the present point, at the head of each chapter I borrowed wholesale Stuart Gilbert's schema for dissecting the episodes of *Ulysses,* but altered his topics—Scene, Hour, Organ, Art, Symbol, Technic—to divisions I felt useful in reading Sterne, namely, Character, Foil, Incident, Document, Activity, Image and -Ism. I remained consistent to these categories in five separate chapters. As I wrote in my introduction, "What appeals to me in so rigid a schematization is precisely its blatant artificiality. It calls attention to the act of 'reading' as an organizing, demarcating, and ultimately limiting exercise."[4] Looking back almost thirty years later, I am happy that I anticipated the present-day foofaraw over the discovery of the act of reading as a theoretical subject; and sad that I used the scheme to suggest a relationship between Sterne and Joyce without engaging in its many complexities.[5]

Now, with the occasion of celebrating fellow Sternean Peter de Voogd, coeditor with me of the two volumes of *Letters* in the Florida Edition of the Works and the incomparable editor of the *Shandean* for all of its history to date, it seems appropriate to acknowledge Peter's second scholarly interest, his career as a Joyce enthusiast, by returning to the Sterne-Joyce conversation across several centuries and paying closer attention to what they might be saying to one another.

I use *conversation* advisedly because it has become my hobby-horse over the past few decades, the idea that great authors (and I insist on *greatness* or *genius,* to the dismay of twenty-first-century levelers) hold conversations with one another that we can sometimes hear over the chatter of our own literary, social, economic, and political concerns.[6] And while I am indulging one hobby-horse let me gallop apace and suggest another: like every author in the Western canon, Sterne and Joyce begin in conversation with Homer—*The Iliad,* chronicling the life of warfare, *The Odyssey,* the life of peace. For Sterne, *Tristram Shandy* is his *Iliad,* not only because of Uncle Toby's military obsession but even more pertinently, Walter Shandy's "opinions," opinions being the originating cause of warfare. Tristram's attempt to chronicle his life and opinions emerges from a world of conflicts and contradictions, however domesticated they have become in Shandy Hall. *A Sentimental Journey* (with an "*odyssey*" already in its title) is, in contrast, a homage to peace, the absence of hostilities between human beings that is the goal of our quest for sociability and love, and eventually the true domesticity associated with going home. I have perhaps too overtly allowed this reading of Sterne to sway my reading of Joyce, but my argument is that *Portrait* is a conversation with *The Iliad,* Stephen being the warrior who emerges from a country at war with itself, and a religion at war with him, while *Ulysses,* with its structural basis in *The Odyssey,* is a narrative of domestic reconciliation, Bloom discovering consolation for his lost son in Stephen and for his lost wife in returning to her bed where he becomes the surprising subject of Molly's magnificent final soliloquy. Sterne's chapter "A Fragment" in *A Sentimental Journey* also puts "love" at the center of his voyage:

> The fire caught—and the whole city, like the heart of one man, open'd itself to Love.
>
> . . . Friendship and Virtue met together, and kiss'd each other in the street . . .
>
> every Abderitish woman left her purple web, and chastly sat her down and listen'd to the song. (*SJ* 45–46)[7]

I will, however, concentrate in this essay on *Tristram* and *Portrait,* the making of artists in times of conflict—and save homecoming for another time. My title echoes Alexander Pope's early thoughts on a literary career, published before he was thirty: "I believe, if any one, early in his life should contemplate the dangerous fate of authors, he would scarce be of their number on any consideration. The life of a Wit is a warfare upon earth; and the present spirit of the learned world is such, that to attempt to serve it (any way) one must have the constancy of a martyr, and a resolution to suffer for its sake."[8] This is a prophecy that will shape both Tristram and Stephen, but perhaps the narrative artist to begin with is Yorick, Sterne's clerical alter ego, whose death allows Tristram room to narrate his life and opinions, unimpeded by the judgmental posture that marks Yorick's relationship with the world: "so that when mention was made of a pitiful or an ungenerous proceeding,—he never gave himself a moment's time to reflect . . . but if it was a dirty action,——without more ado,—— The man was a dirty fellow." His honesty rouses "a swarm of wasps," till, "over-power'd by numbers, and worn out at length by the calamities of the war . . . he threw down the sword" and "died . . . quite broken hearted" (*TS* 1.11–12). And lest it be objected that Yorick is not an "author," we should recall that his return to *Tristram Shandy* is signaled when his sermon is retrieved from the mud and read in volume 2, a sermon that will receive even more importance to Sterne's work when we compare it to the sermon that terrifies Stephen in *Portrait*.

When listening to a conversation between authors long dead, one is prone to imagine an exchange based on the slightest of whispers, which is why I wrote "Yorick" in the margin of *Portrait* when Stephen bravely yet with great trepidation enters the rector's office to report a "dirty action": "He saw the rector sitting at a desk writing. There was a skull on the desk and a strange solemn smell in the room like the old leather of chairs . . . he looked at the skull and at the rector's kindlooking face."[9] In this instance, of course, Stephen is rewarded with a just decree but what is also important is that the incident culminates the early childhood of the author with a hero's "victory": "They [his classmates] made a cradle of their locked hands and hoisted him up among them and carried him along till he struggled to get free. And when he had escaped from them they broke away in all directions, flinging their caps again into the air and whistling as they went spinning up and crying:—Hurroo!"[10] The boys then go off to play cricket, not quite the eight days of sports that Achilles sponsors after killing Hector, but within the context of Stephen's early school days, filled with significance: the Battle of Waterloo was won on the playing fields of Eton, according to popular sentiment.[11]

School is not the only battlefield Stephen encounters; his memories of early childhood center on a Christmas dinner and serve to introduce the warfare of Walter Shandy's library, where opinions are formulated and, most important, proselytized: "What could be wanting in my father but to have wrote a book to publish this notion of his to the world? Little boots it to the subtle speculatist to stand single in his opinions" (*TS* 1.19.63). The quarrels of Dublin involve, of course, inseparable issues of politics and religion: in celebrating the birth of Christ ("Peace on Earth") Dante cannot resist arguing with Simon Dedalus, who responds in kind. Significantly, Scripture is brought to bear on this human quarreling: "*Woe be to the man by whom the scandal cometh! . . . It would be better for him that a millstone were tied about his neck and that he were cast into the depth of the sea*"; what is ignored is Luke 17:3, if one surrenders his opinion, then we should "forgive him." Mrs. Dedalus asks the same question that might occur to Mrs. Shandy: "not even for one day in the year . . . can we be free from these dreadful disputes," seconded by Uncle Charles, "Can we not have our opinions whatever they are without this bad temper and this bad language?"[12]

That *Tristram Shandy* offers "opinions" in its title is not, as we might hope in our enlightened view of sharing equal opinions with our equal neighbors, a declaration in favor of opinions. Rather, in the Shandy world *opinion* is another word for "argument"; one of Sterne's profoundest insights into human behavior is that we are never satisfied with our own opinions until others agree with us. It is to be expected, then, that Walter Shandy is "certainly irresistible" in disputation: "Persuasion hung upon his lips . . . In short, whether he was on the weak or the strong side of the question, 'twas hazardous in either case to attack him" (*TS* 1.19.59–60).[13] In the first five volumes of *Tristram,* dominated by Walter, the word *argument* or its variants appear more than forty-five times; *dispute* (or variants), thirty-eight times. Moreover, it is the progress of argumentation that establishes a particularly important, often overlooked relationship between Walter and Toby: our first line of defense for our opinions is argumentation, the art of rhetoric; the second, when the first line fails (as it too often does), is violence, the art of warfare (persuasion by other means). It is worth observing, in an era of "alternative truth," that Walter Shandy's opinions are in fact usually ridiculous and hence persuadable only by means of the "*Argumentum Baculinum*" (argument with a stick)—an argument Stephen knows well, given Heron and his cane, Boland and his weaponized cabbage stump.[14] Thus, although the brothers have often been praised for reconciling their differences, usually with irenic gestures rather than words, there is an important irony behind these sentimental reconciliations. To the very last chapter in volume 9, the theme remains persuasion and warfare, and the brothers remain at odds; significantly, even the dead Yorick is "rising up to batter the whole [of Walter's] hypothesis to pieces" (*TS* 9.33.807), when Obadiah breaks in with his impotent bull. Opinion remains suspended between Walter's persuasiveness and Toby's military prowess, a vision of human society that reflects a world as old as the *Iliad,* and as recent as yesterday.

It is certainly the world of Dublin in Stephen's time, conflict writ large in the disputes between Ireland and England, Roman Catholics and Protestants, Irish "orators" and English troops. But it is also the world writ small of Stephen's boyhood, where images of conflict abound, beginning perhaps with the childhood reading of works like *The Count of Monte Cristo* or the sea adventures of Frederick Marryat, and progressing to his "ally" Aubrey Mills and their "gang of adventurers," with "short sticks thrust daggerwise" in their belts, fighting "a battle on the shaggy weedgrown rocks."[15] We tend to dismiss such realistic accounts as typical (and indeed they are), but Stephen's entire education is set up as a series of rivalries, whether in determining who will be first in the "weekly essay," to who is the "greatest writer," an argument that ends with Stephen being switched with "a long cabbage stump" to "persuade" him to admit "Byron was no good."[16]

Stephen is a reluctant participant in all this "manly" behavior, and his adolescent struggles with sexuality serve as a contrapuntal melody in *Portrait*: "This spirit of quarrelsome comradeship which he had observed lately in his rival had not seduced Stephen from his habits of quiet obedience. He mistrusted the turbulence . . . which seemed to him a sorry anticipation of manhood."[17] His imagination is now fed with the likes of Mercedes in *The Count of Monte Cristo* and Melnotte in Bulwer-Lytton's *The Lady of Lyons,* but also with the Roman Catholic Virgin Mary, whose litany, taken from Ecclesiasticus 24:17–20, is Eros-tinged with echoes of Song of Solomon, "I gave a sweet smell like cinnamon and aromatic balm: I gave a sweet odor like the best myrrh."[18] The result is a "stream of gloomy tenderness," visions of Emma and Mary entwined in such a manner than when several years after the episode of the tram steps his friends tease him about Emma ("deucedly pretty," "ripping"), Stephen feels an uncharacteristic "shaft of momentary anger" over these "indelicate allusions."[19] His friend Heron tries to force him to confess to admiring Emma by striking him several times with his cane "in jesting reproof," but the anger has already passed, and Stephen by way of mock confession recites the Confiteor.[20]

Given that procreativity and creativity are bound together in *Tristram* and *Portrait,* Tristram's maiming at birth, his window-sash circumcision, his admission of impotence with Jenny (*TS* 7.29.624) all suggest similar impediments to "manliness." At the same time, there are uncanny resemblances between Joyce's portrayal of fraught sexuality in *Portrait*

320 · Textual and Critical Intersections

and Sterne's seemingly freer encounters in *A Sentimental Journey*. For example, Yorick's meeting on the concert hall steps in Milan with the suggestively named Marquesina di F*** (*SJ* 77–78), a "connection" that gives him "more pleasure than any one I had the honour to make in Italy," surely echoes the dance Stephen and Emma enact on the tram steps: "They seemed to listen, he on the upper step and she on the lower. She came up to his step many times and went down to hers again between their phrases and once or twice stood close beside him for some moments on the upper step, forgetting to go down, and then went down. His heart danced upon her movements like a cork upon a tide."[21] Or again, Stephen's recapturing that moment by resting "the tips of the fingers of one hand upon the palm of the other hand, scarcely touching it and yet pressing upon it lightly. But the pressure of her fingers had been lighter and steadier: and suddenly the memory of their touch traversed his brain and body like an invisible warm wave."[22] As many have pointed out, fingers and hands (tactility) are central to Yorick's encounters with women in *A Sentimental Journey*.[23] As for Tristram, while the meeting with Jenny is significant, even more telling is his dancing away from the accommodating Nannette at the end of volume 7, an episode to which I will return.

When Stephen accompanies his father to Cork, Joyce puts heavy stress on Simon's "manliness," his reputation, twenty years later, for athletic and sexual prowess, which drives his son to memories of his sick bed at Clongowes, his dream of being dead and "buried then in the little graveyard of the community."[24] "Alas, poor Stephen" we might respond, as we certainly do when Simon assures his friends that his son is not interested in girls:

> —Then he is not his father's son, said the little old man.
> —I don't know, I'm sure, said Mr Dedalus, smiling complacently.
> —Your father, said the little old man to Stephen, was the boldest flirt in the city of Cork in his day.[25]

It does not take Freud to suggest that Simon is not the best of fathers for the budding artist. Sterne is more subtle, planting seeds of doubt as to whether Walter is Tristram's biological father; blaming Walter for the botched birthing at the application of Dr. Slop's forceps; and for allowing Tristram to be baptized with the "worst" name in the English language. We might add to these shortcomings as a father, his taking an unhealthy interest in sizable noses after his son's has been crushed, and ultimately his

Sterne, Joyce, and Their Portraits of the Artist · 321

faith in auxiliary verbs as the source of his son's education. Everything in *Tristram Shandy*, in fact, points to an estrangement between father and son—yet no reader can seriously doubt that, in every way that matters, Tristram is Walter's intellectual heir, just as Stephen is his father's Irish Catholic son.[26]

It seems to me, then, essential to our understanding of both works that their authors introduce a mediating (and, oddly enough, nonfictional) voice into their fictions at this point, Sterne's own "Abuses of conscience" sermon and Father Arnall's sermon on the four last things, Death, Judgment, Heaven, and Hell. I have written extensively about "Abuses" and will not repeat myself here;[27] suffice to say, that the two sermons would seem to provide a direct confrontation between orthodox Roman Catholicism and orthodox Anglican Catholicism, or, to speak in familial terms, between the father church and its breakaway son.[28] Yet, as with the Shandys and the Dedaluses, the separation is fundamentally illusory; despite differences in setting and tone, both sermons end up at the same place: the judgment seat of God. The stated purpose of both preachers is to "examine the state of our conscience."[29] Sterne, who had delivered the same sermon, with only very minor revisions, to an assize meeting (that is, a congregation primarily of judges, attorneys, and other cogs in the legal machinery) at York Minster in 1750, now directs it toward his readers rather than the auditors in the Shandy Hall parlor. Indeed, the one Catholic in the room, Dr. Slop, falls asleep. Joyce, on the other hand, directs Father Arnall's words toward his captive congregation of "dear little brothers in Christ,"[30] among them Stephen and his very bad conscience; sleepless nights follow for him.

While Sterne's sermon is being read downstairs, Tristram, the artist who will write his own life by defying Horace and all similar appeals to order and decorum, is upstairs being born into the world. Having accompanied the embryo from inception to this moment, the reader is acutely aware of encountering a different sort of author, one who will be as unlike Sterne (Yorick), the author of the sermon, as possible. The death of Yorick entails the death of Sterne and the Christian organization of life as a pilgrimage toward those four last things of Father Arnall's sermon—and, I hasten to add, of the direction of Sterne's forty-five Anglican sermons as well. Life now presents itself as that disordered and directionless chaos celebrated in recent years as an encounter with the directionless indeterminacy of all things, the relativity of all values, the secularization of a society in which the disappearance of Truth (Logos) opens an era even Swift and Sterne were not ready to predict, one in which "alternative truths" take seed and blossom, and we no longer are able to distinguish between harmless and poisonous fruits.

The portrait of Tristram as an artist is limned by a sermon that has no place in Tristram's autobiographical world; still, we find it there, directed toward the readers, much as Yorick's death has also been directed toward them. No matter what Tristram might want to believe about the world he is born into, all will continue to move inexorably toward death; and indeed, death comes calling for him in volume 7. His flight postpones but cannot prevent the conclusion of *Tristram Shandy* some thirty volumes short of the planned work.[31] Yorick, on the other hand, buried and mourned early in volume 1, returns again and again, a source of judgment in a world where it is sorely needed. Sterne, I continue to argue, never loses control of Tristram or of the book his putative author is supposedly writing, an authorial presence indicated pervasively by judgment—his sermon at this point, Yorick's pithy observations at another—and always the measurement that satiric irony creates between what Tristram's words say and what Sterne means. Does anyone believe that Walter's "opinions" are worthy? Does anyone find Toby's bowling green a useful contribution to the nation's defense? Does sentiment justify participation in and endorsement of the ways in which "civilizations" ennoble the killing of others? Phrased as questions, these words will still awaken that quarrelsomeness, mild if possible, malevolent if necessary, that accompanies all human endeavors: no one likes being told what to think.

However, by doing so, even by way of ironic questions, we exhibit our belief in definable Truths, validations of Judgment; and that returns us to those four last things of Father Arnall, who in one stroke makes clear the gulf between human and divine Truth and Judgment: "One single instant after the body's death, the soul had been weighed in the balance."[32] There will be no time to argue one's case; recall that Yorick, the Anglican minister, weighs dishonest actions with the same speed. There is no time for the different perspectives that today we blithely accept as everyone's "right to an opinion," no lengthy appeals to another more favorable court, and not even to the politically attractive "majority rule." Some opinions are wrong, some viewpoints are vicious. The one possibility that Sterne and Joyce endorse with their art—indeed, because of their art—is that Truth exists and, in doing so, Truth must be subjected to final Judgment. I will capitalize Truth throughout to indicate this precise moment of Judgment after our time has expired; whether labeled God or the Word, the Logos or the Spirit, Truth cannot be lost to the artist in a more enlightened world of alternative truths. On this point, I believe the eighteenth-century heteroclite Anglican cleric and the twentieth-century fugitive Catholic agreeably conversed.

I have discussed the place of human justice within the divine scheme in "Single and Double: *Memoirs of Martinus Scriblerus* and *Tristram Shandy*" and will not repeat myself here, except to note that Dr. Slop is present at the birthing of Tristram because Walter believes that headfirst delivery damages the soul, which for him, following the popular distortions of Descartes's theory in Britain, is a physical entity lodged in the pineal gland,[33] while podalic delivery, which Slop will provide, preserves it—a small hint of Enlightenment's undertaking to materialize everything while still insisting, at least nominally, on an abstract, unknowable, ineffable entity labeled *soul*. If someone could have convinced the world of the materiality of soul—or if war could have forced compliance to that opinion—and if death did not present us with the ultimate (and *essentially* meaningless) end of material existence, we might not have evolved, from Moses and Homer onward, into a civilization that found it useful to connect virtue and immortality. This connection, inspired or invented, was by means of an infinite Justice that was infallible in its knowledge of the difference between right and wrong, virtue and vice. Within a religious or political institution infinite Justice was all too finite, all too human; the conscience, the existential manifestation of essential Justice, the religion implanted within us, reflects this imperfection, the message of both Sterne's and Father Arnall's sermons. As a metaphysical necessity, however, a means by which the Truth of both the material and immaterial worlds could be established, the positing of a final Judgment enables one certain earthly manifestation—the works of art that speak to one another over centuries and invite us to listen to their conversations.[34]

That the sermons in both works are embedded within a context of human sexuality is important and here again an uncanny exchange between the two authors revolves around a work both had absorbed, *Aristotle's Masterpiece,* a seventeenth-century birthing manual, still being republished in the twentieth century.[35] When the young Stephen sees the word

Fœtus carved into the "dark stained wood" of a desk in the classroom of Queens College Cork his thoughts wander to the monstrous births and sanguinary illustrations of *Masterpiece:* "It shocked him to find in the outer world a trace of what he had deemed till then a brutish and individual malady of his own mind. His recent *monstrous* reveries came thronging to his memory... wondering always where they came from, from what den of *monstrous* images."[36] That Stephen's awkward sexual awakening, Tristram's account of his own conception (the homunculus), and Walter's theories of healthy birthing all entail consulting *Aristotle's Masterpiece* (and similar manuals) might help us formulate one of the more obvious links between Sterne and Joyce: both deplore a Christian ethic that centers on sexual repression.

The "embryo" from *Aristotle's Masterpiece* is planted in the opening chapter of *Tristram Shandy,* and the birth taking place upstairs will result in Tristram's nose being crushed, putting into question his ability to procreate. As has often been observed, Sterne interweaves procreation and creation in his fiction, so that Tristram's "wound" is aesthetic as well as physical. For Stephen, the delay in sexual maturity is the result of an education at the hands of celibate priests, the guilt-fueled impotence the sermon arouses because he has become, he believes, addicted to the vices of pornography and masturbation. His recourse is worship of the Virgin Mary, in whose chapel, significantly enough, he finds "embossed brasses of the candlesticks upon the altar that gleamed like the battleworn mail armour of angels."[37] The image of warfare, the pun on "mail," perhaps even the phallic candlesticks, together suggest Stephen's need for "manliness" at this crucial moment in his development as an artist; thus, it is no accident that the second day of Father Arnall's sermon retells the Fall in Eden, beginning with Satan's defiance of God: *non serviam.* How much power will be needed to continue that defiance is measured by the vivid descriptions of Hell that follow, Father Arnall outdoing himself within each succeeding paragraph: "And then imagine this sickening stench, multiplied a millionfold and a millionfold again from the millions upon millions of fetid carcasses massed together in the reeking darkness, a huge and rotting human fungus."[38] All the senses are similarly assailed, so that when the day ends Stephen exits the chapel with "his legs shaking and the scalp of his head trembling,"[39] a physical body certainly not at the moment able to confront God with a *non serviam.*

The last part of the sermon ties it closely to Sterne's, detailing the conscience that has failed to do its duty and the resultant eternal separation from God. Human justice is here taken into account, our sense of the unfairness of it all: "Men, reasoning always as men, are astonished that God should mete out an everlasting and infinite punishment in the fires of hell for a single grievous sin,"[40] a thought similar to that of Sterne's sinner, who though "utterly debauched in his principles" rails against "petty larceny, and . . . such puny crimes as his fortune and rank in life" keep him from committing, and thus with an easy conscience faces death without concern (*TS* 2.27.148–49). Dr. Slop awakens at this point to argue that this cannot happen to Roman Catholics, who would be denied the last sacrament unless they eased their conscience in the confessional, quite missing the sermon's point that the conscience is not at all uneasy, since it cannot believe trifling dalliances will be judged sinful enough for damnation. Father Arnall knows better: even if God could end all the evil of the world by permitting, without punishment, "a single venial sin, a lie, an angry look, a moment of wilful sloth, He, the great omnipotent God, could not do so because sin, be it in thought or deed, is a transgression of His law and God would not be God if He did not punish the transgressor."[41] Allowing for differences in tone and style, Sterne's conclusion is similar: "Remember this plain distinction, a mistake in which has ruined thousands,—that your conscience is not a law:—No, God and reason made the law, and have placed conscience within you to determine;—not like an *Asiastick* Cadi, according to the ebbs and flows of his own passions,—but like a *British* judge in this land of liberty and good sense, who makes no new law, but faithfully declares that law which he knows already written" (*TS* 2.27.164).

Stephen's young Catholic conscience is sorely tried by the sermon: "Yes, he had done them, secretly, filthily, time after time, and, hardened in sinful impenitence, he had dared to wear the mask of holiness," but once he decides to confess to a priest, "the ache of conscience ceased."[42] Sterne dismisses the "confessional" with typical eighteenth-century Anglican bite: "if he robs,—if he stabs,——will not conscience, on every such act, receive a wound itself? Aye,—but the man has carried it to confession . . . and in a short time be quite healed up by absolution" (*TS* 2.27.152). Stephen, too, will shortly dismiss the confessional by his decision not to accept a clerical vocation. Juxtaposing Sterne and Joyce helps us to see that both consider the very necessary immaterial soul as an entity vested not in the

326 · Textual and Critical Intersections

received Christianity of either Catholic or Protestant communion, but rather in the essence of an infallible Judgment not of this world. On the other hand, because confession is a sacrament (as Dr. Slop points out) and hence a site of divine visitation, Stephen's immediate sense of relief ("His soul was made fair and holy once more, holy and happy")[43] is the result not, as Sterne's Anglicanism argues, of the priest's absolution but rather of the Holy Spirit's presence. As such, when Yorick in *Sentimental Journey* reveals to the reader the pervasive sexual impulses underwriting his sensibilities, he is also visited: "Wherever thy providence shall place me for the trials of my virtue— . . . let me feel the movements which rise out of it, and which belong to me as a man—and if I govern them as a *good* one—I will trust the issues to thy *justice,* for thou hast made us—and not we ourselves" (*SJ* 124, emphasis added).

The possible bawdiness in that sentence ("movements," "rise," "issues") is echoed in Joyce's language when he returns to the Fall, to the serpent, and then to the "bestial part of the body able to understand bestially and desire bestially. . . . [Stephen's] soul sickened at the thought of a torpid snaky life feeding itself out of the tender marrow of his life and fattening upon the slime of lust."[44] The play on the male organ is not as overt as Tristram's "nose" but more so than Yorick's "movements"; the passage echoes not only Stephen's encounter with the "embryo," but also one of Sterne's most important ethical observations, reserved for the very last chapter of *Tristram Shandy,* where, borrowing from Montaigne by way of his codifier, Pierre Charron, Walter Shandy asks why procreation "should be done by means of a passion which bends down the faculties, and turns all the wisdom, contemplations, and operations of the soul backwards—a passion . . . which couples and equals wise men with fools, and makes us come out of our caverns and hiding-places more like satyrs and four-footed beasts than men" (*TS* 9.33.806).[45]

As already noted, that both authors plant their sermons within a sexual context and assert their hostility toward religion's seeming war on human sexuality as a "bestial" and sinful activity is vital to understanding just how inextricably tied together procreation and creation are within their writings. Sterne's bawdry and Joyce's defiance of the censors speak to their shared urge to challenge earthly judgments by an appeal to a necessary and infinite Judge that validates efforts to create something good and truthful as acts of fertility rather than futility. The literary and spiritual legacy to which they were heirs insisted on the centrality of war and of love, but era after era, society after society, decided to fall in love with war and, simultaneously, to wage war on love as their earthly choices.

From Homer to Sterne and Joyce, art attempts to undo that perversion: the school for the young artists, Tristram and Stephen, is intent on teaching them that a good writer's body and mind must both be open to visitation by Spirit if one's art is to reflect the immortal soul placed within us by that infinite Judge. I borrow here the concept of the Paraclete, but only because John, the sole user of the word in Scripture, is a particularly literary artist among the writers of the New Testament and thus a convenient bridge between Homer and artists of the modern era.[46] Interestingly enough, in *The Oxford Companion to the Bible,* John's convictions are summarized as life being a "struggle between truth and perversity, the sons of light and the sons of darkness, good and evil."[47] I might note that Jesus's first miracle at the wedding in Cana is told only by John, as is also true of Jesus's pardoning of the woman taken in adultery.[48] There is also in John the most vivid display in Scripture of the argumentative nature of society during the life of Jesus. It seems appropriate then, that it is John who delivers this rather un-Pauline sentiment from the mouth of Jesus: "Ye judge after the flesh; I judge no man. And yet if I judge, my judgment is true: for I am not alone, but I and the Father that sent me."[49]

With both sermons concluded, the artists might now seem free to develop their creativity, unimpeded by the teleological world of Judgment. While death still has its sting (Stephen's mother's sickbed, a theme pursued at length in *Ulysses;* Death's knocking at the door in *Tristram Shandy*), Judgment, which in art is so often manifested as selection and choice, is set aside. For Tristram, it begins with his including among his "life and opinions" on alternate pages the Latin of Ernulphus's curse and its English translation, a damning in Augustinian detail of every part of the human anatomy; we might even read it as an ironic post hoc commentary on Father Arnall's sermon, compacted of centuries of Catholic thought. That same freedom from the shaping truth of Logos (to invoke John again) allows Tristram now to place his "Author's Preface" in the middle of the third volume, undoing the meaning of *preface* (Johnson: "something proemial"). It also allows for the discussion of Walter's theory of noses, raised to the overt bawdiness of Slawkenbergius, whose book, we are told, was Walter's recreation and delight at "*matin,* noon, and vespers": "'twas for ever in his

328 · Textual and Critical Intersections

hands,—you would have sworn, Sir, it had been a canon's prayer-book" (*TS* 3.42.285).[50] What seem to be random insertions of documents by Tristram are, in my reading, Sterne's deliberate markers delineating the creation of the modern artist as a scatter-brained ("Shandy") dunce in the tradition of the Scriblerians—but I have said that too many times previously.[51]

In volume 5, and especially after his persuasive arts fail to sway the polemical divines at the Visitation dinner to undo Tristram's christening, the education of his surviving son occupies Walter, that is, the writing of the *Tristrapædia*. The death of Bobby, significantly, concludes the fourth volume—one of several deaths that keep an inescapable truth always within the reader's cognition. But writing, Walter discovers, is no easy task: each thought he generates is accompanied by a tempting devil in the opposite direction, so that, he concludes, in words that will recall another Scriblerian writer, "the life of a writer, whatever he might fancy to the contrary, was not so much a state of *composition,* as a state of *warfare;* and his probation in it, precisely that of any other man militant upon earth,— both depending alike, not half so much upon the degrees of his WIT—as his RESISTANCE" (*TS* 5.16.447).[52] The resultant nonsensical theory of "auxiliary verbs" holds them to be the essence of all knowledge, because they enable "every idea [to] engender millions." Tristram's emerging portrait of the artist as a young man is one in which selection and judgment are displaced by prolixity and multiplicity—when millions of ideas are possible, how can we possibly have the time or the energy to distinguish, much less discriminate among them? This is Walter's triumphant moment, the licensing of his son to say and write anything at all: with ideas pouring forth in infinite abundance, to argue against any single idea is to leave a multitude unanswered, and Tristram's motto from the beginning is now justified: "*De gustibus non est disputandum*" (*TS* 1.8.12). As a philosophy of rhetoric and artistry, the motto and the theory of auxiliary verbs are unanswerable, an argument that stops all argumentation. It is no wonder, then, that Walter is now slowly eased off the stage,[53] and Toby's mixture of love and warfare dominates the last volumes of the work (excepting volume 7, Tristram's flight from death). If words fail us, fists (or nuclear weapons) may not.

Stephen's post-sermon life repeats Walter's theory of writing as strewn with temptations, but here they are more overtly sexual, and his "resistance" an effort to bring "each of his senses . . . under a rigorous discipline," including walking down the street without seeing the life around him, and shunning every encounter with the "eyes of women."[54] (Uncle Toby, we recall, is captured by an eye "full of gentle salutations" [*TS* 8.25.708].) This war within Stephen is replete with images of manliness and warfare: "the idea of surrender," "a new thrill of power," knowing he had not "yielded"; echoing the militant language of Toby's siege warfare Stephen takes consolation in the fact that "frequent and violent temptations were a proof that the citadel of the soul had not fallen and that the devil raged to make it fall."[55]

There is, however, a new temptation, the priesthood, with its promise to expunge sexual temptation. Uncannily, both Sterne and Joyce image forth this moment in the development of the artist with a parody of the epic staple, the "arming of the warrior." Gossip over the damage caused by Tristram's encounter with the falling window sash impels Walter to put his son in breeches, but doing so is complicated by his need to consult the authorities on Roman attire, resulting in several Rabelaisian lists of alternatives (*TS* 6.16–19), derived not from the scholarly tomes Walter says he consults, but from textbooks used by schoolboys like Stephen, when studying Roman history (and the Latin language).[56] Walter concludes his investigation by bouncing among the diverse scholarly opinions concerning the *Latus Clavus,* whether a button, a coat, a color, a fibula, etc., demonstrating that multiple opinions about minute subjects have been part of our world for a very long time. The Florida annotators have no explanation for this obsession, but Sterne's conversation with Joyce may reveal one: Walter is looking for the means to *secure* the flap (the "fly" since the mid-nineteenth century), that would be part of Tristram's trousers. The decision, then, to use "*hooks and eyes*" is a sexual (indeed, priestly) determination, manifesting Walter's suspicion of sexuality, male or female, whether that of Mrs. Shandy, Widow Wadman, Toby, or, in the very last words of *Tristram Shandy,* Obadiah and the Shandy bull.

Clothing is the first subject of Stephen's talk with the director concerning his vocation, Stephen contemplating *les jupes,* the long skirts worn by Belgian monks. The word kindles a "tiny flame . . . upon the cheek" as it invokes "the names of articles of dress worn by women . . . the brittle texture of a woman's stocking . . . within rosesoft stuffs that he dared to conceive of the soul or body of a woman moving with tender life."[57] Joyce then provides his own brief version of Rabelaisian logorrhea: within a single

330 · Textual and Critical Intersections

paragraph, Stephen pictures himself as a powerful priest reenacting the solemn gestures of the Mass, introducing us to the "thurible," "chasuble," "tunicle," "humeral veil," "paten," and "dalmatic of cloth of gold," not all articles of clothing, to be sure, but, like Toby's siege vocabulary, a means of suggesting the verbal isolation of special interests. The words also suggest the fecundity of language that is both an author's necessary milieu—and demonic temptation.

Stephen rolls each clerical word on his tongue, but nevertheless rejects the vocation; in doing so, however, his language continues to resound with the world he spurns. Much as Tristram is not set free by the death of Yorick, who continues to serve as the measure of Truth by which we are to judge him, so Stephen will carry with him the doctrine of the four last things, phrased in the language of Scripture and commentary, from Talmudic scholars to Augustine and Aquinas, and finally, to Father Arnall's sermon. To define his destiny as eluding "social or religious orders," "wandering among the snares of the world," the ways of which are "ways of sin"; to decide that "Not to fall was too hard, too hard" is to take Father Arnall with him as he departs from the church,[58] an indelible scar that I believe shapes Joyce's entire canon. It is to be expected that the "young artist" does not realize the impossibility for him of *non serviam,* but Joyce's distance from his young man is measured by Stephen's new view of the "disorder" he will now embrace as he nears the family home: "the Blessed Virgin which stood fowlwise on a pole in the middle of a hamshaped encampment of poor cottages. . . . The faint sour stink of rotted cabbages came towards him from the kitchengardens. . . . He smiled to think that it was this disorder, the misrule and confusion of his father's house and the stagnation of vegetable life, which was to win the day in his soul."[59] Shandy Hall and Stephen's home are worldly sites of misrule and confusion; and cabbages again play a part in defining for Tristram his own artistic embrace of misrule, the difference between the straight line of cabbage planters and his own linear diagrams of disorder.[60]

While Tristram's name has been discussed early on as part of Walter's theory of names, it is only now that Stephen contemplates his own name as a determinant of fortune, associated not only with Saint Stephen, the first martyr, but most importantly with the myth of Daedalus and his son. After his rejection of vocation, Stephen finds in the name "a prophecy of the end he had been born to serve . . . symbol of the artist forging anew in his workshop out of the sluggish matter of the earth a new soaring impalpable imperishable being."[61] The irony of "imperishable" is quite palpable but even more so within the context of the sin of pride that awaits final Judgment, whether in classical myth or Christian doctrine. Escaping from "childhood and boyhood," and "the pale service of the altar," Stephen imagines himself having shaken the "cerements . . . from the body of death . . . cerements, the linens of the grave. His soul had arisen from the grave of boyhood, spurning her graveclothes."[62] And again, the hope of creating something "beautiful, impalpable, imperishable" recurs,[63] as does his desire to clothe both his body and his ideas: the esoteric "cerements" distance him from death, even as they wrap him about. "Alas, poor Icarus," one is tempted to intone: there was "a splash quite unnoticed / this was / Icarus drowning."

And yet the time is also for Stephen an *epiphanic* moment, Joyce's own significant term for that transcendent insight he claims for himself and, more generally, for the creators of art. That the word is so tightly interwoven with the Christian calendar is important, as is Stephen's ejaculation when he realizes the young girl at the water's edge is returning his stare without "shame or wantonness": "Heavenly God! cried Stephen's soul, in an outburst of profane joy."[64] We do not think of Sterne as driven by epiphanies, but the similarity of this scene and the passage that ends Tristram's flight from Death at the conclusion of volume 7 is startling. Encountering Nannette, with the "slit in her petticoat,"

> I would have given a crown to have it sew'd up—Nannette would not have given a sous—*Viva la joia!* was in her lips—*Viva la joia!* was in her eyes. . . . She look'd amiable!—Why could I not live and end my days thus? Just disposer of our joys and sorrows, cried I, why could not a man sit down in the lap of content here—and dance, and sing, and say his prayers, and go to heaven with this nut brown maid? (*TS* 7.42.651)

Both Stephen and Tristram turn away from potential sexual dalliance and pursue their art instead, but the parallel tracks I have been listening to when I put Sterne in conversation with Joyce diverge in what remains. While much of Stephen's development as an artist up to now has had to do with a conflict between youthful spirituality and adolescent sexuality, Tristram's story has unfolded primarily in consequence of Walter Shandy's opinions. One might hear, in fact, a chiastic interchange at this point, in which Toby's suspension of militancy puts his monkish modesty in the hands of Widow Wadman, the temptress, while Stephen, escaping the protective environment of the church, "seeking fresh woods and pastures new," becomes rather a Shandean fount of opinions.

We soon realize, however, that Toby carries his bowling green with him as he journeys into the world of peace, by way of love and marriage; Stephen, too, has his emerging opinions on art tainted with his continuing priestly warfare against sexual urges. Thus, after numerous digressions, many suggesting, as with Trim and the fair Beguine or Tom and the sausage maker's widow, the softer emotions of domesticity, the affair between Widow Wadman and Toby reaches its unfortunate culmination in her curiosity about the exact location and extent of Toby's groin wound, and Trim's being sent to fetch the map of Namur so that Toby can point to "the very place" (*TS* 9.26–28). In Homeric terms, then, leaving Troy will not be easy for Toby, and when Walter is forced to explain his brother's misconception it leads to one final conflict, an argument about war's justification, interrupted only by Obadiah, the possibly impotent bull, and Sterne's final linking of his nine volumes to the satiric tradition of Scriblerian satire, significantly identified by Yorick, who, when answering Mrs. Shandy's question, "what is all this story about," offers the answer: "A COCK and a BULL, said Yorick——And one of the best of its kind I ever heard" (*TS* 9.33.809).

It is often thought that Sterne bowed to his censorious critics by substituting sentiment for bawdry in these last volumes, but that is not true. The most flagrant sexual humor in the entire nine volumes is in volume 8, chapter 11, Tristram's "furr'd cap" and "finger in the pye," but there is also the fair Beguine rubbing Trim's leg (*TS* 8.22.701–4), and Tom's sausage making ("There is nothing so awkward, as courting a woman . . . whilst she is making sausages" [*TS* 9.7.750–52]), among other indications that this sort of innuendo, which might well be labeled adolescent in the present context, is vital to chronicling the artist's development.[65] That Sterne allows Tristram this license to the very end of the work suggests one reason why Yorick will have to narrate the journey home while Tristram, an author in the modern mode, rejecting order and selection, discrimination and judgment, will have to remain forever at Shandy Hall, amusing us with his father's opinions and his uncle's bowling green, but unable to return to the world Yorick and Sterne have measured him by, the world eternally cognizant of the four last things.

Stephen, on the other hand, seems almost ready to depart, needing only to formulate the role of an artist who has, in his youth, rejected the sustaining opinions of his society. Or to be precise, Stephen wants to believe he "will not serve," although the conclusion of *Portrait,* locked into the church calendar from Maundy Thursday through Easter Sunday, in no way abandons the world of last things that Father Arnall preached. Early in Stephen's college years, his mind, "when wearied of its search for the essence of beauty amid the spectral words of Aristotle and Aquinas, turned often . . . to the dainty songs of the Elizabethans."[66] The sentence encapsulates Joyce's vision of what being an artist entails, from its homage to the philosophers and theologians to its celebration of the bawdy songs of the Elizabethans, and, most importantly, its faith in an *essence* of beauty that underwrites the possibility of Truth. We can quote Keats to validate Joyce at this point, but with equal pertinence address the emergence of John the Baptist (the other John of Scripture) in the closing pages of *Portrait,* who appears to Stephen on Thursday morning within a waking vision of Cranly (his final argumentative opponent), as "the face of a severed head or deathmask, crowned on the brows by its stiff black upright hair as by an iron crown."[67] It is a "priestlike face" and yet, in the debates that follow, we hear echoes also of John the Apostle and his persistent arguments with the Jews, unique to his Gospel retelling.

Anti-Semitism has, in fact, been one charge against John, but I would suggest that Joyce recognized in his Gospel a domestic honesty that is vital to our understanding of the relationship between Jews and Christians. For John, Jesus's life was a "family" affair, a quarrel between Jews and whoever followed this latest messiah; and, as Stephen learns early on, the fiercest arguments concerning our opinions are often family affairs.[68] That a Jew will replace Stephen as the Homeric hero of the voyage home, much as Yorick replaces Tristram, suggests to me Joyce's need to establish his art within its origins, the Greek and Hebrew cultures of his—and Matthew Arnold's—inheritance. While Sterne could offer his own "Abuses of conscience" sermon as a starting point for restoring Truth and Justice to the world, Joyce could not return to Father Arnall, whose rhetoric he ironically dismantled even as he endorsed his meaning. Thus, a new artist, Leopold Bloom, is chosen to accompany Stephen in Dublin, fulfilling the same role Yorick

334 · Textual and Critical Intersections

plays in *A Sentimental Journey,* where he revisits earlier versions of Tristram's relationship with women and desire. Both men seem odd choices to embody that longing for the "*essence* of beauty" that will allow Truth and Justice to exert their necessary presence in art, but one senses in both the essence of Odysseus—the triumph of experience over heroics, perhaps even over "virtue." "They order . . . this matter better in France," Sterne's opening line of *A Sentimental Journey* plays significantly with two primary concerns of Enlightenment, "order" and "matter." The conversation I hear between Sterne and Joyce suggests to me that both found in *order* the Truth of their artistry, despite modernist readers who believe they celebrated *matter* instead.[69]

Before Stephen can test his theological opinions with Cranly, however, his aesthetic ideas are challenged by Lynch. We do not need to consider Stephen a serious aesthetician to realize that he is examining the nature of art in relation to Truth and Judgment, beginning with his attempt to define "improper arts" as those that arouse desire, while "proper" art raises the mind "above desire and loathing."[70] When Lynch protests that he finds the backside of the Venus of Praxiteles exciting his desire, Stephen resorts to "normal" appetites, and in a manner reminiscent of Uncle Toby's explanation of ravelins, has recourse to the "rhythm of beauty": "Rhythm . . . is the first formal esthetic relation of part to part in any esthetic whole or of an esthetic whole to its part or parts or of any part to the esthetic whole of which it is a part."[71] Lynch, rightfully enough, is dubious, and Stephen resorts to Plato: "beauty is the splendour of truth. I don't think that it has a meaning but the true and the beautiful are akin." Again, Lynch is dubious: "But what is beauty? . . . Something we see and like! Is that the best you and Aquinas can do?"[72] Lynch is amused that the unbeliever keeps reverting to Aquinas, but Stephen's absorption of scholastic divisions and discriminations moves him closer to a viable definition of art, and his recourse to Shelley evokes the Western tradition that has sought since the Enlightenment to find a way for art to survive the despiritualizing or secularizing of thought. Hence, in ironic contrast with *enlightenment* Stephen clings to Aquinas's *claritas* (radiance), "the artistic discovery and representation of the divine purpose in anything."[73] It is the "*quidditas,* the whatness of a thing," that leads him to Shelley: "The supreme quality is felt by the artist when the esthetic image is first conceived in his imagination. The mind in that mysterious instant Shelley likened beautifully to a fading coal."

And then a second image to help define a spiritual state, not from Shelley, though it well might have been, "the enchantment of the heart."[74] Lynch is silenced: "a thoughtenchanted silence."

On Good Friday morning Stephen recalls his dreams, repeating an "enchantment of the heart," and, most pertinently, with its echo of John, a belief that "in the virgin womb of the imagination the word was made flesh."[75] Significantly, his waking reverie replays his encounters with Emma, using the images he shares with Sterne; in this case, she dances "away from him along the chain of hands, dancing lightly and discreetly, giving herself to none"; and again, the tram steps are described in some detail.[76] For Stephen this seems to be his final release from the sexual anxieties of his youth, and his attention turns to departure, although now clouded by another woman, his mother, whose plea that he perform his Easter duty he has denied. It is, of course, an issue not resolved until *Ulysses,* but Cranly, picking up the argumentative nature of these final pages, points to Stephen's contradictory conduct: he "will not serve" (again reiterated) and yet cannot but serve if his art is to express the Truth he believes it must. Cranly reminds him of the original speaker of *non serviam* (Satan), forcing Stephen to embrace Joyce's paradox: "I neither believe in it [the Eucharist] nor disbelieve in it." Again, Cranly speaks the obvious: "It is a curious thing . . . how your mind is supersaturated with the religion which you say you disbelieve."[77] And yet again, Stephen repeats for the last time those words of denial, "I will not serve that in which I no longer believe whether it call itself my home, my fatherland or my church,"[78] the futility of which sentiment even Satan is said by both Talmudists and church fathers to have discovered.

The final pages of *Portrait* become a journal, the first entry (Holy Saturday?)[79] devoted to Cranly and his elderly parents, he being "the child of exhausted loins," which certainly returns us to *Tristram Shandy* one final time. The next morning (Easter Sunday?), he recalls while still in bed the phrase "exhausted loins," but now applies it to "Elisabeth and Zachary," the parents of John the Baptist, and it brings him more bodily into his thoughts than heretofore, recalling him as the "precursor," the eater of "locusts and wild honey," and, finally, "a stern severed head or deathmask as if outlined on a grey curtain or veronica. Decollation they call it in the fold."[80] This figure of death (the necessary death into a new "life") is entwined with the Gospel of John, the source of that Platonic commentary

336 · Textual and Critical Intersections

on the Hebrew's ineffable, unknowable God, "In the beginning was the Word, and the Word was with God, and the Word was God" (the Christian version of what Moses heard: "I am that I am"). The certainty of death and the promise of overcoming it: these are the sources of art (Beauty and Truth) that are inescapable for Stephen, raised, as he has been, between John the Baptist and John the Apostle, the patron saints of Joyce's *Portrait of the Artist as a Young Man*. And the entry for the evening of that same Easter Sunday, marked by his refusal of his mother's sickbed request that he take Communion, suggests just how much remains for Stephen to learn on the homeward journey, about both death and love: "Free. Soulfree and fancyfree. Let the dead bury the dead. Ay. And let the dead marry the dead."[81]

When Joyce wanted to explain *Finnegans Wake* to a reader he invoked Sterne: "Time and the river and the mountain are the real heroes of my book. Yet the elements are exactly what every novelist might use: man and woman, birth, childhood, night, sleep, marriage, prayer, death. There is nothing paradoxical about this. Only I am trying to build as many planes of narrative with a single esthetic purpose. Did you ever read Laurence Sterne?"[82] And when he invokes Sterne among a list of Irish writers in *Wake*, he does so in a passage that begins significantly with the word "Home": "Home to go. Halome. Blare no mor ramsblares, oddmund barkes! And cease your fumings, kindalled bushies! And sherrigoldies yessymgnays; your wildeshaweshowe moves swiftly sterneward! For here the holy language."[83] Both quotations suggest to me that when Joyce entered into conversation with Sterne across more than two centuries, he discovered a commonality that I have tried to overhear in this essay. However, having never understood *Finnegans Wake*, I have quite possibly only brought home to myself a marriage of two favorite authors; perhaps literary criticism is always a homecoming.

Originally published in the *Shandean* 33 (2022).

Notes

1 While obviously pertinent to the time in which this essay was being written (2021), the lines in the epigraph are the refrain of a poem quoted twice by Stephen Dedalus, once incorrectly as "*Darkness falls from the air*" and then

remembered correctly as *"Brightness falls from the air."* James Joyce, *Portrait of the Artist as a Young Man*, ed. Chester G. Anderson (New York: Viking/Penguin, 1977), 232, 234. In that I start with Homer, it is perhaps appropriate to cite two other pertinent lines from Nashe's "litany" of the dead: "Dust hath closed Helen's eye" and "Worms feed on Hector brave."

2 See my essays "Proust's Influence on Sterne: A Remembrance of Things to Come," *MLN* 103 (1988): 1031–55; "Three Sentimental Journeys: Sterne, Shklovsky, Svevo," *Shandean* 11 (1999): 126–34; and "Reading Sterne through Proust and Levinas" and "Sterne and the Modernist Movement," reprinted as chapters 7 and 8 in this volume, respectively.

3 Stephen E. Soud, "Blood-Red Wombs and Monstrous Births: *Aristotle's Masterpiece* and *Ulysses*," *James Joyce Quarterly* 32, no. 2 (1995): 195–208. Three years later, in a published letter in *James Joyce Quarterly* 35, no. 2/3 (1998): 549–50, I suggested that Joyce already had *Aristotle's Masterpiece* in mind in *Portrait*, as I come back to later in this essay.

4 Melvyn New, *Tristram Shandy: A Book for Free Spirits* (New York: Twayne-Macmillan, 1994), 26.

5 Cf. Frank Budgen, *James Joyce and the Making of Ulysses* (1934; Bloomington: Indiana University Press, 1960), 71–72: "The prevailing attitude of *Ulysses* is a very humane scepticism—not of tried human values, necessary at all times for social cohesion, but of all tendencies and systems whatsoever. There are moods of pity and grief in it, but the prevailing mood is humour.... The laughter reminds us often of the bright, mocking laughter of Sterne of whom Nietzsche wrote that he [is] the 'freest of all free spirits.'"

6 With a few minimal exceptions, I have not cited herein the vast scholarly output on Sterne and Joyce, in part because of the celebratory occasion for my essay, in part because having spent a lifetime among Sterne critics, I would need another lifetime among Joyceans to balance the account.

7 The glance at Penelope in these lines is overlooked by the Florida editors. Robert Burton's *Anatomy of Melancholy* (1621), where Sterne found this passage (*Anatomy*, 3.2.3.4), also informs *Ulysses*, a twentieth-century anatomy of the love-melancholy that dominates almost all of Dublin's inhabitants on that day in June.

8 Alexander Pope, "The Preface of 1717," in *The Poems of Alexander Pope*, ed. John Butt (New Haven, CT: Yale University Press, 1963), xxvi–xxvii. Interestingly, this is Pope's reflection on the reception of his proposal to translate Homer and not, as might be thought, on his afteryears as the author of the *Dunciad*.

9 Joyce, *Portrait*, 56.

10 Joyce, 58–59.

11 From Rodney Kickham and Nasty Roche, from Stephen's musings about the word *belt* ("And belt was also to give a fellow a belt"), from Cantwell's "Go and fight your match," to the "whirl of a scrimmage . . . their legs were rubbing and kicking and stamping," from the "soldiers' slugs in the wood of the door" to hacking chestnuts, school is certainly as much a test of physical prowess and courage as of mental acumen. Even the math drill conducted by Father Arnall is made into a battle between York and Lancaster: "Bravo Lancaster! The red rose wins." Joyce, 8–10, 12.

12 Joyce, *Portrait*, 32, 34, quoting Luke 17:1–2.

13 That Walter is deemed a master of both "Logick and Rhetorick" (*TS* 1.19.59) surely glances at Plato's various discussions of the antagonistic relationship between philosophy (truth) and rhetoric (persuasion), especially in the *Gorgias* and the *Phaedrus*. Cf. Johnson, *Dictionary* (1755), s.v. "opinion"; "Perswasion of the mind, without proof or certain knowledge"; he illustrates with Ben Jonson's *Timber*: "Opinion is a light, vain, crude and imperfect thing, settled in the imagination, but never arriving at the understanding, there to obtain the tincture of reason."

14 Joyce, *Portrait*, 77–78, 82.

15 Joyce, 63.

16 Joyce, 79, 82. Anderson notes that according to Stanislaus Joyce, this scene was not exaggerated, their mother having had "to mend the rips in his clothes so that he could go to school the following day." Joyce, *Portrait*, 506, n. to 80.19, citing S. Joyce, *My Brother's Keeper: James Joyce's Early Years*, ed. Richard Ellmann (1958; Cambridge, MA: Da Capo Press, 2003), 55.

17 Joyce, *Portrait*, 83.

18 Stephen quotes the entire litany, part of his musing on what he considers "the falsehood of his position," his sexual desires versus his leadership of the "sodality of the Blessed Virgin Mary." Earlier in the work, he had been warned to stay away from Eileen because "protestants used to make fun of the litany. . . . How could a woman be a tower of ivory or a house of gold?" Joyce, 105, 35.

19 Joyce, 69, 77.

20 Joyce, 77–78.

21 Joyce, 69.

22 Joyce, 83.

23 On touch, see, e.g., Anne Bandry, "Les livres de Sterne: Suites et fins," *XVII–XVIII: Revue de la Société d'études anglo-américaines des XVIIe et XVIIIe siècles* 50 (2000): 132–33. The encounters with Maria in both works (*TS* 9.24; *SJ* 149–54) are in harmony with the "gloomy tenderness" of both eighteenth-

century sentimentalism and Stephen's adolescence, especially if one reads Sterne (and Joyce) without an eye toward consistent ironic reversals.

24 Joyce, *Portrait*, 93.

25 Joyce, 94. Admittedly already in his cups, Simon adds, "There's that son of mine there not half my age and I'm a better man than he is any day of the week" (95).

26 On Stephen's name, see below, pp. 330–31.

27 Beginning with my book *Laurence Sterne as Satirist: A Reading of Tristram Shandy* (Gainesville: University of Florida Press, 1969) and ending with my essay "Single and Double: *Memoirs of Martinus Scriblerus* and *Tristram Shandy*," reprinted as chapter 11 in this volume, fifty-two years of holding to the same view of the sermon, perhaps demonstrating that, like Walter, I have been "systematical, and, like all systematick reasoners . . . would move both heaven and earth, and twist and torture every thing in nature to support [my] hypothesis" (*TS* 1.19.61).

28 The occasion for the religious retreat and sermon in *Portrait* is to honor Saint Francis Xavier, cofounder of the Jesuits, "A great *soldier* of God," a "true *conqueror*," and a saint who "has great *power* in heaven." Joyce, *Portrait*, 108 (emphasis added). If one is going to wage a war, the order of Saint Francis Xavier is a worthy ally—but also, a formidable foe, as countless "heathens," equally countless Protestants, and poor Trim's brother, Tom, will readily attest. That there are significant borrowings in Sterne's "Abuses" sermon from Jonathan Swift, the Anglican dean in the heart of Catholic Dublin, should not be overlooked.

29 Joyce, *Portrait*, 109.

30 Joyce, 111. In the constant refrain of the preacher's "dear boys" (Joyce, 110, 118, 124, 134) alternating with Hieronymus Bosch–like images of Hell's torments, Joyce employs, I believe, the judgments by ironic juxtaposition that he would find in Sterne, where Uncle Toby will not kill a fly, but dresses with extra smartness for a particularly bloody battle reenactment (*TS* 6.24.543–44).

31 "I have forty volumes to write, and forty thousand things to say and do, which no body in the world will say and do for me" (*TS* 7.1.576). This is among Tristram's first thoughts when Death knocks on the door to open the volume and chapter.

32 Joyce, *Portrait*, 113.

33 Whether it is Sterne or Walter who embraces this popular British distortion of Descartes's theory, we cannot say, but the discussion here is based, as is so often true of the learning of *Tristram Shandy*, almost entirely on entries in Chambers, *Cyclopædia*, as noted in *TS*, Notes 194–96, n. to 173.14ff.: e.g., "The principal part of [the soul], Des Cartes maintains, is the pineal gland in the

340 · Textual and Critical Intersections

brain, where all the nerves terminate *&c.*" The Florida note also points to the satiric reception of Descartes's "pineal gland" among English writers, including the Scriblerians and Elijah Fenton, who writes in *The Fair Nun* that Cartesians, "Assert that souls a tip-toe stand / On what we call the pineal gland." I suspect Sterne is partaking of this satiric tradition.

34 Scripture is, to my secular mind, a work of art, which, like Homer's poetry, continues to engage all great Western artists in an ongoing dialogue (even denial is a mode of engagement). Pontius Pilate might well have asked Jesus, "What is art?" The answer is as elusive as for Truth and Judgment, but one clue, pertinent to this essay, is Joyce's belief that Gabriele D'Annunzio was one of the great artists of his day. Budgen, *James Joyce*, 180. Like Sterne, who puts on display in *Tristram* the tradition of Western literature, so D'Annunzio gathers in his 1889 novel, *Pleasure* (*Il Piacere*), the equally long tradition of both visual and aural arts (in addition to literature). In both instances, moral judgments inhere in the juxtaposition of the lives and opinions of the characters with the enduring visitations of art, beginning—of course—with Scripture. Joyce will do the same in all his fiction, not a revolt against that tradition but a total absorption into it. In religion this absorption might well be labeled Grace.

35 See Soud, "Blood-Red Wombs and Monstrous Births"; New, letter in *James Joyce Quarterly* 35.

36 Joyce, *Portrait*, 89, 90 (emphasis added).

37 Joyce, 115–16.

38 Joyce, 120. Joyce's brilliant emphasis on "infinite" time and space in the sermon keeps the immateriality of art in front of the reader (and Stephen) throughout the novel; for instance, later in the sermon, Father Arnall asks us to picture a mountain of sand a million miles high and a million miles broad, and a bird who once every million years takes away a grain, "yet at the end of that immense stretch of time not even one instant of eternity could be said to have ended. At the end of all those billions and trillions of years eternity would have scarcely begun." Joyce, 132. The importance of the passage to Joyce is suggested by his repeating it to end the paragraph.

39 Joyce, 124.

40 Joyce, 133.

41 Joyce, 133.

42 Joyce, 137.

43 Joyce, 145.

44 Joyce, 139–40.

45 I have discussed this conclusion and the influence of Charron on Sterne many times, first in "Some Sterne Borrowings from Four Renaissance Authors,"

Philological Quarterly 71 (1992): 301–11, and most recently in "Laurence Sterne and William Falconer: Soldiers and Sailors," *Philological Quarterly* 99 (2020): 229–44. [As is quite apparent in this volume of collected essays, my frequent return to this one passage strongly suggests that, to my mind, it is quintessentially Sterne, both in being a borrowing from the Renaissance and in insistently asserting that any ethical account of humanity must acknowledge—and enjoy—the body in all its functions.]

46 Paraclete is translated as "Comforter" in the KJV and Douay Bible, John 14:16, 14:26, 15:26, 16:7. Stephen had used the word with echoes of John, when contemplating the Trinity during his post-sermon religious exercises. Joyce, *Portrait*, 149.

47 Bruce M. Metzger and Michael D. Coogan, eds., *The Oxford Companion to the Bible* (Oxford: Oxford University Press, 1993), 374.

48 See John 2:1–10 and 8:3–11, respectively.

49 See John 8:15.

50 That the "Tale" is also told (partially) in Latin on pages facing its translation links it to Ernulphus—and further back, to the "Memoire of the Doctors of the Sorbonne," given in French (*TS* 1.20.67), where the baptism of the all-important embryo is discussed.

51 For a generation of Sterne scholars, Wayne C. Booth's essays on Sterne and his *Rhetoric of Fiction* (Chicago: University of Chicago Press, 1961), 323–36, were shaping influences, as with this comment about an author's irony: "Let us then call for the reader's precise judgment on a very elaborate set of opinions and actions in which the hero is sometimes right, sometimes slightly wrong, and sometimes absurdly astray" (324). That this is said in a discussion of *Portrait* rather than *Tristram Shandy* is grist for my mill, as is Booth's insistence that all art requires distinction and discrimination by both artist and reader—art is never amoral, never random, an observation he footnotes with a relevant quotation from Richard Ellmann, who was to Joyce scholars at the time what Booth was to Sterne scholars: "Joyce's court is, like Dante's or Tolstoy's, always in session." Ellmann, *James Joyce* (Oxford: Oxford University Press, 1959), 3.

52 Walter attributes the resistance theory of composition to "*John de la Casse*, archbishop of *Benevento*," but as the Florida annotators indicate, "no evidence" has been found for the attribution (*TS*, Notes 365–66).

53 To be more accurate, after one further attempt literally to gird Tristram's loins for the life of a writer as a warfare on earth, that is, to put him into breeches, Walter is displaced by a "new scene of events," namely Uncle Toby's amours (*TS* 6.20.533).

54 Joyce, *Portrait*, 150.

342 · Textual and Critical Intersections

55 Joyce, 153. Compare *TS* 5.16.447: "all the devils in hell broke out of their holes to cajole him [the writer].—'Twas Term-time with them,—every thought ... was captious;—how specious and good soever,—'twas all one." The devils' lack of discrimination is worth attention; a hallmark of our modern era is to consider *discrimination* an absolute evil; what that does to art (and the *discriminating* taste it once demanded) has not been sufficiently explored (or deplored)—except, I maintain, by artists of genius in conversation with one another.

56 See *TS*, Notes 419, for parallels to Lefévre de Morsan's *The Manners and Customs of the Romans* (1740), one such textbook. Authors like Rabelais and Burton suggest how pervasive in the course of history is the artistic struggle to select content, how foolish to think that a work of art can be randomly produced, even when such art is subsequently purchased by museums.

57 Joyce, *Portrait*, 155.

58 Joyce, 162.

59 Joyce, 162.

60 See *TS* 6.40.571–72, where Tristram invokes Benevento's devils to help him achieve the straight line of cabbage planters, "the *right line,*—the path-way for Christians to walk in! say divines." But, of course, he rejects that line (although reminding us of Yorick's accompanying judgment when he labels it the "line of GRAVITATION"), and volume 7 opens with a most overt deviation (yet ultimately a return to Yorick)—Death's knocking on the door. Tristram returns to these same cabbages in the first chapter of volume 8, but they now symbolize his rebellion; he defies anyone to go on "cooly, critically, and canonically, planting his cabbages one by one, in straight lines, and stoical distances, especially if slits in petticoats are unsew'd up—without ever and anon straddling out, or sidling into some bastardly digression" (*TS* 8.1.655).

61 Joyce, *Portrait*, 169.

62 Joyce, 169–70. Again, I wrote "Yorick" in the margin; the education of the young artist seems to insist on an awareness of death underlying all meaningful creation. That death is signaled by clothing rather than the more traditional memento mori, the skull, is what we expect from Stephen, for whom bodily coverings is a particular obsession; see n. 64, below.

63 Joyce, 170.

64 Joyce, *Portrait*, 171. The "profanity" of his joy is once again clothed: "Her thighs, fuller and softhued as ivory, were bared almost to the hips where the white fringes of her drawers were like featherings of soft white down. Her slateblue skirts were kilted boldly about her waist" (171).

65 Joyce too, despite howls of criticism over the sexual content of *Portrait*, doubled down, so to speak, in *Ulysses*. To call bawdry "adolescent" is of course

a historical anachronism, since "the teen years" is a modern invention. Still, we distinguish, as Sterne notes early on, alluding to Montaigne, a book for a parlor window from one for the closet (*TS* 1.4.5). That Sterne and Joyce and all of us—perhaps even Father Arnall—have a storehouse of bawdy jokes is undeniable, but when embedded within a fiction everything depends on the teller and distance from the narrator.

66 Joyce, *Portrait*, 176.

67 Joyce, 178.

68 Cf. the conversation Frank Budgen reports after Joyce had asked him to name any "complete all-round character presented by any writer." Budgen went through the usual suspects, Balzac, Flaubert, Tolstoy, Shakespeare, and then Faust: "'Faust' said Joyce, 'Far from being a complete man, he isn't a man at all. . . . Where are his home and family? We don't know.'" Ulysses is the complete man for Joyce because he is presented as a father, a son, "a husband to Penelope, lover of Calypso, companion in arms of the Greek warriors around Troy and King of Ithaca." Budgen, *James Joyce*, 16.

69 Much of the thought in this paragraph devolves from my reading coincidentally with the writing of it, Wolfram Schmidgen's challenging *Infinite Variety: Literary Invention, Theology, and the Disorder of Kinds, 1688–1730* (Philadelphia: University of Pennsylvania Press, 2021). Schmidgen listens to conversations primarily between forgotten writers who were attracted to the fecundity of disorder; I am listening, instead, to those who embrace the fecundity of order as necessary to art, artists we continue to read today.

70 Joyce, *Portrait*, 205.

71 Joyce, 206.

72 Joyce, 208.

73 Joyce, 213.

74 Joyce, 213. Joyce is quoting from "A Defence of Poetry," a paragraph beginning "Poetry is indeed something divine." Shelley goes on: "A man cannot say, 'I will compose poetry.' The greatest poem even cannot say it: for the mind in creation is as a fading coal which some invisible influence . . . awakens to transitory brightness." Percy Bysshe Shelley, "A Defence of Poetry," in *The Major Works*, ed. Zachary Leader and Michael O'Neill (Oxford: Oxford University Press, 2003), 696. For a discussion of Shelley's continued reliance on the language of Christianity, see the fine analysis in Richard E. Brantley, *Locke, Wesley, and the Method of English Romanticism* (Gainesville: University Press of Florida, 1984), 168–85, esp. 171–72, where Shelley's argument that poets have been "washed in the blood of the mediator and redeemer, Time" ("A Defence," 699) is traced to John 1:7.

75 Joyce, *Portrait*, 217, quoting John 1:14.

344 · Textual and Critical Intersections

76 Joyce, 219–22.

77 Joyce, 239–40.

78 Joyce, 246–47.

79 The last day before the first diary entry is Good Friday; the journal begins, without explanation, on March 20, which would be Holy Saturday, and thus Easter would be on March 21—but the earliest possible date for Easter is March 22. Whether Joyce misdated the diary, intentionally or otherwise, I do not know. Fortunately, in the argumentative world of alternative truths to which Walter Shandy and literary theory have accustomed us, this is not a problem: "Nature . . . had sown the seeds of verbal criticism as deep within him, as she had done the seeds of all other knowledge,—so that he had got out his penknife, and was trying experiments upon the sentence, to see if he could not scratch some better sense into it" (*TS* 3.37.272).

80 Joyce, *Portrait*, 248. Yorick's skull, "outlined" by the dramatic black leaf (*TS* 1.12.37–38), is Sterne's early device for keeping death before our eyes from the very beginning of his satire.

81 Joyce, *Portrait*, 248.

82 Qtd. in Seon Givens, ed. *James Joyce: Two Decades of Criticism* (New York: Vanguard Press, 1948), 11–12.

83 James Joyce, *Finnegans Wake* (New York: Viking Press, 1965), 256. Cf. Budgen, *James Joyce*, 214: "It [*Ulysses's* "Nausikaa" episode] is a stern tale of Swift swiftly told by Sterne. Joyce always held that these two writers ought to change names."

Coda

"A Genius of That Cast"

Celebrating Sterne

I first read *Tristram Shandy* a half century ago, in graduate school in 1963, but my initial encounter with Sterne was even earlier, as an undergraduate reading *A Sentimental Journey* in the fall of 1957, fifty-six years ago, or one year more than Laurence Sterne's entire lifetime. I offer these chronological tidbits to ask forgiveness preemptively for some of the remarks that follow. They will possibly seem to twenty-first-century ears dated, archaic, passé—or, in the more modern idiom of condemnation, sexist, elitist, paternalistic, nostalgic, imperialistic, and whatever other crime against postmodern sensibilities can be charged against me. Keep in mind, however, as you begin to formulate your charges, that ageism is also a culpable offense.

Perhaps the most important passage to me at the beginning of my career with Laurence Sterne was not a passage from his fictions, but one from his account, in a letter to Eliza, in March 1767, of his meeting with Lord Bathurst, then in his eighty-fifth year. You all know the passage, I am certain, but it gives me great pleasure to read it again at this gathering in Sterne's honor:

> This nobleman is an old friend of mine. You know he was always the protector of men of wit and genius, and had those of the last century, Addison, Steele, Pope, Swift, Prior, &c. &c. always at his table.—
>
> The manner in which his notice of me began, was singular, as it was polite: he came up to me one day, as I was at the Princess of Wales's court—"I want to know you, Mr. Sterne; but it is fit you should also know who it is that wishes this pleasure. You have heard," continued he, "of an old Lord Bathurst, of whom your Pope's and Swift's have sung and spoken so much: I have liv'd my life with genius's of that cast, but have surviv'd them; and despairing ever to find their equals, 'tis some years since I clos'd my accounts, and shut up

my books, with thoughts of never opening them again: But you have kindled a desire in me to open them once more before I die, which I now do—so go home and dine with me" (*Letters* 540).

It is a beautiful literary encounter across generations, and Sterne's retelling of it is filled with obvious pride. For me, it served as a concrete exemplum of the bridge from the Augustans to Sterne, and hence as just the evidence I wanted for my developing argument that Sterne drew his nourishing waters for *Tristram Shandy* from the Scriblerians. This remains a truism for me today, but already I can feel a shudder among you—"Oh no, not Sterne as a satirist yet again—How long, O Lord, how long?" So I will not on this occasion repeat what I have so often written about for forty-five years, except perhaps to note in passing that while working recently on annotations for Sterne's *Miscellanies,* the final volume of the Florida Edition, fortuitously, volume 9, I was struck more than ever before with the notion that when Sterne was writing the two pieces immediately preceding *Tristram—A Political Romance* and the "Rabelaisian Fragment"—he almost certainly had on his desk the four volumes of the Pope-Swift *Miscellanies,* first published between 1727 and 1732. Let us recall some of the works that collection gathered together: Pope's *Memoirs of P.P. Clerk of This Parish,* surely an inspiration for the diminishing satire of ecclesiastical politics of the *Romance;* and Pope's *Key to the Lock,* reflected in Sterne's various allegorical keys to his *Romance;* and the John Bull pamphlets, which suggested the political readings of the Key. And surely everyone now agrees that his "Rabelaisian Fragment," in which he sets out to write an "Art of Sermon-Writing," is a parody in the tradition of Pope's *Peri Bathous*—why else is the narrator named Longinus Rabelaicus? Shall I go on? No!

Rather I will voluntarily—if reluctantly—dismount my hobby-horse, because as you probably have realized over the course of years, once I am astride and galloping, I am as loath to stop as ever were Walter and Toby. But I do so because today I want to talk about an aspect of this encounter with Lord Bathurst that has only lately occurred to me. To once again recall his words: "I have lived among geniuses of that cast." Like the good old Lord, I too have spent a half century with "geniuses of that cast," if not in the flesh, certainly in the spirit. What else is the study of literature, in fact, but the study of genius? Are we not still guardians of the flame, preserving and passing on to future generations the best that has been thought and written in the heritage we take to be our own?

I invoke Matthew Arnold as a shorthand indicator of how dated this notion will seem to those of you educated in the post-age, that is, an age stamped first and foremost by two conflicting notions: (1) genius is a socially constructed and hence politically motivated privileging of the elite over whatever is not elite; and (2) our age has produced, every third year or so, theories applicable to literature that are truly works of genius—but they are theories of history, or sociology, or psychology, or economics, or anthropology. Indeed, genius now thrives everywhere but in the discipline of literary creation and literary study. Our authors are all terribly flawed, our critics inept unless they derive their readings from Foucault, Habermas, or Said (who was a politician, not a literary scholar)—and it greatly reinforces my argument that the three have already been quite superseded by the latest models in fashion. One reads, for example, a recent essay on Sterne's critical future that contains the following laudatory words, all within nine pages: perceptive, standout, fascinating, influential (twice), dense but rewarding, accomplished, deft (twice), impressive, reenergizing, persuasive, nimble, intriguing, remarkable, triumphant, masterful, and delightful. Oddly enough, not one of these wonderful words was applied to Sterne, all being reserved for his critics, each of whom had taken pen to paper within the last decade, all of whom were attuned to the latest cross-disciplinary approaches.

Somewhat paradoxically, this lauding of ourselves is a tendency splendidly anticipated by one of those modernist geniuses of literature, Robert Musil, now little read because he wrote an enduring novel rather than founded a transient paradigm. I'll quote one telling passage from *The Man without Qualities,* written primarily in the 1930s, and unfinished when the author died in 1942:

> It just so happens that the second thought, at the very least, of every person today confronted by an overwhelming phenomenon, even if it should be its beauty that so overwhelms him, is "You can't fool me! I'll cut you down to size!" And this mania for cutting things down to size, typical of our era that not only flees with the fox, but also pursues with the hounds, has hardly anything to do any longer with life's

natural separation of the [secondary] from the sublime; it is, rather, much more a self-tormenting bent of mind, an inadmissible lust at the spectacle of the good being humiliated and too easily destroyed altogether.[1]

What Musil perhaps did not fully anticipate was our pervasive modern practice of carrying out this mania by inflating praise for all of us mediocre critics (how rare, indeed, is literary criticism that rises above the mundane), even while denying it to the rare geniuses we write about.

I do not have sufficient time or, frankly, insight, to unravel the history of this "mania" for cutting things down and eradicating the "separation of the [secondary] from the sublime," but allow me, instead, briefly to adapt a few of the insights of David Hawkes, in his 2012 *Times Literary Supplement* review of the interestingly titled *The Cultural Return,* written by a colleague of mine at the University of Florida, Susan Hegeman. Hawkes takes us back to Gramsci in the 1920s, his campaign to undermine the "hegemony of bourgeois culture" with an alternative culture that would both destroy and then replace it. This intent was inherited by the literary Left, let us suggest, at the moment of the Derridean revolution in both France and America in 1968:

> Even as leftist parties failed at the polls [according to Mr. Hawkes] their cultural surrogates came to dominate, particularly in the most sophisticated and avant-garde movements. The academic discipline of Cultural Studies emerged as the most self-consciously radical of their projects. It challenged the conventional divisions of the humanities, insisting on "interdisciplinarity," and defining itself by its methods rather than its objects of interpretation. Yet more disturbing, it undermined the traditional canon of great works, proclaiming that popular culture, minority cultures, and the cultures of non-Western societies were as deserving of scholarly attention as Michelangelo, Mozart, or Milton.[2]

As Hawkes notes, presumably echoing Hegeman, the project was a huge success, "all that was sacred was profaned" and "almost every research university now has a Cultural Studies programme, while the requirements that once ensured students would study the classics of the Western canon have been abandoned." Neither author nor reviewer, perhaps not surprisingly, has a problem with that success, their point being that despite what may seem to be the cultural bankruptcy of the cultural studies movement in recent years, we are experiencing only a Hegelian antithesis in the upward spiral of a discipline (if we can call it by that old-fashioned name) that will finally triumph in teaching us "that the boundaries between culture and other areas of experience are artificial and best disregarded."[3] In short, the new discipline will teach us to quite disregard—indeed belittle—the separation of what is secondary from what is sublime; it will erase all difference between art and accident, meaningfulness and mediocrity, truth and triviality. As Pope ironically—and prophetically—argued almost three hundred years ago, there is only one small, ultimately insignificant letter standing between *bathos* and *pathos*—why bother ourselves with the difference?

On several occasions while organizing this splendid gathering, Peter de Voogd has insisted that it be a *working* conference. Several bemused participants asked me how that might differ from other eighteenth-century conferences they attended, which set me to wondering the same thing. My conclusion, with apologies to Peter, was that perhaps this conference ought to be one that addresses not only our *work* on Sterne, but the *work* we do for a living (Sterne being a hobby-horse, not a livelihood), and, with a few exceptions, we all do the same work: we all teach students, ranging from the brightest and best to the dimmest and worst. We work in classrooms, we work as educators. I therefore took Peter to mean he would like us to remember that not Laurence Sterne, but teaching literature is our primary work, and a "working conference" would try to come to grips with what it means to teach eighteenth-century literature three hundred years after one of its several geniuses was born.

My own response might begin not with Sterne, but with Swift. A few years ago, a *Scriblerian* reviewer took an author to task for suggesting that the great popularity of Swift's *Tale of a Tub* in the postmodern era was due to readers perceiving and appreciating its amiability to deconstructive practices. The reviewer suggested, with a welcome dose of common sense, that neither Swift nor his *Tale* is at all popular in our age, that, in truth, both are read today by only a very small number of academics and their bonded servants, otherwise known as English majors. Even then, he added, the number of majors reading Swift is steadily diminishing, since Swift competes poorly against media and cultural studies, not to mention feminist, ethnic, postcolonial, animal rights, "thing," and ecology studies.

To his diatribe, I might have added two further observations: first, if Swift is still read, it is more likely *A Modest Proposal* or a book or two of *Gulliver*. *A Tale of a Tub* can be offered to some advanced graduate students specifically studying the first half of the eighteenth century, but few undergraduates I encountered in my last two decades of teaching had the foundations in literary studies, much less in theology, history, or philosophy, sufficient to get through the first ten pages. Second, despite my belief that *A Tale of a Tub* is the epitome of literary genius in the eighteenth century—indeed, in any century—such a claim works against the cultural ambience I outlined earlier. Quite the opposite: it invokes the advocacy of required courses, period courses, necessary readings, structured curriculums, and, worst of all, the notion that a great book is the work of a great genius, and that teacher and student are engaged in the difficult (yet pleasurable) task of paying due homage to both by trying to understand how and why such brilliant works and authors come into being. How absolutely reactionary, pedantic, and, worst of all, authoritarian, such a practice sounds to the modern ear.

We are living, I believe, in a postliterary age, an age of cultural studies, and while I hesitate to dampen the enthusiasm of this celebration of Sterne, I do think it might be useful to contemplate his future in such an age. I do not deceive myself with any notion that Sterne was ever a popular author, at least not since the first few volumes of *Tristram* took London by storm in 1760–61. He has always been the reading of a minute (and highly educated) segment of society; so, for that matter, are now the writings of Swift and Pope, Richardson and Fielding. Double that tiny segment, and you have the audience for some of Johnson's writings; double it again, and for those of Jane Austen—who has been helped immensely by film versions. Neither film nor graphic novel, however, has done very much for the popularity of *Tristram Shandy*. Put another way, *Tristram Shandy* will continue to be read only if it continues to be taught, and it will continue to be taught only as long as a received canon of literature exists. How long and for what reasons such a canon *should* exist, is the question I am trying to explore.

Canon formation is the very first question a teacher confronts, whether a kindergarten teacher preparing his daily lesson plans or a college professor needing to fill a dozen weeks under course rubrics that might range from a single author, to a survey of five hundred years of literature, to a course known only as "Special Topics." I started my own teaching at the

University of Florida in 1966. Two years later, as already mentioned, Derrida, almost certainly without any inkling of the glory to come, descended on Johns Hopkins, upon which American scholars quite mistook him for the Holy Spirit. Rather than return to Gramsci's political program or to Derrida's philosophical one, however, I would prefer to recall the actual physical scene, the US campus in 1968, where students and faculty were in the streets, protesting segregation, Vietnam, and the authorities who had sanctioned both. Nineteen sixty-eight was also, by the by, the year of the Sterne bicentennial conference at the University of York; it is apropos my argument that York seems to house on its faculty today nary a scholar willing to encourage institutional support for this conference—another reason for us all to be very grateful to Judith Hawley and Royal Holloway.

What students wanted in those heady days of protest was a confirmation of their causes, beginning perhaps with their assault on authority. "What is the relevance of *The Rape of the Lock* to the Vietnam War?" and woe betide the professor (authority personified) who could not find a satisfactory answer. For the next four decades, the profession tried to answer that question in all its various guises, in part because many of us thought it was the right question to ask, in part because we believed it was the only way to hold the attention—and tuition fees—of our students, and forestall their drift toward more satisfying areas of study—the hard sciences for the bright ones, the soft sciences for the others. Not only was the classroom our workplace, but our product was English majors, and if we stopped producing them, we would soon be out of work. Yes, even a reactionary English professor can make an occasional economic observation, although please note that I did so without using "commodification" or "wage slavery," thus ensuring my place alongside Adam Smith and other troglodytes.

The intersection between students and professors on the one hand, the paths of Gramsci and Derrida, on the other, is anti-authoritarianism. I believe this to be the crux of the matter, because, unfortunately, professors have to profess something, even if it be only the anti-authoritarianism of the post-age. There must be, in short, a curriculum, an agenda, a purpose to that classroom time in which we do our work. I do know teachers who ask their students what they would like to read for the semester, but as their shop foreman, I would want such teachers dismissed. So, I direct my comments to those who have since the 1960s struggled with the notion of curriculum, for it is precisely here that the map of our profession's future and

354 · Textual and Critical Intersections

Sterne's fate will be shaped. Let me hasten to add that faculty have, in fact, two workplaces in which curriculum planning takes place—the individual classroom and the collective department. Only a few of us in this youthful assembly will remember, I am sure, the freedom-loving days of the 1970s, when departments decided that requirements, basic courses, prerequisites, structured curriculums were all signs of paternalistic authoritarianism, and did away with them. Undergraduates could cherry-pick among our offerings, put together a major of ten or twelve courses of their own choosing, and graduate as English majors ready for graduate school. In a few more hyper departments, graduate students could do the same thing and go out into the world as English professors without ever taking a single course covering material written before 1968. Ah, brave new world!—although our new professors would have no idea who said that first, or why.

And there was yet another important complication, the outcry to expand the canon and thus reshape curriculums, not only because women had been excluded, but because so many of the male writers were wrong-headed people who had nothing to say about Vietnam or slavery or colonialism or gayness or whatever the present interest was—they did have a lot to say about women, but, like Sterne, they were always sexist. Each new interest was, and still is, I believe, indicative of the continuing search for relevancy in the making of our curriculums, but the primary effect is an entropic inclusion of more and more relevant writers, each of whom quickly proves irrelevant to the next wave of timely social or political or economic concerns.

Equally to the point, while we can expand the canon in our research and writing without curricular consequences, perhaps even with some reward, it does not thus happen within the confines of the classroom, unless we expand the time we can spend in the workplace. Our research may well be on Aphra Behn, rather than Pope, but if we add her to the twelve-week semester's worth of reading, do we remove Pope to provide space? I have said this before but will repeat it now: given the limitations of time and eyesight, the canon is never expanded when it functions, as it always does, as the basis of curriculum. The size of the canon remains the same, only the components of it differ, because ultimately the canon becomes those titles that are being taught in the classroom—the space in which we do our primary work. Even more worrisome, few of us have encountered students recently who are able and willing to read more in twelve weeks than they could a generation earlier. Decades ago, we began slimming the curriculum, choosing *Pamela* over *Clarissa* (obviously and sadly enough), *Joseph Andrews* over *Tom Jones, Billy Budd* over *Moby Dick, London Journal* rather than *Life of Johnson*—even, I shudder to say it, *A Sentimental Journey* over *Tristram Shandy*. And length is not the only issue; ease is another, so that one can try to teach students the first two books of *Gulliver's Travels*, but not *A Tale of a Tub*.

The workplace of the teacher of literature has become, perhaps always was, a complicated and convoluted place, and I have touched on only a few of the myriad problems that confront us when we decide what it is we will bring into the classroom to share with those we are asked to teach something rather than nothing. For it turns out that although we have compounded our difficulties with some post-age complications, the curriculum problem has always been unique for the study of literature—in which dubious discipline, to save us from all quibbles, I will include philosophy and theology, even non–studio art and music. Within the university, we cannot help but observe that all other professors have *disciplines,* which word I take to mean the defining principles by which they know what it is they are supposed to teach. This is an oversimplified view of these other disciplines, I am sure, but I believe that in their practitioners' own minds, a set of concrete and definite guidelines of inclusion and exclusion are part of how they know their own curriculums, and how they can separate that within their discipline which needs to be taught (truths) from that which does not (errors). They also have a strong sense, without any underlying nihilism, that all present truths may be proved false at a future date and hence abandoned for new truths. What is important here is that other disciplines are shaped by the very process of inclusion and exclusion, that which belongs (truths) and that which should be excluded (no longer truths). Put otherwise, the word *discipline* suggests the two elements most necessary to almost every other academic study: objectivity and authority. And it is precisely these elements that we cannot locate in our own supposed discipline, the first because it never existed, the second because we have abandoned the concept of *authority*—at times even of *authorship*— in pursuit of relevancy or freedom or whatever other rough beast slouches now toward Bethlehem.

Why do we teach *The Rape of the Lock* rather than a poem by Richard Blackmore? Why teach *Tristram Shandy* rather than *Adventures of a Guin-*

ea? I would suggest that we have never known and never will find a sufficient answer to that question, but will always and everywhere lapse into mysticisms and abstractions by way of answering it, abstractions that can always be reduced to the dreaded sanction of authority. This is the received truth of our literary heritage, that some things are more worthy to be passed on than others, that cultures naturally draw a distinction between the secondary and the sublime, as Musil argues, and that many minds over many years have acquiesced in that sanction and that distinction. It is a dreadful argument to the postmodern mind, but after a half century in the profession I must admit that I have little better to offer. We do not seem to have a discipline comparable to other academic endeavors; we have no significant objective means for measuring inclusion and exclusion.

The fact that our curriculum has changed quite radically over the past half century is not, however, the result of our uniqueness within the academic community. Quite the contrary, it is observable that all the sciences, hard and soft, have probably changed far more than literary studies. If anything, in our desire to imitate these disciplines—somehow more worthy in our eyes than literary studies because they have more overt relevance to modern life—we have tried to mimic their rapid turnover of materials. Every decade in the sciences produces new models, new paradigms, new theories, and we in the humanities have tried to imitate that concept of disciplinary revolution, without, however, instituting its foundational source: the authority of present truth or validation.

Some of my best friends are Aphra Behnites and Charlotte Smithians, so I will avoid Behn and Smith in pursuing my argument and offer my own guilty implication in the history of curriculums I am deploring. Twenty years ago, attracted by a few sentences in a footnote to a study of Israel Zangwill, I started reading a quite unknown late Victorian, Amy Levy, and edited a collection of her work for the University Press of Florida. Levy was a London Jew, one of the first women to attend Cambridge, probably near deaf, probably a lesbian, certainly suffering from depression. At age twenty-seven she committed suicide, leaving behind three novels, three small chapbooks of poetry, and a small collection of essays, literary, political, and social. She was, in short, an ideal author for the postmodernist mind, so relevant in so many directions that one could almost lose track in their abundance. The MLA International Bibliography listed one essay on her in all the decades before my edition appeared in 1993; it has almost forty entries for the nineteen years after 1993, including two full-scale biographies and new editions of two of her novels from Broadview Press. This is not overwhelming, but two entries a year measures quite well against many in the eighteenth century who were once required reading: Addison, Congreve, Prior, Sheridan, Gray, even Goldsmith, all no longer average two entries annually—discounting *Notes and Queries,* perhaps. Of course, as a Levite, I do not regret this; nor should Londoners, who step on her words every time they pace the Queen's Walk along the South Bank—where lines from her poem "London Plane Tree" are enshrined on a pathway memorial along with other London poets such as Wordsworth and T. S. Eliot: to wit: "Green is the plane tree in the square, / The other trees are brown; / They droop and pine for country air; / The plane tree loves the town." But how good is Amy Levy? I taught her in a nineteenth-century novel course, along with Austen, Dickens, George Eliot, and Trollope, and I was embarrassed for her—perhaps for myself as well, since we used my edition. Without doubt, Amy Levy should be preserved, she is too talented an author, too interesting, I think, again to drop totally out of our sights, and I am happy to have helped in her rescue.[4] There are hundreds of writers from 1850 to 1900 who are far less talented; her problem is that there are twenty or thirty or forty who are more talented, and in a course of literature from that period, which author should be dropped to make room for Levy? We can find more room for her, perhaps, in a Jewish literature course, especially in an Anglo-Jewish literature course, even more room for her in an Anglo-Jewish women's literature course, and we must give her a dominant role in an Anglo-Jewish lesbian literature course; indeed, if we add deaf and depressed to that description, she may be the only author we teach. I can, in my more pessimistic moments, imagine we are already on that slippery slope whereby we design our canon based solely on characteristics that we find "interesting" or, rather, "relevant," characteristics we then seek authors to represent. Our curriculum, in short, is determined not at all by literature, much less by genius or the sublime, but solely by our social and political desire to be relevant to our own present concerns.

Let us turn back to those thirty or forty authors who are better than Amy Levy. As with all counting games, all rankings, we are in quite arbitrary territory, most especially because we have no idea what sets those thirty or forty authors apart from all others. (Actually, I do: "Proper words in proper places"—but I doubt if that would pass postmodern scrutiny,

358 · Textual and Critical Intersections

and even I am not at all sure what it means.) For this reason alone, I would like to insist that it is not our own authority, and not even the heavy-handed authority of past judgment, that creates the necessary distinctions, but rather that when the secondary are put in proximity to the sublime, the difference is obvious. The difference between George Eliot and Amy Levy is clear not only to the instructor, but to the instructed as well. Even those who might prefer the easiness of Levy over the difficulty of Eliot, recognize something transcendent in Eliot, lacking in Levy. For this reason alone, Levy is a task for the humanist's study, Eliot for both the study and the classroom.

To be sure, we might offer Levy in a course as a sacrifice, a scapegoat that we use to illustrate the difference between canonical writing and that which is not. To do so, however, will still require, even for just one semester in, say, the Victorian novel, dropping a canonized author. Thus, in *The Cambridge Companion to English Novelists,* published in 2009, the initial table of contents did not contain either Trollope or Smollett, both of whom would certainly have been included twenty years earlier. I assume that protests from contributors like me helped restore Trollope (while keeping Gaskell as well), but Smollett remained excluded. An editor can at times get extra pages for a collection, but we do not have extra hours in our classroom, and while it is worth debating whether Smollett should be replaced by Burney, as in the *Cambridge Companion,* my point is precisely that we are not adding to the canon but rather replacing one figure with another. Moreover, as I said, we are doing so primarily for nonliterary reasons, reasons having to do with our current political and social agendas, which have overwhelmed whatever a "literary agenda" might be. Hence, as I and others have pointed out, the MLA International Bibliography and the pages of the *Scriblerian* both offer ample evidence of seismic shifts in the subjects of academic literary study,[5] shifts almost assuredly reflected in our curriculums. Entries on Behn, Manley, Haywood, in issue after issue of the *Scriblerian* over the past decade, outnumber the work being done on Addison and Steele, Dryden, Congreve, Gay, even Pope—and to be sure, Tobias Smollett. Is this a good thing?

For many of you it is, and all the rapid-fire judgmental comments I am making about rankings and how this author is better than that author are purposeful and designed to keep you very attentive—not necessarily attentive to what I am saying but certainly to the sound of my voice, because as soon as it stops you will want to be on your feet with objections. Let me anticipate the most obvious of them, namely, that I am not offering any objective criteria for what is better or worse, nor any workable definition for what I mean by literary or nonliterary, secondary or sublime, and certainly no validating principles or procedures by which to establish the truth of my belief (or opinion, as Sterne would have it) that George Eliot is a better author than Amy Levy, and Jane Austen a better author than Aphra Behn or Eliza Haywood.

This is, of course, an inartful dodge, pitting one woman against another, when it is obvious that the primary canonical change of our time is that women are replacing men. The operative word is *replacing*, since we cannot add to the canon, but can only substitute one author for another. My point is quite simple: when we make canons by our own choice, we operate in conflict with a canon that has, in large measure, perhaps full measure, chosen itself. It does so, I believe, by the seemingly passive, yet paradoxically very active, process of authors coming into proximity with other authors, who read and—most significantly perhaps—reread them. That is, at any rate, the opinion of Thomas Bernhard, a modern author I very much admire:

> There are some writers . . . who excite the reader much more the second time he reads them than they did the first time. With me this always happens when I read Kafka. I remember Kafka as a great writer . . . but when I reread him I'm absolutely convinced that I've read an even greater writer. Not many writers become more important, more impressive, on a second reading. Most of them, on a second reading, make us feel ashamed of having read them even once. This is an experience we have with hundreds of writers, but not with Kafka, not with the great Russians—Dostoyevsky, Tolstoy, Turgenev, Lermontov—and not with Proust, Flaubert, and Sartre, whom I rate among the very greatest.[6]

I quote at length because the passage turns in so many different directions, typical of Bernhard's writing. On the one hand, surely one test of the *sublime* I have posited in opposition to the *secondary* is precisely the rereadability posited by the narrator of *Extinction*. He is not, however, an always reliable narrator, and I believe Bernhard puts forward two names that, in proximity to the others, might raise questions: Lermontov, who, I believe, after something of an eclipse, has emerged as an equal to the other Russian authors listed; and Sartre, who, to my ear—and I hope to others—sits uncomfortably alongside Proust and Flaubert.

What Bernhard is deliberately demonstrating, I believe, is that the process of canonization certainly allows for changes over time, if only because the canon is constantly narrowed and limited in response to an ever ongoing accumulation. That is to say, it is no accident that the canon comes to us as an inverted cone, whittled down by time from the wide breadth of modernity to the consistently diminishing numbers of the canonized from earlier periods. If we have just so many hours in our classroom, a similar limitation seems to prevail within the passage of time itself, and where we might offer fifty twentieth-century American poets to the canon today, perhaps only five will still be read—and reread—three hundred years from now. This seems quite acceptable; what I suggest is unacceptable is our tendency of late to interfere and impose our own changes, changes of a self-defined and self-defining nature, on what I take to be a most natural process.

The soul selects her own society, says Emily Dickinson. There is a level of literary achievement that defies special pleading and does not need it. An author is included because other authors demand his or her presence so that their own achievement can be sufficiently measured. Such authors talk to one another across time and geographic, political, linguistic, and theological boundaries, and, most vital to the argument I am pursuing, they survive only when placed in contact with authors of equal accomplishment. Sterne depends on Swift and Pope, Fielding and Richardson, Boswell and Johnson, in order for us to grasp and appreciate how his achievement differs from that of lesser lights. In addition to those English authors, he is also talking to Rabelais and Montaigne, Cervantes and Erasmus. He depends on Goethe and Voltaire, Rousseau and Richter. There is more in common between Sterne and Joyce than between Sterne and his contemporaries, say, Richard Griffith or Charles Johnstone or Eliza Haywood, just as there is more in common among Donne, Pope, Austen, Wordsworth, and Browning, than between Pope and Matt Prior or Aphra Behn. That commonality, that conversation, is what I am calling genius, whatever it was that allowed Bathurst to recognize in Sterne a semblance—better, a kinship—with the geniuses he had spent his own life with. Great literature and its authors speak to one another, and as teachers, workers in the field of literature, we must, I think, teach others to listen to that conversation and not just to our own discourse, however interesting and relevant we might be to ourselves, however much we want to find that interest and relevance reflected in second- and third- and fourth-rate writers.

I want to digress for one moment, as Tristram might write, to consider a well-known *second-rate* eighteenth-century poet, William Collins. Poor Collins, as Johnson had it, has always been one of my own best loved poets, so much so that over the course of forty years I collected some forty-five separate editions of his work, now owned by the University of Florida Libraries. He is a fine and important poet, and as I have told many classes, I would much rather have been a poet of the rank of Collins than an English professor. Had he lived longer, perhaps he would have achieved his goal, although neither longevity nor the size of one's canon seems to matter when defining genius and the sublime. Collins deserves to be preserved, deserves to be read by as many people as can be convinced to read him, but William Collins, after having had some discourse with Milton on the one hand, with Wordsworth on the other, no longer was heard as a necessary part of their conversation. We might write articles and books protesting that, but for every Blake (or Lermontov) restored to prominence, hundreds of aspirants continue to fail to make the cut, and rightfully so; canons should be created not by special pleading, but by time and the process of a conversation among authors to which critics need to listen.

For the past forty years, we have been abandoning the task of teaching the great authors because we have not been able to hear the conversation of genius, deafened by our own conversation with ourselves and with our students. We have thus introduced into the classroom, for a plethora of social, political, psychological, and economic reasons, authors who not only cannot sustain this conversation with genius but actually impair our ability to hear it. Without doubt, we continue to produce handbooks and companions, ever more elaborate and scholarly editions of the major— and minor—authors, monographs ad infinitum, but sales are only to a few hundred libraries at most, just as the venue for art is now the museum— and the bank vault. Still, the number of scholarly monographs on major figures diminishes annually, some major publishers telling authors that single-author scholarship is no longer marketable, that one must have more breadth, less depth. This phenomenon, too, drives our curriculum, because as workers we are more efficient when we can combine our study

362 · Textual and Critical Intersections

and our classroom, can teach what we are "working on." For this reason, we too often bring the wrong books to our classrooms, and our final product, our students, will be not educated lovers of literature but undereducated dilettantes of a variety of other disciplines.

I see several reasons for this increasingly bad product. We have allowed the uneducated to dictate to the educated; thus, we allow students to shape curriculums. The teaching of poetry has just about disappeared in America because students do not "like" it. Even the creative writing courses are filled with students who write but do not read poetry; every poetry teacher I have known has told me that their first task is to force students to read more and write less. Students like fiction, but not difficult fiction and not long fiction, and so, as already suggested, we teach shorter works. Students (and their professors) want to be seen as theoretical, but the key is to be so without effort: excerpts replace whole works, and theory is reduced to a single personality rather than, as it truly is, the evolution of thought over generations. To be a Derridean without being able to read French, without having read Descartes and Kant, Hegel and Heidegger, and, I will quickly add, Emmanuel Levinas, is equivalent to being an eighteenth-century scholar—or student—without ever having read *Paradise Lost.* One can fake it, of course, but the problem is that the geniuses of the eighteenth century were in continual conversation with Milton, and unless one has read both generations, one is, to borrow from Swift, spinning out one's own entrails. Or, to return to my economic expertise, to allow students to shape our curriculum is to deal in clipped coin; it passes for the real thing, it drives out the real thing. When one is finally caught, one is hanged.

That we teach to the lowest common denominator in the classroom is not, however, the primary problem. Rather, it is that we are denying a generation of students the means by which they will be enabled to read and appreciate the best literature available in our literary heritage—the works of sublime genius. Again, I will not define my terms, neither literature nor literary, sublime nor genius; perhaps by all those terms I simply allude to the feeling one has in a cathedral rather than in a bedroom; we can certainly make love in both, but at some point even Boswell learned to distinguish between the two. Again, I will invoke poor Matthew Arnold, much maligned nowadays for what I take to be one of the most astute critical insights of the last two hundred years, his touchstone theory of literary appreciation:

Indeed there can be no more useful help for discovering what poetry belongs to the class of the truly excellent . . . than to have always in one's mind lines and expressions of the great masters, and to apply them as a touchstone to other poetry. Of course we are not to require this other poetry to resemble them; it may be very dissimilar. But if we have any tact we shall find them, when we have lodged them well in our minds, infallible touchstones for detecting the presence or absence of high poetic quality.[7]

If readers are given even a single touchstone, Homer or Shakespeare, Greek drama or Milton, they are equipped with a yardstick that enables them to measure what else is offered in the curriculum. If we could still be certain, as we once were, that English majors were familiar with the Bible, we would indeed have students coming to us with a touchstone in place. Students today, however, are almost entirely reliant on whatever curriculum is offered to them in the classroom. Thus, if our curriculum does not cover the best authors, they measure their readings by whatever yardstick they are exposed to; and we all know what Sterne had to say about that: "a dwarf who brings a standard along with him to measure his own size—take my word, is a dwarf in more articles than one" (*TS* 4.25.375).

I have managed, finally, to return to Sterne, but I hope I have been talking about him all this while, digressive and progressive, as is the Shandean manner. In the last volume of *Tristram Shandy*, we recall that Tristram comments on the continued reading of his book by "Posterity": "I say, by Posterity—and care not, if I repeat the word again—for what has this book done more than the Legation of Moses, or the Tale of a Tub, that it may not swim down the gutter of Time along with them" (*TS* 9.10.754). It is, I believe, an echo of that overheard discourse between genius that I have been alluding to, by no means a brash shouting, but instead a complex bit of whispered irony, that depends on our knowing not only both Warburton's and Swift's works, but also Sterne's relationship with the bishop and the dean, his scorn of the one, his admiration of the other. Without doubt, Warburton thought of himself as a genius of his age—and like Bathurst, a companion of genius—but Sterne knew better: by placing the *Legation* in proximity with *A Tale of a Tub,* the latter floats up, the former sinks out of sight. In linking himself thus to Swift as the genius whose company he kept, he is also signaling to readers, at the very end of his work, the genius

364 · Textual and Critical Intersections

with whom he wanted to be compared, because only then would his work be valued for what he believed it to be—a conversation with genius, Swift perhaps first among them. It marks for me, as do Bathurst's comments, a telling trace of that discourse among the great authors we are privileged to overhear if we are sufficiently attentive and sufficiently educated—and if we ask ourselves not whether their conversation is relevant to our own social and political concerns, but rather, whether our concerns are relevant to theirs. If not, perhaps we need a new set of concerns, or, at the very least, we need to remember that Warburton spent many, many hours in the company of Pope, but did not seem to hear a thing: perhaps he talked too much and listened too little.

Why Swift and why *A Tale of a Tub?* I would no more hazard a guess (beyond the forty years of guesses that might be said to constitute my career as a scholar of Sterne) than I would try to guess why James Joyce, when explaining what he did in the unknowable *Finnegans Wake,* invoked Sterne: "Time and the river and the mountain are the real heroes of my book. Yet the elements are exactly what every novelist might use: man and woman, birth, childhood, night, sleep, marriage, prayer, death. . . . Only I am trying to build as many planes of narrative with a single esthetic purpose. Did you ever read Laurence Sterne?"[8] There is a level of understanding here that strikes me as creative rather than critical, enigmatic rather than elucidating, but I am teaching myself to be content with that distant awareness of a discourse of which I can only hope to overhear and comprehend snatches. Still, since the fate of great authors in a postliterate age is that they must be taught before they are read, if we want to continue to have a futurity in which the best that has been thought and written continues to be read we had best try to fashion a readership willing to be attentive to—possessing the necessary tactfulness, in Arnold's formulation, to listen to—voices other than our own, as difficult as that task always is.

Indeed, to find texts relevant to our own interests is, conversely, an incredibly easy task, even more so for a reader with well-honed critical skills, able to make a text speak the modern idiom: that we now read Smollett, if we read him at all, for what he says about imperialistic hegemony or *commodifacational* impulse, is a case in point. Far more difficult is it to find our own relevancy to the discourse of those authors who are conversing over the centuries among themselves, with hardly a nod in our direction. Some of them, like Sterne, can fool us at times into believing that they write for us, but only because they know our egoistic and self-absorbed natures so much better than we know them ourselves, knowledge, I hasten to add, garnered from the writers to whom and for whom they are actually writing. Sterne knows from Swift, for example, that his readers, being human, would like to live in a world without judgment, without discipline and order, a world in which authors speak to the tastes and concerns and interests of readers, "without let or hindrance"; in short, a world in which literature exists solely to support our present concerns and interests, whatever is relevant to our own time and place. And so, like Swift, Sterne pretends to be just such an author, names him Tristram, and plays with our foreknown capacity to turn Tristram progressively into an existentialist (John Traugott), a structuralist (James Swearingen), a deconstructionist (Jonathan Lamb), or a postcolonialist (Carol Watts)—well into the future. Meanwhile, in silent discourse with Swift—with Rabelais before him, and Henry James after him (I am thinking of the many unreliable narrators in James)—Sterne writes a book that he expects will swim down the gutter of time with *A Tale of a Tub*. What splendid, yet hushed, arrogance, as if he already knew that he had spent his time with geniuses of that cast and was indeed one of them.

Originally published in the *Shandean* 26 (2015).

Notes

1 Robert Musil, *The Man without Qualities*, trans. Sophie Wilkins (New York: Knopf, 1995), 330 (translation slightly altered).

2 David Hawkes, review of *The Cultural Return*, by Susan Hegeman, *Times Literary Supplement*, August 15, 2012, 23.

3 Hawkes, 23.

4 The recent tome *Amy Levy: Collected Writings*, ed. Luke Devine (Jerusalem: Library of the Jewish People, 2023), notes its roots in my 1993 edition, referring to it as "a first and monumental collection."

5 See, e.g., Melvyn New, "'Lisping in Numbers': Some Canonical Statistics for the Present Age," *Scriblerian*, 37, no. 1 (Autumn 2004): 64–67.

6 Thomas Bernhard, *Extinction* (1986), trans. David McLintock (1995; New York: Vintage Books, 2011), 70.

7 Matthew Arnold, *The Study of Poetry* (1880), qtd. from *English Prose of the Victorian Era*, ed. Charles Frederick Harrold and William D. Templeman (New York: Oxford University Press, 1954), 1252.

8 Qtd. in Seon Givens, ed. *James Joyce: Two Decades of Criticism* (New York: Vanguard Press, 1948), 11–12.

Permissions

"Sterne and the Narrative of Determinateness," *Eighteenth-Century Fiction* 4, no. 4 (July 1992): 315–29. Copyright © 1992 by the McMaster University journal *Eighteenth-Century Fiction,* https://muse.jhu.edu/journal/324. Reprinted with permission.

"The Odd Couple: Laurence Sterne and John Norris of Bemerton," *Philological Quarterly* 75 (1996): 361–85. Copyright © 1996 by *Philological Quarterly.* Reprinted with permission.

"Laurence Sterne's Sermons and *The Pulpit Fool,*" *Eighteenth-Century Life* 35, no. 2 (2011): 1–17. Copyright © 2011 by Duke University Press, https://www.dukeupress.edu. Reprinted with permission.

"'The Unknown World': The Poem Laurence Sterne Did Not Write," *Huntington Library Quarterly* 74, no. 1 (2011): 85–98. Copyright © 2011 by *Huntington Library Quarterly.* Reprinted with permission.

"Taking Care: A Slightly Levinasian Reading of *Dombey and Son,*" *Philological Quarterly* 84, no. 1 (2005): 76–104. Copyright © 2005 by *Philological Quarterly.* Reprinted with permission.

"Johnson, T. S. Eliot, and the City," in *Samuel Johnson among the Modernists,* ed. Anthony W. Lee (Clemson, SC: Clemson University Press, 2019), 21–40. Copyright © 2019 by Clemson University. Reprinted with permission.

"Reading Sterne through Proust and Levinas," *Age of Johnson* 12 (2001): 329–60. Copyright © 2001 by AMS Press. Reprinted with permission.

"Sterne and the Modernist Moment," in *The Cambridge Companion to Laurence Sterne,* ed. Thomas Keymer (Cambridge: Cambridge University Press, 2009), 160–73. Copyright © 2009 by Cambridge University Press. Reprinted with permission.

"Richardson's *Sir Charles Grandison* and Sterne: A Study in Influence," *Modern Philology* 115, no. 2 (2017): 213–43. Copyright © 2017 by the University of Chicago. Reprinted with permission.

"Boswell and Sterne in 1768," in *Laurence Sterne's "A Sentimental Journey":*

A Legacy to the World, ed. W. B. Gerard and M-C. Newbould (Lewisburg, PA: Bucknell University Press, 2021), 171–93. Copyright © 2021 by Bucknell University Press. Reprinted with permission.

"Single and Double: *Memoirs of Martinus Scriblerus* and *Tristram Shandy,*" *Swift Studies* 36 (2021): 68–97. Copyright © 2021 by Kirsten Juhas and Hermann J. Real. Reprinted with permission.

"'The Life of a Wit is a warfare upon earth': Sterne, Joyce, and Their Portraits of the Artist," *Shandean* 33 (2022): 237–61. Copyright © 2022 by the *Shandean.* Reprinted with permission (shorter version).

"'A Genius of That Cast': Celebrating Sterne," *Shandean* 26 (2015): 9–26. Copyright © 2015 by the *Shandean.* Reprinted with permission.

NB, the essays have been reprinted as they first appeared, excepting all citations to Sterne's writings, which have now been updated to the Florida Edition. Cross-reference to other essays included in this volume, systematization of citation styles, and the correction of typographical and other errors of inadvertency have been made, along with a very few interpolations, set off by brackets. "'The Life of a Wit is a warfare upon earth': Sterne, Joyce, and Their Portraits of the Artist" is an expanded version of the original, which appeared in *Shandean* 33.

Index

Page numbers in *italics* refer to illustrations

Addison, Joseph, 347, 357, 358; *Cato*, 256, 267; *Remarks on Several Parts of Italy*, 221; *Spectator, The*, 71

Anne, queen of England, 71

Annotation, scholarly, 2–3, 18, 23, 36, 181, 212–13, 221–22, 225–26, 237n4, 279, 284–85, 293, 348

Anti-Semitism, 3, 333

Aquinas, Thomas, 47, 299, 330, 333–34

Arbuthnot, John, 282, 291, 299, 311n59, 311–12n68; John Bull pamphlets, 279

Aristophanes, 312–13n73

Aristotle's Masterpiece, 314, 323–24, 337n3. *See also* Joyce, James

Arnold, Matthew, 4, 8, 125, 333, 349, 362, 364. *See also* Criticism, literary

Art (aesthetics), 201–2, 340n34; and (literary) criticism, 106, 110–12, 123–25, 127–28n37; and literature, 105–18, 121–25, 168–69, 326–28, 330–36, 340n34, 340n38, 341n51, 348n56; theories of, 17, 62, 202, 237n4, 318, 340n34, 348; visual, 6, 102–4, 106, 124. *See also* Dickens, Charles; Levinas, Emmanuel

Astell, Mary, 2, 34, 42, 47; *Letters Concerning the Love of God*, 2, 34, 193n47. *See also* Norris, John, of Bemerton

Aubin, Penelope, 220, 234, 241n27. *See also* Richardson, Samuel

Augustine, Saint, 47, 58n27, 60n40, 159n48, 330; *Confessions*, 260

Austen, Jane, 29n29, 216, 234–35, 352, 357, 359, 360

Baldessari, John, 101–5, 111, 124, 129n43

Barbauld, Anna Letitia, 222, 245n60. *See also* Richardson, Samuel

Bathurst, Lord (Allen Bathurst, 1st Baron), 347–48, 360, 363–64

Behn, Aphra, 213, 214, 297, 354, 356, 358–59, 360. *See also* Canon, the literary

Berkeley, Bishop George, 263, 275n41, 310n56

Bernhard, Thomas, 359–60

Bible, the, 30–31n20, 327, 341n46, 363

Blackmore, Richard, 213, 255. *See also* Mediocrity (literary)

Blake, William, 125, 361

Bolingbroke, Lord (Henry St John, First Viscount of), 224, 242n44

Booth, Wayne C., 214–15, 238n10, 282, 341n51

Borrowings, literary, 5, 27n4, 29n13, 35–37, 42, 213–14, 233

Boswell, James: *Account of Corsica, An*, 251, 263, 264, 266, 276n54, 277n58, 277n53; attitude toward women of, 276n53; early life of, 251; encounters with eminent figures of, 252, 255–56, 262–63, 273n22, 275n37, 278; ethical dilemmas of, 258–60, 263, 276n57, 362; "Harvest Jaunt" of, 252, 278; literary celebrity of, 254, 268, 272n14; marriage of, 263, 272n14; reading interests of, 252–53, 272n11, 278–79; in relation to Laurence Sterne (*see under* Sterne, Laurence, in relation to other writers); religious beliefs of, 255, 257–62; Roman Catholicism of, 255; romantic idealism of, 254, 270, 276n50; sexual

370 · Index

Boswell, James—*continued*
encounters of, 254, 258–59, 263; sexually
transmitted diseases of, 254
—travels of, 251, 259, 262–63, 266–67,
275n37; to Corsica, 254–55, 266–68,
272n14, 276n54, 277n58, 277n63; to
France and Italy (Grand Tour), 253,
260–61, 262, 265–66, 274–75n35, 275n37;
276n57; to Germany and Switzerland,
253, 255–56, 273n22; to Holland (The
Netherlands), 253, 258–60; to London,
251–52
—works of: *Boswell on the Grand Tour:
Germany and Switzerland, 1764*, 273n22;
Boswell in Holland, 1763–64, 271n9,
274n24; *Boswell in Search of a Wife,
1766–1769*, 272n14; *Boswell's London
Journal*, 252, 355; *Life of Johnson, The*,
155n13, 156n17, 355
Bradshaigh, Lady Dorothy, 219, 236n3,
240n22, 242n41, 246n62. *See also* Richardson, Samuel
Brantley, Richard E., 1, 5, 156–57n21, 239n18,
273–74n23, 310n56, 343n74
Brown, Reverend Robert (Scottish minis-
ter), 290, 307n36. *See also* Boswell, James
Browne, Hablot Knight ("Phiz"), 9, 101,
103–4, *104*, 105–6, 111–12, 126n3, 126n4.
See also Dickens, Charles
Bulwer, John, 237
Bulwer-Lytton, Edward: *Lady of Lyons, The*,
319
Bunyan, John, 113, 156n17, 263; *Pilgrim's
Progress, The*, 262–63
Burney, Frances, 79n29, 216, 251, 358
Burton, Robert, 342n56; *Anatomy of Melan-
choly, The*, 26, 31n23, 39, 44, 93n6, 94n13,
308n44, 337n7; influence on the Scrible-
rians of, 308n44; influence on Laurence
Sterne of, 16, 20, 24, 31n23, 32n26, 39, 44,
93n6, 94–95n13, 308n44, 337n7. *See also*
Joyce, James; Sterne, Laurence
Butler, Joseph, 310n56
Butler, Samuel, 282; *Hudibras*, 280

Canon, the literary, 6–9, 291; commercial
factors determining, 361–62; criticisms
of, 234, 288, 350, 354, 358–59; exclu-
sions from, 8, 358, 361–62; expansion
of, 354; formation of, 8–9, 234, 251,
271n3, 279, 315–16, 352–53, 359–60; and
misattributions, 8, 92; and pedagogy,
7, 9–10, 352–58, 360–62; in relation to
Truth, 7–8; value of, 7–8, 234–45, 271n3,
350–52, 360–63; Western, the, 315, 350.
See also Mediocrity (literary); Pedagogy
(university)
Cash, Arthur H., 87
Celan, Paul, 107, 193n51
Censorship (political), 10
Cervantes, Miguel de, 29n10, 107, 213, 252,
263–64, 270, 282, 360; *Don Quixote de
la Mancha*, 263–64, 280; influence on
James Boswell of, 263–64, 266; influence
on Laurence Sterne of, 35, 62, 263–64,
276n55
Chambers, Ephraim: *Cyclopædia*, 16, 293,
308n45, 339n33. *See also* Sterne, Laurence
Charron, Pierre, 44, 48, 177, 226, 244n39,
290, 326
—influence on Laurence Sterne of: and
borrowings, 44, 48, 177, 225–26, 232,
244n39, 290, 307n35, 326, 340–41n35;
critical commentary on, 244n39; *Of
Wisdome*, 42, 44, 225–26, 232, 244n39;
and sexuality, 42
Chaucer, Geoffrey, 168
Christianity: and incomplete enjoyment,
223–27, 231–35, 247–48n56; inconsistencies of, 41, 298; influence on literature of,
142–43, 148–49, 153–54, 160–61n53, 208,
213, 235, 239–30, 301, 343n74; influence
on political philosophies of, 143; Jesus
Christ in, 47, 68, 70, 142, 146, 216–18,
259, 296, 327, 333; John the Apostle in,
333, 336; John the Baptist in, 146, 196–97,
333, 335–36; and the New Testament,
146, 218, 327; and the Old Testament,
146; and politics, 59n35; in relation to

philosophy, 16–17, 34, 42–43, 60n40, 78n20, 181, 217–18, 239n18, 310n56; in relation to theology, 4–5, 42–43, 46–47, 51, 56n9, 56n14, 59n35, 63–66, 73–74, 79n28, 142, 159n47, 217–18, 224, 227, 235, 237n6, 242n44, 269, 287–88, 304n20; and Scripture, 30–31n20, 59n35, 60n40, 142, 149–50, 160n52, 213, 217–18, 230, 235, 273–73n23, 274n25, 295–96, 317, 327–33, 240n34; significance in the eighteenth century of, 148–49, 234, 258–59, 261; skepticism toward, (present-day), 149–50, 234, 298, 301; symbols of, 144; and unknowingness, 6, 208

—denominations of: and interdenominationalism, 90; Anglican Catholicism, 321; Anglicanism, 56n9, 59n35, 60n35, 75n6, 234; Baptist Church, the, 64, 89, 94n9; Church of England, the, 59n35; Episcopalianism, 94n9; Latitudinarianism, 37–38, 41, 47, 65, 181, 232, 248n67; Methodism, 159n47, 273n23; Presbyterianism, 67, 69, 70, 77–78n23, 253; Protestantism, 131n61, 228, 229–30, 232, 288, 319, 326, 338n18, 339n28; Quakerism, 47, 64, 70; Roman Catholicism, 47, 64 70, 228, 255, 263, 319, 321, 325

—philosophical concepts of: death, 8, 20–21, 39–40, 65–66, 142–47, 152, 166–67, 174, 204, 223–24, 266, 301, 321–25, 331, 335–36; Eden (as paradisical concept), 142–44, 152–53, 160–61n53, 218, 247n64, 247–48n56, 264, 300–02, 304; Neoplatonism, 39, 78n25; Platonism, 55–56n9, 126n15, 182, 187n6, 193–94n52; skepticism, 16–17, 28n6, 28n8, 49, 149–50. *See also* Norris, John, of Bemerton

—practice of: and *The Book of Common Prayer,* 160n52, 203, 246–47n52, 272n11, 307n36; confession, 255, 257, 325–26; Mass, the, 330

—theological tenets of: afterlife, the, 36–37, 54, 224, 242n44, 257, 301; conscience, the, 60n41, 257, 262, 289, 295–96, 298–

99, 310–11n58, 311n63, 321–25; Fall, the, 51, 144, 146, 153, 204, 217–18, 234, 300–2, 324–26; free will, 254–62; grace, 37–38, 40–41, 59n32, 115, 143, 270, 340n34; Judgment, 38–39, 54, 147, 166–68, 174–75, 186, 321–27, 331, 334, 340n34; peace, 53–54, 68–74; redemption, 153–54, 218, 296; reformation, 270; sin, 20, 39, 59n32, 124, 142–43, 152–54, 204, 254, 261, 266, 287–88, 297, 299, 301, 325, 331; soul, the, 36–37, 57–58n22, 64, 90, 121, 182–83, 187, 217–18, 227–28, 325–26, 229–32, 255–66, 273n22, 293–302, 310n56, 312n71, 322–26, 339–40n33; Trinity, the, 236, 287, 306n31, 308n44. *See also* God; Religion; Secularism; Theology

Cibber, Colley: *Apology for the Life of Mr. Colley Cibber, An,* 76n7

City, the (concept): as allegory, 61, 147–48, 150–51; compared with the country, 144; in the eighteenth century, 139–40, 151, 153–54; negative attitudes toward, 139–41, 145–50, 161n58; in the nineteenth century, 141; pleasures of, 144–45; and religion, 148–50, 152–53, 159n48; in the twentieth century, 141–42; as utopia, 142, 148, 152–53. *See also* Eliot, T. S.; Johnson, Samuel; London

Clarke, Samuel, 35, 293–94

Coleman, George, 251

Collins, William, 361

Comber, Thomas, Dean of Durham, 66–68

Conferences, academic, 351, 353

Congreve, William, 213, 257, 258

Conrad, Joseph: *Lord Jim,* 137

Consciousness, human: eighteenth-century concepts of, 289, 291, 294–98, 309n50; philosophical theories of (general), 60n40, 193n51, 307n34

Conversation, between authors (as critical concept), 4–7, 9, 136–37, 215, 233–35, 238n14, 250–52, 261–263, 271n3, 179–80, 315–17, 341–42n55, 360–64. *See also* Genius, literary

372 · Index

Corsica, 254–55, 266–67, 270, 277n58. *See also* Boswell, James

Coventry, Francis, 214

Criticism, literary: and annotation, 33, 42; and art, 105–6, 110–12; attention to the text as essential to, 121–22, 127–28n37, 183–84, 288–89, 307n33; egotism of the critic in, 112–13, 131n61, 348–51, 364–65; ethical responsibilities of, 105–6, 116–18, 121–25, 130–31n56, 132n67, 183–84, 363–64; and foolishness, 122–23, 307n33; function of, 105–6, 111, 124–25; and gender, 114, 129–30n44, 297; and hobby-horses, 245n56, 315–16, 348–49; influence of political agendas on, 10, 178, 200–3, 207–8, 214–15, 271n3, 315, 353–54, 358, 361, 364; interpretative distortions of, 106–7, 288–89, 364–65; and politics (present-day), 10–11, 137–38, 148–49, 201–3, 315–16, 349, 353–54, 357–58; preoccupations shaping (present-day), 19, 21, 106–7, 113–14, 168–70, 214–15, 222–23, 245n56, 288–89, 315–16, 348–49, 352–53, 356–58, 361, 364–65; and recovery of lesser-known works, 214–15, 251, 343n69, 360–61; and subjectivity, 123–24, 132n67; as supplanting a work of art, 116–17, 169–70

Cross, Wilbur L., 85–87, 89, 93–94n6, 94n9

Cumberland, Richard, 251

Dante Alighieri, 19, 132n78, 156n17, 168, 169, 176–77, 188n10, 263, 317; *Divine Comedy, The,* 156n17, 263

Day, W. G., 88–89. *See also* "Unknown World, The"

Defoe, Daniel, 65, 213, 214, 301

De Morsan, Lefèvre, 23, 342n56, 60n40; *Manners and Customs of the Romans. Translated from the French, The,* 23. *See also* Norris, John, of Bemerton; Malebranche, Nicolas; Sterne, Laurence

Derrida, Jacques, 128n37, 166, 169, 196, 288, 353

Descartes, René, 34, 59n30, 179, 187n6, 263, 293–94, 323, 339–40n33, 362

De Voogd, Peter, 9–10, 315, 351. See also *Shandean, The*

D'Holbach, Baron, 258

Dickens, Charles, 4, 7, 9, 235, 286, 297, 357; artistic achievement of, 106–9, 115–16; collaboration with illustrators of, 103–4, 111 (*see also* Browne, Hablot Knight ["Phiz"]); and concepts of time, 110–11, 123; critical evaluations of, 113, 128n37; ethical considerations in the work of, 105–6, 114–15, 117–21, 132n78; in relation to Laurence Sterne, 101–5, 109–12, 126n3; sentimentalism in the work of, 115. *See also* Browne, Hablot Knight ("Phiz"); Levinas, Emmanuel

—*Dombey and Son:* artistic achievement of, 127n24; artistic shortcomings of, 122–23, 127n28, 131n61, 134n85; conclusion of, 116, 121, 134n89; critical evaluations of, 113–14, 129n43, 132–33n81; deathbed scene in, 109–12; economic discourses in, 133n84; ethical dimensions of, 117–23, 125, 130–31n57; gender criticism of, 114, 129–30n44, 134n85, 134n89; illustrations to, 103–6, 111; sentimentalism in, 108–10, 115, 117, 129n43, 134n85

Dickinson, Emily, 1, 5, 273n23, 360

Diderot, Denis, 68, 258

Disraeli, Benjamin, 156n20

Dodsley, Robert, 292

Donne, John, 21, 360

Doolittle, Thomas, 66–68

Dostoevsky, Feodor, 7–8, 132n78, 286

Draper, Eliza: portrait of, 170, 189n20, 190n28; removal to Bombay of, 172. *See also* Sterne, Laurence

—relationship with Laurence Sterne of, 167–68, 180, 184–85, 187–88n8, 188n10, 189n20, 254, 264, 268, 270, 347; and *Bramine's Journal,* 167–70, 172–76, 188n9, 189n20, 268

Dryden, John, 139, 159–60n49, 358

Dumas, Alexandre (fils): *Count of Monte Cristo, The,* 319

Dunton, John, 65–66, 76n10, 77n21; poetry of, 65–67, 72; as publisher, 65–66, 79n29; in relation to Laurence Sterne, 65, 76n7
—*Pulpit-Fool. A Satyr, The* (*Pulpit-Fool* Part 1), 62–63, 77n21, 79n29; approach toward religion of, 63–64, 69–70, 73, 77–78n23; comment on John Norris in, 72–74, 78n25, 79n28, 79n29; compared with Laurence Sterne's religious practice, 64–65, 70–71, 73–74, 75n5; contemporary references in, 66–69; depiction of preaching in, 63–65, 66–68, 70, 75n2; poetic style of, 63, 66; preface to, 63; satire of the clergy in, 63, 78n24
—*Second Part of the Pulpit-Fool. A Satyr* (*Pulpit-Fool* Part 2), 62–63, 64, 66, 69, 75n1, 77n21; religious attitudes of, 65–72, 78n24; two parts of, 62–63, 64
—works of: *Life and Errors of John Dunton . . . written by himself, The,* 76n7; *Voyage Round the World, A,* 65

D'Urfey, Thomas, 34, 71

Dutens, Louis, 262, 275n37

Editing, scholarly, 2–4, 212–13, 215–16, 356–62; and annotation, 2–3, 17–18, 23–24, 33, 216, 220–21, 226–27, 233; and finding sources, 8, 33, 35–36, 38–39, 92, 213–14, 216–17, 220–21. *See also* Criticism, literary

Eliot, George, 357, 358, 359

Eliot, T. S., 4, 9, 208; approach toward John Milton of, 142, 144, 153–54; and Christianity, 142–43, 153–54, 156n20; influence of Alexander Pope on, 138–39; and London, 140, 145–46, 357; and modernism, 142–43, 147, 160–61n43; political views of, 143, 156n20; works of, *Little Gidding,* 138; works of, *Waste Land, The,* 138–39, 140, 144
—*Love Song of J. Alfred Prufrock, The:* allusions in, 140–42, 156n17, 158n36; attitude toward urbanism in, 141–42, 144–46; and Christianity, 145–47; and London, 141–42; and *London* (poem), 140–42, 144–48, 151, 156n17; and John Milton, 144
—in relation to Samuel Johnson, 137–38; and Christianity, 138–39, 142–43, 148–50, 153–54; and the city (of London), 139–41, 144–46, 148–53, 155n12, 156n20; and literary allusions, 138–40, 143–44; and *London* (poem), 140, 141–42, 144–48, 151, 156n17; and shared ontological vision, 137–38

Enlightenment, the eighteenth-century, 138, 258, 265, 283, 287; definitions of, 176n51, 287; ideals of, 137, 144, 149–50, 153, 159n47, 258, 264–66, 270, 185–87, 290–91, 292–94, 302, 323–34; literature of, 5; relation to modernity of, 138, 283, 187, 287–88, 305n28; secularism of, 154, 265–66, 273–74n23, 288, 290–91, 302, 310n56, 323

Erasmus, Desiderius, 252, 264–65, 276n51, 282, 360; *Praise of Folly, In,* 264

Eusden, Laurence, 213, 237n7

Fawkes, Francis, 251

Fielding, Henry, 27n4, 79n29, 212, 214, 216, 218, 236n3, 279, 301, 352, 360
—works of: *Amelia,* 263n3; *Joseph Andrews,* 355; *Shamela,* 220; *Tom Jones,* 231, 355

Fitzgerald, Percy, 80–81, 85–87, 93n6, 96n23

Flaubert, Gustave, 286, 343n68, 359–60

Forster, E. M., 15, 23, 113

Fountayne, John, Dean of York, 62

Garrick, David, 251, 267

Gaskell, Elizabeth, 358

Gay, John, 139, 282, 358

Genius, literary: concept of, 4–5, 11, 249n71, 348–49, 352, 360–61, 362; nature of, 4, 6–9, 153, 250–51, 271n3, 278, 291, 315, 361–62, 363–64; present-day dismissal of, 7, 155n3, 249n71, 315, 349–50, 352,

374 · Index

Genius, literary—*continued*
  357; scope of, 6–9, 258, 275n37, 342n55,
  349. *See also* Conversation, between
  authors (as critical concept); Mediocrity
  (literary)
Gentleman's Magazine, The, 34, *81–82,*
  85–87, 239–40n19. *See also* "Unknown
  World, The"
Georgic (poetry), 143–45
Gibbon, Edmund, 251
Gide, André, 137; *The Counterfeiters,* 137
Gill, Thomas: *Vallis Eboracensis, 83–84*
God: City of (concept), 61n46, 159n48, 187;
  goodness of, 37, 46, 47–48, 125, 143–46,
  150, 167–68, 225, 268, 273–74n23, 295;
  grace of, 37–38, 41, 158n39, 262; judgment of, 166–67, 284, 321; nature of,
  6, 26, 38–41, 46, 57n19, 59n30, 60n40,
  121–22, 143–44, 157n28, 191n37, 193n47,
  206–207, 287, 301, 304n22, 306n31, 32–
  25; relationship with man of, 26, 36–37,
  40–41, 47, 56n14, 57n19, 143–46, 171–72,
  224, 248n67, 257, 259, 268, 291, 296, 302,
  310n56, 311n63, 324–25; unknowability
  of, 6, 50–51, 55n3, 217, 235–36, 285, 297,
  335–36. *See also* Christianity; Judaism;
  Religion
Goethe, Johann Wolfgang von, 177, 188n10,
  191n34, 210n6, 360
Goldsmith, Oliver, 139, 251, 357
Goodall, William, 214
Gramsci, Antonio, 112, 350, 353
Gray, Thomas, 357
Griffith, Richard, 187n7, 239–40n19,
  245n57, 272n13, 360

Hall, Bishop Joseph, 68–69
Hammond, Lansing Van der Heyden, 33–36
Hawkes, David, 350
Haywood, Eliza, 213, 214, 289, 358–59, 360
Hegel, Georg Wilhelm Friedrich, 200, 209,
  351, 362
Hegeman, Susan, 350
Heidegger, Martin, 119, 200, 362
Hogarth, William, 101–3

Homer, 19, 160n52, 315, 323, 327, 332–33,
  337n8, 340n34, 363; *Iliad, The,* 315–16,
  318; *Odyssey, The,* 178, 315–16
Hume, David, 17, 28n6, 64, 68, 196, 272–
  73n21, 279, 284

Ideation, eighteenth-century concept of,
  259–60, 309n52. *See also* Locke, John
Indeterminacy, in literature. *See under*
  Literature (Western)
Internet, the, as research tool, 10–11, 214–15,
  251; Seventeenth and Eighteenth Century Burney Newspapers Collection, the
  (dataset), 92, 96n22

Johnson, Samuel, 4, 9, 72, 95n17, 96n20,
  215, 221, 263, 352, 360; attitude toward
  John Milton of, 153–54, 157n26; and
  Christianity, 138, 142, 148–50, 157–58n28,
  273n22; concept of perfectibility in the
  writings of, 156–57n21; *Dictionary of
  the English Language, A,* 156–57n21,
  157n26, 221, 299, 312n71, 327, 338n13; and
  Enlightenment thought, 137–38; and
  lexicography, 2; and London, 144–45,
  155n12, 155n13, 159n48, 161n58 (see also
  under *London*); and modernism, 137–38,
  159n48, 161n58; relationship with James
  Boswell of, 155n13, 255, 257, 263, 266,
  277n62, 279; and Laurence Sterne, 137,
  138; views on literature of, 95n17, 155n4,
  263, 361; views on marriage of, 277n62
—in relation to T. S. Eliot, 137–39, 156n17;
  and Christianity, 138–39, 142–43, 148–
  50, 153–54; and the city (of London),
  139–41, 144–46, 148–53, 155n12, 156n20;
  and literary allusions, 138–40, 143–44;
  and *London,* 140, 141–42, 144–48, 151,
  156n17; and shared ontological vision,
  137–38
—*London:* attitude toward urbanism in,
  144–47, 148–50, 161n58; and Christianity, 140, 144–45, 148–50, 152–53; depiction of the French in, 147, 151–52, 156n20;
  and georgic poetry, 143–45; influence on

T. S. Eliot of, 139–40, 141–42, 144–48, 151, 156n17; and Juvenal, 139–46, 148–49, 151–52, 159–60n49, 161n58; and London, 140, 143–45, 147–48, 150–52; and John Milton, 153–54; political orientation of, 145, 147–48, 156n20, 158n30; role of "Thales" in, 157–58n28; as satire, 141, 145–47, 149–50, 158n30
—works of: *History of Rasselas, Prince of Abyssinia, The,* 2, 137, 250, 283; *Irene,* 157n28, 161n54; *Vanity of Human Wishes, The,* 138–39, 148, 224

Johnstone, Charles, 360

Joyce, James, 4, 9–10; aesthetic approach of, 196, 209–10n3, 327, 330, 333, 330n34, 343n68, 343n74, 364; *Finnegans Wake,* 209–10n3, 336, 364; indeterminacy in the works of, 19, 196; and modernism, 196, 305n21; in relation to Laurence Sterne (*see under* Sterne, Laurence, in relation to other writers); significance of Homer to, 316–17, 327; *Ulysses,* 160n53, 315–16, 327, 335, 337n5, 337n7, 342–43n65, 344n83
—*Portrait of the Artist as a Young Man, A:* aesthetic concepts in, 333, 334–35; books mentioned in, 314, 324, 337n3; Catholicism in, 319, 321, 324–25, 329, 338n13; character of Leopold Bloom in, 333–34; character of Stephen Dedalus in, 316–17, 319, 323–25, 328–31, 333, 342n62; childbirth in, 323–24; depiction of Dublin in, 319; depiction of school in, 317, 327, 329, 338n11; and Judaism, 333–34; "manliness" in, 319–21, 324; naming in, 330–31; relation with *The Iliad* of, 316–17; role of religion in, 316–17, 319–20, 325–26, 330–31, 333–36; role of the sermon in, 317, 321, 323–27, 333, 338n28, 339n30, 340n38; Scripture in, 317–18, 340n34; sexuality in, 319–20, 323–24, 326–27, 328–29, 331–32, 338n13, 342n65; structure of, 335–36, 344n79

Judaism, 2, 5, 25, 156n20, 182, 197–98, 208, 287, 333, 356–57

Juvenal, 139–42, 144–46, 148–49, 151–152,

156n20, 159–60n49, 161n58, 282–83. *See also* Johnson, Samuel

Kafka, Franz, 198, 359

Kant, Immanuel, 133, 196, 272–73n21, 362

Keats, John, 6, 29n14, 106, 200, 286, 291, 305n27, 333; and negative capability, 29n14, 305n27

Kelly, Hugh, 251

Keymer, Thomas, 212–15, 227, 236n1, 236n4, 244n54, 245n56, 257, 281–83

Kimber, Edward, 214

Krasznahorkai, László, 305n28

Lamb, Jonathan, 18–19, 24, 28–29n10, 290–91, 365

Law, William, 113, 157n21, 310n56

Lermontov, Mikhail, 359–61

Leslie, C. R., 101–2, *103,* 104–5, 109–12, 126n3, 126n4

Levinas, Emmanuel, 4, 5, 9, 362; ambiguity in the philosophy of, 168–69; approach toward literary criticism of, 106, 111–12, 112–13, 121–25, 127–28n37, 193n51; concept of hospitality of, 114–15; ethical concepts of, 115–18, 119, 121, 123–25, 129–30n44, 167–68, 170, 183–84, 186, 194n56; and expression, 105–6; and gender, 114, 129–30n44, 188n10, 190–91n29, 191n37, 191n38; indeterminacy in the philosophy of, 169–70; love and sexuality in the philosophy of, 174–78, 180–81, 184, 190–91n29, 191n38, 192n44, 192n46, 193–94n52, 194n56; and ontology, 105–6, 107–8, 126n15; political aspects of the philosophy of, 186; rebuttal of negation in the work of, 102–3; in relation to Charles Dickens, 106–7, 108–9, 112–14, 116–19, 128n41; in relation to Marcel Proust, 166, 169–71, 174–75, 177–78, 180–81, 184–85, 189–90n23, 192n46; in relation to Laurence Sterne (*see under* Sterne, Laurence, in relation to other writers); responsibility in the ethics of, 117–18, 130–31n57, 132n67; solitude in

376 · Index

Levinas, Emmanuel—*continued*
the philosophy of, 177–79, 185; subjectivity in the philosophy of, 123–24, 132n67,
132n67, 171–72, 174–75, 179, 190n24;
theory of the novel of, 108–10. *See also*
Baldessari, John; Dickens, Charles
—aesthetic theories of, 105–6; art and
meaning in, 105–7, 113, 123–24, 126n15;
art and mimesis in, 107, 168–69; art in
relation to time in, 110–11, 123; art and
unknowingness in, 107–8, 111, 121–22;
concept of the image in, 110–11, 115–16,
118–19; ethical principles of, 115–18,
123–25; relation of art to criticism in, 106,
111–12, 121–23, 127–28n37; relation of
art to the novel in, 108–110; theological
implications of art in, 107–8, 121–22
—concept of the "other" of, 102–3, 113–15,
127n28, 167–68, 170–71, 174–75, 177–78,
180, 183, 189–90n23, 191n37, 193n50; ethical implications of, 115; and expression of
the face, 102–3, 115
—works of: *Otherwise than Being,* 190n24,
194n56; *Time and the Other,* 188n10,
189–90n23, 193n50
Levy, Amy, 2, 9, 141–42, 155–56n14, 156n20,
356–59
*Life and Memoirs of Mr. Ephraim Tristram
Bates, The,* 214–15, 234
Literature (Western), 3–4, 6, 161n58, 175,
218, 276n51, 286, 340n34; characters
in, 122–23; eighteenth-century, 5, 8, 34,
79n28, 88–89, 213–14, 248n67, 250–51,
281–83, 300–301, 351–52; and indeterminacy, 15–19, 168–70, 306–207, 227,
287–90, 321–22; and literary genius (*see*
Genius, literary); and pedagogy, 3–7, 10–
11, 136–37, 123–45, 238–39n14, 287–88,
351–61 (*see also* Pedagogy [university]);
and reading (as practice), 3–4, 6–7, 16–
17, 63, 115–16, 165–66, 196–97, 215–16,
222–23, 234–35, 238–39n14, 287–88, 291,
301–2, 314–15, 352–53, 359; in relation to
philosophy, 112–13, 248n67 (*see also* Levi-

nas, Emmanuel); in relation to theology,
5–8, 79n28, 142–43, 213–14, 286, 340n34;
relation to Truth of, 6–9, 22, 106, 124–25,
333–36, 340n34; and unknowingness,
7–8, 9–10, 18–19, 251–52, 285–86; value
of, 3–4, 201, 235–56, 286–88, 348–49,
351–52, 360–61, 365. *See also* Canon, the
literary; Criticism, literary
Locke, John, 263; concept of identity in the
work of, 285–86, 295–97, 309–10n52,
310n56, 313n75; and consciousness, 294–
95, 307n34, 310n53, 311n61; empiricism in
the work of, 1, 71, 180; epistemology of,
5, 28n8, 214, 239n19, 285–86, 287, 310n56;
*Essay concerning Human Understand-
ing, An,* 5, 20, 31n22, 34–35, 50, 55n3,
60n41, 71, 214, 218, 248n67, 260, 284,
310n56; and ideation, 55n3; and the limits
of human knowledge, 287, 293–94; in
relation to John Norris, 34–35, 49–50,
55n3, 60n41, 71, 181, 186–87n6, 239n19,
284–86, 305n26; in relation to religion,
28n8, 248n67, 285–86, 297, 310n56; in
relation to Laurence Sterne, 28n8, 31n22,
35, 49–50, 180–81, 238n9, 260, 279, 284–
85, 305n23, 308n40, 309n50, 309–10n52,
314; theory of language of, 305n23
—works of, 55n3, 238n9, 239n19, 248n67;
"Examination of P. Malebranche's
Opinion of Seeing All Things in God,
An," 55n3; *Letter Concerning Toleration,
A,* 248n67; *Reasonableness of Christianity, The,* 218, 248n67; *Two Treatises on
Government,* 248n67
London: in the eighteenth century, 138–
39, 147–48, 150–51, 152–53, 155n13;
eighteenth-century culture of, 45, 170,
225, 253, 352; and fog, 141; Great Fire of,
149–50, 160n52; in literature, 108–9,
138–54, 155n12, 155–56n14, 159n48, 207,
231–32, 251–52, 356–57; in the nineteenth
century, 141; in relation to Laurence
Sterne, 45, 169–70, 225, 252–53, 352; in
relation to religion, 149–50; and science,

140; in the twentieth century, 140–41. *See also* Boswell, James; Eliot, T. S.; Johnson, Samuel

Lucian, 289

Mackenzie, Henry: *Man of Feeling, The,* 251

Malebranche, Nicolas, 34, 55n3, 56n14, 59n30, 69n30, 72, 79n29, 178–79, 182, 187n6, 193n47, 193n51; *Search after Truth,* 79n29. *See also* Norris, John, of Bemerton

Manley, Delarivier, 213, 358

Mann, Thomas, 3, 44; *Magic Mountain,* 3

Maritain, Jacques, 145

Mechanism (philosophical concept), 60n40, 294

Medalle, Lydia. *See* Sterne, Lydia

Mediocrity (literary), 4–7, 250–51. *See also* Canon, the literary; Genius, literary

Melville, Herman, 355

Milton, John, 5, 125, 144, 153–54, 157n26, 161–62n67, 169, 213, 234, 247n64, 301, 350, 361–63; *Paradise Lost,* 121, 142, 153–54, 157n26, 161–62n67, 247n64, 362

MLA International Bibliography, 3, 356–67, 358

Modernism: nature of, 150–52, 196–98, 200–208, 276n51; in relation to post-modernism, 136, 138, 154–55n3, 160n53, 196–97, 206–208, 209–10n3; in relation to religion, 140, 154, 160n53, 208; in relation to Laurence Sterne, 4, 65, 136–38, 197–99, 209–10n3, 314. *See also* Johnson, Samuel; Schulz, Bruno; Woolf, Virginia

Montaigne, Michel de: influence on Laurence Sterne of, 16, 20–21, 28–29n10, 30n18, 32, 35, 44, 177–78, 179, 192n39, 211n22, 236, 290, 307n36, 326, 342–43n65, 360; philosophy of, 20–21, 30n18, 192n39, 236; in relation to James Boswell, 260, 272n11. *See also* Skepticism

More, Henry, 36, 48, 51, 56n14, 59n35. *See also* Norris, John, of Bemerton

Musil, Robert, 235, 349–50, 356; *Man Without Qualities, The,* 235, 349–50

Newman, Cardinal John Henry, 64

Nietzsche, Friedrich, 196–98, 202, 271n7, 315; in relation to Laurence Sterne, 27, 122, 136, 210n6, 315, 337n3

Norris, John, of Bemerton, 71–72, 181, 239n16, 269; career of, 5, 33–34, 72–73; and clerical politics, 59n35; *Letters Concerning the Love of God,* 2, 34, 42, 47, 55n3, 193n47; philosophical thought of, 5, 34, 43–44, 46–47, 59n30, 60n40, 71, 75n25, 79n28, 193n51, 239n18; physical love in the works of, 42–49, 57–58n22, 58n26, 58n27, 79n28, 193n47; poetry of, 72–73, 79n28; in relation to Mary Astell, 2, 48–49; in relation to John Dunton, 70–74, 78n25, 70n29; in relation to John Locke, 5, 34, 50, 55n3, 71, 78n26, 239n18, 305n26; in relation to Laurence Sterne (*see under* Sterne, Laurence, in relation to other writers)
—religious thought of, 36–37, 46–47, 48–50, 79n28, 306; and the afterlife, 53–54, 60–61n46; and the body, 40–41, 47, 57n19, 57–58n22, 58n25, 59n30, 59n31, 60n40; innate goodness of man in, 47; limitations of human knowledge in, 50–52, 59n32, 60n45, 182, 286–87; nature of grace in, 41; Neoplatonism in, 2, 5, 34, 36–37, 47, 51, 55–56n9, 193–94n52; and other denominations, 47–49; and preparedness for heaven, 37–39, 40–41, 53–54, 56n14; in relation to sensual pleasures, 36–37; and salvation, 41
—religious writings of, 34–35, 38–39, 41, 44–45, 51–52, 57n17, 58n27, 71–72, 78n27, 70n29, 216–17, 284–87; comments on sermon writing in, 55n8; Scriptural reference in, 38, 50–51, 60n41
—works of: *Account of Reason and Faith, An,* 34; *Christian Blessedness,* 34, 40, 44, 56, 78n26, 78n27; *Collection of Miscellanies, A,* 34, 58n26, 58n27, 277n61; *Concerning Christian Prudence,* 34, 59n35, 79n29; *Cursory Reflections upon a*

378 · Index

Norris, John, of Bemerton—*continued*
Book Call'd "An Essay on Human Under-
standing," 55n3, 78n26; *Essay Towards the*
Theory of the Ideal or Intelligible World,
An, 34, 60n40, 71, 239n18; *Idea of Hap-*
piness, An, 34, 58n25; *Practical Discourses*
upon the Beatitudes; Practical Treatise
concerning Humility, 34, 41, 72; *Reason*
and Religion, 34, 57n17; *Theory and*
Regulation of Love, The, 34, 42, 47, 57n19,
58n27, 193n47

Oratory: art of, the, 203, 237n4; and
eighteenth-century preaching, 63
Orrery, John Boyle, Earl of, 252, 278;
Remarks on the Life and Writings of Dr.
Jonathan Swift, 278. *See also* Boswell,
James; Swift, Jonathan
Orwell, George, 3, 105
Ovid, 225

Parnell, J. T., 55–6n9, 76n6, 78n25, 212, 214–
15, 226, 236n1, 236–37n4
Pascal, Blaise, 152–53; *Pensées,* 142, 194n56
Pastoral (literary mode), 139–40, 144–46,
152. *See also* Eliot, T. S.; Georgic; Johnson, Samuel; Juvenal
Pedagogy (university), 6, 287–88; and
academic conferences, 10, 351–52; as
academic profession, 351–53, 361–62;
curricula of, 137–38, 287, 353–58, 361–63;
and the literary canon, 7, 9–10, 352–58,
360–62; and literature, 7, 10–11, 136–37,
123–45, 238–39n14, 287–88, 351–61. *See*
also Canon, the literary; Universities
Petrarch, Francesco, 168
Petronius, 225, 289, 312–13n73
Philips, Ambrose, 213, 237n7
"Phiz." *See* Browne, Hablot Knight ("Phiz");
Dickens, Charles
Plato, 41–42, 43–44, 48, 49, 54, 58n25,
58n27, 106–7, 111, 122, 126n15, 128n37, 168,
181–82, 193–94n52, 256, 334–36, 338n13.
See also Levinas, Emmanuel; Norris,
John, of Bemerton

Platonism, Cambridge (Neoplatonism),
34, 38–39, 41, 47–48, 51, 55–56n9, 58n25,
71, 182, 187n6, 193–94n52, 259. *See also*
Christianity; Norris, John, of Bemerton
Politics, in relation to literature. *See under*
Criticism, literary
Pope, Alexander, 169, 309n50, 316, 354,
358, 360–61; and eighteenth-century
literature, 65, 95–96n17, 139, 213, 281–83,
308n44, 347–48, 351–52, 364; in relation
to later literature, 138–39, 234–35; in
relation to Laurence Sterne, 62–63, 205,
281–83, 360; religious sentiment in the
works of, 224, 242–43n45; and satire, 69,
237n7, 251–52, 267, 281–83; writings of,
62, 278–79, 292–93, 302, 337n8, 347–48.
See also Scriblerians, the; Swift, Jonathan
—works of: *Dunciad, The,* 69, 77n21, 214,
221, 279–80, 283, 302, 337n8; *Key to the*
Lock, The, 279, 348; *Memoirs of P.P. Clerk*
of This Parish, 348, 352; *Miscellanies* (with
Jonathan Swift), 252, 278–80, 348; *Peri*
Bathous (The Art of Sinking in Poetry), 62,
230, 252, 278, 279, 283, 348
Postmodernism: nature of, 154–55n3,
160–61n53, 196–97, 207–8; in relation to
modernism, 138, 154–55n3, 196–97, 206–
208; in relation to Laurence Sterne, 136,
209–10n3, 210n5. *See also* Theory, literary
Preaching, eighteenth-century. *See* Sermons
(eighteenth-century)
Prior, Matthew, 95n17, 139, 347, 357, 360
Proust, Marcel, 238, 359–60; approach toward travel of, 178; concept of the other
in the work of, 165, 185–86; homosexuality in the works of, 170; love and sexuality
in the work of, 175–77, 180–81, 192n46;
political sentiments in the works of,
186; in relation to modernism, 165, 177,
202; in relation to Samuel Richardson,
234–35; in relation to Laurence Sterne
(*see under* Sterne, Laurence, in relation
to other writers); sensibility in the works
of, 171, 189n22; solitude in the works of,
178–79. *See also* Levinas, Emmanuel

—*À la recherche du temps perdu: Captive, The* (La prisonnière), 166, 177, 185; character of Marcel in, 185; love and sexuality in, 175–77; motif of captivity in, 185–86; role of Albertine in, 175, 177, 185, 196n21
—in relation to Emmanuel Levinas, 4; and the concept of the other, 168–69, 170–71, 175, 189–90n23, 193n50; and the concept of sensibility, 170–71; and indeterminateness, 169–70; and love and sexuality, 175–77, 180, 192n46; and morality, 170
Publishing, scholarly, 361–62
Pynchon, Thomas, 238; *V.,* 3, 238

Rabelais, François, 192, 342n56; approach toward learning of, 22; *Gargantua and Pantagruel,* 213, 280; humor of, 282; and modernism, 329–30
—influence on Laurence Sterne of, 16, 20, 22, 253, 360, 365; and borrowings, 16, 20, 31n25, 35; and *Tristram Shandy,* 20, 22, 25–26, 62, 202, 308–309n45, 329
Religion: as cultural inheritance, 138; hostility toward sexuality of, 326–27; nineteenth-century, 131n61; and pleasure, 53–54; practice of, 6; seventeenth-century, 65–69, 248n67, 259, 262–63; social dimensions of, 73–74, 248n68; and truth, 208. *See also* Christianity; God; Judaism
—eighteenth-century, 6; and Enlightenment, 258; pervasive nature of, 147; and politics, 317–18; publications relating to, 225; and science, 6, 57n19; and sentimentalism, 258; and theology, 64–65
Restoration drama, 213, 219. *See also* Richardson, Samuel
Richardson, Samuel: bawdry in the works of, 218–20; *Clarissa,* 222–23, 227, 231, 234, 236n1, 239n17, 240n21, 246–47n62, 286; and eighteenth-century literature, 95n17, 226–27, 241n27, 301, 352; and the eighteenth-century novel, 212–214, 216, 236n3, 236n6; literary style of, 240n21; politics in the works of, 247–48n66;

in relation to Henry Fielding, 212, 214, 216, 218–20, 236n3, 301; in relation to Laurence Sterne, 239–40n19 (*see also under* Sterne, Laurence, in relation to other writers); and religion, 79n29, 216–17, 233–36, 238n19, 242n41, 242n44, 246–47n52, 247n54; sentimentalism in the works of, 74, 216–17; sexuality in the works of, 218; social circle of, 218–19, 231, 236n6, 240n22, 245n60, 246–47n52
—*Sir Charles Grandison:* annotation of (scholarly), 212–13; bawdry in, 218–22, 241n23; Cambridge University Press edition of, 2, 212; character of Sir Charles Grandison in, 221, 226–28, 229–31; Christian discourse in, 222–27, 232–33, 242n40; composition of, 245n60; conclusion of, 231–32, 248–49n70; contemporary reception of, 222, 246–47n52; critical appraisal of, 230–31, 345–46n61; gesture in, 212, 236–37n4; literary allusions in, 213; and pastoral, 144; polygamy in (implied), 231–32, 235, 240–41n22; and Restoration drama, 213, 219; in relation to *Clarissa,* 223; in relation to Laurence Sterne, 212, 216–17, 219–35; sentimentalism in, 222–27; sexuality in, 219–2, 243–44n48; travel in, 229–31
—works of: *Pamela,* 231, 355; *Pamela II,* 220
Richter, Johann Paul Friedrich (Jean Paul), 360
Romanticism (English), 138
Rosewell, Thomas, 67–68
Ross, Ian Campbell, 87, 89
Rousseau, Jean-Jacques, 68, 254–59, 267, 276n50, 360; *Émile,* 258–59
Rowe, Elizabeth, 8, 90–92, 93n1, 94n8, 95n17, 95–96n20, 96n22, 96–97n24. *See also* Stogdon, Hubert; "Unknown World, The"
Rowe, Nicholas: *Fair Penitent, The,* 257
Rubens, Albert, 21–23; *De Re Vestiaria Veterum,* 21
Russian Revolution, the, 4, 192n42. *See also* Shklovsky, Viktor

380 · Index

Sacheverell, Henry, 147, 158n42
Sartre, Jean-Paul, 3, 359–60
Satire: classical, 141, 144–46, 160–61n41, 282–83, 289 (*see also* Juvenal); eighteenth-century, 76n7, 139–40, 146–47, 251–52, 278–84, 286, 291–94, 301–2, 308n44; of the eighteenth-century church, 62, 62–64, 70–71, 230, 279, 348; nature of, 22, 213, 252, 280–81, 282–84, 286, 289, 292–93, 296–97, 299, 302, 308n44; twentieth-century, 141–45. *See also* Eliot, T. S.; Scriblerians, the
Schulz, Bruno, 3, 197–98, *205*; in relation to modernism, 4, 9, 207–9; in relation to Laurence Sterne, 4, 9, 136–37, 198–204, 314
—*Street of Crocodiles,* 197–98; father figure in, 198–200, 202; in relation to Laurence Sterne, 198–200; sexuality in, 202–3
—works of: *Messiah, The,* 198; *Sanatorium under the Sign of the Hourglass,* 198
Science: as academic subject, 353, 356; eighteenth-century, 6, 57n19; idealization of, 157n28, 204–7; limitations of, 207–208; nature of, 6, 136, 299; and progress, 136, 140, 142, 155n13, 204–5, 285, 305n23
Scott, Reverend George, 80, 85–88. *See also under* Sterne, Laurence; "Unknown World, The"
Scriblerian, The (journal), 307n33, 351, 358
Scriblerians, the, 9, 76n7, 205, 252, 278, 286–302, 308n44, 309–10n52, 328, 339–40n33, 348
—*Memoirs of Martinus Scriblerus, The,* 280–81, 323; authorship of, 280–81, 300, 309–10n52, 311n59; concept of the soul in, 293–94, 297–98, 310n53, 312n79; in relation to *Gulliver's Travels,* 280–81; in relation to Laurence Sterne, 9, 279–81, 291–92, 297–98, 302, 309–10n52; satire in, 292–94, 300–301
—*Memoirs of Martinus Scriblerus, The,* the "Double Mistress" episode, 291–92, 297; concept of doubleness in, 298–99, 313n75; concept of self-love in, 292–93;

concept of the soul in, 297–300; debates about generation in, 297–98, 312n69; epistemology in, 294–95; form of, 292–93; generation in, 293–94; historical contexts of, 297; legal debates in, 297, 300–301
Secularism, 286, 321–22, 334; in the eighteenth century, 59n30, 63–65, 69–71, 153–54, 214, 216–17, 258, 265; as impediment to discussing literature (especially eighteenth-century), 3–4, 6, 28n8, 51, 258, 260–61, 273–74n21; in relation to the city, 144–46, 150, 156n20, 159n49. *See also* Christianity; Theology
Sensibility: eighteenth-century, 170, 259, 265, 273–74n23, 281; and hospitality, 116–17; nature of, 46–47, 170–71, 181–82, 259, 270; in relation to sentimentalism, 115, 189n22; and sensuality, 190–91n29, 268
Sentimentalism: and economics, 185; eighteenth century, 55–56n9, 63–64, 70–71, 74, 185, 338n23; nature of, 67–68, 189n22, 216–17, 227, 318; reactions against, 108–10, 115, 129n43, 134n85; in relation to secularism, 63, 64, 69, 70–71; in relation to religion, 47, 55–56n9, 167, 216–17, 222–25, 227–33; and sympathy, 174, 185–86. *See also* Dickens, Charles; Sensibility
Sermons (eighteenth-century): different types of, 74; prolific quantity of, 74, 223–24; and pulpit preaching, 65, 67, 75–76n6; rhetorical skill of, 70–71; and sermon writing, 66–71. *See also* Dunton, John; Joyce, James; Norris, John, of Bemerton; Sterne, Laurence
Sermons (seventeenth-century), 66–69, 248n67
Sextus Empiricus, 16, 27
Shaftesbury, Anthony Ashley Cooper, 3rd Earl of, 64, 68
Shakespeare, William, 4, 19, 26, 29n14, 107, 213, 267, 290, 297, 343n68, 363; *Hamlet,* 146, 158n39, 171, 213
Shandean, The (journal), 4, 10, 88–89, 315
Sheridan, Richard Brinsley, 357

Sherlock, Thomas, 242n44

Sherlock, William, 223–24, 225, 232, 242n44; *Practical Discourse Concerning Death, A,* 223–24, 242n44. *See also* Richardson, Samuel

Skepticism, 17, 27, 28n9, 30n18, 44, 49, 55n3, 150, 178, 201

Shklovsky, Viktor, 4, 136, 192n42; *Sentimental Journey, A,* 4, 192n42. *See also* Russian Revolution, the

Slavery (eighteenth-century), 185, 266–67, 276n57, 354

Smith, Adam, 250, 273–74n23, 353, 356; *Theory of Moral Sentiments, A,* 250, 273–74n23

Smith, Charlotte, 356

Smollett, Tobias, 27n4, 151, 212–13, 214, 229, 358, 364, *Adventures of Roderick Random, The,* 2; *History and Adventures of an Atom, The,* 27n4; *Travels through France and Italy,* 214

Sorbonne, the (university). *See under* Sterne, Laurence

Spencer, John, 21, 24–25, 31n24; *De Legibus Hebræorum Ritualibus,* 21, 24

Standen, Joseph, 93n1, 95n17

Steele, Richard, 347, 358; *Spectator, The,* 71

Stephen, Leslie, 64–65

Stearne, Bishop John, 307n33

Sterne, Laurence: adaptations of, 352; aposiopesis in the works of, 53–54, 166, 176, 211n23; attitude toward death of, 20, 39, 54–55n1, 86–87, 166–68, 174, 189n20, 257, 321–22; body in the works of, the, 36–37, 41–42, 47–48, 57–58n22, 181–83, 187n7, 203–204, 216–18, 228–30, 239–40n19, 259–62, 268–70, 289–90, 298–99, 306n32, 308n44, 340–41n45; catalogue of the library of, 31n24; celebrity of, 45, 137, 170, 225, 253, 272n14, 277n58; correspondence of (*Letters*), 30n18, 85–86, 93n4, 94n7, 175–76, 253–54, 290; death in the work of, 344n80; death of, 80, 86, 168, 174, 251, 252, 257, 270; and eighteenth-century literary

culture, 170, 225; and eighteenth-century novels, 27n4, 212–16, 226–27, 236n1, 238n10, 244n53, 250, 259–60, 281–83, 286–87, 300–301; gender in the works of, 176–77, 186, 190n26, 289, 354; humor in the works of, 17–18, 29n16, 177, 192n46, 204, 284, 286, 289, 302, 332; illustrations to the works of, 101–5, 111–12; imitations of the works of, 65; indeterminacy in the works of, 15–26, 27n3, 28–29n10, 29n16, 31–32n26, 49–50, 168–69, 227, 245n56, 283, 289–91, 321–22; internationalism of, 248n69; irony in the works of, 273–74n23, 308n44, 322, 338n10, 339n30, 341n51; and learnedness, 30–31n20, 31n22; and modernism, 4, 65, 136–38, 197–99, 209–10n3, 314; narrative modes of, 16–17, 20–21, 26, 197, 209–10n3, 214, 259–60, 281, 314, 336, 364; physical illness of, 166, 177–79, 185, 203, 214, 254, 268; political issues in the works of, 62, 185–86, 302, 354; posthumous works of, 80, 85–86, 94n7; religious beliefs of, 37–38, 65, 69–70, 75–76n6, 79n28, 166–67, 232–34, 248n67, 257–60, 266, 284, 293–94, 302, 309–10n53 (*see also* Christianity; Norris, John, of Bemerton); as satirist, 19, 22, 62, 205, 210n17, 225–28, 230, 252, 257, 279–86, 289, 291, 296–97, 302, 308n44, 308–309n45, 322, 332, 339–40n33, 348; sensibility in the works of, 30n17, 57n19, 170–74, 181–82, 256–59, 265–70, 273–74n23, 276n57, 281; sentimentalism in the works of, 55–56n9, 57n19, 62–63, 67–68, 70–71, 109, 173–74, 185–86, 216–36, 338n23; *Sermons of Mr. Yorick, The,* 66, 225, 275n36; sexuality in the works of, 192n46; skepticism in the works of, 16–17, 22–23, 27, 28n8, 30n18, 49, 178–79, 199, 201–2; Stapfer fragment, the, 85; travels of, 192n42, 252–53, 254, 275n37

—*Bramine's Journal, The,* 167, 187–88n8; composition of, 170, 176, 254; and Eliza Draper, 167–70, 172–76, 188n9, 189n20, 268; obsessive fantasy in, 170, 172–74,

382 · Index

Sterne, Laurence—*continued*
182, 184, 187–88n8, 188n10, 188n9,
190n26, 264, 268, 270, 315, 347–48;
publication of, 166, 189n16; in relation
to *A Sentimental Journey,* 166–68, 174–
75, 176, 189n20, 254, 268; in relation to
religion, 168; style of, 166–67; unrecip-
rocated sentiment in, 172–75
—Florida Edition of the Works of, the, 2,
241n31; *Letters, The,* 93n4, 315; *Life and
Opinions of Tristram Shandy, Gentleman, The,* 2; *Miscellaneous Writings,*
279–80, 348; *Sentimental Journey
through France and Italy, A,* 256, 258;
Sermons: The Notes, 277n62; *Tristram
Shandy: The Notes,* 18, 23, 38–39, 215,
216–17, 225–26, 276n55, 284, 292–95,
329
—*Life and Opinions of Tristram Shandy,
Gentleman, The:* "Abuses of conscience,
The" in, 21, 24, 275n36, 304n24, 322,
326–27, 339n27, 339n28; annotation of,
18, 24; argumentation in, 298–99, 318;
bawdry of, 17–18, 167, 220, 228–29, 239–
40n19, 289–90, 330–33; borrowings
in, 27n4, 29n12, 29n13, 31n23, 36–39,
42–44, 55–56n9, 182, 213, 290; "*cervantick* tone" in, 266; character of Uncle
Toby in, 9, 16, 19–20, 25, 31–32n26, 43,
64, 105, 176, 198, 199–201, 205–206,
208–209, 211n33, 221–22, 227–28, 243–
44n48, 208, 309n50, 315–18, 328–32,
339n30; character of Walter Shandy in,
16, 24, 71–72, 182, 192n46, 199–204,
208, 229, 232–33, 290, 292–93, 298–300,
315–18, 320–26, 327–32, 341n53, 344n79,
348; character of Yorick in, 23, 25–26,
29n14, 35, 45, 55–56n1, 53–64, 170–71,
213, 316–17; childbirth in, 297–98, 324;
clothing in, 21–24; composition of, 33,
65, 250, 253–54, 281, 292; death in, 39,
54–55n1, 55–56n9, 109, 203–204, 316,
321–22, 327–28, 330–31, 339n31, 342n60,
344n80; documents in, 18–19, 21–26,
199–200; doubling of the self in, 170–

71; "Ernulphus's Curse," 16, 21, 24, 77n21,
327, 341n50; false citations in, 23–24;
false learning in, 25–26, 200–201; fictional influences on (possible), 76n7, 212–16,
226–27, 234, 236n1; fragmentariness in,
198–99; generational theories in, 298–99,
309–10n52, 326; genius of, the, 6, 363–
64; Homeric qualities of, 315–16; human
limitations explored in, 50–53, 203–204,
232–33, 239–40n19, 283–87, 304n20, 322;
illustrations of, 101–106; imitations of,
65; initial reception of, 45, 137, 170, 225,
239–40n19, 253, 272n14, 277n58; listing
in, 21–22; love in, 43–44, 203–204,
227–28; masculinity in, 199–201; narrative modes of, 16–17, 253, 282; narrative
modes of (determinacy), 15–27, 201–204;
narrative modes of (indeterminacy), as
problematic interpretation, 15–27, 27n3,
28–29n10, 31–32n26, 287–91; negative
reactions against, 10–11; opinion in, 199,
318, 341n51; paternal role as depicted
in, 19–20, 50, 227–29, 320–21, 332–33;
and pedagogy, 352–53, 355–56; preaching in, 63–64; rhetorical strategies in,
236–37n4; reader's role in, 18–19, 29n16;
reason in, 36, 38–39; religious discourse
in, 50–51, 64–65, 75–76n6, 79n28, 203,
207–208, 269, 304n24, 329–31; "riddles
and mysteries" in, 28n8, 29n14, 50–51,
282–87, 294; as satire, 279–80, 298–302,
348; sentimentalism in, 109, 186–87n6,
332–33; sexuality in, 48, 180–81, 199–200,
204, 228–29, 289–90, 293, 300, 324,
326–32; skepticism in, 17–18, 28n8, 30n18,
283–85; "Slawkenbergius's Tale," 20–21,
199, 202; Sorbonne, the (university) in,
16, 18–20, 24, 341n50; sources in, 21–26,
212–14, 339–40n33; travel in, 39–40,
228–29, 254; *Tristrapædia,* the, 20, 24,
199, 328; warfare in, 23, 205–6, 207–8,
211n33, 228–29
—*Political Romance, A,* 33, 64, 75n1, 281; as
church satire, 62, 75n1, 230; printing of,
292; Scriblerian influence on, 279

—"Rabelaisian Fragment," the, 237n6, 279; composition of, 33, 62, 213, 230, 281, 348; publication of, 94n7

—relationship with Eliza Draper of, 189n20, 254, 347; ambiguous sexual nature of, 167–68, 184–85; and journal-writing, 264, 268; as obsessive fantasy, 180, 187–88n8, 188n10, 270; significance of portrait to, 170, 189n20, 190n28. See also *Bramine's Journal*; Draper, Eliza

—*Sentimental Journey through France and Italy, A:* ambiguity in, 169, 228; and pedagogy, 354–55; appeal to modernity of, 136–37; borrowings in, 35–36, 39, 256–57, 263–64, 269; censorship of, 10; communication in, 177–80, 183–85, 248n69, 319–20; composition of, 175–76, 245n57, 251, 254; concept of captivity in, 175, 185–86, 234; concept of the other in, 173–75, 178–85; concept of the other in, as egotistical fantasy, 174–75; death in, 166–67; economic aspects of, 194–95n62; ending of, 166–67, 211n23; Enlightenment ideals in, 334; genius of, 278; Homeric qualities of, 316; human limitations as explored in, 58n26; imitations of, 4; identity of the self in, 171–72; isolation in, 179, 274–75n35; literary contexts of, 221–22, 226, 232–33, 255–56; love in, 180–82; publication of, 39, 187n7, 254; quixotism in, 264–65, 270; in relation to *Bramine's Journal,* 166–70, 175–76, 189n20, 254, 268; religious discourse in, 35–39, 79n28, 166–68, 181, 211n21, 225, 228–30, 232–33, 248n69, 262–63, 269; satire in, 181–82; sensibility in, 258–59; sensuality in, 47–49, 57n19, 181–82, 228, 261–62, 274–75n35, 320, 333–34; sentimentalism in, 57n19, 167, 228–30, 251; sexuality in, 166–67, 169–70, 179–85, 194n55, 198–99, 228, 232–33, 261–62, 319–20, 326; travel in, 178–79, 189n20, 232–33

—sermons of: "Abuses of conscience, The," 60n41, 275n36; borrowings in, 33–54,

186–87n6, 277n61, 277n62, 285, 296; contingency in, 235, 246–47n62; earthly vanity in, 51, 59n31, 61–62n46, 186–87n6, 225; happiness in, 43–45, 52–54; human limitations in, 46–47, 49, 52–53, 60n41, 225, 284–85, 296, 304n20, 306n32; love in, 49, 269; occasionality of, 57n20; and practical divinity (vs. polemical), 66, 71–72, 76n11, 237n6; and preaching, 63, 66, 70, 75–76n6, 236–37n4; preparation for the afterlife in, 36–38, 47–47, 53–54, 56n14, 181, 225; publication of, 66, 94n7, 225, 275n36; reason in, 40–41, 52–53, 269; redemption in, 42, 296; in relation to Laurence Sterne's fiction, 28n8, 35–54, 55–56n9, 60n41, 62–63, 79n28; rhetorical style of, 64–65, 67, 69–70; "riddles and mysteries" in, 284–85; self-knowledge in, 304n20; sexuality in, 42–43, 49, 269, 323–27; sources for, 5, 70, 73, 75–76n6, 232, 243n47, 248n67, 277n61, 277n62, 285, 296, 306n32; subscriptions to, 275n37, 276n54; theology of, 75–76n6, 186–87n6, 225, 232, 321; worship in, 306n32. *See also* Dunton, John; Norris, John, of Bemerton

Sterne, Laurence, in relation to other writers

—Boswell, James, 9, 250–302, 360; acquaintance with (unlikely), 252–54, 303n3; contemporaneity of, 250; and parallel travels abroad, 252–54, 260–61, 275n37; and romantic quixotism, 263–65, 268–70; and sexuality, 254, 261–62, 268–69, 274–75n35, 276n53; and shared religious anxieties, 254–55, 257–61, 267–68

—Joyce, James, 4, 9–10, 19, 196–97, 209–10n3, 314–16, 336; and aesthetic vision, 316–17, 322, 331–34; and the conscience, 324–25; and generation, 317–20, 323–24; and masculinity, 319–21; and paternal figures, 319–20, 328–29, 330; and religion, 317–25, 329–30; and sermons, 321–29; and sexuality, 317, 319–20, 323–24, 326–27, 331–32; and shared Homeric qualities, 314–16

384 · Index

—Levinas, Emmanuel, 4, 166, 186–87n6, 216; and aesthetic vision, 102–103; and art, 102, 103; and concept of the other, 166, 168–70, 171–75, 177–80, 183–84, 185–86; and indeterminacy, 166–67; and self-doubt, 170–72, 179, 190n24; and sexuality, 180–81, 183–84, 192n46

—Norris, John, of Bemerton, 5, 33–54, 216–17; critical work on, 33–35, 55–56n9, 75n25, 96–97n24, 277n61; and borrowings, 40–41, 193n51, 304n20; and fiction, 79n28, 181–82, 269; in the "Rabelaisian Fragment," 33; in *A Sentimental Journey,* 35–39, 48–49, 181, 269, 277n61; and sermons, 33–35, 36–37, 44–47, 50–51, 52–54, 60n41, 60–61n49, 79n28, 181–82, 187, 239n18, 269, 284–87; and theology, 59n31, 60–61n49, 73–74, 232, 269, 304n20; in *Tristram Shandy* of, 38–39, 41–43, 50–51, 53, 55–56n9, 182

—Pope, Alexander, 62–63, 205, 281–83, 360

—Proust, Marcel, 3–4, 9, 136, 165, 185, 196, 234, 314; and motif of captivity, 185, 196n21 (see also *Captive, The* [*La prison-nière*]); and *A Sentimental Journey,* 165–66, 185; and sexual desire, 166, 192n46

—Richardson, Samuel, 9, 212–13, 216, 236n1, 279, 360; and bawdry, 218–21, 222–24; and the body, 218–19, 220, 230–33; and Christian sentimentalism, 225–27, 230, 232–33; and gesture, 213–14; and sexuality, 218–20, 230–31; and *Sir Charles Grandison,* 212, 216–17, 219–35, 245n59

—Schulz, Bruno, 4, 9, 136–37, 198–204, 314

—Scriblerians, the, 9; and the "Double Mistress," 291–302; and *The Memoirs of Martinus Scriblerus,* 279–302, 309–10n52; and satire, 279–81, 292, 297–98, 302; and Scriblerian publications, 279

—Swift, Jonathan, 20, 205, 280–81, 307n33, 344n83, 347–48, 360, 365; as influence, 62; as satirist, 280–81; and sermons, 304n20, 339n28; and *A Tale of a Tub,* 363–64; and *Tristram Shandy,* 31–32n26

Sterne, Lydia, 85–86, 88, 92, 94n7, 96n23

Sterne, Richard, Archbishop of York, 68

Stogdon, Reverend Hubert, 80, 89–92, 93n1, 95n15, 95n17, 95–96n20, 96n21, 96n22. *See also under* Sterne, Laurence; "Unknown World, The"

Svevo, Italo, 3–4, 136, 196, 314

Swift, Jonathan, 3, 208, 308–309n45, 322, 351–52, 362; biography of, 252, 278; current popularity of, 351–52; and eighteenth-century literature, 65, 139, 213, 308n44, 347; "Journal to Stella, The," 187–88n8; language academy of, 20; and materiality, 206, 211n27, 308n44; parodic work of, 31–32n26; in relation to Laurence Sterne (*see under* Sterne, Laurence, in relation to other writers); as satirist, 20, 205, 251, 280–82, 392–92, 302; as satirist of modernity, 252, 309–10n52; scatology in the works of, 302; sermons of, 304n20, 306n31, 311n65, 339n28; and Stella (Esther Johnson), 168, 188n10; and theology, 287, 312n71

—*Gulliver's Travels,* 302, 355; in relation to *The Memoirs of Martinus Scriblerus,* 280; as satire, 280–81; satirical ambivalence of, 280–81

—*Tale of a Tub, A,* 3, 279, 302; and aesthetic criticism, 112–13; approach toward language in, 309–10n52; diminished popularity of, 351–52; hobby-horses in, 211n33; and matter, 206, 211n27

—works of: *Battle of the Books, The,* 292; *Discourse concerning the Mechanical Operation of the Spirit, A,* 292; "Letter to a Very Young Lady," 252, 278; *Miscellanies* (with Alexander Pope), 252, 278–80, 348. *See also* Pope, Alexander; Scriblerians, the; Sterne, Laurence

Talon, Henri, 113–16, 129n43

Tate, Nahum, 213, 237n7

Teaching (university). *See* Pedagogy (university)

Temple, William Johnson, 259, 264, 272n14, 276n50. *See also* Boswell, James

Theology: Anglican, 5, 132n79; eighteenth-century, 55–56n9, 59n35, 63–64, 159n47, 217–18, 224, 227, 242n44; practical vs. scholastic, 237n6; in relation to literature, 5, 79n28, 142, 272–73n21, 352; in relation to philosophy, 42–43, 79n28, 107–8, 217–18, 355; seventeenth-century, 66–68. *See also* Christianity; God; More, Henry; Secularism

Theory, literary: biases of, 4–5; deconstruction, 65, 283–87, 307n37, 351, 365; feminist, 351; French, 113 (*see also* Derrida, Jacques); Freudianism, 134n89; and judgment, 123–24; narrative, 26; political (American), 59n35; postcolonial, 351; postmodernist, 154–55n3. *See also* Postmodernism

Thomson, James, 213

Tillotson, John, 33–36, 56n11, 232, 284–85. *See also* Norris, John, of Bemerton; Sermons (seventeenth-century)

Times Literary Supplement, The, 142, 350

Toldervy, William, 214

Tolstoy, Leo, 286, 341n51, 343n68, 359

Trollope, Anthony, 286, 357, 358

Truth: and aesthetics, 6–8, 106–7, 322–23, 333–36; and divinity, 6, 47, 51, 70, 193n51, 295–96, 321–23, 330, 333–35; and literature, 6–8; and Plato, 106; and unknowingness, 6–9, 22, 39, 340n34. *See also* Christianity; Malebranche, Nicolas

Turgenev, Ivan, 359

Universities: and cultural politics, 196–97, 350–51, 352–53, 355; and pedagogy, 6–7. *See also* Pedagogy (university)

"Unknown World, The," 8, *81–84;* authorship of, 8, 80, 89, 93n1, 95n17, 96n21; critical evaluations of, 80, 85–89, 93–94n6, 96–97n24; publication of, 80, 85–88, 89, 92, 94n9; and religion, 8; textual transmission of, 85–88, 91–92; typographic symbols in, 87–88, 94–95n19

Voltaire, 255, 276n50, 360, *Candide,* 137, 250, 280, 283; *Dictionnaire philosophique,* 255; meeting with James Boswell of, 254–56, 257, 258; secular beliefs of, 260, 273n22

Walker, Obadiah, 19, 29n12

Walpole, Robert, 145, 149, 158n30

Warburton, Bishop William, 19, 25, 29n13, 31–32n26, 363–64

Ward, Caesar, 292

Wilkins, John, 30–31n20; *Ecclesiastes: or, A Discourse Concerning the Gift of Preaching,* 30n20

William III, king of England, 71, 232

Wollaston, William, 243n47; *Religion of Nature Delineated, The,* 225

Woolf, Virginia, 4, 9, 136, 138, 209, 305–6n28; *Mrs. Dalloway,* 197–98, 204–8; in relation to Laurence Sterne, 136–37, 198, 204, 210n5, 211n33, 314; *Waves, The,* 127n28. *See also* Modernism

Wordsworth, William, 140, 267, 283, 357, 360–61

World War I, 143, 305–6n28

World War II, 143

Xavier, St. Francis, 339n28

York, in the eighteenth century, 266; and the church, 62, 68, 230, 279, 321; newspaper press of, 86–87; and politics, 62; printing houses of, 292, 304n20

Yorkshire, in the eighteenth century, 87, 96n22, 204, 225, 251, 266, 279; Coxwold (village), 80, 85–86

Young, Edward, 213, 224, 237n5, 243n46

Zangwill, Israel, 356

Melvyn New, professor emeritus, University of Florida, was general editor of the nine-volume Florida Edition of the Works of Laurence Sterne. He co-edited the Cambridge Edition of Samuel Richardson's *Sir Charles Grandison,* published in four volumes; and coedited *Notes on Footnotes: Annotating Eighteenth-Century Literature.* Some recent essays not included in this volume are (with Robert G. Walker) "Who Killed Tom Cumming the Quaker? Recovering the Life-Story of an Eighteenth-Century Adventurer"; "Ethics of Eighteenth-Century Comedy"; "Laurence Sterne and William Falconer: Soldiers and Sailors"; "John Baldessari and Laurence Sterne"; "A Room of One's Own on Main Street"; and "In Quotes: Annotating Maria Edgeworth's *Belinda.*" He is the book review editor, emeritus, of the *Scriblerian,* having served that role for some twenty years.

Printed in the United States
by Baker & Taylor Publisher Services